Presidential Campaign Rhetoric in an Age of Confessional Politics

LEXINGTON STUDIES IN POLITICAL COMMUNICATION
Series Editor: Robert E. Denton, Jr., Virginia Polytechnic Institute and State University

This series encourages focused work examining the role and function of communication in the realm of politics including campaigns and elections, media, and political institutions.

Titles in the Series

Presidential Campaign Rhetoric in an Age of Confessional Politics

Brian T. Kaylor

LEXINGTON BOOKS
Lanham • Boulder • New York • Toronto • Plymouth, UK

Published by Lexington Books
A wholly owned subsidiary of The Rowman & Littlefield Publishing Group, Inc.
4501 Forbes Boulevard, Suite 200, Lanham, Maryland 20706
www.rowman.com

10 Thornbury Road, Plymouth PL6 7PP, United Kingdom

British Library Cataloguing in Publication Information Available

Library of Congress Cataloging-in-Publication Data

Kaylor, Brian.
Presidential campaign rhetoric in an age of confessional politics / by Brian T Kaylor
p. cm. -- (Lexington studies in political communication)
Includes bibliographical references and index.
ISBN 978-0-7391-4878-5 (cloth : alk. paper) -- ISBN 978-0-7391-4879-2 (pbk. : alk. paper) -- ISBN
978-0-7391-4880-8 (electronic)

1. Communication in politics—United States—History—20th century. 2. Rhetoric—Political as-
pects-United States—History—20th century. 3. Political campaigns—United States—History—20th
century. 4. Communication in politics—United States—History—21st century. 5. Rhetoric—Political aspects—United States—History—21st century. 6. Political campaigns—United States—History—21st century. 7. Presidents—United States—Election. 8. United States—Politics and government—1945–1989. 9. United States—Politics and government—1989– I. Title.
JA85.2.U6T39 2011
324.701'4—dc22
2010041559

Printed in the United States of America

Contents

Acknowledgments

Although this book and the dissertation it is derived from represent the input and wisdom of many individuals, the strongest influence has been that of my doctoral advisor, Dr. Mitchell McKinney. In addition to offering advice and encouragement, his invaluable input has greatly improved my writing in this and other research projects. I am also grateful for the advice and encouragement I received from my doctoral committee members: Dr. Bill Benoit, Dr. Debbie Dougherty, Dr. Richard Callahan, Dr. Michael Porter, and Dr. Sharon Welch. Their guidance during graduate courses and the dissertation process has enhanced my research efforts. Additionally, I am appreciative of the many other faculty members and staff at the University of Missouri and Southwest Baptist University who also imparted me with wisdom and offered encouragement and assistance along the way. Among the many professors that helped prepare me for graduate studies and encouraged my academic research, I am especially grateful for the affirmation, prodding, and lessons I received from Dr. Josh Compton, Shannon Dyer, Dr. Brett Miller, and Dr. Rodney Reeves. I will also cherish the memory of being able to start this manuscript while sitting in the same office at the University of Missouri that Dr. Bob Derryberry occupied four decades earlier.

I am also thankful to Dr. H. K. Neely and Dr. Jim Hill for supporting me during my graduate studies, as well as my other colleagues at ChurchNet who encouraged me along the way (especially Verlyn Bergen, Veronica Kramer, Jeanie McGowan, Marilyn Nelson, Bob Perry, Gary Snowden, and Owen Taylor). Over the past couple of years, I have been fortunate to be part of a welcoming and inspiring academic community at James Madison University. I am thankful for my colleagues there who have encouraged and assisted me. I have also been grateful for the encouragement I received from the University of Missouri and from the Religious Communication Association, both of whom awarded an earlier version of this work with their top award for doctoral dissertations.

Throughout this endeavor, I have been fortunate to have the support and encouragement of my family, including my parents, Doug and Carol Kaylor, and my in-laws, John and Dr. Ronda Credille. I must also thank my grandfather, Dorsey Derrick, for first inspiring me to consider doctoral studies when I was in second grade. Most of all, I have been blessed by my wife Jennifer. Her love and support throughout the process has been invaluable, and I am thankful she has put up with all my graduate school and research efforts!

Chapter One

Introduction

During a Republican presidential primary debate on June 5, 2007, moderator Wolf Blitzer asked Rudy Giuliani about recent remarks by a Catholic bishop that compared Giuliani's position on abortion to Pontius Pilate's actions during the crucifixion of Jesus. As Giuliani started his response, his microphone cut in and out, making several words inaudible. Blitzer quickly explained that lightning from a storm was disrupting the system. After a brief moment, Giuliani looked upward in surprise and then the candidates standing near him backed away as the audience erupted in laughter. Before returning to the original question about the bishop's attack, Giuliani remarked, "Look, for someone who went to parochial schools all his life, this is a very frightening thing that's happening right now." In responding to the question, Giuliani claimed that in addition to relying on the U.S. Constitution for his guidance in governing, he would also "consult my religion" to answer public policy issues like abortion.

Despite the constitutional directive of no religious test for holding public office, Giuliani found himself under fire from religious leaders of his own faith as he attempted to pass their rhetorical religious test and convince voters that he was religious enough to serve as the nation's leader. Far from the lack of a religious test for holding public office, Giuliani not only faced judgment from religious leaders and perhaps voters, but the proverbial judgment from God also seemed at hand. Giuliani was not the only candidate singled out for questioning regarding his religious commitment, as other candidates who jokingly backed away from him during the debate faced questions during the 2008 campaign about their own religiosity and church attendance. As in other recent presidential elections, questions about candidates' church attendance and religious beliefs were frequently raised with candidates seeking to convince the electorate to have faith in them as a suitable leader of the nation.

Although religious questions to presidential candidates are nothing new in U.S. politics, the direction of this line of questioning seems drastically different than the interrogation of Democratic nominee John F. Kennedy during the 1960 campaign. Kennedy—and before him the 1928 Democratic presidential nominee Al Smith—faced suggestions that they were *too* Catholic and would be told how to govern by the Pope or other Catholic leaders. However, Giuliani—and before him the 2004 Democratic presidential nominee John Kerry—faced accusations that they were not Catholic or religious enough to be elected president and thus they were encouraged to allow their faith to play an even greater role in their governing decisions. As Kerry argued in 2007, "President Kennedy's challenge was to prove that he was not so Catholic that he could be president. My challenge was to prove that I was Catholic enough that I could be president" ("Faith and the public dialogue," 2007, ¶99). Although Kennedy and Smith found themselves mostly attacked by Protestant ministers, Catholic clergy joined their evangelical Protestant brethren in criticizing Giuliani and Kerry. The concerns now are no longer that the Pope would tell politicians how to govern; instead, politicians now are routinely chastised for not following the dictates of their faith or adequately listening to the Pope or other religious leaders when making public policy decisions. Even Protestant candidates now declare they would seek the Pope's advice while president, as Bob Dole claimed in 1996 and George W. Bush did in 2004.

Whether it be comparisons to Pilate or announcements by bishops that they would deny communion to Kerry, Giuliani, or other pro-choice politicians, political candidates today appear to have a religiosity test they must pass, a test that covers much more than the specific issue of abortion that plagued Kerry and Giuliani. Indeed, the recent history of presidential politics reveals a rather tight coupling of religion and politics. In 1976, a self-professed "born-again" Christian, Jimmy Carter, was elected president of the United States. In the late 1970s and early 1980s, a minister, the Reverend Jerry Falwell, created and led the Moral Majority, a political empire designed primarily to influence political leaders in adopting policies in line with Falwell's evangelical Christian ideals. In 1980, Carter lost his bid for reelection to the new champion of the "Religious Right," Ronald Reagan. In 1984 and 1988, the Reverend Jesse Jackson sought the Democratic nomination for president, fairing particularly well in the South. Also in 1988, another minister, the Reverend Pat Robertson, the leader of a religious media empire, sought the Republican presidential nomination. Robertson garnered a surprise second-place finish in the Iowa caucus and placed ahead of U.S. Vice President and eventual nominee George H. W. Bush. Robertson has maintained his voice on political issues through his nationally televised cable television program *The 700 Club* and other media outlets. Christian activists have been perennial candidates for the Republican presidential nomination, including Alan Keyes in 1996, 2000, and 2008, and Gary Bauer in 2000. In 2008, former Arkansas Governor Mike Huckabee, a former Southern Baptist pastor and past president of the Arkansas Baptist State Convention, sought the Republican nomination and won several states. During the campaign he frequently preached in Baptist churches on Sundays.

Although 2008 Republican candidate Mitt Romney's Mormonism was frequently mentioned as a possible hindrance to his presidential bid, his father's Mormonism was not raised when his father sought the 1968 Republican presidential nomination (Gilgoff, 2007d). Today, Republican presidential candidates speak at religious schools like Bob Jones University, Jerry Falwell's Liberty University, and Pat Robertson's Regent University to gain the favor of religious conservatives and the schools' religious leaders that are seen as influential voices. During the 2000 presidential campaign, Republican candidate George W. Bush credited famed evangelist Billy Graham with his spiritual conversion and soberness from alcoholism (Hart and Pauley, 2005); and during the 2008 campaign, Democratic candidate Hillary Clinton credited Graham with helping her following her husband's public admission of sexual involvement with Monica Lewinsky (Luo, 2007a). James Dobson, the founder of the influential Christian organization Focus on the Family, spent his early career focused on nonpolitical family counseling for Christians; yet Dobson now offers frequent proclamations about which political candidates are acceptable Christians with millions listening to his daily radio program (Gilgoff, 2007a). Throughout this period, religious leaders have become important "kingmakers" and candidates seem compelled to bare their souls to the populace in hopes of gaining electoral salvation. Clearly, substantial changes have occurred regarding the religious rhetoric in presidential campaigns since Kennedy's attempt to assure religious leaders and voters that his faith would play no part in his governing decisions.

In the 1960 campaign, John F. Kennedy attempted to dispel concerns about his Catholicism during a speech to the Greater Houston Ministerial Association, a group of mostly protestant ministers. Kennedy proclaimed:

> I believe in an America where the separation of church and state is absolute; where no Catholic prelate would tell the President—should he be Catholic—how to act, and no Protestant minister would tell his parishioners for whom to vote; where no church or church school is granted any public funds or political preference, and where no man is denied public office merely because his religion differs from the President who might appoint him, or the people who might elect him. (Kennedy, 1960a, ¶4)

Kennedy further argued that it would be "unreasonable" if someone voted against him because he was Catholic (Kennedy, 1960b, ¶47), and that the questioning of his religion suggested that some people felt Catholics became inherently disqualified to serve as president "on the day they were baptized" (Kennedy, 1960a, ¶24). Although the assembled ministers asked Kennedy several questions following his speech, none questioned if he was religious enough to be president. Instead, the ministers worried that he would answer to the bishops on important public policy issues. To ease their concerns, Kennedy mentioned several issues where he had voted differently from the desires of Catholic leaders and stressed his firm belief in the separation of church and state.

Four decades later, the rhetorical demands for our nation's would-be leaders have completely changed in how they are expected to talk about religion and persuade voters regarding their personal faith. In attempts to communicate that they would sufficiently adhere to the dictates of their religious faith, John Kerry talked about being an altar boy and Rudy Giuliani mentioned that he had considered at one point becoming a priest. As Mitt Romney delivered a speech on faith in America that was billed by many commentators as his JFK moment, Romney proved that he—like Giuliani, Kerry, and most other recent presidential candidates—was no Jack Kennedy. In stark contrast to Kennedy, Romney spoke to a friendly audience and took no questions. More significantly, Romney confessed his personal religious beliefs, argued that he would rely on these beliefs to govern, and attacked some interpretations of the principle of separation of church and state. Romney offered what he called "a confession of my faith" and declared, "I believe that Jesus Christ is the son of God and the savior of mankind" (Romney, 2007, ¶25, 28). Clearly, between 1960 and today an important shift has occurred in how politicians talk about their faith. Presidential campaign discourse has been publicly baptized, with religion becoming a key feature of campaign communication and an important voting criterion for a significant portion of the electorate. What are the rhetorical features of this change? Why has this change occurred? What does this increase in candidates' religious talk mean for American political campaigns and our democracy? This study provides answers to these important questions.

STUDY JUSTIFICATION

Although often considered the two taboo topics for polite dinner discussion, religion and politics are becoming increasingly intertwined. This study examines these connections in order to explore the religious rhetoric of modern presidential nominees. Such an endeavor is important for a number of reasons, including the need to better understand the impact of religion in modern presidential campaigns, to understand the influence of religious leaders in contemporary politics, the importance of analyzing the rhetoric of presidential candidates, and, finally, the need to critically examine the role of religious rhetoric in American democracy.

Mixing of Religion and Politics

Religious issues—including the perceived religiosity of candidates and voters—have repeatedly garnered attention in political analyses during recent elections. George W. Bush's overwhelming support in both the 2000 and 2004 elections from voters who frequently attend church has been deemed the "God gap" in the American electorate by many commentators. In 2000, Bush won 63 percent of the vote from those who attend church more than once a week and 57 percent of those who attend weekly. Democratic nominee Al Gore, on the other hand, won support from 61 percent of those who never attend church and 54 percent of those who attend only a few times a year ("Religion and the presidential vote," 2004). Similar results occurred in 2004 as Bush won 64 percent of those who attend church more than once a week and 58 percent of those who attend weekly; Democratic nominee John Kerry won 62 percent of those who never attend church, and 54 percent of those who attend only a few times a year ("Religion and the presidential vote," 2004). In both elections, the vote of those who attend church monthly was evenly split. The proportion of the electorate who attend church at least weekly (just over 40 percent) remains roughly equal to those who seldom or never attend. This so-called God gap in presidential politics first appeared in 1972, exploded in 1992, and has increased since then (Page, 2004). Among white voters this voting pattern is more significant than the "gender gap," and has replaced previous religious divides that once cut across denominational lines (Page, 2004). As a result, *Time* magazine senior editor Amy Sullivan (2008) argued, "Trying to understand American politics without looking at religion would be like trying to understand the politics of the Middle East without paying attention to oil" (p. vii).

Not to be outdone by their Republican counterparts, Democratic candidates and strategists have experienced what Bill Clinton's former press secretary Mike McCurry called "a Great Awakening" (Berlinerblau, 2008, p. 96) as they seek to use religious rhetoric to follow in the footsteps of Bible-quoting Southern Baptists Jimmy Carter and Bill Clinton. Al From, chairman of the Democratic Leadership Council, argued during the 2004 primary season, "We went for years in the Democratic Party without recognizing God, and we pay a price for that" (Swarns and Cardwell, 2003, ¶9). Senator Joe Lieberman, an Orthodox Jew and one of the more openly religious candidates during the 2004 Democratic presidential primary, stated:

[Democrats] have been very hesitant to talk about faith . . . and in doing so we have lost a connection with a lot of people. Democrats ought to pay attention to the fact that the two Democrats who have been elected president since Johnson were Jimmy Carter and Bill Clinton . . . and both talked a lot about their faith. (VandeHei, 2003, ¶3)

The most recent crop of Democratic candidates—including Barack Obama, Hillary Clinton, and John Edwards—heeded this advice by talking about their spiritual beliefs and participating in religious forums sponsored by evangelical Christians. Obama reiterated this advice for Democrats:

I have said it's important for Democrats to reach out to the faith community. And the reason is because 90 percent of Americans believe in God. It's a source of values. It's a source of their moral compass. And I know it's a source of strength for me and my family. (Obama, 2007d, ¶69–70)

During the 2008 Democratic primary race, Obama spoke at the fiftieth anniversary meeting of the United Church of Christ, Obama and Clinton spoke at meetings hosted by conservative evangelical leader Rick Warren, Edwards joined Obama and Clinton in talking about their personal faith during a Presidential Forum on Faith, Values, and Poverty sponsored by CNN and the liberal evangelical Christian organization Sojourners, and Obama and Clinton gathered for another night of religious Q&A at the Compassion Forum sponsored by CNN and the liberal group Faith in Public Life. Other candidates in 2008 while on the stump talked about their favorite Bible verses and shared their personal faith in efforts to reach out to religious voters, all seemingly in an effort to pass catechism courses and achieve confirmation in order to win a political election.

As a result of the increased religious appeals by politicians and their campaigns, and also due to the rise of evangelical Christians as an influential voting bloc, scholarly examination of the prominence and functions of religion in political discourse is needed. What religious messages are politicians sending in hopes of persuading voters? Have there been changes in politicians' religious rhetoric as the "God gap" has become larger and more influential? This study seeks to answer these important questions.

Influence of Religious Leaders

Although religious rhetoric in presidential campaigns often originates from the candidates and other party leaders as a political strategy, religious leaders also initiate religious discussions during presidential campaigns. In 1996, Republican nominee Bob Dole initially turned down an invitation to address a meeting of the Christian Coalition, but appeared before this audience after receiving intense criticism that he was ignoring the concerns of conservative Christians (Gray, 1996). The Christian Coalition's leader, Ralph Reed, had warned Dole that if he wanted "to have any chance at all of gaining the White House, you had better not retreat from the pro-life and pro-family stands that made you a majority party in the first place" (Gray, 1996, ¶8). During the 2000 Republican primary race, televangelist Pat Robertson sponsored automated phone attacks on candidate John McCain in order to help George W. Bush win the nomination. This prompted McCain to attack Robertson and Jerry Falwell, labeling them and Nation of Islam leader Louis Farrakhan as "agents of intolerance" (Bruni and Mitchell, 2000, ¶17). McCain also described Robertson and Falwell as "forces of evil," for which he later apologized (Bruni and Mitchell, 2000, ¶1). McCain offered these attacks even as he attempted to reach evangelical voters by touting the endorsement of evangelical Christian leader Gary Bauer, who had recently dropped out of the race for the Republican presidential nomination (Bruni and Mitchell, 2000). During the 2008 Republican primary campaign, influential evangelical leader James Dobson questioned Republican candidate Fred Thompson's faith and stated that he could not vote for Thompson. Dobson also proclaimed to his followers that he could not vote for Rudy Giuliani and hinted that he would support a third-party candidate if Giuliani became the Republican nominee (Dolbee, 2007). Dobson later endorsed Mike Huckabee and announced that he would not vote for Republican nominee John McCain or Democrat Barack Obama (Gorski, 2008a). During the general election, however, Dobson changed his mind and announced his support of McCain, particularly after McCain's choice of Alaska Governor Sarah Palin as the Republican Vice Presidential candidate.

On other occasions, a candidate's close association with a religious leader or church created political controversy for which the candidates had to give an accounting. In 1976, Democratic nominee Jimmy Carter faced questions days before the election over his church's refusal to accept African Americans as members. Carter voiced his opposition to his church's racial policies but refused to resign as a member of his church (Carter, 1977); however, just days after leaving the White House he joined a different church in his hometown that during his presidency had split away from his former church in protest over the segregationist position (Carters join, 1981). In 1984, Reverend Jesse Jackson received criticism from his Democratic primary opponents and the media for his close ties to controversial Nation of Islam leader Louis Farrakhan (Sawislak, 1984). During the 2000 Republican primary, John McCain attacked George W. Bush for speaking at Bob Jones University, which had a long history of segregationist policies and whose leader had made anti-Catholic remarks. During the 2008 campaign, both Barack Obama and John McCain faced questions about their ties to controversial and outspoken preachers—Obama because of his long relationship to his former pastor Jeremiah Wright and Chicago Catholic priest Michael Pfleger and McCain for seeking and receiving endorsements from televangelists John Hagee and Rod Parsley (Gorski, 2008b). After controversial remarks by these preachers emerged, the two candidates distanced themselves from the remarks then eventually repudiated the religious leaders and rejected their support. These controversies demonstrate that when political candidates associate themselves so closely with their religion and specific religious leaders, their religious affiliations become fodder for political attacks. Although candidates may employ religious rhetoric as a political strategy, often the talk of religion in campaigns is actually sparked by the political activism or controversial comments of religious leaders.

In particular, evangelicals have risen to prominence in American politics and society. Since evangelicals play a substantial role in this analysis, it is important to clarify the term. *Newsweek* magazine famously declared 1976 to be "the year of the evangelical" in large part because of the political success of evangelical Christian Jimmy Carter. Since then, evangelicals have maintained a strong role in presidential campaigns, with Ronald Reagan, Bill Clinton, Al Gore, George W. Bush, and Barack Obama among the presidential candidates who would be considered evangelicals. However, there has been confusion about who evangelicals are and what they believe—despite the fact that at over one-third of the population, evangelicals are the largest religious group in America (Carter, 2000). John C. Green (2007), political science professor at the University of Akron and senior fellow at the Pew Forum on Religion and Public Life, explained the four key doctrines of evangelicals:

> 1) faith in Jesus Christ is the only way to salvation; 2) individuals must accept salvation for themselves (i.e. must be "born again"); 3) it is imperative to proclaim this message of salvation and make converts among nonbelievers; and 4) the Bible is the inerrant Word of God, providing the authority for the previous doctrines and other matters. (p. 25–27)

He also explained that evangelical beliefs lead to:

> high levels of religious devotion, with an emphasis on personal, unmediated relationship with Christ; extensive personal involvement in local congregations of like-minded believers; an intense focus on "evangelizing," that is proselytizing to make converts; and a strong emphasis on preaching and reading the Bible. (p. 27)

Highlighting similar characteristics of evangelicals, former President Jimmy Carter (2006) explained his view of evangelicals:

> The term "evangelical" is often misused or distorted, but I consider the two primary meanings (*Random House Dictionary of the English Language*) to be quite adequate: (*a*) "belonging to or designating Christian churches that emphasize the teachings and authority of the scriptures, especially of the New

Testament, in opposition to the institutional authority of the church itself, and that stress as paramount the tenet that salvation is achieved by personal conversion to faith in the atonement of Christ"; or (*b*) "designating Christians, especially of the late 1970s, eschewing the designation of fundamentalist but holding to a conservative interpretation of the Bible." (p. 19)

In essence, evangelicals are Protestant Christians who hold to traditionally orthodox views of God and salvation, preach that one must have a "born-again" experience in accepting Jesus as Lord, expect that a Christian will publicly profess their commitment to Jesus, and who attempt to evangelize others.

Evangelicals are not, however, inherently fundamentalists, although there remains some overlap between the two groups. Green (2007) noted that only about 10 percent of evangelicals are fundamentalists. Liberal evangelical preacher and author Tony Campolo (1995) argued that evangelicals differed substantially from fundamentalists since evangelicals believe that "fundamentalism was majoring in minors with its legalisms and had overlooked some weightier concerns such as racism and poverty" and "deplored the anti-intellectual attitudes of fundamentalism" (p. 80). He added that evangelicals were more likely to be involved in social action "to transform society," instead of the fundamentalist approach of withdrawing from seeking societal changes (p. 80). Evangelicals like Jimmy Carter, Tony Campolo, and Jim Wallis also demonstrate the fallacy of viewing the term "evangelical" as synonymous with "conservative." Since there are many evangelicals in both major political parties, they remain an influential group in our current political system. During the 2008 presidential primaries, for instance, one-third of white evangelicals voted for a Democratic candidate, making white evangelicals as significant a Democratic voting bloc as African Americans (New post-election, 2008).

As a result of the prodding of religious leaders—especially evangelical ones—to get politicians to open up spiritually, scholars must also examine the broader cultural conditions in which religious-political rhetoric occurs. What role do religious leaders play in the religious rhetoric found in presidential campaigns? Are these instigators of such talk reflective of a broader societal change that demands more personal religious rhetoric of our potential leaders? This study seeks to answer these important questions.

Importance of Campaign Rhetoric

The modern presidency is a rhetorical institution. As Medhurst (2006) argued, "A president cannot escape rhetoric—as much as some would like to do so. For good or ill, all presidents are rhetorical presidents" (p. ix). Even Mike Huckabee, a 2008 Republican presidential candidate, observed in an ironically ineloquent manner during a December 12, 2007, Republican primary debate, "The second most job of importance to the president—second to being Commander-in-Chief—is to be the Communicator-in-Chief." Due to their position as the nation's leader, presidents hold a unique and powerful rhetorical position. As a result of the president having a "privileged voice in our public or civic conversation," the president has the power to "help people interpret the social and political realities" (McKinney and Pepper, 1999, p. 79). The president is able to use their privileged voice, or "the symbolic supremacy of the presidency" (Denton and Hahn, 1986, p.125), to interpret reality for the public, which allows them to define who we are and how things are as they see it.

The president therefore serves the nation's "interpreter-in-chief" Stuckey (1991) explained that as the "nation's chief storyteller," presidents tell "us stories about ourselves and in so doing . . . tell us what sort of people we are" (p. 1). Beasley (2002) concluded that presidents "teach reality" by reminding "listeners who they *ought* to be" (p. 82, emphasis in original). She added that their rhetoric should be viewed as "both influencing and reflecting cultural norms" (p. 81). This includes on matters of religion and faith. Goldzwig (2002) utilized Stuckey's language when he declared that "George W. Bush has played a key role as interpreter-in-chief of the new American civil religion of the twenty-first century" (p. 112). Presidents have used this rhetorical role to continue, as Campbell and Jamieson (2008) described it, "creating the presidency." The authors explained that this power is "enhanced in the modern presidency by the ability of presidents to speak when, where, and on whatever topic they choose and to reach a national audience through coverage by the electronic media" (p. 6). Presidential rhetoric is indeed a powerful act.

Some scholars even argue that a "rhetorical presidency" has arisen where the president has assumed a more powerful position in American governance. For instance, Tulis (1987) argued that President Woodrow Wilson—with President Teddy Roosevelt as a transitionary figure—brought a new approach to the presidency where the primary leadership role of the president today is a rhetorical function. Although the constitutional powers and equality were not technically changed, Tulis maintained that a "Second Constitution" was imposed on top of the first where the rhetorical president became the most powerful individual rather than a system with power shared across three equal branches of government. Some scholars argue that Tulis and others have exaggerated the shift that occurred (e.g., Laracey, 2002; Medhurst, 2008), and even Tulis (2008) has admitted that the transition was not abrupt as he originally described it. However, it is clear that the modern presidency is a more rhetorical one where presidents communicate more with the public and in a different manner. For instance, Lim (2002) analyzed the tone of all presidential inaugurals and state of the union addresses (from George Washington to Bill Clinton) and argued that there is a significant change in these addresses starting with President Teddy Roosevelt. He found that presidents beginning with Roosevelt were more conversational, democratic in their appeals (defined as compassionate and focused on the people), and more abstract in their language (defined as poetic and religious).

Due to the necessity of their public rhetoric, presidential candidates must now demonstrate an ability to handle the rhetorical throne. Kaid, McKinney, and Tedesco (2000) argued that in presidential elections, the "battle for votes is waged with competing candidate messages" and therefore becomes a "struggle for *interpretative dominance*" (p. 8, emphasis in original). Thus, the authors argued, Stuckey's (1991) concept of the president serving as our "interpreter-in-chief" should "extend . . . to an aspiring chief-executive" since these "would-be leaders" also attempt to "take on the role of chief storyteller" (p. 9). The authors added, "Viewing the campaign as a struggle for interpretative dominance allows a focus on the competing messages of candidates, and the visions they offer for citizens to compare and to accept or reject" (p. 9). Tulis (1987) even credited Woodrow Wilson with helping create a new rhetorical presidential campaign as he "was the first victorious presidential candidate to have engaged in a full-scale speaking tour during the campaign" (p. 182). Tulis added:

> In Wilson's view, the rhetorical campaign was intended not only to downgrade the role of parties in the selection process, but to prepare the people for a new kind of governance—the rhetorical presidency. . . . It is increasingly the case that a president's most important governmental advisors will be those who managed his electoral strategy. Since that strategy is increasingly rhetorical, the skills imported into the White House are more and more those needed to fashion popular appeals. (p. 183)

As a result, the current political campaign system is "a proving ground for the very skills necessary to govern well, a rhetorical fitness test" (Tulis, 1987, p. 184).

Kernell (2006) suggested the presidential rhetorical strategy of "going public" has transformed not only presidential governance, but also presidential campaigns: "No aspect of the presidency has escaped this transformation. It encompasses how candidates seek their party's nomination, how they campaign in the general election, and which kinds of candidates enjoy a competitive edge at both enterprises" (p. 50). He noted that the changes in presidential candidates particularly began in the early 1970s as the nomination process moved toward a primary system that required candidates to go public in order to attract the support of the people of their party. Kernell (2006) argued that this second rhetorical shift toward a strategy of "going public" began with Richard Nixon and Jimmy Carter, and Lim (2002) also noted a change in presidential rhetoric starting around the time of Gerald Ford as presidents were becoming even more personal and relying even more heavily on the tactic of "going public." Interestingly, this shift to presidential "going public" appears to coincide fairly closely with the increase in religious rhetoric of presidential candidates examined in the present study and traced to Jimmy Carter's first White House run. Additionally, Carter's election in 1976 made him the first evangelical elected president since Woodrow Wilson (Boller, 1979).

Presidents and would-be presidents must make "choices about what to say, how to say it, where and to whom to say it" (Medhurst, 2006, p. ix). These rhetorical cues offer insights into what politicians value and how they will govern. Although scholars have examined the rhetorical power of the presidency to push legislation through Congress (e.g., Crockett, 2003; Kernell, 2006; Welch, 2003) or create bipartisanship (e.g., Sigelman, 1996), other scholars examined the commitment of a president or candidate to policies or issues based on what they talk about or not. Since saying is doing for the rhetorical president, the act of addressing certain topics is viewed as a sign of one's commitment. As Medhurst (2006) concluded:

> Failure to think and act rhetorically not only results in failure to communicate one's ideas. It can also result in the attribution of all kinds of negative inferences, based not only on what one says and how one says it, but also on what is left unsaid and what audience needs are left unmet. (p. 200)

Presidential rhetoric—as well as the rhetoric of our would-be presidents—powerfully establishes the priorities and agenda of the individual politician. Thus, the policy preferences of presidents and candidates are often judged according to their rhetoric. Scholars must therefore consider the rhetorical decisions of would-be presidents seeking the mantle of our nation's "interpreter-in-chief." Such analysis can offer insights into their commitments and decisions, even moral ones. As Shogan (2006) concluded, "The modern rhetorical presidency is not limited to policy concerns. Instead, the rhetorical purview for modern rhetorical presidents is all-encompassing; every aspect of democratic life becomes worthy of a moral pronouncement" (p. 174).

As our nation's would-be leaders seek our support in today's political system filled with rhetorical expectations, how they build that case communicates their ideals, priorities, and their perception of what they need to say to win over voters. When it comes to matters of religion and faith, what are our candidates talking about? How are they discussing these issues? What insights do their campaign confessions of faith offer regarding their religious commitments and priorities?

Civil-Religious Contract

The growing fusion of religion and political campaigns has garnered the attention of numerous scholars. Generally, this body of research seeks to understand how religious rhetoric functions in politics and democracy, and the impact of this discourse on campaign rhetoric. However, despite the scholarly attention given to the important issues of religion in politics, many gaps in the scholarship remain. Perhaps one of the most dominant perspectives used for examining the religious rhetoric of the early modern presidency is the civil-religious contract proposed by Roderick Hart in *The Political Pulpit*. Hart (1977) explored the relationship between religion and politics and attempts by political leaders to balance the two. While the two are interrelated, Hart argued that politicians should not be "overly religious," and religious leaders should not be "overly political" (p. 44). When the political rhetor does incorporate religion or religious ideals into their discourse, it should be done in a nonpartisan and nondenominational fashion and to the betterment of both church and state, but in a way that maintains the separation of the two. He also argued that this relationship or "contract" between the two groups is inherently enshrined in American democracy.

In his analysis, Hart drew from the influential work of sociologist Robert Bellah on "civil religion." Bellah (1975) argued that "any coherent and viable society rests on a common set of moral understandings about good and bad, right and wrong, in the realm of individual and social action" (p. ix). He added:

> these common moral understandings must also in turn rest upon a common set of religious understandings that provide a picture of the universe in terms of which the moral understandings make sense. Such moral and religious understandings produce both a basic cultural legitimation for a society which is viewed as at least approximately in accord with them and a standard of judgment for the criticism of a society that is seen as deviating too far from them. (p. ix)

Bellah (1967) also explained that "American civil religion is not the worship of the American nation but an understanding of the American experience in the light of ultimate and universal reality" (p. 18). Although Bellah (1975) believed that American society had lost much of that "common set of understandings" and "the religious framework for the traditional morality," he believed that "no matter how undermined, a remnant of the older morality provides much of what coherence our society still has" (p. x–xi, xiii). It is this common religious framework serving as our basic cultural foundation that Bellah terms "civil religion." Thus, civil religion is "a collection of beliefs, symbols, and rituals with respect to sacred things and institutionalized in a collectivity" (Bellah, 1992, p. 104). He particularly pointed to John

F. Kennedy's rhetoric as an exemplar of civil religion. Bellah (1992) argued that for a republic, "civil religion is indispensable. A republic as an active political community of participating citizens must have a purpose and a set of values" (p. 176). He added that civil religion has been "absolutely integral" to "our existence as a republican people" (p. 179).

West (1980) explained that civil religion is not a formal or institutional religion, but rather:

> A civil religion is a set of beliefs and attitudes that explain the meaning and purpose of any given political society in terms of its relationship to a transcendent, spiritual reality, that are held by the people generally of that society, and that are expressed in public rituals, myths, and symbols. (West, 1980, p. 39)

Thus, traditional or institutional religions may both support and challenge a nation's civil religion. As West (1980) explained, "A church is likely to be one of the exponents or agents of a nation's civil religion; however, it will likely not be the only one and may, at times, even oppose the civil religion" (p. 39). Hughes (1980) argued that civil religion helps a nation by providing "meaning in the face of apparent absurdity, acceptance in the face of apparent condemnation, and life in the face of apparent death" (p. 76). He added, "a civil religion is the theological glue that binds a nation together by binding it simultaneously to the dimensions of the transcendent" (p. 76). He stressed that it is not the worship of the nation as some critics have suggested, but "simply a way of providing a context of meaning for a given society" (p. 77).

Hart argued that the "significance of the phenomenon Bellah discovered" was that presidential rhetoric reflects "what the people in the United States find to be most important, to be most right, to be most true" (Hart and Pauley, 2005, p. 16). Hart (1977), however, critiqued Bellah's conception of civil religion as really being an exploration of civic piety. Bellah 1992) acknowledged that had he chosen a different term (e.g., public theology, public piety) there likely would be less criticism and confusion surrounding his work. Hart argued that Bellah's discovery was not a religion but "interesting religious assertions" (Hart and Pauley, 2005, p. 39). Hart believed that Bellah "perhaps overreacted" and "sacrificed his analytical skills to speak solemnly and idealistically of the religion he found, and, later, loved too well" (pp. 39–40). Hart insisted that Bellah's findings were not because of a civil religion but rather the rhetorical features of a unique relationship between religion and politics in American society. Hart thus built upon the idea of civic piety in the development of his civil-religious contract in order to focus attention upon the rhetorical functions and characteristics of religious-political discourse.

Although a few presidential rhetoric scholars have questioned if the civil-religious contract still exists (Medhurst, 2002) or ever existed (Gring, 2002), the notion of such a contract has been utilized as a guiding theoretical perspective and affirmed by numerous scholars (e.g., Erickson, 1980; Goldzwig, 1987; Hostetler, 2002; Mitchell and Phipps, 1985; O'Leary and McFarland, 1989; Powell and Neiva, 2006). The scholarly impact of Hart's civil-religious contract sparked a special issue of the *Journal of Communication and Religion* (e.g., Eidenmuller, 2002; Lee, 2002; Marvin, 2002; Ofulue, 2002), followed by a new edition of *The Political Pulpit* (Hart and Pauley, 2005) that included essays from the special JCR issue edited by John Pauley. Reviewing Hart's original theorizing, Brockriede (1978) labeled *The Political Pulpit* "a work of art" (p. 203). Goldzwig (2002) proclaimed that Hart's analysis "remains a landmark work in rhetorical studies" that still resonates even twenty-five years later, and Friedenberg (2002) argued that the civil-religious contract remains intact and "will largely hold true for the foreseeable future" (p. 46).

Although many scholars continue to use the civil-religious contract to guide explorations of religious-political discourse, its original development and application is now over thirty years old. In his initial analysis, Hart examined presidential rhetoric through President Gerald Ford's administration; and although Hart studied the 1976 bicentennial celebration, he offered no discussion of the 1976 presidential election that thrust an evangelical Sunday school teacher into the White House. As Medhurst (2002) noted:

> 1977 was a long time ago. Indeed, many aspects of that world no longer exist. Those that do still exist have been, in many instances, radically transformed. It hardly seems fair, therefore, to expect that a "contract" published so long ago should be expected to remain in full force some 25 years later. (p. 87)

In fact, the changing role of religion in American politics even made the 2007 version of "Beloit College's Mindset List," an annual list of reminders about the experiences and events that incoming freshman may or may not know because of their age. For the class of 2011 (those born in 1989), the list included, "Religious leaders have always been telling politicians what to do, or else!" (Beloit College's," 2007, ¶13).

Even Hart admitted in the new edition of his work that "[m]uch has changed since of 1977" and noted that Jimmy Carter and George W. Bush "serve as bookends for an era that has worried constantly about matters of church and state" (Hart and Pauley, 2005, p. 5, 8). However, despite briefly noting numerous examples of the mixing of religion and politics over the thirty years since his original conception of civic piety, Hart maintained that the contract is still in place today and that even President George W. Bush "follows [the rules] carefully" (Hart and Pauley, 2005, p. 11). He added that "[h]eads continue to roll in the United States when politicians become too confessional or preachers too ideological" (pp. 137–38). He offered as proof of the contract's continued existence that Bush had not been successful in getting his "batch of right-wing jurists" confirmed by the U.S. Senate (Hart and Pauley, 2005, p. 188–89), and that religious leaders like Jerry Falwell and Ralph Reed had been pushed to the background of the Republican Party. Hart concluded, "Political compromise, not sectarian creeds, is the dominant language of America politics" (Hart and Pauley, 2005, p. 189). Interestingly, his argument was advanced prior to Bush's success in getting justices John Roberts and Samuel Alito confirmed to the U.S. Supreme Court, and the withdrawal of his nominee Harriet Miers largely because of complaints by conservative religious leaders. Despite the fact that Hart's (1977) original analysis was conducted prior to the rise of the Moral Majority or the elections of proclaimed born-again candidates like Jimmy Carter and George W. Bush, most religious-political scholars continue to apply the civil-religious contract as an appropriate framework for analyzing political-religious discourse.

Although a few have questioned its validity, none have undertaken a more substantial analysis across time to test whether or not the contract still holds. But does the contract really still remain in force despite the increased mixing of religion and politics? If not, what type of religious-political rhetoric has replaced the contract? This study seeks to answer these important questions. In order to so, the rhetoric of the presidential candidates included in this study is compared with Hart's key tests for considering if politicians' or religious leaders' rhetoric violated the contract. He provided these guidelines and examples of acceptable and offending discourse to distinguish between "official" and "unofficial" civil-religious rhetoric. Hart argued that scholars should not merely dismiss those rhetors who do not "align closely" with Bellah's (1975) "American civil religion" as "a 'heretical byway,'" but instead claimed that the discourse of these "[u]nofficial religionists" should be examined to compare the differences between the "religious in-groups and out-groups" (Hart and Pauley, 2005, p. 24–25). He explained that rhetors who promote an unofficial civic piety "are those political animals who stalk the American people from lairs far removed from 1600 Pennsylvania Avenue" (Hart and Pauley, 2005, p. 24). In other words, those who rhetorically violate the contract during the period he examined were not the power-brokers or mainstream religious or political leaders, but those acting from the fringe and therefore not actually leaders of the contractual parties.

Hart identified three features of unofficial civil-religious rhetoric—discourse that violates the civil-religious contract—that distinguishes it from the official and acceptable religious-political rhetoric. First, this discourse is sectarian, or advocates a particular faith or church. Rather than speaking about a God in general terms that could satisfy those of various backgrounds, these rhetors openly proclaim their theological doctrines and commitment to an exclusive and specific faith. Second, unofficial civil religious rhetoric is marked by activism. These rhetors are "distinctively partisan" with their religious discourse as they "act out their political and religious convictions" (Hart and Pauley, 2005, p. 28). Finally, unofficial civil-religious discourse includes overt ideology. With this, religion is used to promote one's political agenda or nationalism is used to promote a religious agenda. Hart argued that for official civil-religionists, the use of ritualistic religious rhetoric by politicians comes with "certain ground rules" that "must be observed when deploying such themes" (Hart and Pauley, 2005, p. 78). His rules are: "(1) they must be brief, (2) they must commence or terminate an address (but usually not both), and (3) they must normally (i.e., during peacetime) be appended to ceremonial, as opposed to policymaking or policy-endorsing, speeches" (Hart and Pauley, 2005, p. 78). These rules and the characteristics of unofficial civil-religious discourse provide a guide for systematically examining if the religious rhetoric of presidential campaigns has shifted since Hart's (1977) original conception of the civil-religious contract.

Although Hart's (1977) premise accurately captured the nature of religious-political rhetoric in the decades prior to the mid-1970s, thirty years of campaigns demands a closer examination to determine if such a contract still exists. Does the civil-religious contract really still hold despite the increasing mixing of religion and politics by our presidential candidates? If not, what type of religious-political rhetoric has replaced the contract? This study seeks to answer these important questions.

Democracy and Confessional Politics

A popular claim often made about the so-called American dream is that anyone can grow up to be president someday. As Carol Moseley-Braun, an African American female politician and former U.S. senator from Illinois who unsuccessfully sought the 2004 Democratic presidential nomination, explained in her address announcing that she was running for president:

> Just last week, my little 9-year-old niece Claire called me into her room to show me her social studies book. Turning to the pages on which all of our Presidents were pictured, she looked at me and complained: But Auntie Carol, all the Presidents are boys! . . . This campaign is our way of fighting to give Claire and every American girl or boy not only the opportunity to become President of this great country, but the freedom to decide to lead a quality private life if they choose to do so. (Moseley-Braun, 2003, ¶37, 39)

The American myth that anyone can be president persists despite the fact that every president has been a male, usually fairly wealthy, all but one have been white, and all but one have been Protestant Christians. Although Obama's election broke the racial barrier to the White House and the appeal of 2008 candidates Hillary Clinton and Sarah Palin suggests that the gender barrier may also be broken someday soon, religious diversity among our nation's Commander-in-Chiefs seems much less likely to occur anytime soon.

Although some presidents were likely marginal believers at best, all have at least professed to be Christians, and John F. Kennedy remains the only non-Protestant occupant of 1600 Pennsylvania Avenue. Only three Catholics—Kennedy, Al Smith, and John Kerry—have even received their party's nomination for president, only one Jewish candidate—2000 Democratic Vice Presidential nominee Joe Lieberman—has ever been nominated on a major-party national ticket, and no candidate who professed another or no faith has received or even come close to their party's nomination. Nearly 61 percent of Americans think presidential candidates should be religious (Cole, 2007), and 62 percent said they would not vote for an atheist, including 78 percent of Republicans (Elder, 2007). Another poll found that a candidate who claims to not believe in God was the top factor that would make voters less likely to vote for the individual (Luo, 2007b), topping factors such as never having held elective office, being a homosexual, lacking college education, and taking antidepressants. Even 2008 Republican presidential nominee John McCain argued that since "this nation was founded primarily on Christian principles" that he would vote for a Christian instead of a Muslim for president because he would "prefer someone who I know who has a solid grounding in my faith" (Gilgoff, 2007e, ¶2).

Indeed, furor erupted shortly after the 2006 election of Keith Ellison of Minnesota to the U.S. House of Representatives, which made him the first Muslim elected to national office. Criticism of Ellison particularly focused on his decision to take his oath of office with a Qur'an instead of a Bible (Sacirbey, 2006), although he eventually used a Qur'an that had been owned by Thomas Jefferson. Virginia U.S. Representative Jim Goode urged Americans to "wake up" or else "there will likely be many more Muslims elected to office and demanding the use of the [Qur'an]" (Lindsey, 2006, ¶5). Goode added that stricter immigration laws were needed to prevent this and "to preserve the values and beliefs traditional to the United States of America" (Lindsey, 2006, ¶4). In 2007, a current U.S. Representative, Peter Stark, became the highest-ranking officeholder to publicly admit to being an atheist, which led some supporters to declare they might not vote for him again (Artz, 2007). Later in 2007, Rajan Zed became the first Hindu clergyman to pray at the start of a U.S. Senate session. His prayer, however, was repeatedly interrupted by loud heckling from conservative Christians in the Senate gallery who shouted "this is an abomination" (Babington, 2007, ¶2). As they were being removed by police officers, one protestor declared, "we are Christians and patriots"(Babington, 2007, ¶3). The intensity and level of controversy would likely be substantially larger if a major presidential candidate professed to be Muslim, atheist, or Hindu. In fact, it is almost certain in today's political-religious environment that a person of such or no faith would not be considered a viable candidate for the presidency. During the 2008 campaign, Barack Obama repeatedly attempted to overcome Internet and viral email rumors that he is a "secret" Muslim or had been raised as one (Alessi, 2008). Although the claim is false, the fact that it was considered by the Obama campaign to be a vicious slur, with some voters even reporting the rumor led them to question supporting Obama, demonstrates that a professed Muslim candidate would not have a prayer of being elected president in today's religious-political climate.

With American voters now closely inspecting the religiosity of their would-be leaders, presidential candidates are now openly proclaiming their faith. After listing a few examples of 2008 Republican presidential candidates talking about their personal faith, the *Los Angeles Times* declared, "These confessions reflect the clout of Christian conservatives" ("Into the wilderness," 2007, ¶3). The *Sacramento Bee* argued that President George W. Bush's reelection in 2004 was in part because of his "born-again professions of faith" (Rosen and Dobbin, 2004, ¶8). Much as worshippers might recite a confession of faith during a church service in order to prove the sincerity of their faith, presidential candidates appear to proclaim their faith in the public square in order to inspire voter confidence. As a result of these more personal and sectarian declarations of faith and the influence of religious voters, it is possible that otherwise qualified presidential candidates may be excluded from consideration. Additionally, candidates may feel forced to answer the religious questions from religious leaders and reporters out of fear that they will otherwise be rejected by voters at the ballot box. In the current study, Michel Foucault's work on the confession is utilized as a critical lens to explore the broader social implications of the interjection of religious discourse into presidential campaigns. Foucault used the setting of the Catholic Church to explore issues of disciplinary power and normalization in society. This project seeks to democratize, or re-baptize, Foucault's work to critique broader issues related to religious discourse in political campaigns. Particular attention is given to an examination of who is defined as nonviable in our society as a result of confessional politics, and also a critique is offered suggesting the negative impact of such religious-political rhetoric on American democracy.

Article VI of the U.S. Constitution declares that "no religious test shall ever be required as a qualification to any office or public trust under the United States." However, our nation today appears to demand that our presidential candidates not only believe in God but do so in a fairly orthodox Protestant Christian manner. Although a literal religious test has not been adopted, there does appear to be a *rhetorical* religious test presidential candidates must now pass. What impact does the expectation of public proclamations of faith have on candidates, the public, and American democratic campaigns in general? Is our nation's current confessional style of politics healthy and appropriate for our democracy? This study seeks to answer these important questions.

Nature of Religious-Political Rhetoric

Scholars of religious-political communication have argued for the importance of a rhetorical analysis in order to explore the nuances and functions of specific discourse. Pauley (2002) echoed Hart's (1977) call for a "rhetorical perspective" in examining civil-religious discourse because the "data" being analyzed by "sociologists or theologians" was "primarily presidential speeches—the stuff that rhetorical scholars are most uniquely qualified to analyze" (p. 2). Analyzing comments by Jerry Falwell and the Moral Majority, Mitchell and Phipps (1985) argued "the rhetorical perspective . . . provides special insights into the interrelationships between American political and religious life" (p. 60). They added that "examining the rhetorical artifacts of speakers" helps scholars "understand more fully the blending of politics and religion" (p. 60).

Even religious leaders and political commentators have noted the rhetorical nature of religious discourse in presidential campaigns. Welton Gaddy, a Baptist minister and president of the Interfaith Alliance, argued, "Political leaders in this nation have learned that attaching religious rhetoric to political initiatives gains great support" (Farrelly, 2003, ¶6). Gaddy added that he wanted to see religious "values impact our politics and our political rhetoric, rather than letting our political rhetoric influence our religious conversations" (Farrelly, 2003, ¶10). Duke Divinity School professor Stephen Chapman noted that one hope for Democrats in 2004 was that Vice Presidential nominee John Edwards could help reach religious citizens because "he would know how to use religious language and imagery in a way that people could recognize" (Sabar, 2007, ¶60). Jim Guth of Furman University argued that Democrats had come to recognize the importance of "making it clear they're comfortable with the language of faith" in order to win "in a very closely divided electorate" (Feldmann, 2007a, ¶4). Republican presidential hopeful Mike Huckabee went so far as to argue that his understanding of religious language was a prime reason that religious conservatives should vote for him:

> But let me say that it's important that people sing from their hearts and don't merely lip-sync the lyrics to our songs. I think it's important that the language of Zion is a mother tongue and not a recently acquired second language. (Huckabee, 2007, ¶24–25)

As a former Southern Baptist pastor and a past president of the Arkansas Baptist State Convention, Huckabee clearly knows how to talk the talk.

Often these religious references—or the language of Zion—in politics can be subtle allusions to scriptural passages or religious terms (such as Zion). As Bruce Lincoln (2003) argued, President George W. Bush often uses religious allusions that work powerfully with those who know the reference but might be seen as insignificant by others. Lincoln explained:

> Rather, for those who have ears to hear, these allusions effect a qualitative transformation, giving Bush's message an entirely different status. . . . These allusions are instructive, as is the fact that Bush could only make these points indirectly, through strategies of double coding. (pp. 31–32)

Lincoln (2004) added, "Bush employs Biblical citation to communicate with his base, using signs so subtle as to be the linguistic equivalent of winks and nudges" (¶11). Domke and Coe (2008) posited that "[s]uch language does not inevitably carry religious meanings for all listeners, but there is a vocabulary of faith embedded in American culture that conveys religious sentiment to anyone listening for such cues—and millions are doing so" (p. 31). The subtle nuance of these types of allusions can make it more difficult to thoroughly examine candidates' religious rhetoric. For instance, Shogan's (2006) analysis of religious governance discourse of presidents included a content analysis that only coded for "*explicit* moral and religious argumentation" but not "*implied* or *tacit* moral or religious allusions" because of the difficulty that doing so would add to creating a workable coding scheme that could be replicated (p. 21, emphasis in original). Thus, she did not include "biblical passages that were not explicitly attributed to the Bible" (p. 22), even though many auditors of this discourse would have made the connection. Ultimately, along with her content analysis she decided to conduct a more interpretative analysis of presidential governance rhetoric because of "[t]he inability of the quantitative measures to explain rhetorical patterns" (p. 9).

As a result of the importance of rhetoric in the modern presidency and the significance of religious nuance, this study employs a rhetorical analysis of the religious communication of presidential nominees and religious leaders. The analysis includes an exploration of the functions and forms of this discourse and situates it within the broader cultural milieu. Does presidential religious-political campaign rhetoric follow general forms or function in similar ways? Are there rhetorical differences between Republicans and Democrats? This study seeks to answer these important questions.

SUMMARY

This study examines the religious rhetoric of modern presidential candidates in order to explore possible changes in and influences on candidates' religious-political rhetoric, and also to explore implications of this discourse on American presidential campaigns and society. A dramatic shift in the nature of religious rhetoric in presidential campaigns appears to have occurred since Kennedy's campaign a half-century ago. Since the late 1970s, religion has played an increasingly important role in electoral voting behavior, and candidates have been openly confessing their faith as religious leaders interject themselves into political campaigns. These changes question the validity of the civil-religious contract and suggest the potential need for a new framework to understand and critique our new age of confessional politics.

Due to the nature of presidential campaigns, one would be unable to collect all campaign communication. Numerous campaign speeches and remarks are made throughout the country that, especially in the case of nonincumbent presidents, are often not documented but heard only by those physically present. However, a candidate's stock stump speech often includes the same basic messages—and even the very same script—as particularly noticed when one explores the campaign speeches of incumbent presidents recorded in the *Weekly Compilation of Presidential Documents*. This study analyzed the primary forms of campaign communication, including campaign rally and stump speeches, media interviews, campaign debates, television advertisements, campaign announcement speeches, and convention acceptance addresses, with texts collected for each major party presidential nominee from 1976 through 2008. The primary texts for analysis were collected from several databases: LexisNexis, *Weekly Compilation of Presidential Documents*, Federal News Service, www.americanrhetoric.com, and various book anthologies of campaign speeches; also relevant texts were pulled from secondary sources that quoted candidates' campaign discourse, including books, magazines, and newspaper articles. Overall, 5,387 campaign speeches and interviews were collected and analyzed, along with 163 campaign debates, and 1,053 campaign ads. The religious statements identified were evaluated to determine key themes that emerged in the analysis, which were then compared with those of the texts analyzed by Hart and others during the previous era of presidential discourse.

Chapters 2 through 4 analyze the religious rhetoric of our modern presidential nominees from 1976 until 2008. These chapters offer a descriptive analysis of how religious rhetoric is used by presidential nominees, with attention given to the major rhetorical themes employed during their primary and general election campaign speeches, debates, and ads. Although some studies have explored religious rhetoric in presidential governance discourse (e.g., Coe and Domke, 2006; Lim, 2002) or examined a single campaign's religious rhetoric (e.g., Detwiler, 1988; Hahn, 1980; Medhurst, 1977; Porter, 1990), the current project provides a more comprehensive look at the campaign discourse of modern presidential campaigns. Chapter 2 considers the era of Jimmy Carter and Ronald Reagan by examining the 1976, 1980, and 1984 campaigns. Chapter 3 explores the era of George H. W. Bush and Bill Clinton by analyzing the 1988, 1992, and 1996 campaigns. Chapter 4 examines the George W. Bush and the start of the Barack Obama era by considering the 2000, 2004, and 2008 campaigns. Chapter 5 builds on the rhetorical themes identified in chapters 2, 3, and 4 by identifying and describing the elements of a confessional style of religious-political discourse. This chapter also contrasts these rhetorical features to the tenets of the civil-religious contract that guided analysis of presidential discourse prior to 1976. The proposed features of the confessional style outlined are: Testimonial, Partisan, Sectarian, and Liturgical.

The sixth chapter explores possible reasons for changes in the religious-political campaign rhetoric identified in chapter 5. In addition to examining important societal shifts in the American religious-political landscape, the impact of religious leaders is also considered. Finally, this chapter seeks to understand why the confessional political rhetoric identified in chapter 5 is successful in today's presidential campaigns. The societal shifts considered are: Changes in Catholicism, Civil Rights Movement, Religious Shift, Court Decisions, Aftermath of Watergate and Vietnam, Religious-Political Activism. Chapter 7 critically evaluates the changes of religious rhetoric in electoral politics, examining the impact of these changes on American democracy and presidential campaigns. Guiding this chapter's analysis is Michel Foucault's work on the confession, which is recast for a more democratic context in order to explore the impact of cultural pressures placed upon candidates to publicly profess their faith. This chapter also critiques the problems for U.S. democracy created by this new style of confessional politics. The eighth and final chapter summarizes important implications from this study regarding both the content of religious-political rhetoric and theoretical developments related to the civil-religious contract and Foucault's conception of the confession. This chapter also briefly considers the potential impact of the confessional political system on the 2012 presidential election.

Chapter Two

Carter and Reagan

In January of 1977, Jimmy Carter placed his hand on a Bible and became the thirty-ninth president of the United States. Carter had moved from being a little-known peanut farmer and one-term governor of Georgia to the leader of the nation in less than two years. His seemingly improbable election as the first president to emerge from the deep South since prior to the Civil War ended eight years of Republican leadership that had been rocked by Watergate and other scandals. Pledging to always tell the truth to the American people and to lead with integrity, Carter's image as a trustworthy leader was enhanced by his public professions of being a born-again Christian and a Sunday school teacher. Even many conservative evangelical leaders like Pat Robertson offered their support to his candidacy. Ironically, most of these evangelical leaders would turn on Carter only four years later to enthusiastically support Ronald Reagan, who also claimed to be an evangelical and often spoke to Christian groups. Later, another evangelical Southern Baptist Democrat from the South—Bill Clinton—would win two terms as president, as would an evangelical and religiously outspoken Republican—George W. Bush. Finally, our current president is Barack Obama, whose church—although part of the mainline United Church of Christ—has more in common with the evangelical African American tradition than the churches within the mostly white denomination. Although only four of the thirty-eight presidents prior to 1976 identified as evangelicals—James Garfield, Benjamin Harrison, William McKinley, and Woodrow Wilson (Boller, 1979)—five of the six presidents since 1976 have been evangelicals—Jimmy Carter, Ronald Reagan, Bill Clinton, George W. Bush, and Barack Obama.

Carter's 1976 election marked a substantial shift from just four years earlier as he openly talked on the campaign trail about his faith and his service in the church, including earlier missionary service. In 1972, however,

Democratic nominee George McGovern avoided mention of his previous service as a Methodist minister and even attempted to hide photos from that time from the media (Hart and Pauley, 2005). McGovern, whose father was also a Methodist minister, graduated from Dakota Wesleyan and then studied at Garrett Evangelical Seminary, during which he served as a pastor of a Methodist church (Balmer, 2006). He also briefly taught classes at Dakota Wesleyan before beginning his political career. In an examination of a 1972 campaign speech by McGovern at Wheaton College, an evangelical Christian school, Medhurst (1977) noted that McGovern used biblical passages and talked about his childhood as a minister's son. However, Medhurst (1977) argued that McGovern gave the "humanist's plea for material well-being and social justice" instead using more evangelical rhetoric about "change of soul" (p. 32); Medhurst further argued that McGovern's rhetoric was ultimately unsuccessful because he did not identify with the values of his audience.

Indeed, the 1972 election saw the so-called God gap emerge for the first time in presidential politics as President Richard Nixon was favored among those who attended church more frequently and McGovern won those who never or rarely attended church (Page, 2004). Four years later, a man who had unsuccessfully lobbied to be McGovern's running mate—Jimmy Carter—would not repeat McGovern's mistakes when it came to the use of religion as a campaign appeal, but instead openly professed his personal faith and his born-again conversion. Carter's God-talk on the campaign trail took him all the way to 1600 Pennsylvania Avenue. Far from candidates shying away from past ministerial service, the Sunday school teacher-turned-president was followed over the next three decades by competitive runs for the White House by ministers Jesse Jackson, Pat Robertson, and Mike Huckabee. Incidentally, George McGovern would become one of the first targets of the Moral Majority as he was defeated for reelection to the U.S. Senate during his 1980 campaign, as was Idaho U.S. Senator Frank Church, who was one of the men who Carter out-God-talked to defeat in the 1976 Democratic presidential primaries. When McGovern mounted his long-shot bid for the 1984 Democratic presidential nomination, he frequently targeted President Ronald Reagan for inappropriately using religion for political purposes.

Beginning especially with Carter's campaign in 1976 and continuing through the 2008 contest, presidential candidates have employed religious-political rhetoric in their campaign appeals by talking openly about their personal faith and how their religious beliefs inspire and inform their public policy positions. This chapter and the next two examine this rhetoric by considering how the major-party nominees used religious references, God-talk, and Scriptural citations in their primary and general election campaign discourse. Specifically, within each presidential election from 1976–2008, the religious-political appeals from the major-party nominees is discussed, noting common themes or important differences. Additionally, contextual attention is given to religiously significant "also-ran" candidates like Jesse Jackson, Pat Robertson, Mitt Romney, and Mike Huckabee. This chapter will examine how the confessional political system began through the rhetorical efforts of Jimmy Carter and Ronald Reagan by considering the campaigns of 1976, 1980, and 1984.

1976

President Gerald Ford faced a stiff challenge for the Republican nomination in 1976 from California Governor Ronald Reagan. Ford, who had assumed the presidency following President Richard Nixon's resignation in August of 1974, upset many voters by pardoning Nixon, was seen by conservatives as weak in fighting communism, and was viewed as a weak incumbent since he had not been elected nationally. Although Ford won earlier primaries, Reagan mounted a comeback in North Carolina and eventually won several southern and western primaries. Ford entered the Republican convention with a slight lead in delegates but had not yet secured the nomination. Although Ford went on to win the nomination on the first ballot, Reagan received over 47 percent of the delegate vote. Ford chose Senator Bob Dole of Kansas as his running mate, rather than the more moderate and current Vice President Nelson Rockefeller.

Although a virtual unknown nationally, Georgia Governor Jimmy Carter slowly captured the Democratic nomination by winning primaries and defeating better known candidates. Carter bested all other candidates in the Iowa caucuses (although he placed second to uncommitted), which provided him with national media attention. He then proved he could gain support from more liberal Northeastern voters by winning New Hampshire. Other key victories forced major opponents out of the race, including Alabama Governor George Wallace in North Carolina, Washington Senator Henry "Scoop" Jackson in Pennsylvania, and Arizona Congressman Morris Udall in Wisconsin. Late in the primary season, Senator Frank Church of Idaho and California Governor Jerry Brown entered the nomination race as western liberals worried about the conservatism of the southern Carter. Despite Church and Brown winning several late primaries, Carter captured enough delegates to secure the nomination. Carter chose Senator Walter Mondale of Minnesota as his running mate.

During the primary, Carter received the greatest scrutiny and attention from a religious standpoint based on the fact that he campaigned as an outspoken born-again Christian Sunday school teacher. However, Jackson and Wallace were also both former Sunday school teachers, and Brown once studied for the priesthood at a Jesuit seminary. Several of the candidates, particularly Carter and Jackson, spoke at churches during the campaign. In fact, the Catholic Church distributed a newsletter in Iowa backing Carter because of his stand against abortions. Carter went on to win Iowa—and the Catholic vote—by a large margin (Steele, 1976). As Carter's public professions of faith garnered attention during the primary, some of his opponents dismissed his God-talk as inappropriate. Scoop Jackson said Carter's talk about his personal religion was in "bad taste" and claimed, "It's [a] deeply personal matter, and I deeply resent it. When people go around telling how religious they are, I generally get suspicious" (Politicians are discovering, 1976, ¶8). Jackson added, "I've taught Sunday school, but I'm not making my relationship with the Lord an issue in this campaign" (Meyer, 1978, p. 59).

During the general election, Carter ran as the Washington outsider and as a trustworthy person needed to clean up in the Capital after President Richard Nixon and the Watergate scandal. Although Carter recorded a 33 percentage point lead over Ford in the polls following the Democratic convention, his lead nearly completely disappeared by election day due to such missteps as Carter's interview with *Playboy*, his promise to pardon Vietnam draft dodgers, and Ford's strong performance in the first presidential debate. During the second presidential debate, however, Ford inaccurately claimed that eastern Europe was not under Soviet domination and therefore lost his momentum in the campaign. At one point during the campaign, Ford's campaign contacted popular evangelist Billy Graham to see if Ford could join Graham on the platform during one of his mass crusades as a way to appeal to religious voters. Graham, however, rejected the offer and said that Ford and Carter were both welcome to sit in the crowd (King, 1997). Ford did speak at annual meetings of the American Jewish Committee, Southern Baptist Convention, the Jewish group B'nai B'rith and a joint meeting of the National Association of Evangelicals and National Religious Broadcasters, while Carter addressed meetings of the National Conference of Catholic Charities and B'nai B'rith. Additionally, both candidates spoke at the Alfred E. Smith Memorial Dinner that raises money for Catholic charities. In November, Carter narrowly won the election 50.1 to 48 percent, but captured over 55 percent of the electoral college vote as he carried nearly all of the southern states.

Gerald Ford

Although President Gerald Ford did not often initiate discussion of his *personal faith* during the 1976 campaign, he was frequently asked about his spiritual beliefs. However, he usually offered ambiguous answers about his "commitment" and such questions occurred frequently in the month after which Carter's professions of being "born-again" garnered significant media attention. For instance, Ford was asked if he believed the Bible was the "inspired Word of God," if he had personally accepted "Jesus Christ as King of your life," and if he would follow Christ as his standard in policy decisions. He responded again describing his somewhat vague "commitment":

> The answer, without getting into the details, is yes. I have been, as a part of my own parents' family and as a part of our family, I think, deeply committed. I have especially committed myself, and I think the decisions that I make every day have to be related to a higher authority than just what we as humans do. (Ford, 1976d, p. 724)

During the campaign Ford was also asked, "Mr. President, I am a Baptist minister and my question is this, sir: Why is it that we haven't had a President in the White House since Herbert Hoover that has mentioned Jesus Christ's name publicly?" (Ford, 1976c, p. 424). Ford responded:

> Mrs. Ford and—my oldest son, Mike, is studying the ministry up at Gordon Conwell Seminary in Massachusetts. He has taken a commitment and so have I, and I am proud of him, and I am proud of our commitment. (Ford, 1976c, p. 425)

Ford, again, claimed a somewhat vague "commitment" and pointed to his family's faith as evidence of his own religious qualifications.

On a few occasions, Ford did offer a more personal glimpse into his religious beliefs. He argued that he shared a faith in God at a prayer brunch for athletes, "You are also special because of your love of God, your faith in Him, a love and a faith that Betty and I share" (Ford, 1976a, p. 266). In June of 1976, Ford became the first president to personally address the Southern Baptist Convention. To identify with this audience of conservative Christians, he noted that his son graduated from the Baptist-affiliated Wake Forest University and that he himself spoke at the graduation ceremony. He added, "Although our religious denominations are different, I have long admired the missionary spirit of Baptists and the fact that you strive to keep the Bible at the center of your lives" (Ford, 1976f, p. 1058). In several different speeches, Ford offered an example from his own religious background with reference to a biblical lesson he was taught as a child:

> I was taught early in my life by a wonderful Sunday school teacher that the beauty of Joseph's coat is its many colors. The strength of our great country is the fact that we are all different, that we share that same great hope of freedom, of liberty not only for ourselves but for all mankind. (Ford, 1976m, p. 1643)

Speaking about suddenly becoming president, Ford cited a biblical passage to explain how he spiritually managed in the aftermath of President Richard Nixon's resignation:

In the few hours before this responsibility was suddenly thrust upon me, I was asked what verse I wanted the Bible open to when I took the oath of office. I turned to the Bible, which had been given to me when I became Vice President by my oldest son, Mike, who is a divinity student in Massachusetts. Ever since I was a little boy I have used a very special verse in the Bible as a prayer. . . . It comes from the Book of Proverbs and it says, "Trust in the Lord with all thine heart, and lean not unto thine own understanding. In all thy ways acknowledge Him, and He shall direct thy path." (Ford, 1976e, p. 926)

Although Ford was often asked about his personal religious beliefs, his answers usually referenced a rather vague "commitment," and only on a few occasions did he speak of his religious beliefs in a more personal manner. With his answers, Ford demonstrated that although he attended church and believed in God, he was not nearly as comfortable with talking publicly about his private faith as Carter.

Most of Ford's religious-political discourse during the campaign period dealt with the United States bicentennial celebrations and his belief that America had a *special relationship* with God and that our nation had been divinely blessed. Throughout the year, Ford talked about how America's founders had trusted God, how God had blessed America through conflicts and difficulties, and why America needed to continue to recognize God's blessings. In an address to a joint meeting of the National Religious Broadcasters and the National Association of Evangelicals, Ford focused on the upcoming bicentennial and 200 years of American history:

The commandments and the laws of God were of very special importance to our Founding Fathers and to the Nation that they created. . . . We are taught in the Psalms, that blessed is the nation whose God is the Lord. I believe that very, very deeply, and I know you believe it, too. (Ford, 1976b, p. 270)

At a Jewish high school he argued, "God has blessed our great land. With this blessing goes a great responsibility: As a free people, we must remember that the price of freedom is eternal vigilance" (Ford, 1976j, p. 1491). At the Alfred E. Smith Memorial Dinner that raises money for Catholic charities, he spoke of "[t]he Jewish-Christian tradition from which this great country emerged" (Ford, 1976k, p. 1553). Ford clearly articulated that he believed America had been divinely created and blessed. In doing so he not only endorsed a Christian interpretation of American history—especially its founding—but also encouraged Americans to join him in worshipping God.

As Ford preached about America's blessings from God, he also linked his campaign to a *spiritual mission* as he claimed a revival was needed to keep America strong. In addressing public cynicism and disillusionment in the wake of the Watergate scandal, Ford urged Americans to worship God. In an address to a joint meeting of the National Religious Broadcasters and the National Association of Evangelicals, Ford claimed that governmental problems could be solved by placing faith in God:

> We hear so much about the corruption of government and business and labor. We sense so much distrust in our basic institutions of society. Too many people are complaining we don't know who or what we can believe in. My answer is we can believe in God. We can believe in the faith of our Fathers. (Ford, 1976b, p. 271)

In his speech to the Southern Baptist Convention, Ford argued that trust in God was needed to help government officials avoid corruption and govern morally:

> Public officials have a special responsibility to set a good example for others to follow—in both their private and public conduct. . . . Jesus said, "Unto whomsoever much is given, of him shall much be required." Personal integrity is not too much to ask of public servants. . . . To remedy these abuses, we must look not only to the government but, more importantly, to the Bible, the church, the human heart. (Ford, 1976f, p. 1059)

With these remarks to Southern Baptists, Ford attempted to distance himself from the moral failures of his predecessor and respond to an argument advanced by his opponent—the Southern Baptist Sunday school teacher. In fact, Ford began his speech at this meeting by praising Carter as a good Southern Baptist. Throughout the campaign, Ford expressed his belief that God was the answer for our nation's problems and therefore Americans— especially America's leaders—should follow God's decrees. As he developed this spiritual mission during the campaign, Ford preached a prosperity type of gospel that taught as long as Americans would trust and follow God the nation would continue to be blessed and strong.

Only on a few occasions did Ford link his religious beliefs to specific *public policy* positions. With these remarks, Ford suggested that his religious beliefs and scriptures would serve as a guide for governing. In his address to a meeting of the Jewish group B'nai B'rith, Ford referred to a slingshot and small stone used by David in the Bible to defeat the giant warrior Goliath to explain his advocacy for the development of a stronger national defense system: "I seem to recall that the shepherd boy David was both tough and muscular. It is a good thing he also had the most advanced weapon system of that day" (Ford, 1976h, p. 1321). Explaining his position opposing most abortions, Ford told a meeting of Catholic leaders, "The supreme value of every person to whom life is given by God is a belief that comes to us from the holy scriptures confirmed by all the great leaders of the church" (Ford,

1976g, p. 1253). Although Ford used religious teachings with these comments to justify specific public policy positions, he did not often invoke religious beliefs or scriptures during policy discussions on the campaign trail

During the campaign, Ford also dealt with issues of *church and state* as he talked about the importance of religious freedom while also arguing for governmental support of religion. As a result, his rhetoric often appeared caught in a tension between advocating governmental support of religion while not crossing the line separating church and state. He argued, "The United States is a nation where each and every one of us has an opportunity to participate—to participate in government, to pray to God, to have our own religion, and strengthen the character of America" (Ford, 1976l, p. 1582). Although Ford talked about the importance of religious freedom, he also advocated greater governmental support of religion. On the issue of providing funding for private schools, he stated:

> I think we have to give some tax relief to those individuals who, as a matter of choice, want to send their children to nonpublic schools, whether they are Lutheran or Catholic or Christian Science or Jewish or whatever the sponsorship. (Ford, 1976i, p. 1471)

Just days before the election, Ford also pushed for a constitutional amendment allowing prayer in public schools:

> In my view, we lost a great, great American tradition when the Supreme Court ruled out voluntary prayer in public schools. Every child should have the opportunity for voluntary prayer in school, and I strongly support a constitutional amendment that would permit voluntary prayer in public schools. (Ford, 1976n, p. 1641)

During the campaign, Ford preached the need for religious freedom while also advocating policies that the Supreme Court had ruled violated the separation principle. Ford, however, did not acknowledge or attempt to resolve this contradiction.

As an Episcopalian—a mainline Protestant denomination whose membership is often considered reserved in publicly discussing their faith—Gerald Ford clearly struggled to articulate his private religious convictions openly on the campaign trail. With the media focusing considerable attention on Carter's open professions of being "born-again," Ford appeared uncomfortable answering similar questions about his personal faith. Ford did, however, suggest that his religious beliefs would influence his public policy decisions and that he was on a spiritual mission to restore America's faith. Ford also struggled with finding a balance between church and state. When it came to religion, Ford could most often be heard preaching about America's special relationship with God and the divine blessings Ford believed had been be-

stowed upon the nation. In many ways, Ford represented an earlier generation of politicians as he avoided discussing private religious beliefs. As a
result, he seemed unable to easily adjust to the challenge of his more religiously outspoken opponent—an evangelical Christian who seemed more than
willing to break the American taboo of talking publicly about private religious matters.

Jimmy Carter

During both the 1976 primary and general election, Jimmy Carter spoke
frequently and openly about his *personal faith* and spiritual practices. Far
from the religiously shy Ford, Carter seemed not only comfortable but even
proud to discuss his Christian credentials. In fact, in announcing his candidacy, Carter began his speech by identifying himself as a Christian:

> We Americans are a great and diverse people. We take full advantage of our
> right to develop wide-ranging interests and responsibilities. For instance, I am
> a farmer, an engineer, a businessman, a planner, a scientist, a governor and a
> Christian. (Carter, 1974, ¶1).

To further strengthen his religious credentials, Carter also identified himself
as "a born-again Christian Baptist Sunday-school-teacher deacon" (Matthews, 1975, ¶6) and mentioned he read Christian theologian Reinhold Nie-
buhr. Carter spoke of "a profound religious experience that changed my life
dramatically" (Politicians are discovering, 1976, ¶3) and proclaimed, "The
most important thing in my life is Jesus Christ" (Smith, 2006, p. 293). Carter
boasted that he prays "about 25 times a day, maybe more" and reads the
Bible in Spanish because "I could do it [in English] in three minutes. . . . It
wasn't a challenge" (Fraker, 1976, ¶3). He said of his time as governor: "I've
spent more time on my knees than all other times put together, because my
decisions affected people" (Schlesinger, 1976, p. 18). He also spoke about
the religious insights he would seek once in the Oval Office:

> If I'm elected President, I would join the nearest Baptist church and go there
> every Sunday and play down any sort of show about it. . . . I wouldn't hold a
> Catholic service and a Jewish service and a Moslem service and a Presbyterian
> service in the White House. (Fraker, 1976, ¶3)

Asked about previous comments he had made when describing the strong
influence of a specific sermon that lead to his born-again conversion, Carter
explained:

> And one day the preacher gave this sermon. I just remember the title which
> you just described—"If You Were Arrested for Being a Christian, Would
> There Be Any Evidence to Convict You?" And my answer by the time that

sermon was over was no. I never had really committed myself totally to
God. . . . I formed a much more intimate relationship with Christ. And since
then I've had just about like a new life. (Carter, 1977, p. 94)

After being questioned about his Baptist beliefs, Carter responded by reiter-
ating his faith and commitment to the teachings of Christ: "If people want to
know about it, they can read the New Testament. . . . I can't change the
teachings of Christ! I believe in them, and a lot of people in this country do
as well" (Carter, 1977, p. 182–83). Asked about a statement that he does not
fear death, Carter explained, "It's part of my religious belief. I just look at
death as not a threat. It's inevitable, and I have an assurance of eternal life"
(Carter, 1977, p. 187). Throughout the campaign, Carter often spoke about
his personal religious faith, which garnered him much media attention and
support. Attention to his declarations of being "born-again" particularly
gained attention and public support in the spring of 1976 just as he was
moving from long-shot to front-runner in the primary campaign. Carter not
only remained open about his private religious beliefs, but seemed to adopt a
stance of what the biblical writer Paul called "boasting in the Lord" as he
proudly proclaimed his prayer and Bible reading habits.

Carter expressed his belief that God had blessed America and that America had a *special relationship* with God. As his Republican opponent also
argued, Carter declared that America's strength came from God and that
America was God's chosen nation. He stated during his October 6, 1976
general election debate with Gerald Ford:

We'll never have that world leadership until we are strong at home, and we can
have that strength if we return to the basic principles. . . . It ought to be a quiet
strength based on the integrity of our people, the vision of the Constitution, an
in—innate strong will and purpose that God's given us in the greatest nation
on earth—the United States.

Carter stated about his belief of a divinely blessed nation:

God's blessed us with wide open fields and great land and mineral deposits
and access to the oceans, and pure streams, and good harbors, and pure air.
And God's blessed us too with the finest system of government on earth.
(Carter, 1978b, p. 1079)

He also spoke of the "economic strength that God gave us" (Carter, 1978b, p.
824). Clearly, Carter's religious-political rhetoric included the belief that
America had been blessed by God, although he did not develop this theme as
strongly or frequently as his Republican opponent. He declared that God not
only had bestowed upon America great resources, but also protected and
guided America.

Carter, at times, connected his religious beliefs to *public policy* positions. As he attempted to explain and justify his position on issues or his calls for reforming government, Carter would invoke God or quote scripture. Describing his overall approach to governing, he explained, "I hope my decisions as President would be guided by the religious principles in which I believe" (Gannon, 1976, p. 14). In the announcement of his candidacy, Carter linked his promise to reform government and reduce the levels of bureaucracy to a biblical teaching:

> The Bible says: "If the trumpet give an uncertain sound, who shall prepare himself to the battle." As a planner and a businessman, and a chief executive, I know from experience that uncertainty is also a devastating affliction in private life and in government. . . . There is no clear vision of what is to be accomplished, everyone struggles for temporary advantage, and there is no way to monitor how effectively services are delivered. (Carter, 1974, ¶42)

Carter told those present at a Disciples of Christ laymen's conference that "men of faith" were needed in government (Carter urges, 1976, ¶19). He added, "I believe that if we can demonstrate this kind of personal awareness of our own faith, we can provide that core of strength and commitment and underlying character that our nation searches for" (Carter urges, 1976, ¶22). In addition to invoking religion to call for government reform, Carter also used religion to explain his position on various issues. Regarding his foreign policy, Carter stated, "I think the establishment of Israel . . . is a fulfillment of Biblical prophecy. I think God wants the Jews to have a place to live" (Fraker, 1976, ¶11). He called homosexuality "contrary to the Bible's teachings" (Politicians are discovering, 1976, ¶12). On another occasion, he told those at a campaign rally, "The Bible says that adultery and fornication are wrong. I believe in the Bible. I believe that premarital and extramarital sex are wrong" (Meyer, 1978, p. 73). As Carter sought the bully pulpit of the presidency, he demonstrated that he would often be guided by teachings from the religious pulpit in his decision-making while president.

A prominent religious-political theme Carter frequently developed in his campaign appeals was his support for religious freedom when addressing issues of *church and state*. Although Carter often talked about his religion and even cited scripture to justify political positions, he insisted that he respected the religious freedom of all Americans and the principle of separation of church and state. Carter stressed that he understood and respected "very clearly the requirement of separation for church and state" (Fraker, 1976, ¶5). He explained to a Jewish group that an "important tenet of my own Baptist faith is an absolute and total separation of church and state" that he believes in "very deeply" (Mohr, 1976b, p. 22). He added, "I worship the same God you do. . . . We study the same Bible you do" (Mohr, 1976b, p. 22). He also connected this theme of separation to his opposition to religious prejudice. He argued at the Alfred E. Smith Memorial Dinner, "I think everyone here will agree that Al Smith would have made a great President. But he was denied that office, and we were denied his service, partially because of religious prejudice" (Carter, 1977, p. 237–38). In a speech to the National Conference of Catholic Charities, Carter also compared his own religious-political struggle to that of John F. Kennedy:

> John Kennedy, speaking in 1960 to a meeting of ministers in Houston, said that while it was he a Catholic who faced suspicion that year, it would someday be, as he said, a Jew or a Baptist. His prediction has come to pass. This year it is a Southern Baptist who faces the intense scrutiny. And I've not the slightest doubt that this year once again our national tradition of tolerance and fairness will prevail. (Carter, 1977, p. 208)

Although Carter's public professions of his faith garnered substantial attention during the campaign, he offered his assurances—especially when addressing different religious groups like Jews and Catholics—that he would respect their religious rights and uphold the separation of church and state.

During the 1976 campaign, two church-related conflicts became political issues—one during the primary campaign with attacks against a Carter opponent, and the other during the general election with attacks on Carter's own hometown church. A prominent Carter supporter attacked Morris Udall during the Democratic primary campaign because Udall's Mormon denomination did not allow African Americans to be ministers. Udall claimed he had already left the Mormon church because of "a deep-seated conscientious difference with the church doctrine regarding blacks" and "a lack of feeling any need for organized religion" (Politicians are discovering, 1976, ¶22). Carter, however, refused to repudiate the remark of his supporter and Carter's spokesman instead attacked Udall's campaign for suggesting Carter was using religion for political gain (Mohr, 1976a).

Another religious issue that developed late in the general campaign occurred when Carter's home church in Plains, Georgia, closed on the Sunday two days before the election in order to prevent a black minister and activist from attending. Carter, who was away from Georgia campaigning at the time, held a press conference to deal with the issue and argued that there was an effort to disrupt his church in Plains because of his presidential run. He blamed the controversy on a Republican from out of state trying to hurt his campaign and divide his church. When asked why he did not leave his church to protest its position on race—a position that he disagreed with—Carter explained:

I can't resign from the human race because there's discrimination. I can't
resign as an American citizen because there's still discrimination. And I don't
intend to resign from my own church because there's discrimination. I think
my best approach is to stay within the church and to try to change the attitudes
which I abhor. (Carter, 1977, p. 249)

He added that he could not "quit my lifetime of worship habit and commitment" as a result because "this is not my church, it's God's church" (Carter,
1977, p. 249). As Carter walked a fine line in defending and critiquing his
church, he offered further insights into his religious beliefs and how a candidate's religion should be judged within a political campaign. For the first
time in sixteen years since John F. Kennedy was questioned by Protestant
ministers, a candidate's church attendance became a political issue and potentially even a liability to his campaign.

As Carter moved from a little-known one-term governor of Georgia to the
front-runner in the 1976 presidential campaign, his frequent public professions of faith garnered media attention and attracted the attention of evangelical Christians across the nation. Although Carter proudly talked about his
theological beliefs and personal spiritual habits and how his religious beliefs
would inform his political decisions, he also stressed his belief in the separation of church and state and his belief in religious freedom for all Americans.
Carter also advocated that America was divinely blessed. Portending problems for later candidates who would be attacked because of the church they
attended, Carter was confronted with a racial conflict in his longtime spiritual
home. In handling the situation, Carter—who talked about his church service
as proof that he could be trusted to lead the nation—argued that his church
membership should not be held against him as he promised to work toward
reforming the congregation.

In the wake of the Watergate scandal and the resignation of both the
President and Vice President, a peanut farmer tapped into the nation's desire
for moral leadership by testifying about his personal religious beliefs and
practices. Catching many of his Democratic opponents and the sitting President off guard, the Bible-quoting Sunday school teacher soon found himself
with his hand on the Bible while taking the oath of office to become the
nation's thirty-ninth president. In contrast to Gerald Ford's private approach
to religious beliefs, Jimmy Carter proudly confessed his faith and his sins.
The religious rhetoric of the unlikely Democratic candidate seemed to many
to be a stark and refreshing contrast to our nation's recent government scandals. While Carter embraced religious rhetoric as a way of gaining media
attention and the public's trust, Ford remained hesitant and uncomfortable in
talking about his personal faith—even when asked. The candidates also differed substantially on issues of church and state. Ford attempted to balance
the rhetorical tension between his affirmation in separation of church and

state while also advocating positions that violated such separation. Mean-while, Carter strongly expressed his support for separation of church and state and his respect for religious freedom of all Americans. Although both candidates proclaimed that God had specially blessed and protected America and suggested that they would use religion in their consideration of public policy positions, Carter's public professions clearly established him as the religious candidate in the race and helped him unseat the incumbent President.

1980

A number of problems, including a sagging economy, resulted in President Carter receiving low approval ratings from the American public and led Senator Edward Kennedy of Massachusetts to announce in late 1979 that he would challenge Carter for the Democratic nomination. Despite early polls showing Kennedy beating Carter nearly two-to-one, the numbers shifted dramatically by the time the Democratic primaries began the following year. Kennedy's inability to clearly articulate why he should be elected president and Carter's initial handling of the Iran hostage crisis that erupted in December of 1979 boosted Carter's approval ratings during the Democratic primaries. Unlike Carter, Kennedy virtually avoided religious references during the campaign. After Carter strongly defeated Kennedy in both the Iowa caucuses and the New Hampshire primary, he easily won most remaining primaries until Kennedy claimed a few late states when public opinion began to shift regarding Carter's handling of the Iran hostage crisis. However, Carter and Vice President Walter Mondale went on to secure the Democratic nomination before the convention.

On the Republican side in 1980, Ronald Reagan stood as the apparent front-runner after nearly beating incumbent President Gerald Ford for the nomination four years earlier. As a result, Reagan avoided participating in many early party events and forums, which allowed George H. W. Bush, former chairman of the Republican National Committee and former director of the Central Intelligence Agency, to gain attention and support. After winning the Iowa caucuses, Bush appeared to be a serious contender for the nomination. However, with strong debate performances, Reagan managed to win New Hampshire and most other states. Reagan later chose Bush as his running mate.

As the first Republican primary held after the creation of the Reverend Jerry Falwell's Moral Majority, the 1980 primary featured pronounced religious rhetoric. Conservative Christian organizations focused their support on Reagan and former Texas Governor John Connally, although they also liked

Representative Phil Crane of Illinois (Witt, 1979). During the campaign, the Republican candidates often spoke to religious groups. For instance, Bush spoke to the National Conference of Christians and Jews, Crane addressed the National Religious Broadcasters, and Representative John Anderson of Illinois and Bush spoke at the evangelical Wheaton College. Some candidates, like Connally, Bush, and Anderson, spoke in local churches during the campaign. In fact, Connally's campaign was accused of making a deal to give more than $70,000 to the African Methodist Episcopal Church in return for a promise of 100,000 African American votes in the South Carolina primary, a charge pushed by Bush's campaign but denied by Connally (Smith, 1980). The attacks by Bush apparently backfired as he dropped in the South Carolina polls and Connally's support rose (Martin, 1980).

In the general election, John Anderson, who ran unsuccessfully for the Republican nomination against Reagan, launched an independent run against Reagan and Carter. This set up a race where all three major candidates professed to be "born-again" Christians (Benson, 1981). Although gaffes by Reagan sometimes hurt his image, the economic problems and Iran hostage crisis greatly hurt Carter's electoral chances. Carter refused to debate with Reagan if Anderson was also included, and therefore Carter did not attend the first presidential debate hosted by the League of Women Voters. Reagan beat expectations and held firm against Anderson in the debate, which likely contributed to a dramatic decline in the polls for Anderson. Two weeks before the election, Carter and Reagan finally agreed to a one-on-one debate. Reagan's strong performance in the debate turned a slight Carter lead in the polls into a large Reagan victory on election day. During the campaign, both Carter and Reagan addressed religious audiences, such as the biennial meeting of the Jewish group B'nai B'rith, the Alfred E. Smith Memorial Dinner, and different meetings of the National Religious Broadcasters. Carter spoke in several churches and Reagan addressed a group of evangelists in Dallas, where he famously told the group, "I know you can't endorse me . . . but I want to know that I endorse you and what you are doing" (Balmer, 2008, p. 119). Reagan captured 50.7 percent of the popular vote to Carter's 41 and Anderson's 6.6, but Reagan received a landslide electoral college victory with over 90 percent of the votes.

Throughout the 1980 campaign, John Anderson offered a unique religious voice as he forcefully criticized the mixing of religion and politics. A lay minister and Bible teacher in the Evangelical Free Church, Anderson had proposed a Constitutional amendment three times in the 1960s to recognize "the authority and law of Jesus Christ, savior and ruler of nations" (Alpern, et al., 1980, ¶16). However, by the 1980 campaign, he admitted that it was "a mistake and I regret it. It does not represent my current thinking" (Alpern, et al., 1980, ¶16). He also said it was "one of the stupidest things I ever did" and that he had since become "much more tolerant" (Hornblower, 1980, ¶27). On a few occasions during the campaign, Anderson talked about his personal religious background and beliefs, but he rejected the open approach of Carter. During his September 21, 1980, general election debate with Ronald Reagan, Anderson declared that his religious faith was "important" but "a very deeply personal matter." He also claimed he did not "wear his religion on his sleeve" (Macpherson, 1980, ¶51). Anderson argued that the answers to America's spiritual crisis were not "sectarian" and that he did not believe there was "something exclusive about the brand of salvation offered by a particular denomination or religious belief" (Briggs, 1980a, ¶26). He argued, "I'm not a narrow, sectarian, denominational kind of religious person. . . . I can see some very good things in all of the religions" (Rosenthal, 1980, ¶28).

One of Anderson's main religious-political arguments was his strong expression of support for the principle of separation of church and state. Not only did he repudiate his previous positions on constitutional amendments recognizing Christianity or allowing prayer in schools, but he also strongly argued for the need for separation. He argued, "Religion has no place in a political campaign, and I vigorously affirm the principle of separation of church and state" (Foley, 1980, ¶25). Anderson argued during a February 20, 1980 Republican primary debate:

> On the question of prayer in the schools, I believe that when mother sends Johnny and Suzy off to the classroom in the morning, she ought to whisper in their ear and tell them, "Now be sure and say a prayer before you begin your school day." But I certainly don't want the state writing and composing that prayer for Johnny and Suzy to recite.

Anderson also often employed religious-political rhetoric as he attacked his two political opponents and others involved in the campaign. He criticized both candidates for interjecting religion into politics, thus repeating his claim that religious beliefs should remain a private matter. Anderson attacked Jerry Falwell and the Moral Majority as "that kind of extreme fundamentalism that has some dangerous tendencies because it is totally intolerant of anyone else's point of view" (Briggs, 1980a, ¶21). He added, "To the extent that they see themselves as part of the evangelical branch of the church, I think I've tried to distance myself from that point of view" (Briggs, 1980a, ¶21). He especially attacked the evangelical religious leaders for trying to violate the separation of church and state:

> Unfortunately, our constitutional balance is now under broad attack. . . . This August, 15,000 Protestant fundamentalists gathered in Dallas. Many of the speakers who addressed them advocated to what amounted to an American version of Ayatollah Khomeini's Iran. They invoked the scriptures as the sole

source of political guidance and authority. They described secular political forces as satanic. And they were determined to repress all those who disagreed with them. (General news, 1980, ¶5–6)

Anderson also attacked Carter: "I wish he would open up that heavy Bible that he so ostentatiously carries on Sunday morning as he goes to and from the classroom of the Sunday school at the Baptist church" (Reynolds, 1980, ¶6). On another occasion he referenced scripture in his critique of Carter's policies: "Jimmy Carter, you have been weighed in the balances and you have been found wanting" (Phillips, 1980, ¶13). Throughout the campaign, Anderson strongly defended the separation of church and state and attacked his opponents for mixing religion and politics.

Jimmy Carter

During the 1980 campaign, Jimmy Carter continued many of his religious-political themes from the 1976 campaign, although he also offered a few important changes in his religious-political appeals. Once again he proudly talked about his *personal faith* as a prominent part of his life. He frequently discussed his religious service and leadership over the years and how important his religious beliefs were to him. In an election where he was being attacked by conservative Christians through the newly created Moral Majority, Carter found himself in the unusual position of having to stress that he, too, was a devout Christian:

> I grew up as a little boy who went to Sunday school every Sunday morning. . . . When I went to the U.S. Naval Academy as a midshipman for 3 years, I taught Sunday school. It was an extra chore for me, but it was one that I enjoyed. . . . When I got on a submarine, on a ship, quite often Sunday mornings, certainly on Easter Sunday and so forth, I would hold religious services for other crew members on the ship, who wanted me, as a young officer, to tell them about Christ, about my religion. (Carter, 1980s, p. 2592)

He added:

> When I was elected Governor, the first day I moved to Atlanta I shifted my church membership to a nearby church. And I became a deacon in the church, taught Sunday school to a senior citizens group. When I moved to Washington as a President, immediately I joined a church, First Baptist Church in Washington. . . . I teach Sunday school still. (Carter, 1980s, p. 2592)

He also talked about his private devotional life: "Every night I read a chapter in the Bible, with my wife when we're together; we read the same chapter when we're separated. It's part of my existence. I've done it for years" (Carter, 1980q, p. 2509). Carter, who claimed during the 1976 campaign to pray as often as twenty-five times a day, stated during the 1980 campaign: "I have prayed more since I've been President than I ever did before in my life, because I feel the need for it more" (Carter, 1980n, p. 2388). On another occasion, he said, "God knows I pray as deeply and frequently as anyone on Earth that we will have continued peace" (Carter, 1980f, p. 1414). Throughout the campaign, Carter talked about his religious background and his personal religious beliefs. Much as with 1976, he confessed his faith and testified about his spiritual prayer and meditation habits. In attempting to refute attacks by the newly created Moral Majority and other conservative Christians that his presidency was not sufficiently religious, Carter emphasized how religion was still part of his life as he prayed regularly in the White House and still taught Sunday school.

As in 1976, Carter talked about the divine blessings that he believed God had bestowed upon our nation as a result of America's *special relationship* with God. He continued to stress that America's natural resources and greatness came from God. Carter told those at a national 4-H Club meeting, "God has blessed us, as you know, with unbelievably fertile land and with natural resources far beyond the dreams of any other people on Earth, and we've taken good care of that land over which we have stewardship" (Carter, 1980d, p. 701). On several occasions the former peanut farmer talked about farming as part of God's blessings and praised farmers: "You've been blessed by God with productive land, and you've utilized it to the highest as good stewards of what God has given you" (Carter, 1980t, p. 2618). He also talked about "the beauties that God has given us" (Carter, 1980a, p. 51) and that "we've been overly endowed by God with those material blessings" (Carter, 1980a, p. 50). Carter argued, "I want to make sure that we never forget . . . to thank God who gave us all our blessings" (Carter, 1980k, p. 2148). Speaking to a group of black ministers, Carter claimed "And I might add that as President of this country, I think the United States of America was created by God with a purpose—on a purpose." (Carter, 1980p, p. 2429). With his religious-political rhetoric, Carter strongly argued that God had blessed our nation and thus Americans should praise God for those blessings. He declared that America had a special mission and that God had given our nation resources to accomplish that purpose.

Rather than merely continuing his 1976 claim that God had specially blessed America, Carter adapted the message in 1980 to include the claim that there were limits to God's blessings and that the nation needed to rely on God while making needed sacrifices. Carter called on the nation to adapt to the global energy crisis by being wise stewards of God's blessings rather than assuming that God would continue to offer more. He argued, "For the first time in our history, we now have to realize that there are indeed limits on what God has given us to use or to use up or to waste" (Carter, 1980e, p. 829). Addressing the energy crisis with a group of ministers, Carter linked his call for energy conservation to biblical teachings:

> It might seem strange to some, not to you, that the conservation of oil has a religious connotation. But when God created the Earth and gave human beings dominion over it, it was with the understanding on the part of us, then and down through the generations, that we are indeed stewards under God's guidance, to protect not only those who are fortunate enough to grasp an advantage or a temporary material blessing or enjoyment but to husband those bases for enjoyment and for a quality of life for those less fortunate in our own generation and especially for those who will come after us. (Carter, 1980a, p. 50)

In another speech he also compared those criticizing his call to sacrifice to the Israelites that complained in the Old Testament and suggested that conservation was indeed part of God's will:

> Like the children of Israel, we cannot always know where the road will lead. God does give us guidance, but he does not provide roadmaps with a sure and certain destination. Our Nation now is faced with serious challenges and choices which may require sacrifice, even from those assembled here in this great hall. . . . It is not a sacrifice to give up waste. It's not a sacrifice to submit to God's will. (Carter, 1980b, p. 182)

With this analogy, Carter becomes like Moses and his critics are cast as those who challenged Moses and thus God's will. During the campaign, Carter argued that God had blessed America, but—unlike 1976—he now argued that there were limits to those blessings and thus Americans had to make sacrifices. As a result, Carter called on the nation to trust in God to provide the blessings and strength needed for the nation to endure struggles, sacrifices, and difficult times.

During the campaign, Carter often connected his religious beliefs to his *public policy* positions. As he had done in 1976, Carter not only connected specific policies to religious teachings but also his overall governing philosophy. He explained his political philosophy in Christian terms during a town hall meeting:

> To alleviate hunger, suffering, deprivation, discrimination, hatred, to me, is compatible with God's teachings. To promote peace for ourselves and around the world, to me, is part of Biblical admonition and teaching. Also, human rights in the broadest sense of that word, to me, is in accordance with God's teaching. (Carter, 1980n, p. 2388)

In addition to framing his energy crisis policies in terms of trusting in God while sacrificing, Carter also suggested that prayer was a key focus of his foreign policy toward Iran, claiming he prayed every day about the crisis. Carter even stated he prayed for the Iranian leader Ayatollah Khomeini:

> The Bible says even the worst sinners love and pray for their friends, the ones who love them. . . . Every day, I pray for the Ayatollah Khomeini. Every day I pray for the kidnappers who hold our innocent Americans. . . . It's not easy to do this, and I have to force myself sometimes to include someone on my list, because I don't want to acknowledge that that person might be worthy of my love. (Carter, 1980c, p. 277)

With this argument and his claim to pray for the Ayatollah, Carter offered a more inclusive view of prayer than that offered by many of his religious critics, and he suggested that prayer could be an important way to help bring the hostage crisis to an end. Carter also invoked religion with his discussions of domestic policies. About eliminating the marriage tax, he argued, "It's very important that we don't overlook the principles and ideals and religious faith that preserves the sanctity of the marriage vows and also let the family be stable in its relationship to one another" (Carter, 1980i, p. 2083–84). In a speech at an African American Baptist church, he also pushed for more civil rights progress:

> And many times in my own church at home we've sung the old hymn, "There is a Balm in Gilead; sometimes we get discouraged and think our work's in vain." But I tell you that together, as Democrats, we have moved forward. We're on the right road. We're making good progress. (Carter, 1980m, p. 2367)

On other occasions, however, Carter claimed that there are some issues that could not be answered based on the Bible. This was not a line he developed during his 1976 presidential bid, but a message he developed during the 1980 campaign in opposition to arguments from the Moral Majority. He argued at the Alfred E. Smith Memorial Dinner:

> My religion is an important part of my life. I've studied the Bible all my life. But nowhere in the Bible, Old or New Testament, are there instructions on how to balance the budget or how to choose between the B-1 bomber and the air-launched cruise missile. What I do find is, "Judge not that ye not be judged," and the commandment "to love my neighbor." (Carter, 1980l, p. 2315)

Although he denied a biblical position on some specific issues, he still argued that the Bible's teachings should be used as a guide for making decisions in general. Additionally, Carter did use biblical arguments and even a church hymn to justify some of his specific policy positions.

One of Carter's main messages—as in 1976—was his rhetoric on *church and state* issues as he again offered his strong support for the principle of separation of church and state. Despite his emphasis on his personal faith and how his religious beliefs at times informed his political positions, Carter stressed that he respected the religious rights of all Americans. Perhaps in response to the religious-political efforts of the Moral Majority, in 1980 Carter articulated his belief in the separation principle even more forcefully and frequently than in his 1976 campaign. He argued, "I have never found any incompatibility between my own religious faith and my duties as President, and I believe in the separation of church and state" (Carter, 1980h, p. 2010). On the political issue of school prayer, which was being pushed by the Moral Majority, he noted:

> The thing that I'm against, as President—and as a Baptist, coincidentally—is the Government telling people they have to worship at a certain time and in a certain way. To me that violates the constitutional separation of church and state. (Carter, 1980g, p. 1621)

He also connected his belief in the separation principle with his understanding of America's founding at the Alfred E. Smith Memorial Dinner:

> Those who originally created the promise of America were firm in their convictions. They believed in religious tolerance. They believed in tolerance for the views of others. They believed in separation of church and state. They believed that government should not decree or interfere with any person's worship or freedom of conscience. That was not because they considered religion unimportant, but because they considered it too important for government to try to influence or control. (Carter, 1980l, p. 2315)

Additionally, Carter did not endorse the idea that America had been created as a "Christian nation," despite his strong rhetoric about God blessing America. After being asked what he would do to "protect Christians" since "this Nation was built on a Christian foundation," Carter responded in direct opposition to beliefs of the Moral Majority and other conservative Christians:

> Timothy, as a Christian and a Baptist myself, I can tell you that this Nation was not founded just on the Christian religion. This Nation was founded on the proposition that there would be no special religion designated by the Congress or the United States—this is in the Constitution of the United States—either by Congress or any state representing the establishment of religion or singling out a particular religion as being favored over any other. (Carter, 1980n, p. 2387)

Despite Carter's strong advocacy for separation, he did urge religious leaders to be involved with the political process. He told a group of ministers five days before the election to not only vote "and preach a sermon on Sunday outlining the differences that will be decided on Tuesday," but to campaign and get people registered (Carter, 1980r, p. 2531). Carter frequently cited his belief in the separation of church and state during the campaign, especially as he worried that the mixing of religion and politics during the campaign was going too far. Although there remained some of the tension from 1976 because of his openness about his religious beliefs and their political impact, Carter's rhetoric of 1980, overall, offered more suggestion of inclusiveness toward other positions and he was on the offensive—instead of the defensive as in 1976—on the issue of separation of church and state as he attacked the Moral Majority for crossing this line.

Carter also used his religious rhetoric to offer *political attacks* against Ronald Reagan and his Moral Majority supporters, often for going too far in mixing religion and politics. The use of religious rhetoric to attack his political opponents likely further alienated many Christian conservatives. About the efforts of the Moral Majority he offered:

> I respect the right of even Reverend Falwell to express his views, even from the pulpit. But when you start putting a measuring stick on a political figure and saying he is or is not an acceptable person in the eyes of God, I remember the admonition in the New Testament: "Judge not that ye be judged" and "God is love." (Carter, 1980q, p. 2509)

Carter also suggested that if Reagan won the election, America would be divided religiously: "Americans might be separated, black from white, Jew from Christian, North from South, rural from urban" (Carter, 1980j, p. 2093). This statement created controversy and counterattacks from Reagan and his supporters. With these attacks, Carter criticized the religious-political views of his political opponents and used religion as another political weapon.

Ronald Reagan

With the Moral Majority and other evangelical Christian groups campaigning for Ronald Reagan during the 1980 campaign, religion played a significant role in his election. Reagan not only often spoke to meetings of evangelical religious groups, but also espoused many of their religious-political themes. While Reagan talked some about his own *personal faith* and beliefs, he was not nearly as open about his private spiritual beliefs as Carter. Asked if he was "born-again," Reagan offered this interpretation of his own personal conversion experience:

I know what many of those who use that term mean by it. But in my situation, in the church I was raised in, the Christian Church, there you were baptized and you yourself decided that you were, as the Bible says, "born again." In the context of the Bible, by being baptized you were born again. (Hyer, 1980, ¶24)

On another occasion, he pointed to his decision to join his local church at age twelve as part of accepting Christ and added, "If that's what you mean by born-again, you could call me born-again" (Smith, 2006, p. 336). Although Reagan did not fully embrace the term "born-again," he was presented throughout the campaign as an evangelical even though the two terms are generally considered to be synonymous. Although Reagan did not often talk about his personal faith, he did profess his belief in God and made it clear that he considered himself a Christian.

Reagan's dominant religious-political theme during the campaign was his belief that America had a *special relationship* with God. Reagan spoke often about how America's founders had trusted and relied on God and about how God had guided and blessed America throughout the years. Reagan spoke frequently of America's "Judeo-Christian tradition" (President Reagan, 1981, p. 93). In his acceptance speech at the Republican National Convention, Reagan declared, "It is impossible to capture in words the splendor of this vast continent which God has granted as our portion of His creation" (Reagan, 1980, ¶90).He stated during the September 21, 1980 general election debate with Anderson, "Our Government, in its most sacred documents—the Constitution and the Declaration of Independence and all—speak of man being created, of a Creator. That we're a nation under God." In a televised address the night before his election, Reagan claimed, "It is not bombs and rockets but belief and resolve—it is humility before God that is ultimately the source of America's strength as a nation" (Reagan's final speech, 1980, ¶4). In the announcement of his candidacy, Reagan famously quoted a Puritan minister who quoted Scripture to declare America as a divine "city on a hill":

We who are privileged to be Americans have had a rendezvous with destiny since the moment in 1630 when John Winthrop, standing on the deck of the tiny Arbella off the coast of Massachusetts, told the little band of Pilgrims, "We shall be a city upon a hill. The eyes of all people are upon us so that if we shall deal falsely with our God in this work we have undertaken and so cause Him to withdraw His present help from us, we shall be made a story and a byword throughout the world." (Reagan, 1979, ¶42)

Throughout the campaign, Reagan expressed his belief that God had divinely created and blessed America and that America's founders—as he did—trusted in God to lead the new nation. Unlike Carter's 1980 rhetoric suggesting there were limits to God's blessings even if we remained faithful, Reagan offered no such caveats.

Reagan also often compared his campaign and political goals to a religious revival, thus casting his campaign as a *spiritual mission*. With this framing, his political campaign became a religious crusade designed to keep America following in God's will. Speaking at a fairground in California before a gospel concert, Reagan insisted, "I think this country is hungry today for a spiritual revival" (Gerstenzang, 1980, ¶10). He argued that throughout the nation there was "a hunger in this land for spiritual revival, for a return to belief in moral absolutes—the same morals upon which the nation was founded" (Cornell, 1980, ¶8). He told the evangelists in Dallas, "Religious America is awakening, perhaps just in time for our country's sake" (Hunt, 1980, ¶7). Reagan added that he thought the American people held "a belief that law must be based on a higher law" and wanted "a return to traditions and values that we once had." Throughout the campaign, Reagan used religious-political rhetoric to cast his campaign as a spiritual revival designed to bring political salvation to the nation. With this rhetoric, Reagan casts himself as spiritual leader seeking to redeem a struggling nation beset by crises at home and abroad.

Reagan also explained his positions on various *public policy* issues in religious terms. He not only claimed that the Bible should be the guide to making governmental decisions, but also offered specific examples of how he would allow his scriptural interpretations to inform his policy decisions. About the Bible, Reagan told the evangelists in Dallas, "Indeed, it is an incontrovertible fact . . . that all the complex and horrendous questions confronting us at home and worldwide have their answer in that single book" (Raines, 1980, ¶8). Speaking of his overall governing goals, Reagan stated during the announcement of his candidacy:

> [Americans] want someone who believes they can "begin the world over again." A leader who will unleash their great strength and remove the roadblocks government has put in their way. I want to do that more than anything I've ever wanted. And it's something that I believe with God's help I can do. (Reagan, 1979, ¶40)

During a February 23, 1980, Republican primary debate he connected his anticommunist position with the godlessness of the Soviet Union and placed his faith in America's victory because of God's blessing. Reagan's religious-political rhetoric in 1980 also foreshadowed a debate that would later gain even more significance in American politics as he told the evangelists at the

National Affairs Briefing in Dallas that human evolution was merely a theory, and added, "If it was going to be taught in the schools, then I would think that also the biblical theory of creation, which is not a theory but the biblical story of creation, should also be taught" (Lewis, 1980, ¶14). Throughout the campaign, Reagan offered assurances that he would rely on the Bible and his spiritual beliefs as he made policy decisions. This perspective of the Bible as a complete guidebook for governing perfectly matched the beliefs of many of his conservative Christian followers.

An uneasy contradiction developed in Reagan's religious-political rhetoric as he dealt with issues of *church and state*. Reagan spoke frequently about his desire to see greater religious influence in politics and government, specifically offering his support for prayer in public schools and tuition tax-credits for parents with children in parochial schools. At the same time, Reagan both claimed he was not violating the separation of church and state while also attacking interpretations of the principle. Asked if his proposals violated the historic principle of separation of church and state, he told reporters:

> Because you are professional, I know how much you respect and strongly support—as I do—the separation of church and state. . . . This is one of our most important traditions and it must continue to be protected in the future. (Curtis, 1980, ¶8)

On other occasions, however, he criticized the separation concept and urged greater mixing of religion and politics. He told the evangelists at the Religious Roundtable's National Affairs Briefing:

> When I hear the First Amendment used as a reason to keep traditional moral values away from policymaking, I am shocked. . . . The First Amendment was written not to protect the people and their laws from religious values, but to protect those values from government tyranny. But over the last two or three decades the Federal Government seems to have forgotten both "that old time religion" and that old time Constitution. (Raines, 1980, ¶3)

While speaking in favor of tuition tax breaks for parents with children in parochial schools on another occasion, a heckler cried out that the plan was unconstitutional. Reagan responded, "Separation of church and state does not mean we have to separate ourselves from our religion" (Carroll, 1980, ¶25). In a speech to the National Religious Broadcasters meeting, Reagan voiced his support for school prayer and criticized Supreme Court decisions ruling such prayers to be unconstitutional violations of separation of church and state:

> I would be absolutely opposed to a state-mandated prayer, but I have always
> thought that a voluntary, nonsectarian prayer was perfectly proper, and I don't
> ever think we should have expelled God from the classroom. (Cannon, 1980,
> ¶6)

Despite telling reporters that he believed in the separation of church and state, Reagan often advocated positions that the Supreme Court had ruled violated such a principle and he frequently attacked the principle in speeches to religious groups. Reagan appeared to balance his conflicting positions— the promise to respect the separation of church and state while advocating positions contrary to the principle—by attacking specific interpretations of separation and thus advocating for political and religious leaders to follow a much looser standard.

Although Reagan did not often speak of his personal religious beliefs, he did offer assurances that he believed in God and promised voters he would look to the Bible for political advice. Reagan also assured his religious supporters by preaching about the special place America has in God's heart and by calling for a spiritual revival to come about through his election. On issues of church and state, Reagan countered criticisms that he was violating the separation of church and state because he attacked interpretations of the principle in order to justify his support of issues like prayer in school. Such a nuanced interpretation on separation matched the opinion of many conservative Christians who felt that the Supreme Court had gone too far in enforcing the church-state line.

As Americans considered three evangelical Christians for president in 1980, they were presented with three very different options. One—Jimmy Carter—spoke openly about his personal faith but attempted to offer a more inclusive perspective that balanced his reliance on biblical teachings with a respect for separation of church and state. Another—Ronald Reagan—spoke little of his personal faith but frequently used religious rhetoric to cast his campaign as a crusade to save America, to praise America as God's divinely chosen nation, and to advocate positions that violated traditional interpretations of church and state. The final candidate—John Anderson—argued that one's religion should remain private, there should be a strong line of separation between church and state, and thus he attacked his opponents for interjecting religion into the campaign and even repudiated his own past religious-political zeal. Americans chose the candidate that seemed to best represent their overall religious-political goals and spoke the most about these shared religious values and texts—Ronald Reagan. Although Carter testified more about his personal beliefs, his rhetoric about limits to God's blessings, the need to respect the line between church and state, and his attempt to offer more inclusive religious statements ran counter to the evangelical passion of many Christians. Additionally, Anderson's religious-political rhetoric put him even further outside this perspective as he became a strong critic of the increasing role religion was playing in politics. This left Reagan to assume the role of religious champion despite his infrequent discussion about his personal spiritual beliefs. He did, however, strongly preach about America's special relationship with God, cast his campaign as a spiritual mission, link his policy positions to biblical teachings, and call for greater governmental acknowledgment of the Christian faith.

Overall, Reagan more strongly advocated the need for religious values to guide political and social decisions. While Reagan was likely the least personally committed of the three candidates, he most strongly preached the importance of bringing religion into the public policy arena. Four years later, Reagan explained his 1980 victory in spiritual terms in an address to the National Association of Evangelicals, contrasting his optimistic message about God's blessings with Carter's message:

> Public officials at the highest levels openly spoke of a national "malaise." All over the world America had become known not for strength and resolve, but for vacillation and self-doubt. . . . But the Almighty who gave us this great land also gave us free will, the power under God to choose our own destiny. The American people decided to put a stop to that long decline, and today our country is seeing a rebirth of freedom and faith, a great national renewal. (Reagan, 1984d, ¶17–18)

Thus, with his hopeful American theology, Reagan used religious rhetoric to oust the Baptist Sunday school teacher from the Oval Office.

1984

President Ronald Reagan ran unopposed for the Republican nomination in 1984 and was renominated along with Vice President George H. W. Bush. The Democratic race featured several candidates with strong religious backgrounds. Former Vice President Walter Mondale, the son of a Methodist minister, attended a Presbyterian college and married the daughter of a Presbyterian minister. Senator Gary Hart of Colorado studied at a Nazarene college and at Yale Divinity School as he considered becoming a pastor or theologian before entering Yale Law School. Reverend Jesse Jackson, a civil rights activist, was the first African American to become a top contender for a major party nomination and also the first minister. He studied at Chicago Theological Seminary and often preached in churches as he worked to advance civil rights. Even some of the "also-ran" candidates touted their religious credentials. Florida Governor Reubin Askew, a born-again Christian who took a more conservative position on abortion and homosexuality, was a

Presbyterian church elder known for being a "teetotaler" who abstained from alcohol and smoking on moral grounds (Witt, 1983). A homosexual activist was expelled from Askew's announcement speech for denouncing him as "the Moral Majority's Democratic candidate" (Peterson, 1983, ¶11). Askew's campaign offered fliers at churches in Iowa that highlighted him as the only pro-life candidate in the Democratic primary race (Schram and Sawyer, 1984). Other candidates, such as Senator John Glenn of Ohio, Jackson, and Mondale, also spoke at churches during the campaign. And the 1972 Democratic nominee George McGovern, the son of a Methodist minister and who had briefly studied to become a pastor, ran once more for his party's nomination. As one of the first victims of the Moral Majority who targeted and helped defeat him in his U.S. Senate reelection campaign in 1980, McGovern often lashed out against Reagan and conservative Christians for politicizing religion.

Walter Mondale entered the Democratic race as the front-runner, but faced strong challenges from Jackson and Hart. Although Mondale won the Iowa caucuses, Hart gained a surprise victory in New Hampshire and went on to win more states than Mondale, but lagged slightly behind Mondale in the delegate and popular vote counts. However, Mondale's strength in the Midwest and Northeast—along with support from the newly created Democratic superdelegates—provided him with enough delegates to gain the nomination. Jackson won the primaries in two southern states and the District of Columbia. Mondale chose Representative Geraldine Ferraro of New York as his running mate, making her the first female to be nominated nationally by a major party.

Reverend Jesse Jackson frequently campaigned in churches, such as in one event where the choir sang the spiritual "Sign me up," which took on a new connotation as Jackson would soon formally announce his presidential bid (Raines, 1983). Jackson often framed his campaign as a religious mission. In a sermon at a church prior to officially announcing his campaign, Jackson stated, "We are starting this journey, this pilgrimage, in the right place—in church on Sunday morning" (Langer, 1983, ¶4). During the announcement of his candidacy, Jackson quoted a Christian children's song in comparing his presidential run to the biblical story of David versus Goliath:

> Little David, little David, little David. Took off his unnecessary garments, Little David. Didn't want to get weighted down with a lot of foolishness, little David. Took what God gave him, a sling shot and a God biscuit, a rock. . . . Pick up your sling shot, pick up your rock, declare our time has come, a new day has begun! Red, yellow, black and white, we are all precious in God's sight! Our time has come! (Jackson, 1984, ¶12, 20)

Jackson also called his campaign a "crusade" (Lardner, 1984, ¶14) and declared, "I am not a politician. I am a prophet on a political mission" (Magruder, 1983, ¶6). At times Jackson also became the target of religious-political attacks due to his connection with controversial Nation of Islam leader Louis Farrakhan. Refusing to repudiate Farrakhan's support of his candidacy, Jackson stated, "I do not have the moral authority as a Christian to quite go that far" (Sawislak, 1984, ¶3). Mondale and Hart condemned Farrakhan and criticized Jackson for not denouncing Farrakhan's controversial remarks attacking Israel, prompting Jackson to eventually offer mild criticism of Farrakhan.

Throughout the general election, Ronald Reagan held a wide and consistent lead over Walter Mondale in the polls. After Reagan's poor performance in the first of two presidential debates, commentators began to question if Reagan—who was already the oldest U.S. president—would be able to serve another four years. However, Reagan's strong showing in the second debate put aside these questions, especially when he joked, "I will not make age an issue of this campaign. I am not going to exploit, for political purposes, my opponent's youth and inexperience." During the campaign the two candidates appealed to a number of religious audiences. Reagan spoke at annual meetings of the National Association of Evangelicals, Baptist Fundamentalists, and the Jewish organization B'nai B'rith, as well as Jewish and Catholic gatherings. Mondale spoke at the meetings of B'nai B'rith and the predominately African American National Baptist Convention, USA, where he was introduced by former rival Jesse Jackson. Unlike Reagan, Mondale regularly attended and even spoke in churches during the campaign. However, Mondale cancelled his speech at the Alfred E. Smith Memorial Dinner in New York that raises support for Catholic charities, a routine stop for presidential candidates of both parties. His decision to withdraw from the program prompted criticism from Catholic organizers (Hampson, 1984) and left Reagan as the lone presidential candidate at the dinner. Mondale's campaign also ran ads on the Christian Broadcasting Network (Beamish, 1984). On election day, Reagan won a forty-nine state landslide and captured a record number of electoral college votes. Reagan defeated Mondale 58.8 to 40.6 percent in the popular vote and took nearly 98 percent of the electoral college votes.

Ronald Reagan

Although Ronald Reagan did not talk much about his personal religious background during the 1984 campaign, he did offer a lot of discussion about religion and how he felt religious teachings influenced his political positions and philosophy. Reagan's religious-political rhetoric thus followed closely that of his 1980 campaign. Yet, during the 1984 campaign—as in 1980—he did talk on a few occasions about his *personal faith* and connection with God. When asked during his October 7, 1984, general election debate with Mondale if he was born again, Reagan stated:

> Well, I was raised to have a faith and a belief and have been a member of a church since I was a small boy. In our particular church, we did not use that term, "born again," so I don't know whether I would fit that—that particular term. But I have—thanks to my mother, God rest her soul—the firmest possible belief and faith in God. . . . So, it does play a part in my life. I have no hesitancy in saying so. And, as I say, I don't believe that I could carry on unless I had a belief in a higher authority and a belief that prayers are answered.

When asked about Geraldine Ferraro's claim that his budget cuts hurt the poor and thus demonstrated that Reagan was not a good Christian, he remarked, "Well, Helen, the minute I heard she'd made that statement, I turned the other cheek" (Reagan, 1984m, ¶29), a retort which not only suggested he was a good Christians but demonstrated familiarity with the teachings of Jesus. Although Reagan did not speak much about his personal religious practices, he did clearly espouse his belief in God and biblical teachings. By this point, however, Reagan's reputation as a "good" Christian was already firmly ensconced among conservative Christians.

As with his previous presidential campaign, Reagan's primary religious-political message dealt with the *special relationship* America had with God and the blessings Reagan believed God had granted America. Reagan preached that America's founders relied on God and that God had blessed America throughout its history. Reagan, after all, was the politician who popularized the phrase "God Bless America" as a staple of political campaign addresses (Klope, 2002). Reagan endorsed the idea of America being divinely founded:

> If you take away the belief in a greater future, you cannot explain America— that we're a people who believed there was a promised land; we were a people who believed we were chosen by God to create a greater world. (Reagan, 1984b, ¶8)

In his address to the National Association of Evangelicals, Reagan claimed that God's blessings on America could be seen in the victories of the Civil War and World War II, as well as the success of the civil rights movement (Reagan, 1984d). As a result of this belief, Reagan argued that Americans must live up to their special God-given mission. He stated on another occasion, "Together, with the other good and decent people of this country, we can make certain that America is the kind of place, the shining light of opportunity and freedom, that God intended it to be" (Reagan, 1984c, ¶34).

At a meeting of the Jewish group B'nai B'rith, he spoke of the "fundamentals of our Judeo-Christian tradition" (Reagan, 1984u, ¶14). He stated at a prayer breakfast held in conjunction with the Republican National Convention: "Without God, there is a coarsening of the society. And without God, democracy will not and cannot long endure. If we ever forget that we're one nation under God, then we will be a nation gone under." (Reagan, 1984p, ¶27). Thus, Reagan urged Americans to maintain a faith in God in order to continue to prosper as a nation. Another message Reagan developed was that our freedom and liberty come from God. He called freedom "God's greatest gift" (Reagan, 1984l, ¶2). In one of his campaign speeches, Reagan argued democracy was biblical and suggested America's democratic experiment had been divinely created:

> More and more, the world is reawakening to the fact that freedom is better than tyranny, that democracy is better than the iron fist of dictators, that freedom is the one condition in which man can flourish. And man was meant to flourish, was meant to be free. And that is why we were created. That's why it's been said that democracy is just a political reading of the Bible. (Reagan, 1984k, ¶26)

For Reagan, believing in God and democracy were synonymous. With these arguments he declared America to be God's specially blessed nation and claimed that America would remain strong because of God's protection.

Reagan cast his political campaign and governance as a *spiritual mission*, much as he had during the 1980 campaign. By rhetorically baptizing his political activities, Reagan offered his presidency as a ministry and important part of helping to bring about a national revival. Reagan likened government work to ministry service: "I believe the halls of government are as sacred as our temples of worship, and nothing but the highest integrity is required of those who serve in government" (Reagan, 1984g, ¶19). He even quoted Scripture when describing what he would continue to do as president: "For the sake of our children and the millions on Earth who look to America for hope, I know that we'll fight the good fight, we'll keep the faith" (Reagan, 1984q, ¶20). Reagan argued at a prayer breakfast for greater merging of religion and politics in governmental decision-making:

> The truth is, politics and morality are inseparable. And as morality's foundation is religion, religion and politics are necessarily related. We need religion as a guide. We need it because we are imperfect, and our government needs the church, because only those humble enough to admit they're sinners can bring to democracy the tolerance it requires in order to survive. (Reagan, 1984p, ¶23)

Reagan here seems to imply that nonreligious individuals would destroy democracy if allowed to govern. He also pointed to our nation's spiritual revival as one of his presidential achievements:

> America has begun a spiritual awakening. Faith and hope are being restored. Americans are turning back to God. Church attendance is up. Audiences for religious books and broadcasts are growing. On college campuses, students have stopped shunning religion and started going to church. . . . One of my favorite Bible quotations comes from Second Chronicles: "if My people who are called by My name humble themselves and pray and seek My face, and turn from their wicked ways, then will I hear from heaven, and forgive their sin and heal their land." Today Americans from Maine to California are seeking His face. And I do believe that He has begun to heal our blessed land. (Reagan, 1984d, ¶20–21)

Thus, for Reagan his political campaign and governance were cast as a religious mission. When Reagan ran in 1980, he likened his campaign to a religious revival and argued that America needed a spiritual revitalization. In 1984, he continued this theme but argued that his presidency had helped bring about the spiritual healing and awakening that he had called for four years earlier. With such arguments, Reagan cast himself as the nation's shepherd and asked for four more years to serve as the nation's spiritual leader.

In several speeches Reagan moved from his general statements about religion and God to offer specific examples of how his religious beliefs influenced his *public policy* decisions. With these claims, Reagan moved from using religious rhetoric in a merely ceremonial manner to using religious beliefs and scriptural teachings as guides for making policy decisions. Reagan began his address at the Baptist Fundamentalism Annual Convention by claiming that the answers to all our world's problems could be found in the Bible:

> Reverend Falwell, ladies and gentlemen, thank you very much, for there are no words to describe a welcome such as you've given me here. It's a real pleasure to be with so many who firmly believe that the answers to the world's problems can be found in the Word of God. (Reagan, 1984h, ¶1)

Demonstrating this belief that the Bible provided answers for any problem he faced as president, Reagan used the Bible to justify his position on specific policy issues. He connected his military buildup with scripture at a gathering of Jewish youth:

> Since taking office, our administration has made significant headway in rebuilding our defenses and making America more secure. Perhaps you remember the 29th Psalm in which King David said, "The Lord will give strength to

His people; the Lord will bless His people with peace." Well, today America once again recognizes that peace and strength are inseparable. (Reagan, 1984e, ¶23)

In another speech he quoted the words of Jesus to defend efforts to propagate U.S. ideals in Eastern Europe:

And that's why we're modernizing Radio Free Europe, Radio Liberty, and the Voice of America. Our radio programming is becoming the mighty force for good that it was intended to be. As the Scriptures say, "Know the truth and the truth will make you free." Well, our broadcast will carry the truth to captive people throughout the world. (Reagan, 1984o, ¶29)

Reagan often used religious language—especially biblical quotations—to justify his political decisions. Even more than during his 1980 campaign, Reagan used the Bible in his speeches as a political guidebook.

One of Reagan's main policy proposals he frequently talked about during the campaign was his support for a Constitutional amendment supporting school prayer, thus repeating his 1980 position on issues of *church and state*. As with his 1980 campaign, Reagan attempted to balance his support for greater governmental support of religion with an attempt to defend himself against charges that he was violating the separation of church and state. On allowing school prayer, he claimed:

I deeply believe that the loving God who gave us this land should never have been expelled from America's classrooms. If the Congress can begin its day with prayer, children can, too. Not that Congress maybe doesn't need it more than the children do. . . . Passage of the amendment would reaffirm one of the most fundamental American values—faith. (Reagan, 1984a, ¶24, 26)

In another speech, he argued, "Let us come together, citizens of all faiths, to pray, march, and mobilize every force we have so the God who loves us can be welcomed back into our children's classrooms" (Reagan, 1984b, ¶36). He argued that such legislation did not violate the First Amendment: "My administration will continue our efforts to allow government to accommodate prayer and religious speech by citizens in ways that do not risk an establishment of religion" (Reagan, 1984f, ¶4). Reagan claimed that his proposal was simply "asking that the Constitution be restored to neutrality with regard to religion. The government is to neither be an advocate of, nor a controller of, or preventer of the practice of religion" (Reagan, 1984g, ¶71). In another speech, Reagan argued:

All we asked for was to recognize that the Constitution, with that wall of separation between church and state, is interfering with the private individual's right to the practice of religion when it says you cannot pray if you want to, voluntarily, in a school. And we want that changed so that you can. (Reagan, 1984w, ¶57)

In this statement, Reagan suggested that there was indeed a problem with the Constitutional principle of separation of church and state, and thus seemed to admit that his amendment would change that historic principle. Although Reagan paid lip-service to the importance of separation of church and state, he often advocated positions the Supreme Court had ruled violated the separation principle.

Throughout the 1984 campaign, Reagan repeated much of his religious-political arguments from his 1980 run. Although Reagan talked little about his personal religious background, he did speak of his belief in God and offered some theological reflections. Additionally, Reagan proclaimed that America had been founded with a faith in God and had been blessed throughout the years by God. Reagan slightly augmented his 1980 rhetoric that compared his campaign to a religious revival by arguing that his first term had actually ushered in the start of a spiritual awakening in America and urged citizens to allow him to continue to serve as the nation's revivalist. Reagan also used the Bible as a policy handbook on several important public policy decisions, and continued to embrace the apparent contradiction in his church and state rhetoric as he endorsed policies running counter to the separation of church and state while claiming he was not crossing the line. Unlike Carter, whose religious-political rhetoric changed substantially when he ran for reelection, Reagan's sermons remained consistent—much to the delight of the Moral Majority and other conservative Christians who remained solidly in his congregation.

Walter Mondale

Although Walter Mondale spoke out on religious issues during the 1984 campaign, and even talked about his personal religious background, much of his religious-political discourse served as a critique of Ronald Reagan's use of religion in politics and of the Republicans for going too far in mixing religion and politics. Despite this main line of attack, Mondale still found himself testifying about his *personal faith* as he was repeatedly asked questions about his faith. Most of these comments, however, dealt with his family's faith background instead of his personal religious beliefs. Mondale at times introduced himself as "a preacher's kid" (Lynn, 1983, ¶8) or as "a minister's kid" (Weinraub, 1983, ¶8). He said of his father: "He believed Christ taught a sense of social mission and this was heavily given to me throughout my childhood" (Weinraub, 1983, ¶9). When asked during his October 7, 1984, general election debate with Ronald Reagan if he was born again, Mondale answered:

> I am a son of a Methodist minister. My wife is the daughter of a Presbyterian minister. And I don't know if I've been born again, but I know I was born into a Christian family. And I believe I have sung at more weddings and more funerals than anybody ever to seek the Presidency. Whether that helps or not, I don't know. I have a deep religious faith. Our family does. It is fundamental. It's probably the reason that I'm in politics.

Mondale argued in a rather unconfident manner: "I'm a Christian. . . . I think my faith is very important to me" (Blosser, 1983, ¶2). He also insisted about his personal faith: "I don't use it politically . . . and I don't like to see religion used for political purposes. I think it weakens our faith" (Blosser, 1983, ¶3). On several occasions during the campaign, Mondale talked about his religious background by pointing to the religious family he grew up in. He awkwardly answered the question about being "born-again" by noting he was "born into a Christian family," an answer which actually pitted him against the evangelical perspective that places importance in one's second birth instead of one's literal birth. Mondale also insisted that religious beliefs should remain private, thus connecting even discussions of his own faith to his larger religious-political argument that politics was becoming too religious.

Mondale talked at times about how his religious beliefs influenced his *public policy* positions, but usually expressed these arguments in vague terms. Although he argued that religion should be private and criticized Reagan for bringing religion into politics, Mondale himself cited scripture and invoked God on occasion to justify some of his policy views. He explained that "my faith unmistakably has taught me that social justice is part of a Christian's responsibility" (Broder, 1984, ¶6). Mondale cited Scripture during a speech at an African American Methodist church as he urged congregants to remember that "by their fruits ye shall know them" and that his record proves that he has been involved in "every tough fight there's been for justice" (Carroll, 1984, ¶27). Mondale connected his position on abortion by saying he had "prayed over" it (Lawsky, 1984, ¶4). Although Mondale did not often explicitly connect specific policy positions to his faith, he did express that his religious philosophy influenced how he tried to lead politically. In particular, he claimed, albeit quite vaguely, that the social justice focus of his religious background guided him as he made policy decisions.

One of Mondale's main religious-political arguments dealt with issues of *church and state* as he clearly argued for the importance of maintaining the historic separation of church and state. With this discussion, Mondale adopted a strict separation position in stark contrast to his Republican opponent and one closely related to Jimmy Carter's position in the 1980 campaign. Mondale particularly argued that religion should not be corrupted by politics. He declared that in the Constitution the concept of "separation of church and state was spelled out with particular clarity" (Blosser, 1983, ¶5). Mondale argued for maintaining the separation of church and state during his October 7, 1984, general election debate with Ronald Reagan:

> This nation is the most religious nation on Earth—more people go to church and synagogues than any other nation on Earth—and it's because we kept the politicians and the state out of the personal exercise of our faith. That's why faith in the United States is pure and unpolluted by the intervention of politicians. And I think if we want to continue—as I do—to have a religious nation, let's keep that line and never cross it.

He added that Reagan's support for a constitutional amendment on school prayer specifically crossed that line:

> Who would write the prayer? What would it say? How would it be resolved when those disputes occur? It seems to me that a moment's reflection tells you why the United States Senate turned that amendment down, because it will undermine the practice of honest faith in our country by politicizing it.

Mondale's consistent focus throughout the campaign was that church and state should remain separate in order to protect both, but especially religion from politics. Offering a stark contrast to Reagan, Mondale preached the need to keep the two domains separate for the betterment of both.

Mondale's other main use of religious rhetoric came when he often used religion to level *political attacks* against Ronald Reagan and other conservatives with religious language, usually for going too far with interjecting religion into politics. During the October 7, 1984, debate, Mondale attacked Reagan and the Republicans for using religion for political gain:

> What bothers me is this growing tendency to try to use one's own personal interpretation of faith politically, to question others' faith, and to try to use the instrumentalities of government to impose those views on others. All history tells us that that's a mistake. When the Republican platform says that from here on out, we're going to have a religious test for judges before they're selected for the Federal court, and then Jerry Falwell announces that that means they get at least two Justices of the Supreme Court, I think that's an abuse of faith in our country.

After citing attacks on his faith, Mondale stated in an address to the Jewish organization B'nai B'rith:

And what I am doing here today is something that in 25 years of public life I never thought I would do. I have never before had to defend my political—my religious faith in a political campaign. I have never thought it proper for political leaders to use religion to partisan advantage by advertising their own faith and questioning their opponent's. (MacNeil and Lehrer, 1984, ¶11)

Although Mondale often attacked Reagan, Falwell, and others for bringing religion into politics, Mondale himself sometimes quoted scripture to attack Reagan's policies for failing to live up to biblical standards. Mondale stated during a February 11, 1984, Democratic primary debate:

I was taught that to discriminate was a sin, and I believe it is. I think what we're talking about is not policy and differences over policy; we're talking about a radical assault on the right of children of God to be treated as equals in American society.

Mondale attacked Reagan for being "out to lunch" on the issue of "social justice," which Mondale argued was "part of a Christian's responsibility" (Broder, 1984, ¶6). He also cited Scripture in another attack: "By their fruits ye shall know them. . . . And the fruits of this administration have been the grapes of wrath" (Knutson, 1984, ¶10). With these comments, Mondale not only attacked Reagan for mixing religion and politics but also used the Bible himself to attack Reagan's positions. With these two types of attacks, Mondale's use of religion during the campaign often consisted of a critique of Reagan and other conservatives for being too religious.

Although Walter Mondale had campaigned with Jimmy Carter during the previous two campaigns, he took a starkly different approach in his own campaign as he argued in a speech to a meeting of the National Baptist Convention, an African American denomination: "We're proud of our faith, but I never thought you ran for office by bragging about your faith. . . . That is not the way I read our Bible" (McQuillan, 1984, ¶6). Mondale, who had been chosen to bring balance to Carter's ticket, was clearly unable to fill Carter's religious-political shoes. Although Mondale mentioned his church background, he talked more about his father being a minister than his own personal religious beliefs. He did at times connect his religious beliefs to his political positions, but remained virtually silent on Ronald Reagan's main religious-political argument—and one that Carter had espoused, particularly in 1976—that America was a divinely blessed nation. Instead, Mondale focused his religious-political discourse on demanding a strict line of separation between church and state, and on attacking Reagan and conservative Christian leaders. These positions likely further alienated Mondale from many voters.

On his way to a record electoral college defeat—winning only his home state of Minnesota and the District of Columbia—Walter Mondale took a decidedly different approach to religious-political discourse than Ronald Reagan, or even his former running mate Jimmy Carter. Mondale and Reagan differed particularly on the issue of separation of church and state. While Reagan proposed greater governmental support of religion, Mondale demanded a strict separation. While Reagan preached about America's special relationship with God and about the spiritual mission of his campaign, Mondale remained quiet. While Reagan clearly connected some of his public policy positions to religious teachings, Mondale offered vague attempts with such religious-political connections. Thus, Mondale found himself without a prayer of acceptance from an electorate that supported Carter and then Reagan in large part because of their religious appeals.

SUMMARY

Although Ronald Reagan is often credited or blamed—depending on one's perspective—for injecting more religion into politics (e.g., Domke and Coe, 2008; Wood, 1980), this analysis demonstrates that Carter first embodied this substantial rhetorical shift on personal religious matters. Carter's ascension to the presidency may seem at first glance to be one of the most improbable in modern American politics. A one-term governor of Georgia running for president just a decade after rampant civil rights violations were a common occurrence in his state and attempting to become the first president who hailed from the deep South since before the Civil War. With such odds stacked against him, Americans today should still be saying what many did at the start of his campaign: "Jimmy who?" In most election cycles, someone like Carter would likely have easily been topped by other candidates. But 1976 turned out to be the perfect year for Carter. With the fallout of the Watergate scandal, Democrats were poised to reclaim the White House. However, the nature of the scandal and the growing cynicism about all things Washington led many Americans to look for an outsider. Suddenly, Carter's experiences outside the beltway were a plus. Additionally, his squeaky-clean image as a Southern Baptist Sunday school teacher and his down-to-earth persona as a toothy-grinned peanut farmer made him appear as the exact opposite of a Richard Nixon at precisely the time when Americans were looking for someone completely unlike Nixon.

Part of Carter's persona that resonated with American voters was his openness to talk about his personal religious faith. His ease at doing so as an evangelical further distanced him from the image of the sinful and crude Nixon. For Carter—like many evangelicals—such rhetoric came naturally, which helped him appear genuine and likable. What seemed to be merely an expression of who he was quickly became a critical part of the campaign strategy. When Reagan defeated Carter four years later, it was not with a new religious campaign strategy, but rather by co-opting Carter's earlier model. Reagan bested Carter in the ballot boxes in part by implementing Carter's 1976 playbook. Interestingly, Carter actually toned down his religious appeals during his reelection campaign. As Reagan rhetorically and literally reached out to evangelicals, many of Carter's former evangelical allies campaigned for Reagan. When Reagan placed his hand on the Bible in January of 1981 to become the fortieth president of the United States, it marked the second straight election when the most *rhetorically* religiously candidate won. Reagan had out-God-talked the Sunday school teacher and helped cement the new rhetorical expectations for office. Now, political success by invoking God was not just a fluke or the strategy of one political party.

Chapter Three

Bush and Clinton

As Ronald Reagan prepared to ride off into the sunset, politicians in both major parties scrambled to replace him. Among the many politicians—including his own Vice President, the Senate Minority leader, the Governor of Massachusetts, and several U.S. Senators and Representatives—were two preachers. While Reagan and Jimmy Carter were politicians who often seemed to be running for the role of the nation's pastor, two preachers were now running for the role of being the nation's Commander-in-Chief. Jesse Jackson reprised his role from the 1984 Democratic presidential primaries by again running competitively in several Southern states, moving from a third-place finish in 1984 to a second-place finish in 1988. On the other side of the political spectrum, Pat Robertson mounted a bid for the Republican presidential nomination. After a surprise second-place finish in the Iowa caucuses, Robertson won four states and received third-place in the nomination race as he beat more mainstream candidates like U.S. Congressman Jack Kemp.

Although neither Jackson nor Robertson captured their party's nomination, both proved their political savvy and impacted their party's platform. Additionally, both preachers would continue to exert political influence in the years to come—Jackson through his Rainbow/Push Coalition and Robertson through his Christian Coalition. Far from hiding their religious backgrounds like George McGovern, these two candidates mounted competitive bids for the presidency based in large part on their images as religious activists, despite the fact that neither had previously held elected public office. Their competitive bids energized religious voters, placed increased pressures on the more traditional candidates to address these concerns, and helped further expectations that presidential candidates should address issues of religion and faith. Yet, their losses also point to limitations concerning the role of religious rhetoric in the presidential primaries. Although the more rhetorically religious candidates in the general elections were winning, this trend was not always true in the primaries. Jackson and Robertson out-God-talked the more mainstream candidates, but each failed to find political salvation.

1988

Although Vice President George H. W. Bush was the front-runner for the 1988 Republican nomination—especially since he enjoyed President Ronald Reagan's support—other Republican candidates challenged Bush for the nomination. In the Iowa caucuses, Bush came in third place behind Senator Bob Dole of neighboring Kansas and televangelist Pat Robertson. Bush, however, rebounded in New Hampshire after numerous television ads attacking Dole. Bush easily won New Hampshire and then went on to win the nomination as his campaign's organizational strength paid off once many states began voting in rapid succession. Bush chose Senator Dan Quayle of Indiana as his running mate. Throughout both the primary and general election, Bush struggled to recreate the level of enthusiasm among evangelicals that his predecessor Ronald Reagan enjoyed. Bush was not the natural candidate for many conservative Christians, such as Reverend Jerry Falwell and Phyllis Schlafly, who in 1980 had unsuccessfully urged Reagan not to choose Bush as his running mate but instead pick someone more appealing to conservatives (Clendinen, 1980).

On the Democratic side, the race was more divided. In 1987, former Senator Gary Hart of Colorado was the front-runner until he was caught having an extramarital affair. Although he dropped out of the race in May of 1987, he reentered in December but failed to regain much support. Senator Joe Biden of Delaware dropped out of the race after being accused of plagiarizing a speech. Congressman Dick Gephardt of neighboring Missouri won the Iowa caucuses, with Senator Paul Simon of Illinois and Massachusetts Governor Michael Dukakis coming in second and third respectively. Dukakis won New Hampshire and eventually most other states, although civil rights activist Reverend Jesse Jackson and Senator Al Gore of Tennessee each won several states. Dukakis selected Senator Lloyd Bentsen of Texas as his running mate.

With Pat Robertson in the race, issues of religion garnered significant attention, particularly after his surprise second-place finish in the Iowa caucuses. Other candidates also attempted to reach out to evangelical Christians, especially Jack Kemp. Bush spoke to a meeting of the National Religious Broadcasters, and in the lead-up to the primary campaign he even courted religious leaders like Jim Bakker and Jerry Falwell (Blumenthal, 1990). Other than Robertson, most of the other candidates spoke very little about their personal faith. Robertson stated, "I'm a deeply religious person. I'm a person of prayer. I'm a person who believes deeply in God and believes in the Bible. And so my ethics and my statements will reflect that" (MacNeil and Lehrer, 1987, ¶6). He also claimed during the campaign that he was the victim of anti-Christian bigotry in the media and compared his situation to John F. Kennedy's in 1960:

> Kennedy in 1960 was ruled out as a president because they said, "Well, he'll be nothing but a tool of the Pope in Rome." He put that to rest down in Houston to the Ministerial Association. And now in 1988 we're seeing the same thing with me. They say, "You're a strong evangelical Christian. You have deep faith in God and Jesus Christ. And therefore you can't be president." Well, that's a type of bigotry, and I think it isn't appropriate in 1988. So I wanted to show the people you elected Kennedy and you can take a shot on Pat Robertson and not lose. (Sullivan, 1988, ¶20)

Robertson also cast his run as a spiritual mission: "I have a direct call and a leading from God to run for president" (Blumenthal, 1990, p. 98). Although his religious credentials and message catapulted him to the top tier of Republican primary candidates, his prophesy failed to materialize.

The Democratic primary featured relatively little religious rhetoric compared to other cycles. Even some of the candidate who would run again—such as Joe Biden, Dick Gephardt, and especially Al Gore—spoke less about religion during this campaign than during their later presidential runs. During the campaign, Jesse Jackson once again preached in churches as a base for his campaign and continued many of his religious-political arguments from 1984. On a few occasions, candidates spoke about their personal religious beliefs or background. Although Jackson often interjected religion into the primary campaign, his Democratic opponents mostly avoided discussions of their personal faith.

During the general election, Bush painted Dukakis as too liberal, while Dukakis attempted to connect Bush to Iran Contra and other foreign policy controversies. Dukakis's image was damaged, however, when a press stunt in a tank backfired and resulted in him being mocked. Quayle's inexperience and gaffes were attacked by Democrats, while Dukakis was attacked over a prison inmate—Willie Horton—who raped while on furlough from a Massachusetts prison. Throughout the campaign, both Bush and Dukakis spoke to a meeting of the Jewish group B'nai B'rith, and Bush spoke during the primary at a meeting of the National Religious Broadcasters. On election day, Bush easily beat Dukakis in the popular vote and overwhelmingly in the electoral college. Bush captured 53.4 percent of the popular vote over Dukakis's 45.6, and took over 79 percent of the electoral college vote.

George H. W. Bush

During the 1988 campaign, Vice President George H. W. Bush struggled to relate to conservative Christians in the way that his predecessor Ronald Reagan had. Although he attempted to make inroads with evangelicals, Bush often appeared uncomfortable talking about religion and his spiritual beliefs. Bush did, however, open up more about his *personal faith* than his Democratic opponent. Bush recounted how his faith had helped him survive during war and he made it clear that he believed and trusted in Jesus. Talking about being shot down during World War II, Bush noted during a January 8, 1988, Republican primary debate:

> I was a 19–20-year-old kid shot down and scared to death. Lost to comrades in arms, and the government felt I did the mission pretty well, pretty well. And what I said was that my mind turned to faith—my faith in God—and to family.

On another occasion he offered a more personal glimpse into his religious beliefs: "I am guided by certain traditions. One is that there is a God and He is good, and His love, while free, has a self-imposed cost: We must be good to one another" (Bush, 1988c, ¶57). Bush told the National Religious Broadcasters:

> I believe that pursuit of truth will always lead to Christ, who is the Truth. And I want to tell you a true story in closing, a story that shows how bright His light is. A remarkable thing happened at the funeral of Soviet leader Brezhnev. . . . And I happened to be off the corner of the great wall, just in the right spot to see Mrs. Brezhnev. And she walked up, and she took one last look at her husband, and there—this is the gospel truth—there in the cold, gray center of that totalitarian state, she traced the sign of the cross over her husband's chest. I was stunned; I was deeply moved. . . . In that simple act, Christ had broken through the core of the communist system. And it became clear to me, decades, even centuries, of harsh secular rule can never destroy the intuitive faith that's within us. (Bush, 1987, ¶20–21)

With these comments, Bush claimed that he believed in and relied on God. He not only argued that he relied on God's help, but talked about the importance of the love and sacrifice of Christ—even becoming fairly evangelistic as he addressed the National Association of Evangelicals.

Throughout the campaign, Bush used religious rhetoric to describe his political philosophy and specific *public policy* positions. With these statements, Bush invoked God—albeit often in vague terms or with a passing reference—to make the claim that his religious values would impact his governing decisions. Bush connected the importance of religious values to his "points of light" theme. Claiming that "[a]n election that is about ideas and values is also about philosophy," Bush argued that an important part of his philosophy was recognizing the importance of "our culture, our religious faith, our traditions and history" (Bush, 1988c, ¶54). On winning the war on drugs, he argued that religion was one weapon with which to fight. He called not only for "[m]ore planes, boats, and helicopters," but also the need for "faith in God and in one's self" (Bush, 1988b, ¶8). On the issues of abortion and adoption, Bush spoke of a christening church ceremony for his adopted granddaughter during his acceptance address at the Republican National Convention: "Barbara and I have an adopted granddaughter. On the day of her christening we wept with joy. I thank God that her parents chose life" (Bush, 1988c, ¶90). Rather than merely talking about abortion or adoption in policy terms, Bush described his joy and praise at his granddaughter's christening service, thus also alluding to the importance of his personal religious beliefs. Bush also talked about the Bible to justify his opposition to banning certain books from the public schools. In his speech to the National Religious Broadcasters—many of whom disagreed with Bush on this issue—Bush used the Bible as an example of why books should not be banned just because they contain content with which one disagrees:

> Closing our children off to the outside world isn't going to protect them. The Bible itself is an honest book, extremely honest. God's prophets never sheltered their readers from the ugliness of life. As you know far better than I, there are horrible stories of massacre and rape in the Bible, and the Bible doesn't protect children from the dangers or the injustices or the evils of the world. To that small minority, I say simply, don't take away generally accepted books now that you have greater influence. (Bush, 1987, ¶17–18)

As Bush talked about his political philosophy and goals, he occasionally invoked God and his religious faith. However, Bush did not offer the specificity of such a religious influence that Reagan had offered in his campaign rhetoric.

During the campaign, Bush's rhetoric on *church and state* issues found him attempting to walk a fine line between offering support for separation of church and state while also advocating positions that the Supreme Court ruled violated that principle. With this rhetorical balancing act, Bush's campaign rhetoric followed the pattern Ronald Reagan had adopted during his 1980 and 1984 campaigns. Bush told the meeting of B'nai B'rith that he agreed with them in holding a "reverence for the principle of separation of church and state" (Bush, 1988d, ¶8). He also insisted that he supported the religious liberty of all Americans: "We're a nation that was founded for liberty and human rights, for the freedom to speak and to assemble and to worship each in his own way. And that's our heritage, one that must never be abandoned for expediency" (Bush, 1988a, ¶10). Bush declared in another speech, "I'm for an America where values like faith and respect are honored—and where every child should have the right to say a voluntary prayer at the beginning of the school day" (Bush, 1988b, ¶53). He also advocated providing tax credits for parents that send their children to religious institutions for child-care. Bush even connected these positions to his attack on Dukakis. During their September 25, 1988, debate, Bush invoked church-state issues as he attacked Dukakis for being a member of the ACLU:

> But I don't agree with a lot of—most of the positions of the ACLU. . . . I don't think they're right to try to take the tax exemption away from the Catholic Church. I don't want to see the kiddie pornographic laws repealed; I don't want to see "under God" come out from our currency. Now, these are all positions of the ACLU.

Although Bush claimed he supported the separation of church and state, he also advocated for prayer in public schools, tax credits for parents with children in religious child-care, and keeping sectarian statements on U.S. currency.

As Bush attempted to succeed Ronald Reagan, he struggled to gain the mantle of hero of conservative Christians. Bush often spoke uncomfortably about his personal faith—although he did offer some insights—and vaguely referenced how his faith might impact his presidential decisions. Additionally, Bush did not continue Reagan's most consistent religious-political theme about the divine blessings bestowed upon America. Bush did, however, continue Reagan's calls for prayer in public schools and other governmental recognitions of religion while also claiming to support the separation of church and state. In this area, Bush—a former Reagan opponent—managed to capture part of Reagan's religious-political message in a manner that marked the strongest shift in Bush's rhetoric. When Bush unsuccessfully challenged Reagan for the 1980 Republican nomination—before later joining Reagan on the Republican ticket—he offered much of the same religious-political appeals in 1980 that he did in his 1988 quest for the presidency. The 1980 Bush remained quiet about his personal faith and only vaguely interjected religion into his campaign discourse on rare occasions. However, unlike Reagan's rhetoric or Bush's in 1988, Bush did not initially advocate prayer in public schools or other governmental attempts to bring religion into the public square. For example, Bush claimed during a January 5, 1980 Republican primary debate that he did not "believe that morality can be legislated" and stressed that he strongly believed in the separation of church and state. He added that he did not believe pornography and similar moral concerns should be governed at the national level. And during a 1980 communion breakfast at the National Shrine of Our Lady of Czestochowa, Bush argued the government should work "to preserve our great religious diversity" (Bush stresses, 1980, ¶2). By 1988, as he attempted to win the support of conservative Christians who had supported Reagan during the previous two campaigns, Bush adjusted his rhetoric on issues of church and state to offer a more Reaganesque message of advocating for more governmental recognition of religion.

Michael Dukakis

Although Michael Dukakis used virtually no religious rhetoric during the 1988 Democratic primary, he did offer some religious-political discourse during the general election. Raised Greek Orthodox, he married a Jew yet neither remained very religious in their adult life. In fact, his wife stated during his campaign, "None of us is very religious" (Sullivan, 2008, p. 88). Only on a few occasions did Dukakis speak about his *personal faith*, and even then with only passing and minor references. He mentioned relying on prayers during his military service in the demilitarized zone of Korea:

> All we wanted and all we expected was to be well trained, to have weapons that worked, a mission that we understood, and to know that we were being remembered and supported in the thoughts and prayers of those back home. (Dukakis, 1988c, ¶17)

Speaking to the Congressional Hispanic Caucus Institute, Dukakis stated:

> I'll never forget that morning in San Antonio, just two days before Super Tuesday when Kitty and I were joined by many of you at a beautiful mass and I read the scriptures in Spanish, and went off to speak to more than 5000 people in that historic city. (Dukakis, 1988b, ¶15)

He also made a passing reference in a different speech to attending a meeting honoring his archbishop. When Dukakis made references to his religious background, such statements were not only rare but vague.

Dukakis on a few occasions invoked religion as he discussed his *public policy* views. With these statements he suggested that scripture and his beliefs about God would guide his presidential decisions. In a speech to the Congressional Black Caucus, he talked about how everyone in society should be valued, which he described as "an idea that echoes down the ages from the Old Testament prophets to the Sermon on the Mount" (Dukakis, 1988d, ¶9). As he advocated environmental conservation policies, Dukakis argued:

> I want to protect the people, and protect our air and water and forests and beaches and all of the wonderful natural environment God gave us—not as a gift but as something we hold in trust for the future. (Dukakis, 1988f, ¶47)

As Dukakis explained and justified his political positions, he sometimes used God-talk, but much less frequently than his opponent or even his recent Democratic predecessors Jimmy Carter and Walter Mondale.

The strongest religious-political theme used by Dukakis dealt with *church and state* issues as he voiced support for religious freedom and the principle of separation of church and state. Here, he continued lines of argument made during the previous campaign by Walter Mondale, although Dukakis did not address these matters as frequently as Mondale. Dukakis spoke of the importance of separation of church and state in his address to B'nai B'rith:

> Those who came to Ellis Island believed in the dream of liberty, and we must defend that dream against all adversaries, against those who would threaten us from abroad, against those strident voices from the radical right who would undermine the constitutional principles of individual liberty and the separation of Church and state here at home. (Dukakis, 1988a, ¶10)

He added, "And you understand how important the constitutional separation of church and state is" (Dukakis, 1988a, ¶40). The main message Dukakis developed with his religious rhetoric was the importance of religious freedom and the principle of separation of church and state. Although he made clear his strong support for strict separation, he did not detail this position as frequently as his Democratic predecessors Jimmy Carter and especially Walter Mondale. Additionally, Dukakis advanced this argument from purely political terms instead of developing the religious theme that Mondale offered by claiming the importance of separation was to protect the prophetic voice of the church or the religious frame offered by Carter who connected his belief in the separation principle to his personal faith.

Dukakis also used religious rhetoric to level *political attacks* on George H. W. Bush and Dan Quayle during the campaign. For example, Dukakis used an issue raised by other Democratic presidential primary candidates to attack George H. W. Bush's claims to not have been heavily involved in meetings where controversial foreign policy decisions were made. In one of these meetings, President Ronald Reagan signed a Bible that was to be sent by a Christian group to the Iranian Ayatollah, which sparked criticism that Reagan and his administration allowed their evangelistic zeal to interfere with making appropriate foreign policy decisions. Dukakis used Bush's presence at this meeting to question his priorities and understanding of foreign policy (Shaw, 1988). Dukakis also used religion to attack Dan Quayle, who had much more acceptance with conservative Christians than Bush, and who Bush had chosen in part to secure support from this important voting bloc: "And Dan Quayle asks us to believe that, if he ever had to fill in for George Bush, [America] could get by on a right wing and a prayer" (Dukakis, 1988e, ¶5). With these comments—especially the latter—Dukakis used religion to attack his political opponents. Although he did not attack his Republican opponents nearly as frequently in religious terms as the Democratic nominees had in the previous two elections, Dukakis still turned to religion to find political ammunition.

Michael Dukakis has been called the most secular major party nominee in recent presidential elections. Based on his campaign rhetoric, he was clearly the least religiously expressive nominee in the period from 1976 to 2008. Dukakis rarely talked about his personal faith or religious background, and connected religion to his political positions only on a few occasions. Additionally, Dukakis did not develop a larger religious-political theme about the special relationship between America and God—remaining silent on this issue as Walter Mondale had four years earlier. Although Dukakis continued arguments by Mondale and Jimmy Carter in supporting the separation of church and state, he did not make this argument as frequently or religiously. During the campaign, Dukakis took credit for the economic growth in his home state, which he described as a "Massachusetts Miracle." Much as with the rest of his campaign rhetoric, any sort of heavenly divine was absent from his so-called Massachusetts Miracle.

While in no way did George H. W. Bush compare to Ronald Reagan or even Jimmy Carter when it came to the use of religious-political discourse, he still seemed like a rhetorical saint compared to the even more religiously reserved Dukakis. Although neither candidate talked very explicitly about their personal faith, how it would impact their public policy, or about God's blessings on America, Bush did offer more insights into his religious beliefs than Dukakis. Additionally, while Dukakis proclaimed a strict interpretation of separation of church and state, Bush offered a message closer to Reagan's as he advocated prayer in public schools and greater governmental recognition of God. While Dukakis attacked Bush and his running mate Dan Quayle for being too religious, Bush attacked Dukakis for being a proud member of the ACLU—an organization viewed by many conservative Christians as trying to remove God and religion from the public square. Thus, despite lacking the public professions of piety of Carter or the revival sermons of Reagan, Bush was able to defeat the "card-carrying member of the ACLU."

1992

Despite being the sitting president, George H. W. Bush faced a serious challenge for the 1992 Republican nomination from conservative commentator Pat Buchanan. In the announcement of his candidacy, Buchanan cast his political mission as also being a religious mission:

When we say we will put America first, we mean also that our Judeo-Christian values are going to be preserved. . . . But at the root of America's social crisis, be it AIDS, ethnic hatred, crime or the social decomposition of our cities, lies a spiritual crisis. . . . Men have forgotten God, not in the redistribution of wealth, but in the words of the Old and New Testaments will be found not only salvation, but the cure for a society suffering from a chronic moral sickness. . . . We need God's help, and we will need your help. (Buchanan, 1991, ¶16, 18)

Although early results in New Hampshire showed that Buchanan might actually win the primary, Bush managed not only to win New Hampshire but also every other primary. Even though he was overwhelmingly defeated by Bush, Buchanan amassed a loyal following of conservative supporters during his primary bid and was allowed to deliver a key address at the Republican National Convention during which he focused on our nation's so-called culture wars.

On the Democratic side, former Senator Paul Tsongas of Massachusetts emerged as the early front-runner. Senator Tom Harkin of Iowa won the Iowa caucuses, but failed to gain a boost since other candidates skipped the state's race. Arkansas Governor Bill Clinton, who was hit by sex scandals, managed to finish a strong second in New Hampshire behind the favored Tsongas. The finish, which earned Clinton the nickname "the comeback kid," provided him with momentum. Although Tsongas won additional primaries, he had difficulty raising necessary campaign funds. After Clinton began to win a few of the early primaries, and former California Governor Jerry Brown started to pull second in many of these races, Tsongas dropped out. Although Brown won the Connecticut primary and managed to collect delegates in a few other states, Clinton easily secured the nomination. Clinton chose Senator Al Gore of Tennessee as his running mate.

During the primary, Clinton, a Southern Baptist who studied at the Catholic Georgetown University, and Brown, who attended Catholic schools and even studied for the priesthood at a Jesuit seminary, both spoke openly of their religious beliefs. Brown connected his religious background to his political views, such as during an April 6, 1992, Democratic primary debate when he talked about his "Catholic social tradition" and referred to "encyclicals and in bishop's letters." Other candidates also used religious rhetoric, but less frequently than Clinton and Brown.

In the general election, the two major-party tickets also faced a strong third-party challenge from Texas billionaire Ross Perot. Although Perot actually led all candidates in the national polls in June of 1992, he dropped out of the race in July before reentering several weeks later. The move hurt his standing in the polls, as did his claim that Republican operatives had attempted to disrupt his daughter's wedding. Perot chose former Vice Admiral James Stockdale as his running mate. Most of the election centered on economic issues as Clinton and Perot attacked Bush's handling of the economy. During the general election, Bush and Clinton addressed several religious audiences: Bush spoke at meetings of the National Religious Broadcasters and the National Association of Evangelicals, while Clinton spoke at meetings of the National Baptist Convention, USA, and the African Methodist Episcopal Church. Although the three-way race resulted in no candidate winning a majority of the popular vote, Clinton won a plurality of the vote as well as a large majority of the electoral college. Clinton beat Bush in the popular vote with 43 to 37.4 percent, but won nearly 69 percent of the electoral college. Perot, who finished third and received no electoral college votes, garnered 18.9 percent of the popular vote to become the most successful third-party candidate in the popular vote since former President Theodore Roosevelt in 1912.

During the 1992 campaign, Ross Perot rarely used religious rhetoric—especially compared to his two opponents. In several speeches he mentioned attending church as a child, but it was usually a passing reference about a lesson his father taught him. On only a couple of occasions did Perot cite a scripture or Christian hymn, such as when he addressed the Salvation Army, a Christian organization:

> You live the words from the Bible, "Not even a sparrow falls to the ground without God's care." There's a hymn, it was one of my grandmother's favorites: "I sing because I'm happy, I sing because I'm free. His eye is on the sparrow and I know He thinks of me." I think that summarizes a lot of what you are. (Perot, 1992, ¶13)

With this and other statements in the speech, Perot attempted to relate to his Christian audience as he indicated a certain level of familiarity with traditional Christian passages. During the campaign, Perot cast himself as different from the major party candidates and a significant break from traditional politics. His lack of religious rhetoric did represent a substantial difference between his campaign rhetoric and that of his opponents.

George H. W. Bush

During the 1992 campaign, President George H. W. Bush spoke of his personal faith and how his religious beliefs influenced his politics. Offering more discussion about his *personal faith* than he did during his 1988 campaign, Bush attempted to demonstrate an association with conservative Christian leaders in a campaign that sought to highlight such leaders. For instance, Bush referred to friendships with influential religious leaders James Dobson of Focus on the Family and Southern Baptist pastor W. A. Criswell. Bush also referred to praying with evangelist Billy Graham as they waited together to hear the news of the first strike of the Persian Gulf War:

> I remember the night of Desert Storm. Barbara and I had Dr. Billy Graham
> over for dinner there in the White House. In the family, we still say the
> blessing at night, so we said our little prayer together, enjoyed some conversa-
> tion. (Bush, 1992m, ¶19)

On other occasions, Bush opened up about his personal religious background, although usually in generic terms or by referring to church attendance instead of explaining his personal spiritual beliefs. He told the Knights
of Columbus: "I think my parents were like yours. They brought me up to
understand that our fundamental moral standards were established by Almighty God" (Bush, 1992i, ¶9). During his acceptance address at the Republican National Convention, Bush declared:

> There are times in every young person's life, when God introduces you to
> yourself. And I remember such a time. It was back, many years ago, when I
> stood watch at 4:00 a.m. up on the bridge of a submarine, the United States
> Finback, U.S.S. Finback. (Bush, 1992k, ¶185)

Bush made it clear through these speeches that he believed in God and that
religious faith was important to him. Indeed, Bush offered a more personal
look at his religious beliefs than he had four years earlier, but even with his
more open approach he was still out-God-talked by his 1992 Democratic
opponent.

Another religious-political theme that Bush had not offered in 1988 was
the idea that America has a *special relationship* with God. Borrowing from
Ronald Reagan's most consistent religious-political theme, Bush argued in
1992 that America is blessed by God and that our nation was created and
sustained by those who trusted in God. Bush claimed that the writers of the
U.S. Constitution were "steeped . . . in the faith and philosophy of the Judeo-
Christian tradition" (Bush, 1991a, ¶10). During his acceptance address at the
Republican National Convention, Bush declared:

> And I believe that America will always have a special place in God's heart—
> as long as he has a special place in ours. And maybe that's why I've always
> believed that patriotism is not just another point of view. (Bush, 1992k, ¶185)

On another occasion, Bush recounted:

> I thought of our country yesterday, as Barbara and I attended our little church,
> little Easter service there in a little tiny church in Maine, and as I looked
> around our church we gave thanks for all that has truly blessed America.
> (Bush, 1992c, ¶9)

With these comments, Bush captured some of Reagan's religious-political
rhetoric that Bush had virtually ignored in his 1988 campaign.

Bush also sometimes mentioned how his religious values informed his positions on various *public policy* issues. With these statements, Bush indicated that he turned to religion and the Bible to aid him in making policy decisions, as he did on occasion in 1988. In his reelection effort, he told a group of religious leaders at a church in New Jersey: "I will fight for the faith" (Bush, 1992h, ¶22), thus quoting scripture to describe his dedication to continue working hard as president. He also connected the Persian Gulf War with his religious beliefs:

> And in the Persian Gulf we fought for good versus evil, it was that clear to me, right versus wrong, dignity against oppression. And America stood fast so that liberty could stand tall. And today, I want to thank you for helping America, as Christ ordained to be a light unto the world. (Bush, 1992a, ¶4)

Here, Bush not only justified his foreign policy in terms of good and evil but depicted U.S. military action as a light from Christ. In addition to the Persian Gulf War, Bush also connected domestic policy to religion. In a speech at the Sequoia Grove Trail in California regarding his policies to protect the environment, Bush explained:

> Some of these sequoias—I was reminded by Dale as we walked through the grove—were already seedlings by the time Christ walked the earth. And I think back to Sequoia himself. The first time he saw the Bible he called it talking leaves, and I think those leaves have something to teach us today. In Revelations we learn that the leaves of the tree were for the healing of the nations. (Bush, 1992g, ¶17)

In his campaign addresses, Bush only occasionally connected his public policy positions and leadership to his religious beliefs. Although he did not frequently make such arguments, his connections between policies and religious teachings were more explicitly religious than during his 1988 presidential bid.

One of the major campaign issues for Bush dealt with *church and state* issues as he frequently mentioned his support for prayer in public schools, despite concerns that such actions violate the separation of church and state. As with his rhetoric in 1988 and Ronald Reagan's in 1980 and 1984, Bush attempted to balance these contradictory positions during the campaign. Bush assured those at the annual meeting of the Jewish organization B'nai B'rith that he believed in separation of church and state despite his advocacy for school choice that would include funding for religious schools:

> But the underlying point is, certainly any President of the United States must
> be always concerned that nothing he or she might do should blur this line of
> separation between church and state. It is very, very fundamental to our sys-
> tem. And I hope that I can stand up credibly on my record for that principle.
> (Bush, 1992l, ¶48)

On other occasions, however, he advocated allowing a time for prayer in
public schools:

> But prayer in school on a voluntary basis, I simply can't understand why it's
> not permitted. In the Senate, and heaven knows they need it, but in the Senate
> and in the House they open with prayer every single day and nobody com-
> plains about that. (Bush, 1992e, ¶63)

Bush told a group of Christian educators that he supported a constitutional
amendment allowing prayer in public schools because our nation needed "the
faith of our fathers back in our public schools" (Bush, 1991b, ¶10). Bush's
promotion of prayer—especially in a setting that had been declared unconstitutional by the U.S. Supreme Court—not only resulted in Bush advocating a
position other than separation of church and state, but also maintaining a
position that could be used to discriminate against those of minority faiths or
of no faith.

Throughout his 1992 reelection campaign, Bush built on his 1988 religious-political campaign rhetoric as he seemed more comfortable in general
talking about religion, especially through more explicit appeals to religious
conservatives. He still did not talk often about his personal faith or how his
religious beliefs influenced his political positions, but the comments he did
offer were more explicitly religious—particularly with more Christological
references. Bush also expanded his 1988 arguments as he added Reaganesque comments about America's special relationship with God. Additionally, he continued his 1988 rhetorical contradiction by simultaneously arguing for the separation of church and state and for policies the Supreme
Court declared violated that principle. Although Bush increased his religious-political messages from his previous campaign, he also faced a much
more religiously outspoken and eloquent opponent than he had four years
earlier. Instead of a "card-carrying member of the ACLU," Bush faced a
Bible-quoting Southern Baptist.

Bill Clinton

Bill Clinton often invoked religious references and biblical passages in his
campaign speeches and often spoke about his personal religious faith. Like
the most recent Democratic president, Jimmy Carter, Clinton was not only
the governor of a southern state but also an evangelical Southern Baptist.
Clinton often talked about his *personal faith* as a Southern Baptist and his

experiences with Catholic schools, both of which he used to offer insights into his religious devotion. In a speech at the Olivet Institutional Baptist Church, he talked about his family values and personal spiritual life:

> I—you know, it's sort of funny to be told that you don't have family values unless you're a right-wing Republican. My little 12-year-old girl gets on her knees every night and prays to God and when I'm home I do it with her and I wonder what she thinks on her knees when her president tells her that [her] parents don't have family values because they're Democrats and they want him to leave his job. (Clinton, 1992f, ¶11)

In another speech, Clinton not only talked about his personal religious background but argued—in a far cry from candidates during the civil-religious contract period—that it was acceptable for political candidates to wear their religion on their sleeves:

> Like most [Americans] I go to church on Sunday, and until I lost my voice early in this campaign I sang in my choir. My faith is a source of pride to me, but far, far more important it is a source of humility because it teaches that none of us is a stranger to sin and to weakness. It is a source of hope because it teaches that each of us is capable of redemption. And it is a source of challenge because it teaches that we must all strive to live according to our beliefs. We all have the right to wear our religion on our sleeves, but we should also hold it in our hearts and live it in our lives. (Clinton, 1992k, ¶25)

With these references, Clinton clearly identified himself as a Christian who prays and practices his faith in private while also trying to live out his faith in public. Clinton's openness about his personal faith far surpassed previous Democratic candidates Walter Mondale and Michael Dukakis. Although Mondale and Dukakis had argued that religion should remain private, Clinton not only spoke about his personal faith but argued that it was okay for candidates to wear their religion on their sleeves.

On many occasions, Clinton cast his campaign as a *spiritual mission* as he borrowed religious language to describe his overall political philosophy and vision. In his acceptance speech at the Democratic National Convention, Clinton talked about his goal of creating a "New Covenant." Such language draws from the biblical new covenant established by Jesus. As Clinton described his governing vision, he quoted biblical passages:

> In the end, my fellow Americans, this New Covenant simply asks us all to be Americans again. . . . We can renew our faith in each other and in ourselves. We can restore our sense of unity and community. As the scripture says, "our eyes have not yet seen, nor our ears heard, nor our minds imagined what we can build." (Clinton, 1992d, ¶183)

In another speech he talked about the importance of building community as he listed the lessons taught in each of the various genres of the biblical books:

> It is a spirit that draws upon our Judeo-Christian tradition. Everything in the Old Testament concerns not isolated individuals but a people, a community. The books of law governed them. The books of history recounted their wanderings, their troubles and their triumphs. And the prophets are the great poetic voice that recalled them again and again to the meaning of "the people of God." In the Christian tradition, that emphasis on community continues since the Acts, the Gospels and the Epistles all come from early Christian communities and recount to us their problems, their failures, their strengths, but above all, their unity. Echoing down the ages is the simple but powerful truth that "no grace of God was ever given me for me alone." To the terrible question of Cain, "Am I my brother's keeper?," the only possible answer for us is God's thunderous yes. (Clinton, 1992k, ¶30)

Although this speech was not delivered to a primarily religious audience or occasion, Clinton offered lessons in this campaign address more likely to be found in a theology course than a political speech. In a speech at Notre Dame University, Clinton pointed to a religious document as inspiration for his political priorities if elected:

> If I could select a watchword for America, it would be the title of a recent pastoral letter by the National Conference of Catholic Bishops, "Putting Children and Families First." . . . I want to see us share the values expressed in the Bishops' pastoral letter on the economy, that every institution and every economic decision in our society must be judged by whether it protects or undermines the dignity of the person. (Clinton, 1992k, ¶35, 37)

In another speech Clinton called his political campaign a "crusade" for "social and spiritual renewal" (Clinton, 1991, ¶83). With these remarks, Clinton's political agenda was baptized in religious imagery and theology. With his political philosophy imbued with religion, Clinton not only offered more rhetorical evidence of his religious beliefs but also offered a connection between religion and political philosophy that other Democratic candidates had generally avoided.

On several occasions during the campaign, Clinton explained his *public policy* positions by talking about his religious beliefs. These comments moved beyond simply describing his overall political vision in religious terms to using his religious beliefs to justify specific policy commitments. Clinton argued that God would give him the guidance he needed to lead as president:

I became convinced that I had enough experience, enough ideas, enough energy, enough ability to do the job, and that if I were elected to the position, that God would give me the strength to make the decisions that I have to make at the appropriate time. (Clinton, 1992j, ¶4)

In other speeches, Clinton offered examples of how his religious beliefs would influence specific policy decisions. Clinton justified his political policies to provide health and education opportunities for children in religious terms with scriptural allusions:

On any day, at any time, at any place, violence is wrong, bigotry is wrong, abandoning children is wrong, but our religious traditions teach us more than thou shalt nots. In our role as citizens, we should not see ourselves only as our brothers' and sisters' keepers, but also as our brothers' and sisters' helpers. If we truly believe, as almost everyone says, no matter what they believe on certain issues, that children are God's most precious creation, then surely we owe every child born in the United States the opportunity to make the most of his or her God-given possession. (Clinton, 1992k, ¶33)

Speaking about decisions as governor to support the death penalty, Clinton spoke about his private religious struggles:

Three times as governor I have had to sit up through a long night. Three times I have had to search my soul. Three times I have prayed in private, not in public, for the souls of the condemned as well as for those whom they killed. . . . And I prayed that I had not made the wrong decision. (Clinton, 1992a, ¶29)

Clinton referred to his religious background and alluded to biblical passages in order to justify some of his political positions during the campaign. Although he did not often make direct connections between his religious values and his political positions, he did so more explicitly and frequently than his Democratic predecessors Walter Mondale and Michael Dukakis, as well as his Republican rival.

During the campaign, Clinton dealt with *church and state* issues by promoting freedom of religion and arguing that everyone be allowed to worship as they please. As with Southern Baptist Jimmy Carter, Clinton connected this argument with his Baptist faith. He argued in a speech at Notre Dame University:

I am grateful that I was born in a country where my faith can be powerful because it is a voluntary offering of a free and joyous spirit. As that great American Baptist, Roger Williams, understood so well, without the freedom to say no, the word "yes" is meaningless. . . . That is the promise of the First

Amendment's guarantees of freedom of religion and separation of church and state, guarantees that—my Southern Baptist church traditionally have supported strongly. (Clinton, 1992k, ¶21–22)

In addition to connecting his belief in religious liberty to his own religious background, Clinton also argued that this freedom had helped America remain a more religious nation, which was similar to an argument made by Water Mondale in 1984:

Here in our country more people believe in God, more people go to church or temple, and more people put religion at the center of their lives than in any other advanced society on earth, and that is a tribute to the genius and the courage of the American experiment, that our government can be the protector of the freedom of every faith because it is the exclusive property of none. (Clinton, 1992k, ¶22)

During the campaign, Clinton articulated a position firmly in line with the historic principle of church and state separation in order to guarantee true religious freedom. However, Clinton connected his belief and approach to governing to his personal religious faith more than Democrats Walter Mondale and Michael Dukakis had, instead following more of the pattern set by Carter. Unlike the three previous Democratic nominees, however, Clinton spoke more about religious freedom than separation of church and state. For instance, while the other Democrats specifically cited separation in their opposition to school prayer, Clinton instead cited generic law and spoke of the need for freedom of religious expression:

Remember what the law of the land is, though. A lot of people came to this country so they could have freedom of religious expression, and therefore you can't have prayer in the schools if it's official and if it forces other people who may or not want to be a part of it to do it. (Clinton, 1992e, ¶95)

Although he advocated the same position as recent Democratic candidates and remained in strong opposition to the Republican position, his rhetoric about church and state issues represented a substantial shift from that of Mondale and Dukakis.

Clinton also used religious rhetoric to issue *political attacks* on Republicans, particularly in response to Republicans and religious conservatives' attacks of Clinton and other Democrats regarding their religion and family values. In the highly polarized election year—especially following the "culture wars" speech by Pat Buchanan at the 1992 Republican National Convention—responding to attacks questing his values became a major religious-political theme for Clinton. In a speech at the Olivet Institutional Baptist Church, he talked about the attacks from Buchanan, Pat Robertson, and Jerry Falwell on his wife and himself for supposedly not supporting family values:

In biblical times, the people who did that were called the Pharisees. They sit on the corner and pointed their finger and looked down their nose and hid their hardened hearts. There were sanctimonious money changers in the temple until Jesus ran them out. . . . I tell you, the God I believe in teaches me to be humble. And says that we come into the house of the Lord not because we're saints but because we're sinners; not because we're strong, but because we're weak and we should bind up our wounds and go forward together because we are more together than we are apart. (Clinton, 1992f, ¶12)

In a speech to the Arkansas State Democratic Convention, Clinton connected such attacks to his belief in religious liberty:

Then they tried to say they were the party on God's side and we weren't. . . . Thomas Jefferson would roll over in his grave to think that the head of a major party would claim that God was on their side. Thomas Jefferson taught freedom of thought, freedom of religion, freedom of association, freedom to be left alone from government. Our Founders knew that God was not a Republican or a Democrat, a liberal or conservative, and that nobody had a monopoly on religion or patriotism. That's how this country got started. How dare them try to change it now. (Clinton, 1992h, ¶23)

With these comments, Clinton not only strongly attacked Bush and other Republicans politically, but he also attacked them religiously by painting them as opponents of Jesus. Thus, while arguing that political campaigns should not be so religious, he interjected his religious appeals into the campaign.

In his effort to unseat a sitting president—who had achieved record presidential approval ratings the previous year following the success of the Persian Gulf War—Clinton adopted the religious voice of fellow Southern Baptist Jimmy Carter instead of the more secular rhetorical approach of Walter Mondale and especially Michael Dukakis. Clinton frequently talked about his personal faith and how it would influence his public policy decisions, and he did so more often and more explicitly than Mondale, Dukakis, or his Republican rival. Although many of George H. W. Bush's surrogates and supporters often injected religion into the campaign, Clinton actually invoked God and quoted scripture more comfortably and eloquently than Bush. Clinton also linked religion to his political philosophy and used religion to counterattack his Republican opponents. Additionally, while Clinton continued the long-standing Democratic positions on church and state issues, he augmented these arguments by speaking more about religious liberty than simply separation of church and state. Although he used the argument in the same way—and did occasionally cite the separation principle—he usually spoke about the principle in different terms than had Mondale or Dukakis, and Clinton connected it to his personal faith more than the two previous Democratic nominees.

After twelve years of Republicans in the White House, the Democrats' prayer for accession to the Oval Office was answered by a candidate who shared more in common with the last Democratic president than the last two Democratic nominees. The Bible-quoting Southern Baptist Bill Clinton brought religion back into the Democratic presidential campaign repertoire and thus succeeded where Michael Dukakis and Walter Mondale failed. Aiding Clinton in this victory was the fact that, unlike Jimmy Carter in 1980, Clinton did not face a candidate who could eloquently and naturally talk about religion. Although George H. W. Bush offered more religious messages and seemed more comfortable with God-talk than he had in 1988, he still failed to reach the level of his predecessor Ronald Reagan. Other than rhetorical finesse, the most substantial difference between Clinton and Bush occurred on church and state issues. Bush continued Reagan's attempt to claim support for separation of church and state and also for policies that violated the principle, while Clinton advocated his support for separation, albeit often masked in the language of religious liberty. With the exception of Bush's theme on the special relationship between God and America, Clinton out-God-talked Bush in all the other areas, including discussions of personal faith, how religious values influenced his overall political philosophy and specific policy positions, and in using religion to politically attack the opposition. As a result, a second Southern Baptist and little-known governor defeated his better known Democratic opponents before eventually unseating a sitting Republican president.

1996

President Bill Clinton faced no serious challenge for the 1996 Democratic nomination and ran again with running mate Al Gore. Ross Perot faced a challenge for the nomination of his Reform Party from former Colorado Governor Richard Lamm. After Perot won the nomination, he choose economist Pat Choate as his running mate. For the Republicans, Senate Majority Leader Bob Dole quickly emerged as the front-runner. However, he faced a strong challenge from conservative commentator Pat Buchanan who won New Hampshire and three other states. Businessman and *Forbes* magazine editor-in-chief Steve Forbes also won two states. After a few early losses, Dole regained the lead and easily won the nomination. He chose former New York congressman and cabinet member Jack Kemp as his running mate. Some of Dole's primary opponents sounded more like preachers calling for moral and religious revival than candidates running for a political office. In a March 8, 1996, Republican primary debate, Buchanan referenced a theological document from his religious background: "I was raised in a Catholic heritage. And what Steve is saying is a pretty good principle of subsidarity, which was in the Encyclical Rerum Novarum in 1891." Forbes repeatedly called for a spiritual renewal in the nation that he argued was needed to accompany an economic renewal, and activist Alan Keyes often preached about the need for America to acknowledge and follow God's laws.

Both nominees spoke to religious audiences, with Clinton addressing meetings of the National Baptist Convention, USA, Women's International Convention of God in Christ, United Jewish Appeal, and Dole addressing meetings of the Christian Coalition and the Catholic Press Association. Throughout the general election, Clinton maintained a strong lead over Dole and Perot, the latter of whom was left out of the fall presidential debates. Clinton easily won the popular vote and overwhelmingly won the electoral college. Clinton captured 49.2 percent of the popular vote over Dole's 40.7 percent, and won over 70 percent of the electoral college vote. Although Perot received substantially fewer votes than he did in 1992, he still garnered a strong third-party showing of 8.4 percent of the popular vote.

As with the 1992 campaign, Perot rarely used God-talk and did so much less frequently and explicitly than his opponents. Only on rare occasions did he mention God while campaigning and he did not talk about his personal religious beliefs other than a few passing references to attending church as a child. Perot did, however, quote scripture when addressing religious audiences, such as during his speech to the Christian Coalition when he alluded to religious teachings from Jesus and the biblical book of Proverbs to encourage more civil discourse:

> Our religions teach us to love your enemies, be good to those who hate you, bless them who curse you, and pray for those who despitefully use you and persecute you. Now, if we had that attitude across our country, what a difference it would make. As people with strong religious convictions working to solve these problems, we must never forget these words as we deal with others who may disagree with us: "A soft answer turneth away wrath, but grievous words stir up anger." (Perot, 1996, ¶31)

With these quotations, Perot clearly attempted to identify with his Christian audience. As in 1992, Perot's 1996 rhetoric was short on religious references, with the rare biblical quotation appearing in an address to a Christian organization.

Bill Clinton

President Bill Clinton frequently quoted biblical passages and invoked religious language during his reelection campaign, developing the same themes as he had during his 1992 campaign. Clinton offered insights into his *personal faith* as he mentioned his Christian faith and his belief in God. Although he did not talk as explicitly about his personal religious beliefs as he had in 1992, he still made it clear that he was a believer. On several occasions he spoke about the importance of worshipping God. He stated in a speech to the annual meeting of the Women's International Convention of God in Christ that he joined them in affirming Jesus as savior: "But when [we] deny our responsibility and when we are divided, we defeat ourselves. Long before Abraham Lincoln said it, our Savior reminded us that a city or a house divided cannot stand" (Clinton, 1996c, ¶16). During a ceremony honoring Billy and Ruth Graham, he spoke about his personal faith:

> I asked for Billy Graham's prayers for the wisdom and guidance of God—that is a part of his ministry as well. . . . I'll never forget that when Billy Graham came back to Little Rock 30 years later, probably the best well known man of God and faith in the world, he took time out one day to let me take him to see my pastor, whom he had known 30 years before, because he was dying. . . . For all that, as president, and in my personal role as a citizen and a Christian, I am profoundly grateful. (Clinton, 1996b, ¶7, 13, 15)

Here Clinton connected himself to the famed religious leader and expressed his belief that he needed God's help. During several campaign speeches, Clinton quoted scripture or mentioned religious stories, thus demonstrating his familiarity with the Bible. For instance, at a rededication service for Mount Zion African Methodist Episcopal Church, which had burned down, Clinton employed familiar religious allusions:

> This is—this church is Shadrach, Meshach and Abednego: they could burn the building down, but they couldn't burn the faith out. And so we celebrate the triumph of the faith of the members of this church. We celebrate those who have walked from the fire unharmed, goaded by God's faith. We see in the rebuilding of this church that the false idols of hatred and division did not win. (Clinton, 1996d, ¶14)

Clinton's ease in using biblical allusions and quotations provided rhetorical assurances to his religious audiences that he, too, was a devout believer. Although he did not often explicitly announce his Christianity, his scriptural familiarity would be evident to Christians in his audience.

On a few occasions, Clinton connected his overall goals for American society with religion. As he had done in 1992, these remarks cast his campaign as a *spiritual mission* as he imbued his political vision with a spiritual context. Clinton argued for a spiritual renewal to match the economic progress that resulted from his governmental policies: "Yes, we do need more economic advancement, but that may not be our biggest need, for it is said in the Scriptures—and we must remember—that 'man does not live by bread alone'" (Clinton, 1996c, ¶30). He also connected his signature campaign theme of "building a bridge to the twenty-first century" to his religious beliefs:

> The Scripture commands us, in Nehemiah, to rise up and build, and strengthen our hands for the good work. Today, I ask your help in building that bridge to the twenty-first century I have been talking about all across America; a bridge that is wide enough and strong enough to carry every American across. (Clinton, 1996g, ¶18)

Clinton's messages indicated a desire to change American society spiritually in addition to politically. In 1992, Clinton ran on the theme of a "New Covenant" that borrowed explicitly from biblical language. In 1996, he ran with the more secularly sounding "Bridge to the Twenty-first Century," but still justified this vision with scriptural citation.

Clinton also linked selected *public policy* positions to his religious beliefs as he quoted scripture and invoked God to justify his view on these issues. As in 1992, Clinton did not frequently make such connections but, once again, still did so more often and more explicitly than his Republican opponent. He explained his signing of legislation supporting the television V-chip, technology to block selected programming, by stating:

> The Bible asks, "If your child asks for bread, would you give him a stone? If he asks for fish, would you give him a serpent? If he asks for an egg, would you give him a scorpion?" Our children are what we give them, what we teach them. We dare not forget that basic truth. Their lives and our common future depend upon it. (Clinton, 1996a, ¶14)

Clinton also mentioned his support for environmental action in religious terms as he talked about the importance of preserving God's creation: "God created the mountains of Yellowstone and the minerals beneath them, but it is up to us to preserve them" (Clinton, 1996e, ¶28). With these remarks, Clinton tied specific policy decisions with his personal religious beliefs. In doing so, he suggested that the Bible was an important policy handbook that he consulted as the nation's leader.

Clinton also used his political position on *church and state* issues to advocate for religious liberty and the right to worship—or not—as one saw fit. As with his 1992 campaign rhetoric, Clinton framed his argument in terms of religious freedom instead of separation of church and state. With this approach he continued the line of argument of previous Democratic candidates Jimmy Carter, Walter Mondale, and Michael Dukakis, but framed this issue differently. During his October 16, 1996, general election debate with Bob Dole, Clinton talked about his work to promote religious expression:

> One of my proudest moments was signing the Religious Freedom Restoration Act, which says the Government's got to bend over backwards before we interfere with religious practice. So I changed a Justice Department effort to get a church to pay back a man's tithe because he was bankrupt when he gave it.

He also mentioned in a few speeches an example dealing with a Native American religious tradition as proof that he had fought for the right of all people to worship in their own faith. Additionally, Clinton urged respect for all houses of worship in several speeches during the summer of 1996 when many churches were being burned down. He argued that everyone—Christian, Jew, and Muslim—has the right to worship, which is why he said he "reacted so strongly against the church burnings of black churches—and the burnings of white churches, and the people who deface the mosques and the synagogues of this country" (Clinton, 1996f, ¶30). Although Clinton's remarks about his own faith place him squarely within the evangelical Christian tradition, he made it clear throughout his campaign that he believed the freedom of religion must extend also to Jews, Muslims, Native Americans, and others. Clinton also avoided the traditional Democratic language about separation of church and state and instead advocated the same basic position with language about religious freedom for all. In fact, Clinton avoided the separation language even more than he did in 1992 and his firm position on religious freedom for people of all faiths once again placed him in opposition to his Republican opponent.

With strong poll numbers throughout the campaign, the popular Clinton was easily reelected. On his way to another term in the White House, Clinton reiterated his religious-political themes that led him to electoral success four years earlier. He again discussed his personal beliefs and how they impact his public policy decision-making—out–God-talking both of his Republican opponents in these areas. Clinton also once again discussed his political philosophy and campaign theme in religious terms and preached the need for religious liberty. On the latter point, Clinton moved rhetorically even further from his Democratic predecessors, even though his argument remained as ecumenical in asserting the religious rights of those of minority faiths. With this religious rhetoric—and another religiously quiet opponent—Clinton succeeded in his reelection bid where Jimmy Carter failed, thus marking the third election in six cycles where an evangelical Southern Baptist Democrat found political redemption at the ballot box.

Bob Dole

Throughout the general election, Bob Dole spoke about the importance of faith in America and voiced his strong support for greater public religious expressions. However, his religious rhetoric remained less frequent and much more ambiguous than that of his Democratic opponent. On several occasions Dole mentioned his *personal faith* and religious background, but usually only in passing references or about religious experiences from many years earlier. Dole explained during the announcement of his candidacy: "As a young man in a small town my parents taught me to put my trust in God, not government, and never confuse the two" (Dole, 1995a, ¶4). Dole also credited God with his recovery following injuries in World War II. In his acceptance address at the Republican National Convention, he explained, "My life is proof that America is a land without limits. And with my feet on the ground and my heart filled with hope, I put my faith in you and in the God who loves us all" (Dole, 1996b, ¶149). He also cited scripture as he argued to the Christian Coalition that he relied on God:

> And there is a strength that has carried probably all of us and myself through many of life's challenge. It's a strength that always reminds me daily as best expressed in Proverbs 3, verses 5 and 6: Trust in the Lord with all thine heart, and lean not on thy own understanding. In all thy ways acknowledge Him, and He shall direct thy path. (Dole, 1996c, ¶6)

Dole indicated the importance of his faith in God from his upbringing and throughout his life. However, much as with fellow World War II veteran George H. W. Bush, Dole often seemed uncomfortable talking about his personal religious faith.

On a few occasions, Dole declared America to be a Christian nation with a *special relationship* with God. Although this had been a prominent theme for Ronald Reagan in 1980 and 1984, and George H. W. Bush in 1992, Dole did not develop this theme very much throughout his campaign. In one speech, he argued:

> And I'm certain people here remember and understand that we are a nation conceived, born and nurtured by faith. From the hours of our founding to the centuries of our growth, we have always been a nation which recognized its reliance on God. Our faith is declared in our Constitution, affirmed on our currency, and tested in our lives. . . . It is the faith we reject at our peril. (Dole, 1995c, ¶9)

Declaring our Christian nation had remained strong because of trusting in God, Dole argued that America must remain faithful to God. At other times, however, Dole proved he lacked the religious-political eloquence of Reagan. In one speech, Dole awkwardly argued:

> So we want to reconnect the government with your values—your values—hard work and decency and respect for God and country and the church and the Bible, and everything else that goes with it—respect for life. That's the message. (Dole, 1995b, ¶40)

Here Dole insisted that his campaign message had something to do with God and country, but failed to clearly express the relationship. Although Dole occasionally spoke of the special relationship that America had with God from its founding until the present, he did not develop the theme nearly as clearly or strongly as Reagan had or even as Bush had four years earlier.

At times, Dole linked his *public policy* decisions to his personal religious beliefs. With these remarks, Dole claimed that he would look to God—or religious leaders—when deciding how to govern. Taking a position far from that of Catholic John F. Kennedy in 1960, Dole said he would look to the Pope for wisdom on governing decisions concerning abortion: "Though I am not a Catholic, I would listen to Pope John Paul II, who calls the practice a 'brutal' act of inhumanity" (Dole, 1996a, ¶46). Rather than claiming he would not allow religious leaders to tell him what to do as president, Dole bragged that he would seek out their advice. In his speech to the Christian Coalition, Dole cited his 100 percent rating from the organization, which demonstrated that he adopted the same public policy positions that the organization justified as the appropriate Christian positions. With these comments, Dole indicated that his faith guided his policy positions. Although Dole offered a stark contrast to presidents a generation ago—proclaiming he would look to the Pope for guidance on policy issues—he still connected his faith to his policy positions less than his Democratic opponent.

One of Dole's main religious-political messages during the campaign dealt with his position on *church and state* issues. Throughout the campaign, Dole urged support for prayer in schools and greater mixing of religion and politics. However, unlike previous Republican candidates Ronald Reagan and George H. W. Bush, Dole did not contradict this message with claims that he still believed in the separation of church and state. He argued, "I also believe it's permissible to have voluntary prayer in school, and I support an amendment to do that" (Dole, 1996d, ¶26). During a speech to the Christian Coalition, Dole argued that religious groups and individuals should have influence on American politics. In doing so he endorsed a proposed constitutional amendment that, in the name of free exercise of religion, would endorse sectarian prayer in public schools and other religious practices usually considered to violate the principle of separation of church and state:

> And I am particularly interested in continuing the effort to draft a religious equality amendment that will protect our religious freedoms. . . . There are those who believe that attending church and getting involved in politics should be mutually exclusive activities. The liberals tried many tactics during last year's elections when they realized that their number was up. (Dole, 1995c, ¶4–6)

In addition to calling for greater governmental endorsement of religion, Dole attacked Democrats for trying to keep conservative Christians from being involved in politics. Although Dole spoke of the importance of religious freedoms and endorsed prayer in public schools, he dropped the attempt by previous Republican nominees to still claim to respect the separation of church and state.

After two previous attempts in 1980 and 1988, Dole finally secured the Republican presidential nomination. As with his previous two campaigns, Dole did not often invoke religion and seemed uncomfortable when he did. Although Dole did talk about his religious background, about America's special relationship with God, and how religious principles would inform his public policy decisions, he did so less frequently and with less specificity than his Democratic opponent. Additionally, Dole augmented the church and state argument of Ronald Reagan and George H. W. Bush. Although he continued to advocate policies like prayer in public schools, he did not attempt at the same time to insist that he respected the separation of church and state. Despite this adjustment, Dole lacked the rhetorical finesse of Ronald Reagan or Bill Clinton when injecting religion into his campaign discourse.

As Clinton soared to reelection, he once again demonstrated his rhetorical ease and ability in out–God-talking his Republican opponent. In discussing his personal faith and how it influenced his public policy decisions, Clinton offered more frequent and explicit religious discourse. Additionally, Clinton invoked religion to discuss his campaign theme—"a bridge to the twenty-first century." Although Dole spoke of America's special relationship with God, he did so infrequently and with much less clarity than Ronald Reagan had offered. Clinton and Dole also differed in how they addressed issues of church and state, although both differed from the traditional arguments of candidates of their parties. Dole continued the Republican argument for prayer in public schools but dropped giving lip-service to separation of church and state, while Clinton continued to oppose prayer in public schools but spoke more about religious freedom than separation. Along the way, Clinton preached his way to another electoral victory.

SUMMARY

As the lone nonevangelical to capture the White House since the mid-1970s, George H. W. Bush's level and nature of religious rhetoric pales in comparison to that of other recent presidents. Bush clearly attempted to "talk the talk"—as evangelicals might put it—but it came out less naturally and often. Yet, in one general election Bush was easily the most religiously outspoken candidate and in the other he was easily out-God-talked by his Democratic opponent. Compared to Michael Dukakis—the most secular modern candidate to receive a major party presidential nomination—Bush almost seemed to gush about his private faith. However, once he was sharing the campaign spotlight with Bill Clinton, Bush appeared reticent and uneasy discussing his personal religiosity. As an Episcopalian, Bush was part of the faith tradition that claims the most presidents (11) but is the only one elected since Franklin Roosevelt (Gerald Ford was also one). Meanwhile, Dukakis failed in his attempt to become the first president who was a member of the Greek Orthodox Church. Clinton brought the number of Baptists to reach the nation's highest office to four. Along with Jimmy Carter, he helped double this number in just sixteen years after seeing none since Harry Truman.

Although Bush was a member of a denomination whose members are not known for openly discussing their private religious lives, he easily beat Dukakis, who was marginally part of another denomination famous for segregating the public and the private realms. Four years later, Bush was ousted by a candidate steeped in a religious tradition where public confessions of one's faith were not only commonplace but expected. As an evangelical Southern Baptist, Clinton—like Carter before him—could speak of God and quote scriptures with ease. Thus, although both elections saw the most rhetorically religious candidate win the general election, Bush still serves as somewhat of an anomaly for the past three decades. His style on discussing religious matters—along with that of Ford—appears almost as a hybrid between other recent presidents and those of the modern presidency prior to Carter.

Chapter Four

W. Bush and Obama

The first decade of the twenty-first century saw three highly charged elections filled with polarizing arguments and religious rhetoric. The two candidates to emerge victoriously from these contests represent two vastly different wings of the evangelical Protestant community. George W. Bush, a conservative white evangelical, shares few political positions with his successor, Barack Obama, an African American liberal evangelical. However, both men share a similar story of experiencing a religious conversion as an adult and joining a congregation where they were taught to rely on the Bible's teachings and to publicly proclaim their faith. Despite their differences on public policies, both men claim that the Bible impacted their positions on various public policy issues. Despite their ideological differences, both men openly confess their faith in Jesus on the campaign trail, even telling their conversion stories and talking about their personal religious beliefs and struggles. Although neither would likely admit a close similarity—especially since Obama essentially ran as the anti-Bush candidate in 2008—their religious rhetorical styles share striking similarities. Thus, Bush and Obama demonstrate the diversity of evangelicals, who might disagree on specific policies or doctrines but still draw from a common rhetorical style. Unlike the "Religious Right," which is often wrongly treated synonymously with "evangelical" by journalists and scholars, evangelicals cross party lines and can often serve as critical swing voters.

2000

The sitting Vice President, Al Gore, was challenged for the 2000 Democratic nomination by former Senator Bill Bradley of New Jersey, but Gore easily won the nomination as he won every primary and caucus. He chose Senator Joe Lieberman of Connecticut as his running mate, making Lieberman the first Jewish candidate on a major-party ticket. During the Democratic primary, Gore used religious rhetoric much more often than Bradley, who argued that religion should remain a private issue but did sometimes still invoke religion in his campaign rhetoric.

As the race for the Republican nomination neared, Texas Governor George W. Bush emerged as the front-runner. Bush won the Iowa caucuses, but Senator John McCain of Arizona won the New Hampshire primary. Millionaire Steve Forbes and Christian activists Alan Keyes and Gary Bauer all finished ahead of McCain in Iowa but were unable to compete elsewhere. Bush rebounded with a win in the South Carolina primary. Although McCain won a few more states, Bush easily secured the nomination. Bush chose former Secretary of Defense Dick Cheney as his running mate.

After Bush spoke at the religious Bob Jones University in South Carolina, McCain's campaign attacked him for aligning with someone who held anti-Catholic positions. Meanwhile, televangelist Pat Robertson sponsored automated phone attacks on candidate McCain, which prompted McCain to denounce Robertson and Jerry Falwell as "agents of intolerance" and "forces of evil" (Bruni and Mitchell, 2000, ¶1, 17). Although McCain openly criticized religious leaders, he often couched these criticisms with his own attempts to reach out to religious conservative voters. Not only did he declare America to be "a Judeo-Christian principled nation" (McCain, 1999, ¶94), but he urged religious conservatives to join his campaign:

> The overwhelming numbers of people in the Christian right, we want them back, we want them to join us, but they have to reject these leaders that are on the extremes that have caused, frankly, a very harmful impact on not only the American people but our party. (McCain, 2000b, ¶25)

Bush linked himself to the only Catholic U.S. president as he attacked McCain for making an issue of his speech at Bob Jones:

> It's the kind of politics that John F. Kennedy rejected in the 1960s. It's the kind of politics that we thought we put behind us in America. It's the kind of politics that continues to persist today because of Senator McCain. (Bush, 2000b, ¶9)

Due to McCain's attacks on religious leaders and the campaign involvement of religious leaders on behalf of Bush in South Carolina, Bush was able to win the critical first southern primary. However, McCain's campaign highlighted Bush's Bob Jones speech in Michigan to activate the state's large Catholic voting bloc. After McCain's Michigan victory, Bush confessed his error in not repudiating the anti-Catholicism of Bob Jones in a letter to Cardinal John O'Connor of New York, which Bush's campaign released publicly. Bush managed to eventually put the sectarian conflict behind him and capture the Republican nomination. With this controversy, McCain and Bush used religious attacks during the campaign to generate political support among religious voters.

In the general election, conservative commentator Pat Buchanan ran as the Reform Party's candidate and activist Ralph Nader ran as the Green Party's candidate. Bush campaigned on the promise of restoring character to the White House and attempted to paint himself as a Washington outsider while linking Al Gore to Bill Clinton's scandals. Gore distanced himself from the still popular Clinton while pointing to the successes of the Clinton administration. Both Bush and Gore spoke at prayer breakfasts for ministers during the campaign. As the votes were cast on election night, the race remained too close to call. In the early hours of the next morning, the networks called Florida—and thus the election—for Bush, even though Gore won the national popular vote. Although Gore had initially privately conceded to Bush, he rescinded his concession in hopes that a recount of Florida's votes would change the election results. After weeks of legal maneuvering that eventually went to the U.S. Supreme Court, the Florida results were certified for Bush and he was elected by the electoral college. Gore bested Bush in the popular vote with 48.4 to 47.9 percent; but with Florida in his column, Bush collected just over 50 percent of the electoral college vote. Although Nader garnered less than 3 percent of the popular vote, many commentators believed the votes he captured in Florida were enough to keep Gore from winning Florida and therefore the election.

Al Gore

During the 2000 election, Al Gore quoted scriptures and talked about the importance of religion as he sought to succeed fellow Southern Baptist Bill Clinton. Gore spoke about his *personal faith* and religious background during the campaign as he made it clear that he believed in God and knew the Bible's teachings. He talked about his parents during his acceptance address at the Democratic National Convention: "My parents taught me that the real values in life aren't material, but spiritual. They include faith and family, duty and honor and trying to make the world a better place" (Gore, 2000c, ¶54, 56). During a prayer breakfast in Tennessee just days before the election, Gore pointed out that he "studied religion at Vanderbilt," a university in Tennessee that began as a Methodist school (Gore, 2000c, ¶61). Referring to the Columbine High School shooting tragedy, Gore opened up about his personal faith and quoted Scriptures. In the speech he assumed the role of a preacher as he introduced, explained, and applied a biblical text:

> I read Genesis chapter 4 verse 6 and 7 and found a new way of reading it after that Columbine event. It's the story of Cain and Abel. Both give offerings to God and God rejects Cain's offering and accepts Abel's offering. Biblical scholars say it's a metaphor for the shift from pastoral agriculture to planting. . . . But in any case, the words used in the King James version is God had respect for Abel's offering. God had no respect for Cain's offering. And then God says to Cain right after that, why are you angry? Why has your countenance fallen? If you do well, will you not be accepted? And if you do not do well, sin lieth at your door and its desire is for you, but you must overcome it. (Gore, 1999a, ¶233)

In several speeches, Gore offered insights into his religious beliefs, his familiarity with scripture, and his religious background. Although he seemed more at ease discussing his personal religious beliefs than some presidential candidates (such as Democrats Walter Mondale and Michael Dukakis and Republicans George H. W. Bush and Bob Dole), his fluency with God-talk did not compare to Democrats Jimmy Carter or Bill Clinton, or, even more importantly, his Republican opponent.

During the campaign, Gore connected his religious beliefs with some of his *public policy* positions. With these remarks, Gore indicated that he would look to biblical teachings to decide how to govern. Gore suggested that the nation's spiritual quest was even more important than political matters: "The answer to the economic question depends on the answer to the spiritual question. The political question is relevant, but the spiritual question is the principle one" (Gore, 2000d, ¶67). In his speech introducing Lieberman as his running mate, Gore linked environmental policies to their religious beliefs: "He believes, as I do, that the Earth is the Lord's and the fullness thereof" (Gore, 2000b, ¶54). In another speech, he cited a biblical passage to stress the need to address the problem of media violence:

> On this question of the role of culture and the media, I remembered a parable in my faith called the parable of the sower. And it is a story about sowing seeds. And the seeds sometimes fall on barren ground, sometimes on ground clotted with thriving plants, sometimes on fertile soil, and there the seeds put down roots and bear fruit. And the parable is about seeds of faith, but I think it applies to this case. (Gore, 1999a, ¶230)

During his October 11, 2000, general election debate with Bush, Gore declared in a discussion of gun policies: "I also believe in the Golden Rule." And in a speech at a prayer breakfast, Gore quoted scripture to explain why he wanted to continue the policies of the Clinton administration:

> The Apostle Paul, in reference to that passage, wrote not once but twice, once to Galatians and then in his second letter to Thessalonians: "Be not weary in well-doing. Ye shall reap if ye faint not." Some people are tired of prosperity. Some people are tired of the 22 million jobs. They look back to a period eight years ago and they say we were better off then than we are now. I don't agree. (Gore, 2000d, ¶33–34)

On several occasions while campaigning, Gore cited scriptures to convince voters that they could trust him to rely on biblical teachings when making public policy decisions. Gore made these religious connections to his policies more explicitly and frequently than most recent candidates had, including his opponent George W. Bush.

Although Gore frequently invoked religious allusions and scriptural references, he also offered assurances at times that he would not go too far in mixing *church and state*. He talked about his commitment to the principle of separation of church and state in a December 17, 1999, Democratic primary debate:

> I strongly support the separation of church and state. The bedrock principle on which our nation was founded, was the search for religious freedom, which clearly meant freedom from government interference in religion.

Gore applied the separation principle to specific issues during a January 5, 2000, Democratic primary debate: "I strongly support the separation of church and state. I strongly support the First Amendment, the Establishment Clause. I oppose, for example, the teaching of creationism in the public schools. I think that violates that provision of our Constitution." However, Gore did not hold to a strict separation position as earlier Democratic candidates Walter Mondale and Michael Dukakis had. For instance, Gore stated, "I believe strongly in the separation of church and state . . . but freedom of religion need not mean freedom from religion" (Mansfield, 2003, p. 105–6). He also voiced his belief that government should support faith-based organizations: "If you elect me your president, the voices of faith-based organizations will be integral to the policies set forth in my administration" (Mansfield, 2003, p. 106). On other occasions, Gore continued Bill Clinton's approach of talking about religious freedom. Gore did not address issues of separation or religious freedom as often as his Democratic predecessors Carter, Mondale, Dukakis, or Clinton; when Gore did talk about it, he did not take as strong a position on separation as Mondale or Dukakis, or link it to his religious beliefs like Carter or Clinton.

Throughout the campaign, Al Gore quoted scriptures and talked about God, often with religious zeal and detail. Gore discussed his personal religious beliefs and invoked the Bible and God to justify public policy positions. He also claimed to support the separation of church and state, although he offered caveats that his Democratic predecessors had not voiced. Gore's rhetoric placed him closer to the model of fellow Southern Baptists Jimmy Carter and Bill Clinton rather than that of Walter Mondale and Michael Dukakis. However, unlike Carter in 1976 or Clinton in 1992 and 1996, Gore faced an evangelical opponent who proudly and frequently testified about his faith.

George W. Bush

George W. Bush often talked openly about his religious beliefs during the campaign, even testifying about his belief in Christ. As Bush sought the support of conservative Christians during the Republican primary and then the general election, he made it abundantly clear that he not only shared their beliefs but also was one of them because of his conversion and *personal faith*. He stated, "I'm comforted by the fact that I've got great faith, that I believe in a supreme being. And that gives me great comfort" (Matthews, 2000, ¶26). Bush famously declared during a December 13, 1999, Republican primary debate that the philosopher he most identified with was "Christ, because he changed my heart." He added, "When you turn your heart and your life over to Christ, when you accept Christ as the savior, it changes your heart. It changes your life. And that's what happened to me." On *Larry King Live*, Bush later explained his statement and why he felt it was an appropriate comment for a presidential campaign:

> I just was responding to a question to let people know about me, and if they want to know about me, they want to know the kind of person I am, then they need to know that fact, that Christ has had a huge influence in my life. . . . It was a way for people to get a sense for who I am, and it's the right answer. (King, 1999, ¶288)

Bush claimed on another occasion: "I'm going to value my religion, and I'm going to rely upon my religion to bring me strength in life" (Bush, 2000a, ¶22). Throughout the campaign, Bush openly discussed his theology, making it clear that he believes in the Christian God. As Bush articulated his personal religious faith, he demonstrated much more comfort with the subject than previous Republican candidates like Bob Dole and even Bush's own father.

At times Bush spoke about America's *special relationship* with God and how the nation was divinely blessed. With these remarks, Bush attempted to capture the hallmark of Ronald Reagan's religious-political rhetoric. Bush argued, "We're all Americans. We all live in the greatest land that God has put on the face of the Earth, one nation, indivisible and under God" (Bush, 2000f, ¶31). Although Bush—like his father in 1992—only developed this theme on occasion and did not match the rhetorical eloquence or frequency of Reagan, he did make the point more clearly than Bob Dole in 1996 or his father in 1988.

During the campaign, Bush also connected his religious beliefs to his *public policy* positions. With these remarks, Bush offered that he would look to God and the Bible when making decisions as president. Bush stated in a January 6, 2000, Republican primary debate: "I would take an expression in the Oval Office of 'Dear God, help me.'" In describing his view of America's post–Cold War foreign policy, Bush declared, "We are defending the nobility of normal lives, lived in obedience to God and conscience, not to government" (Bush, 1999b, ¶43). He also stated why he believed creationism should be taught in public schools along with evolution: "None of us will actually know what the ultimate truth is, but many of us do believe God created the Earth, and I think that needs to be explained clearly to students" (Bush, 2000b, ¶58). With these comments, Bush mentioned how he would make public policy decisions after looking to God for guidance. While he did not often make a specific connection between his religious beliefs and many of his political policies, Bush did spend much of his time advocating for greater governmental support of faith-based initiatives. Although his advocacy of government-funded faith-based organizations represented Bush's merging of religion and government policy, he seemed to go even further than past candidates as he often assumed the role of an evangelist.

With his rhetoric supporting government-funded faith-based initiatives, Bush suggested that his campaign was attempting to accomplish a *spiritual mission* and not just governmental reform. When arguing that government should assist faith-based organizations in doing their religious work, Bush often downplayed the importance of government. With this line of argumentation, Bush not only preached the need for religious groups to spiritually transform the nation, but also urged the government to support such spiritual renewal efforts: "Government can encourage people of faith and goodwill and good heart to love a neighbor, just like they'd like to be loved themselves" (Bush, 2000e, ¶5). Bush also argued that teaching religious values was a more effective way to deal with public problems than governmental action. During his October 11, 2000, debate with Gore, Bush quoted the "golden rule" as he discounted Gore's call for greater governmental laws to solve societal problems:

It's really a matter of culture. It's a culture that somewhere along the line we've begun to disrespect life. . . . So gun laws are important, no question about it, but so is loving children, and character education classes, and faith-based programs being a part of after-school programs. . . . But there's a larger law. Love your neighbor like you would like to be loved yourself. And that's where our society must head if we're going to be a peaceful and prosperous society.

In another speech he declared, "It's fitting that we be at a prayer breakfast . . . because it reminds us that while government can feed the body, it cannot nourish the soul" (Bush, 2000d, ¶13). Although Bush did not link as many of his political positions to his religious beliefs as his Democratic opponent, Bush did more frequently call for allowing government support of faith-based organizations. As Bush pushed his proposal, he downplayed the importance of the very institution he was hoping to lead. Instead, Bush urged the government to assist religious groups in their important mission of helping others, thus transforming his campaign into something of a spiritual mission.

Bush's rhetoric on *church and state* issues was largely characterized by rhetorical silence when compared to Republican candidates throughout the previous two decades, and also to his Democratic opponent. Although Bush talked a lot about church and state issues, especially his faith-based initiatives, he did not usually frame these matters in separation doctrine terms. In addition to pushing for greater governmental support of religious groups with his faith-based initiatives, Bush also offered support for the public display and teaching of the Ten Commandments, prayer in public schools, and for character education and the teaching of creationism in public schools. He argued during a January 15, 2000, Republican primary debate: "I think districts ought to be allowed to post the Ten Commandments no matter what a person's religion is there's some inherent values in those great commandments that would make our society a better place for everybody." Throughout the campaign, Bush offered strong support for more governmental support and recognition of religion. However, unlike many previous Republican candidates—such as Ronald Reagan and George H. W. Bush—the younger Bush did not voice any support for the separation of church and state. Other than a few statements regarding the lack of religious liberty in China, Bush ignored issues of separation or religious liberty.

Throughout the 2000 campaign, Bush testified about his personal religious beliefs, his belief that America had a special relationship with God, how his religious beliefs would impact his public policy, and how he desired to see greater governmental support of religious organizations in order to bring about spiritual change in the nation. Bush also found himself embroiled in a religious conflict with Republican challenger John McCain that, overall, worked to Bush's favor as conservative Christian leaders rallied to his side and helped him secure the nomination. With his strong religious rhetoric,

Bush clearly avoided the model of his father and the most recent Republican nominee, Bob Dole, and instead placed himself closer to the sermonizing style of Ronald Reagan.

Al Gore more closely followed winning models of his fellow Southern Baptists Bill Clinton and Jimmy Carter than that of Democrats Walter Mondale and Michael Dukakis. In doing so, Gore injected religion more frequently and explicitly than he had during his failed 1988 presidential run. Despite such proclamations—and a popular vote victory—Gore remained unable to capture the White House. In what seemed to many commentators and strategists to be a Democratic year—following eight years of relative peace and prosperity under a popular Democratic president—George W. Bush ascended to the throne of his father. On his way to the Oval Office, however, Bush rejected the reserved approach to religion that his biological father followed and instead more fully embraced the language of his Heavenly father.

2004

President George W. Bush faced no serious challenge for the 2004 Republican nomination. On the Democratic side, several candidates fought to represent their party against Bush. Former Vermont Governor Howard Dean emerged as the front-runner during the summer of 2003, with strong poll numbers and fundraising as the year came to an end. However, Dean placed a distant third in the Iowa caucuses to Senator John Kerry of Massachusetts and Senator John Edwards of North Carolina. A disappointing fourth-place finish drove Representative Dick Gephardt of Missouri out of the race. When Kerry won New Hampshire and Edwards won South Carolina, the race essentially narrowed to the two. After Kerry swept the Super Tuesday states, Edwards dropped out and Kerry secured the nomination. He later chose Edwards as his running mate.

During the general election campaign, Bush stressed foreign policy issues, opposition to same-sex marriage, and attacked Kerry as a flip-flopper. Kerry focused on how Bush had damaged America's relationship with many other nations, and specifically Bush's execution of the Iraq war. Both candidates spoke in churches during the campaign. Additionally, Bush addressed the annual meetings of the Southern Baptist Convention and the National Association of Evangelicals, and Kerry addressed the annual meetings of the National Baptist Convention, USA, and the African Methodist Episcopal Church. On election night, Bush narrowly captured the popular vote and the electoral college. He beat Kerry 50.7 to 48.3 percent in the popular vote and won over 53 percent of the electoral college vote. Although activist Ralph Nader ran again as the Green Party nominee, neither he nor any other third-party candidate won more than one-half of 1 percent of the popular vote.

George W. Bush

During the 2004 campaign, George W. Bush frequently preached the importance of supporting religious organizations and doing God's work here on earth by bringing freedom to Iraq. As with his 2000 campaign, Bush talked openly of his *personal faith* and religious beliefs. In commenting about the central role of prayer in fulfilling his presidential duties, Bush noted:

> From an individual perspective, as a person, I rely upon faith to give me the strength necessary to do my job. One of the interesting parts of the job, something that I discovered as President, is the fact that a lot of people pray for me. That's a very humbling thought when you think about little old me. People pray for George W. and his family. . . . I believe in prayer, and I appreciate the prayers of people. (Bush, 2004d, ¶283, 286)

Bush would make similar remarks on numerous occasions during the campaign about how he appreciated the prayers of Americans. Referring to a painting he hung in the Oval Office and the hymn he claimed inspired the painting, Bush stated:

> The hymn was sung at my first inaugural church service as governor. Laura and I are Methodists. One of the Wesley boys wrote the hymn. The painting is based upon the hymn called, "A Charge to Keep." . . . The hymn talks about serving something greater than yourself in life. I—which I try to do, as best as I possibly can. (Bush, 2004j, ¶153)

Bush also talked about his personal devotional readings during the campaign. With these remarks, Bush offered insights into his private faith and clearly proved himself to be more comfortable discussing religion than his Democratic opponent. Like the other president most open about his personal spiritual habits—Jimmy Carter—Bush testified less about his personal faith during his second campaign than in his first, although Bush interjected more religious rhetoric in other parts of his campaign appeals.

Throughout the campaign, Bush cast his presidency—and thus his campaign for reelection—as part of an important *spiritual mission*. As Bush defended his handling of the Iraq War, he depicted the conflict as an important way for America to bring about God's will. He frequently declared in speeches that a nation's freedom comes from God: "I believe all these things, not because freedom is America's gift to the world, but because freedom is the Almighty God's gift to every man and woman in this world" (Bush, 2004m, ¶60). This phrase, or similar versions, was used by Bush in numerous campaign speeches. By casting the Iraq War as an attempt by the United States to bring the Iraqi people God's gift of freedom, Bush declared the major work of his administration to be part of an important spiritual mission to do God's will on earth. Bush later explained that he—and not a speech-writer—first coined the line about freedom being God's gift to the world: "As a matter of fact, I was the person who wrote the line, or said it. I didn't write it, I just said it in a speech. And it became part of the jargon. And I believe it" (Albright, 2006, p. 5). Thus, for Bush this line united both his religious and political beliefs and justified his actions in perhaps the most contentious issue of the 2004 presidential election. Bush even connected this philosophy—that the Iraq War was an important spiritual mission—with his frequent use of the phrase "God bless America." On several occasions Bush told the story of an Iraqi man, who had been tortured by Saddam Hussein's troops, writing "God bless America" in Arabic. This story connected the phrase with his primary religious-political message—bringing freedom to Iraq. For Bush, his political decision to commit troops to Afghanistan and Iraq was founded on his religious belief that God wanted America to bring freedom and democracy to all nations.

Closely related to Bush's claims about God's gift of freedom was his assertion that America has a *special relationship* with God. Bush clearly articulated that he believed that God had blessed America throughout its history: "And we're a great country because we are blessed by the Almighty God" (Bush, 2004h, ¶12). He also linked this belief to his call for Americans to continue to trust God: "Together, Americans are moving forward with confidence and faith. We do not know God's plan, but we know His ways are right and just. And we pray He will always watch over this great country of ours" (Bush, 2004b, ¶27). In Bush's campaign rhetoric he made it clear that he believed that God had blessed America and that America's greatness endured because it was a free nation trusting in God. Although Bush did not develop this theme as frequently as Ronald Regan had, Bush did use it more than his Democratic opponent and his own 2000 campaign.

At times, Bush used religious allusions and references to promote specific *public policy* positions. He stated his opposition to stem-cell research by explaining: "Human life is a creation of God, not a commodity to be exploit-ed by man" (Bush, 2004b, ¶18, 20). He used religious-political rhetoric in speeches on poverty and education, but usually in reference to his faith-based programs. Like Jimmy Carter, Bush took an approach drastically different from John F. Kennedy as he met with the Pope and pointed to the Pontiff as an important guide for making decisions:

> I had the privilege of visiting His Holy Father Pope John Paul II at the Vatican. It was my third meeting with His Holy Father since I took office, and for those of you who have ever met him, you know I'm telling you the truth when I tell

> you being in his presence is an awesome experience. . . . He has challenged our
> nation, and the entire world, to embrace the culture of life. He's called upon us
> to uphold and affirm the dignity of every person, rich and poor, able and
> disabled, born and unborn. (Bush, 2004l, ¶16–17)

Although Bush did not invoke religion in his discussion of many public
policy decisions, one of his most consistent campaign messages was his
support for faith-based initiatives. This policy—which he promised during
his 2000 campaign to enact—resulted in considerable attention given to issues of church and state during his reelection campaign.

Bush dealt with issues of *church and state* as he continued calls for
greater governmental support and acknowledgment of religion. One of
Bush's main campaign issues in 2000 was his plan to provide government
funding to faith-based programs—social and educational programs operated
by churches and religious organizations; in 2004, he continued to talk about
these programs and how much his initiative was helping society. Several of
his 2004 campaign speeches were focused almost entirely on this subject.
Bush argued that support of faith-based programs was necessary because of
the people that would be helped: "All of you know the power of faith to
transform lives, you're answering the call to love and to serve your neighbor"
(Bush, 2004b, ¶10). He also frequently stated that if the government did not
actively assist faith-based groups, this would actually constitute "government
discrimination against people of faith" (Bush, 2004a, ¶137). Bush, speaking
in the third person, even linked his faith-based support to his eventual presidential legacy: "I want people to look back and say that George W. Bush
understood the power of faith-based programs to change America one heart
at a time" (Bush, 2004n, ¶469). Although Bush would often make a point to
talk about how government funds were available to Christian, Muslim, Jewish, or any other religious groups, many of his statements were explicitly
Christian. In one speech he told a story about his visit to a prison faith-based
program when he was Governor of Texas:

> And so I went to see it as the governor. And out comes the prison choir. And
> one of my favorite hymns is "Amazing Grace." Of course, I've got a lot of my
> mother in me, so I immediately jumped in line with the prisoners singing
> "Amazing Grace," you know, like 10 white suits and me. (Bush, 2004i, ¶91)

Bush's support of faith-based initiatives sparked frequent criticism that he
was violating the principle of separation of church and state. Although Bush
only mentioned the principle explicitly in a few campaign addresses, each
time he did so it was in the context of defending his faith-based initiative.
Bush argued that while he respected the separation principle, the government
should be allowed to give public funds to support religious organizations and
programs:

> Look, I fully understand it's important to maintain the separation of church and state. We don't want the state to become the church, nor do we want the church to become the state. . . . But I do believe that groups should be allowed to access social service grants so long as they don't proselytize or exclude somebody simply because they don't share a certain faith. (Bush, 2004g, ¶99)

Bush also argued that his faith-based programs would not blur the line between church and state. However, Bush spent much more time talking about religious freedom than the separation of church and state:

> Let me just talk about religion and politics. First—first—first, it is essential that this country never abandon the principle that people can worship the way they want to. That you can worship, that you can choose to worship or not worship and be equally patriotic. . . . The second principle is that if you choose to worship, you're equally American if you're a Christian, Jew, Muslim, Hindu. That's an important part of our society. It's essential that we always honor that. That's called freedom of religion. It's an integral part of the American past, present and future. The state should never be the church, and the church should never be the state. (Bush, 2004k, ¶401, 403–4)

With his Manichean mindset, there seemed only two rather extreme positions that Bush needed to avoid: we must avoid either a state-run church or a church-run state. Thus, *anything* in between should not be regarded as a violation of the separation principle. This interpretation allowed Bush to stake out positions on church-state issues he found acceptable but many others viewed as crossing the church-state line. As Bush continued his 2000 campaign focus on promoting faith-based initiatives, he attempted to defend his policy against charges that he was violating the separation principle. However, Bush most often preached more about the need to ensure religious freedom than maintaining church-state separation. Although Bush spoke more about separation of church and state than in his 2000 campaign, his church and state message was essentially the same with his continued call for greater governmental support of religious organizations.

As Bush sought reelection, he continued many of his religious-political themes from the 2000 campaign. Bush once again talked about his personal religious faith, connected his beliefs to his public policies—especially faith-based initiatives—and justified his position on church and state issues with greater governmental support of religious organizations. A few changes occurred from his 2000 campaign discourse. Bush talked less about his personal religious beliefs, much more about faith-based initiatives, and more about the principle of separation of church and state as he attempted to defend his faith-based initiatives. Bush also offered a substantially new message compared to his previous campaign as he compared his Iraq foreign policy to a spiritual mission designed to deliver God's gift of freedom to the world. Throughout the campaign, Bush found himself in a similar position as Ronald Reagan in 1984 with the strong support of conservative Christians who literally preached the need for his reelection. Although Bush had faced a close contest four years earlier against an evangelical Southern Baptist, this time he faced a northeastern Catholic who was more reticent about publicly proclaiming his personal faith.

John Kerry

John Kerry used religious-political rhetoric throughout his campaign, but often appeared less comfortable talking about issues of religion—except when attacking Bush. At times, Kerry discussed his *personal faith* and religious background as commentators and Democratic strategists argued that he needed to do so in order to reduce the so-called God gap that led frequent churchgoers to strongly support Bush. Most of Kerry's personal religious comments dealt with his childhood and experiences in Vietnam:

> It all began with my parents who, in addition to making sure I learned and lived my faith, also taught me at an early age that we are all put on this earth for something greater than ourselves. What they taught me was truly put to the test when I was in Vietnam. Faith was as much a part of our daily lives as the battle itself. Some of my closest friends were killed. I prayed. And I even questioned how all the terrible things I'd seen fit into God's plan. But I got through it. I came home with a sense of hope and a belief in a higher purpose. For more than 30 years, as a soldier, a prosecutor, a senator, and now as a candidate for president, I have tried to live that belief. (Kerry, 2004g, ¶11–12)

Kerry also mentioned being an altar boy, claimed he once considered the priesthood, and stated, "Faith is central to my life" (Smith, 2006, p. 379). However, he did not speak much about his personal religious beliefs or current spiritual practices. He even seemed to downplay such confessions on a few occasions, such as during his acceptance address at the 2004 Democratic convention, "I don't wear my religion on my sleeve, but faith has given me values and hope to live by, from Vietnam to this day, from Sunday to Sunday" (Kerry, 2004c, ¶252). He added on another occasion, "I fully intend to continue to practice my religion as separately from what I do with respect to my public life" (Smith, 2006, p. 380). Compared to his Republican opponent and recent Democratic candidates Al Gore and especially Bill Clinton, Kerry seemed uncomfortable talking about his personal religious beliefs.

On a few occasions, Kerry offered his belief that America has a *special relationship* with God. However, unlike his Republican opponent or most other recent presidential nominees, Kerry suggested that there were limits to God's blessings—thus aligning himself closer to the rhetoric of Jimmy Carter in 1980. Near the end of the campaign, Kerry proclaimed:

> We always end our speeches in campaigns like this by saying "God bless
> America." But it seems to me that we should also say to God, "Thank you for
> blessing America in so many ways." May America always have God's bless-
> ing. (Kerry, 2004g, ¶35–36)

This comment took a more traditional and ceremonial civil religious remark
"God bless America" and infused it with greater religious meaning. In other
speeches, however, Kerry suggested that God had deliberately limited America's natural blessings:

> And so one of the things John [Edwards] and I are going to do is recognize that
> as long as the United States of America only has 3 percent of the world's oil
> reserves, that's all God gave us. I think he sent us a message when he did that.
> And the message is, if we want to control our own security, and hold our
> destiny in our own hands, then I want America's energy to depend on our
> innovation and our ingenuity, not the Saudi royal family. (Kerry, 2004d, ¶68)

As Kerry urged Americans to hear the message God was sending through
providing a limited supply of oil, his message on the relationship between
America and God matched Carter's 1980 limited blessings argument that was
derived from the same issues—energy and oil. With this significant caveat to
the traditional message about God's blessings, Kerry offered a sharp contrast
from the rhetoric of George W. Bush, who argued that it was God's will that
America democratize other nations—especially oil-rich nations.

Kerry connected his *public policy* positions with his religious beliefs,
often in very explicit ways. As he quoted scripture and invoked God, Kerry
demonstrated that he would allow his religious values to impact his presidential decisions—an argument far different from that espoused by fellow Catholic John F. Kennedy four decades earlier. Often these highly religious remarks dealt with domestic issues like the environment, education, race, social security, and poverty. During an October 13, 2004, debate with George
W. Bush, Kerry explained:

> And I think that everything you do in public life has to be guided by your faith,
> affected by your faith, but without transferring it in any official way to other
> people. . . . That's why I fight to clean up the environment and protect this
> earth.

During his acceptance speech at the Democratic National Convention, Kerry
advocated his policy position against privatizing social security by quoting
scripture: "We believe in the family value expressed in one of the oldest
Commandments: 'Honor thy father and thy mother'" (Kerry, 2004c, ¶167).
Similarly, he explained his support for economic issues like raising the mini-
mum wage and enacting welfare reform:

> The Bible tells us that in others we encounter the face of God: "I was hungry
> and you fed me; thirsty and you gave me a drink. I was a stranger and you
> received me in your homes; naked and you clothed me. I was sick and you
> took care of me. I was in prison and you visited me." (Kerry, 2004g, ¶20)

Kerry often cited biblical passage to connect his public policy positions with
his religious beliefs. In policy discussions, Kerry included religious references more frequently and explicitly than his Republican opponent or even
most recent presidential nominees.

On issues of *church and state*, Kerry offered his clear affirmation for the
doctrine of separation of church and state. With these arguments, Kerry's
position contained less ambiguity than his Republican opponent's and
marked a return to the strong support for strict separation that Democratic
nominees Walter Mondale and Michael Dukakis had proclaimed. As with
Mondale, Kerry often used discussions of separation to attack the policies of
the incumbent Republican president. About the principle of separation, Kerry
said, "And I as president will uphold the oath of office, the Constitution of
the United States which the founding fathers smartly and brilliantly made
clear separates affairs of church and state. And we must honor that in this
country" (Kerry, 2004e, ¶439). Additionally, he attacked Bush for crossing
that line: "There's nothing conservative about crossing that beautiful line
drawn by the Founding Fathers that we've lived with for 229 years that
separates church and state in the United States, but they do" (Kerry, 2004a,
¶135). Kerry specifically singled out Bush's faith-based initiatives for violating the separation principle: "I draw a line that George Bush doesn't draw,
which is the line of separating the religious activity itself and prosyletizing
from the service of soup kitchen or a counseling or whatever" (Kerry, 2004e,
¶453). With these remarks, Kerry offered a rhetorical position closer to that
of Walter Mondale and Michael Dukakis than more recent Democratic candidates Al Gore and especially Bill Clinton. While Clinton spoke more of
religious liberty and joined Jimmy Carter in connecting this view to his
personal religious beliefs, Kerry simply preached a clear message of separation.

As Kerry attempted to unseat a relatively unpopular president, he struggled to articulate his personal religious beliefs in order to connect with voters
looking for such professions of faith. Additionally, he augmented the more
optimistic message about America's special relationship with God to suggest
there were limits to divine blessings, and he offered a strong stand for the
separation of church and state. In each of these ways, Kerry differed from the
religious-political approach of Democrats like Bill Clinton and Al Gore, and
appeared closer to the religious-political model of Walter Mondale and Michael Dukakis. Although Kerry did surpass his Democratic predecessors in

connecting his public policy decisions to his religious beliefs, and even did so on more issues than his Republican opponent, he failed to match Bush's evangelistic zeal in all other areas.

Even though George W. Bush was a relatively unpopular president leading an increasingly unpopular war, Kerry remained unable to oust the incumbent president from the White House. As Bush frequently preached the need to support religious organizations in their work through his faith-based initiatives, Kerry reverted back to the strict separation argument of Walter Mondale and Michael Dukakis. Bush openly and frequently discussed his religious beliefs, while Kerry seemed uncomfortable talking about his personal religious faith. In the end, Kerry's attempt to defeat an incumbent Republican President more closely resembled the religious-political campaign appeals of Walter Mondale in 1984 than Bill Clinton's more successful rhetoric in 1992. Christian conservatives replaced their somewhat hesitant support of Bush in 2000 with much more enthusiastic support in 2004, providing their chosen candidate an Oval Office second coming.

2008

With sitting Vice President Dick Cheney not seeking the presidency, the 2008 nomination for both major political parties was wide open. The race for the Republican nomination remained without a clear front-runner for much of the primary campaign. Although former New York City Mayor Rudy Giuliani appeared to be the national front-runner, he failed to garner substantial votes in any of the early primary states. Former Arkansas Governor and Southern Baptist minister Mike Huckabee scored a surprise victory in the Iowa caucuses, followed by Senator John McCain of Arizona winning New Hampshire and former Massachusetts Governor Mitt Romney winning Michigan. After McCain won South Carolina and Florida, Giuliani and former Senator Fred Thompson of Tennessee dropped out. Romney left the race after McCain's stronger showing on Super Tuesday, but Huckabee remained in the race for another month after winning most of the Southern states on Super Tuesday. He finally dropped out after McCain received enough delegates to secure the nomination in early March. McCain, still struggling to prove his evangelical credentials, chose as his running mate the little known Alaska Governor Sarah Palin, who quickly became a star among conservative evangelical Christians.

Among the four early front-runners, two—Romney and McCain—talked about their faith much more often than the other two—Giuliani and Thompson. The campaigns of the latter two fizzled without any primary wins as the former Southern Baptist minister, Huckabee, emerged as a first-tier candidate with his campaign discourse heavily characterized by religious rhetoric. Although McCain received fewer questions in debates and interviews about his faith than did Romney on Mormonism or Huckabee on his previous life as a Baptist pastor, McCain joined them in frequently inserting religion into the campaign dialogue. Much of the religious rhetoric during the campaign resulted from the influence of evangelical organizations. Each candidate attended the Family Research Council's Values Voter Summit, and several attended a Values Voter debate cohosted by several evangelical organizations. Huckabee, who ran ads declaring himself to be "a Christian leader," argued that religion defined him and should be used as an important criterion by voters. He claimed during a January 24, 2008, Republican primary debate, "My faith grounds me. It gives me some sense of direction and purpose. . . . It's who I am. And so if it gives some people a queasy feeling, then they'll have to deal with it." Huckabee told Tim Russert:

> I'm appalled, Tim, when someone says, "Tell me about your faith." And they say, "Oh my faith doesn't influence my public policy." Because when someone says that, it's as if they're saying my faith isn't significant, it's not authentic, it's [not] so consequential that it affects me. (Russert, 2007, ¶28)

While boasting about his Christian credentials, Huckabee soared from a little-known governor to the front of the Republican pack as his flock of Christian supporters propelled him to victory in several contests.

On the Democratic side, Senator Hillary Clinton of New York appeared to be the front-runner throughout the year before the primary contests. However, she placed a surprising third-place in the Iowa caucuses behind Senator Barack Obama of Illinois and former Senator and vice presidential candidate John Edwards of North Carolina. Clinton rebounded to beat Obama in New Hampshire and then Nevada before losing overwhelmingly to Obama in South Carolina. Before Super Tuesday, Edwards and most of the other candidates had already dropped out, leaving Clinton and Obama to fight head-to-head. The two split a number of primaries and caucuses over the next couple of months as Obama slowly increased his delegate lead over Clinton, with Obama finally securing the nomination in early June on the last day of the primaries. Obama chose as his running mate a former Democratic primary opponent—Senator Joe Biden of Delaware.

The 2008 Democratic primary featured more religious rhetoric than any Democratic race in the previous thirty years, perhaps suggesting Democratic candidates are realizing, as their Republican counterparts have for some time, that God-talk in campaigns seems to make for an appealing argument. Unlike many contests where only one Democratic candidate openly talked about religion—such as Jimmy Carter in 1976 or Jesse Jackson in 1984 and 1988—all three major Democratic candidates and most of the "also-rans" testified frequently about their personal religious beliefs and how those beliefs would inform their public policy positions. Obama was joined by Clinton and Edwards at two different forums broadcast nationally on CNN devoted entirely to matters of religion. Edwards discussed his faith more freely and explicitly than in 2004 and Clinton frequently divulged details of her personal prayer life, such as when she claimed:

> I have said many times that I, fortunately, was raised by parents who believe in the power of prayer. So I was taught to pray and encouraged to pray every day. If I had not been a praying person when I got to the White House, after having been there a short period of time, I would have become one, I can guarantee you. (Clinton, 2007, ¶67–68)

Other candidates—including New Mexico Governor Bill Richardson and Senator Joe Biden of Delaware—also talked openly about their religious beliefs. However, no one testified as often, comfortably, or explicitly as the eventual Democratic nominee, Barack Obama, setting up a race between a Democrat very comfortable talking about his private faith and a Republican who is much less comfortable with such rhetoric. Obama had declared in his keynote address during the 2004 Democratic National Convention, "We worship an awesome God in the blue states" (Obama, 2004, ¶80) and he seemed intent on proving it during the 2008 presidential contest. His reference to "an awesome God" is drawn from a popular evangelical worship song.

The first joint forum with the two presidential hopefuls during the general election took place at a church. The bestselling evangelical author and pastor Rick Warren served as the moderator as the candidates answered questions about faith, politics, and society in Warren's Saddleback Community Church that is affiliated with the Southern Baptist Convention. The two candidates would meet again for another forum and three debates. Throughout the general election, Obama preached his messages of hope and change while McCain attempted to focus on issues of experience and foreign policy. Once the nation's economy took a dramatic turn downward, McCain saw victory fade away from his grasp. On election day, Obama bested McCain in the popular vote by a 52.9 percent to 45.7 percent and overwhelmingly won the electoral college 365 to 173. Overshadowed by Obama's status as the first African American president was that Biden become the first Catholic Vice President, although five Catholics were previously major-party running mates.

John McCain

During the 2008 campaign, John McCain talked about religion and its impact on his policy positions as he worked to convince conservative Christians to trust him. He discussed his *personal faith*, usually with references to his service in Vietnam. McCain told the Family Research Council that faith got him through his captivity in Vietnam:

> That faith helped me not only to endure, but to understand and respect the values it encompassed. Thus, in a moment of unexpected compassion that God ordained, I could learn the most valuable lesson of all—how to forgive and how to escape the bitterness that could have destroyed my life. (McCain, 2007c, ¶19)

In this speech, McCain shared the story about a guard who would loosen the ropes that tied McCain down when no other guards were around. This same guard then walked over close to McCain on Christmas Day and drew a cross in the dirt with his sandal. McCain, who had previously used this story during his 2000 campaign, would repeat it frequently during the 2008 campaign. McCain featured this story—and the drawing of a cross in the dirt—in a television ad that played during Christmas of 2007 just days before the Iowa caucuses. When asked of his faith, McCain answered, "The most important thing is I'm a Christian" (Billups, 2008, ¶3). On another occasion, McCain said of his faith:

> I was very slow in maturing. . . . I knew right from wrong; I knew the Bible; I knew the Nicene Creed and the Apostles' Creed and the tenets of my faith. And although I neglected them, the time came that I could fall back on them as a net, as a way of salvation, literally. (Reston, 2008, ¶13)

Although McCain did not talk about his faith as openly as his Democratic opponent or George W. Bush, he did articulate his faith more clearly than other Republican candidates like Bob Dole and George H. W. Bush.

McCain argued in the campaign that America has a *special relationship* with God. In addition to talking about how God had blessed America, McCain asserted that our nation had been divinely founded. McCain declared the nation was built upon Judeo-Christian principles on several occasions, including in his address to the Family Research Council where he connected that belief to his pro-life position: "Our Founding Fathers were informed by the respect for human life and dignity that is the foundation of the Judeo-Christian tradition" (McCain, 2007c, ¶7). On another occasion, he argued that "the Constitution established the United States of America as a Christian nation" (Gilgoff, 2007e, ¶4). McCain also talked about the ways God had blessed America:

> One of my favorite pastimes is to visit and experience the Grand Canyon. It is a special, sacred place whose timeless beauty moves me. Not only is it a place from which I draw personal renewal, it is a monumental inspiration regarding our obligation to be faithful stewards of all the natural blessings that God has so richly bestowed. (McCain, 2008d, ¶17)

With these comments, he clearly identified himself with the religious-political philosophy that America was created as a Christian nation and has been divinely and uniquely blessed. Although he did not develop the theme as strongly as Ronald Reagan had, McCain did so more frequently and explicitly than his Democratic opponent.

On several occasions, McCain used his religious beliefs to explain and justify his *public policy* positions. He even invoked God to advocate positions opposed by many within his own political party. For example, McCain advocated greater environmental efforts to save God's creation:

> The world is already feeling the powerful effects of global warming, and far more dire consequences are predicted if we let the growing deluge of greenhouse gas emissions continue, and wreak havoc with God's creation. (McCain, 2007a, ¶16)

He also justified his immigration stance with God-talk as he described various individuals dying trying to cross the Mexican-American border:

> As a country deeply rooted in a tradition of religious faith, we're taught to love our neighbors as ourselves. . . . Kalea Valez Squez Gonzalez, 16, carried a Bible in her backpack. She was number 109. John Doe, number 143, died with a rosary encircling his neck. His eyes were wide open. . . . But these people are also God's children who wanted simply to be Americans. And we cannot forget that humanity God commands of us as we seek a remedy to this problem. (McCain, 2007b, ¶68, 71–72, 74)

McCain even referred to the fact that the nation of Georgia was "one of the world's first nations to adopt Christianity as an official religion" as he urged the United States to stand against the Russian military operations in Georgia (McCain, 2008c, ¶2), thus suggesting that a nation's Christianity might be a factor in his foreign policy decisions. As McCain articulated his positions on important campaign issues, he pointed to God as his political guide—especially on issues that McCain struggled to have accepted by his own political party. Although McCain made these policy connections to his faith more strongly than some previous nominees—like Bob Dole and George H. W. Bush—he did not do so as frequently or explicitly as his Democratic opponent.

On issues of *church and state*, McCain pushed for greater governmental recognition of religion and attacked judges for ruling against public religious displays. At the same time, however, McCain attempted to balance his calls with an acknowledgment of the importance of religious freedom. He stated before the Family Research Council:

> My friends, if America stands for anything, it stands for the freedom to follow our own hearts, to determine our own relationship with God. Our Constitution did not establish a national religion, but neither did it banish any worship. Religious freedom does not require Americans to hide their faith from public view or that communities must refrain from publicly acknowledging the importance to them of faith. Judges should not legislate from the bench and actually restrict religious freedom by banning its expression in the public square. (McCain, 2007c, ¶24–25)

With these comments, McCain clearly offered his opposition to some aspects of the separation of church and state as he advocated governmental posting and display of religious symbols and attacked judges who ruled against such displays. However, unlike previous Republicans such as Ronald Reagan and George H. W. Bush, McCain did not refer to the separation of church and state. Instead, he voiced his support for religious freedom, terminology that had been used widely by Bill Clinton and George W. Bush. For instance, McCain declared:

> No society that denies religious freedom can ever rightly claim to be good in some other way, and no person can ever be true to any faith that believes in the dignity of all human life if they do not act out of concern for those whose dignity is assailed because of their faith. (McCain, 2008a, ¶7)

Despite these calls for religious liberty, McCain asserted that the government should encourage and use sectarian religious symbols and declarations.

Eight years after condemning prominent ministers Pat Robertson and Jerry Falwell as "agents of intolerance" (Bruni and Mitchell, 2000, ¶17), John McCain sought political redemption as he needed the support of conservative Christians to make it to the White House. In doing so, he often addressed religious groups and sought the endorsements of televangelists like John Hagee and Rod Parsley. However, after controversy erupted surrounding controversial statements by both Hagee and Parsley—although Hagee had supported George W. Bush in 2000 without attracting controversy—McCain first repudiated their comments and then went on to reject their endorsements. The ordeal managed to only highlight the tensions between McCain and many conservative Christians. Although McCain is no George W. Bush or Ronald Reagan, he clearly surpassed George H. W. Bush and Bob Dole in seeming comfortable discussing religion, connecting his religious beliefs to his public policy decisions, and proclaiming America's special relationship with God. Additionally, McCain continued the Republican argument for greater governmental acknowledgment of religion, but did not provide lip-service to the principle of separation of church and state. As McCain struggled to match the religious zeal of George W. Bush, he also failed to match that of his religiously outspoken Democratic opponent.

Barack Obama

Barack Obama frequently, explicitly, and eloquently invoked religion during his presidential campaign. He often testified about his *personal faith* and spiritual practices. Obama particularly made frequent professions of his Christian faith as e-mails and conservative media falsely claimed he was a secret Muslim. Obama said of his religious conversion: "I learned that my sins could be redeemed. I learned that those things I was too weak to accomplish myself, He would accomplish with me if I placed my trust in him" (Gerson, 2007, ¶2). Obama also claimed, "I am a Christian, and I am a devout Christian. I believe in the redemptive death and resurrection of Jesus Christ. I believe that that faith gives me a path to be cleansed of sin and have eternal life" (Pulliam and Olsen, 2008, ¶18). On another occasion, he stated, "I'm a Christian, I'm a member of Trinity United Church of Christ on the south side of Chicago, and I love my congregation" (Obama, 2007e, ¶155), although he would leave the church during the campaign because of controversial preaching by his former pastor and a guest preacher. Responding to an e-mail claiming he was a Muslim, Obama confessed in a campaign speech:

> I've been a member of the same church, Christian church, praying to Jesus Christ, our lord and savior, I've been praying—I've been in church for almost 20 years, same church, the church I was married in to Michelle, the church where my children were dedicated. (Obama, 2008b, ¶84)

During the primary contest, Obama's campaign held gospel music concerts in South Carolina with top Christian gospel artists. Obama's campaign even distributed a brochure that declared him to be a "committed Christian" and "called to Christ," included quotations from Obama about the importance of his faith and photos of him speaking in churches with a large cross and stained-glass window behind him. Obama frequently and clearly expressed his personal faith and Christian commitment during the campaign. As he boasted about his faith, Obama not only out-God-talked his Republican opponent when it came to talking about his private religious faith and conversion experience, but he also surpassed every previous Democratic nominee since Jimmy Carter.

Obama at times appeared to assume the role of preacher as he likened his political campaign to a *spiritual mission*. In commemorating the civil rights movement, Obama strongly utilized biblical allusions that cast himself as the new Joshua who could lead the people to their promised land by standing on the shoulders of the great civil rights heroes—such as Martin Luther King, Jr.—who had served as the movement's Moses:

> Like Moses, they challenged Pharaoh, the princes, powers who said that some are atop and others are at the bottom, and that's how it's always going to be. . . . They wandered through a desert but always knowing that God was with them and that, if they maintained that trust in God, that they would be all right. . . . I thank the Moses generation; but we've got to remember, now, that Joshua still had a job to do. As great as Moses was, despite all that he did, leading a people out of bondage, he didn't cross over the river to see the Promised Land. God told him your job is done. . . . We're going to leave it to the Joshua generation to make sure it happens. There are still battles that need to be fought; some rivers that need to be crossed. (Obama, 2007b, ¶12, 15, 25–26)

Not only did Obama clearly demonstrate his familiarity with the biblical text, but he cast his campaign—as one who would eventually become the first African American nominee of a major political party—as an important part of the second phase of the spiritual mission. Similar to George W. Bush, Obama also emphasized the role of religious institutions over the government in several of his political speeches:

> We know that government can't solve all our problems. We don't want it to. . . . We know that we've been called in our churches, in our mosques, in our synagogues, in Sunday school, to love one another as ourselves, to be our brother's keeper, to be our sister's keeper. We have individual responsibilities, but we also have collective responsibilities to each other. (Obama, 2007c, ¶28–29)

As he campaigned for our nation's highest political office, Obama also preached the need for people to follow biblical commands and accomplish what could only come from a spiritual movement and not from government.

Unlike most of his Democratic predecessors seeking the White House, Obama at times spoke of America's *special relationship* with God. In particular, he articulated his belief that America had been specially blessed by God. He declared during one speech:

> When you travel to all 48 states in the continental United States and then, you know, you're crisscrossing east coast, west coast, north, south, you realize what a magnificent country this is. From sea to shining sea, we've got spectacular mountains, and spectacular oceans, and deserts and just an amazing land that we have. It's a true blessing from God. (Obama, 2008g, ¶11)

Obama, however, subtly suggested that there might be limits to God's blessings, but did not make the argument as strongly as had Jimmy Carter in 1980 or John Kerry. Obama mentioned God's blessings as a reason why Americans should support environmental protection policies:

> I don't want to see a country that failed to invest in our ability to compete, that didn't give our children the kind of education they need, that mortgaged their future on a mountain of debt, that wasn't dealing with our environment, this precious land that God has given us. (Obama, 2008h, ¶96)

With these remarks Obama referred to America's natural landscape to claim God had specially blessed the nation and that Americans should therefore protect God's blessings.

On several occasions, Obama linked his *public policy* positions to his religious beliefs. With these remarks, Obama fleshed out how his frequently cited Christian faith would inform his governing decisions. He claimed that his religious beliefs influenced him to run for president so he could use this position to implement his values:

> And my faith informs my values. So there's no doubt that part of the reason I think it's important to look after people who are poor, part of the reason that I think it's important to help those in need is because of my faith. (Obama, 2007e, ¶156)

Obama used religious-political rhetoric to advocate changing education policies during a speech at Martin Luther King, Jr.'s former church:

> The Scripture tells us that we are judged not just by word, but by deed. And if we are to truly bring about the unity that is needed, that is so crucial in this time. . . . We can pass a law called No Child Left Behind and then leave the money behind. That is not a serious effort in bringing about the unity that is needed. (Obama, 2008a, ¶39)

Justifying his support for same-sex unions, Obama stated, "If people find that controversial then I would just refer them to the Sermon on the Mount, which I think is, in my mind, for my faith, more central than an obscure passage in Romans" (Jeffrey, 2008, ¶2). During the campaign, Obama used religious terms and biblical passages to explain his public policy views and did so more frequently and explicitly than his Republican opponent.

Obama also attempted to rhetorically balance his positions on *church and state* issues. Although he offered his support for the separation of church and state, Obama also called for more religious involvement in the public square. He argued that religion should play an important role in public discussions:

I think the mistake that's been made with respect to the religious right is a literalism that is so rigid that it does not allow for the possibility of somebody of a different faith or nonbeliever to engage in a dialogue. And, on the other hand, I think it's important for us not to presume that faith has no part in the public square. (Obama, 2007d, ¶73–74)

On another occasion Obama even attacked some interpretations of the separation principle:

Doing the Lord's work is a thread that's run through our politics since the very beginning. . . . And it puts the lie to the notion that the separation of church and state in America—a principle we all must uphold and that I have embraced as a constitutional lawyer and most importantly as a Christian—means faith should have no role in public life. (Brachear, 2007, ¶4)

However, Obama insisted that he respected separation of church and state even as he held campaign outreach meetings at churches:

Now, whenever we do this outreach, we make sure that it's consistent with the concepts of separation of church and state. And I'm very clear and unequivocal about the belief that that separation strengthens our religious life and church, as well as make—ensuring that the state doesn't become captives to a particular set of religious beliefs. But I think the idea that people of faith should be involved in the public square in the debate is something that I've talked about for a long time. (Obama, 2008f, ¶85–86)

Although Obama stressed the importance of separation of church and state, as had many Democrats before him, he also stressed the importance of not pushing religion out of the public square altogether and that the separation principle was designed to protect the church from government intrusion. With these views, Obama sought to maintain support for separation while also rhetorically downplaying the principle.

During the campaign, Obama found himself embroiled in religious controversies because of his church affiliation and the comments of his former pastor. After video clips from sermons of Obama's longtime pastor at Trinity United Church of Christ, Reverend Jeremiah Wright, surfaced, controversy erupted. In the brief video segments, Wright attacked the U.S. government for being racist, creating the AIDS virus to kill African Americans, and being responsible for causing the September 11, 2001, terrorist attacks. As a result of these beliefs, Wright decried the nation as "U.S. of KKK A." and declared "God damn America." Obama, at first, defended Wright by saying, "I can no more disown him than I can disown my white grandmother" who he claimed also had espoused racist sentiments (Obama, 2008c, ¶40). Obama added that he had associated himself with Wright and stayed at the church because the "snippets" running "in an endless loop on the television sets and YouTube" created "caricatures" of Trinity and Wright but were not the person or church he knew and loved (Obama, 2008c, ¶27). Obama also expressed his disagreement with Wright's comments and insisted that he had not been present at the church when the controversial statements were made. After Wright further spoke out in several interviews and speeches, Obama declared Wright's remarks to be "divisive and destructive" and said it did not represent the man he had known for over twenty years (Obama, 2008e, ¶3). He added that he found the "outrageous remarks" to be "appalling" and "antithetical" to his beliefs (Obama, 2008e, ¶11–12).

Later in the campaign, a guest preacher and longtime advisor of Obama spoke at Trinity—while Obama was away campaigning—and mocked Obama's then-Democratic primary opponent Hillary Clinton with racially tinted remarks. Shortly thereafter, Obama resigned as a member of the church. Obama claimed that although he still loved the church community, his candidacy had become a distraction for the church and those attempting to worship there. With these controversies, religion became a potential political liability for Obama—just as Jimmy Carter had faced a racial controversy in his home church during the 1976 campaign. However, the controversy developed much earlier in Obama's campaign and he was unable to manage the controversy while also remaining a member of his longtime church.

As the first African American to be nominated for president by a major political party, Barack Obama frequently, explicitly, and comfortably invoked religion and scriptures in his campaign appeals. More than any Democratic candidate since Jimmy Carter, Obama opened up about his personal religious beliefs. As with Bill Clinton and Republicans like George W. Bush and Ronald Reagan, Obama cast his campaign as part of a spiritual mission. Obama also continued the efforts of recent Democrats like Clinton and Al Gore to emphasize issues of religious freedom instead of the strong focus on separation of church and state as offered by Michael Dukakis and Walter Mondale. Additionally, Obama linked several of his public policy positions to his religious beliefs. In citing scriptures and testifying about his religious beliefs, Obama interjected religious rhetoric into the campaign much more often and comfortably than John McCain.

SUMMARY

Barack Obama and George W. Bush hail from opposite ends of the political spectrum but share a similar rhetorical religious style, one which has dominated presidential elections since 1976. As seen in this chapter and the previous two, successful presidential candidates during the past three decades have often testified about their personal faith, used scripture to justify their public policy decisions, proclaimed America's special relationship with God, compared their campaigns to a spiritual mission, and addressed the issues of separation of church and state. When discussing their *personal faith* and private spiritual practices, none have surpassed the Southern Baptist Sunday school teacher Jimmy Carter, but several joined Carter in publicly professing their faith, particularly George W. Bush, Barack Obama, and Bill Clinton. As the candidates sought to become our nation's chief executive, they testified about their Christian conversion and personal prayer habits.

Several candidates developed the theme that America has a *special relationship* with God, with none surpassing Ronald Reagan with this particular message, yet still a theme strongly articulated by George W. Bush, Gerald Ford, John McCain, and Jimmy Carter during his 1976 campaign. This mostly Republican argument presented America as a Christian nation founded by Christians and blessed by God above all other nations. A few candidates offered a variation on the special relationship theme by suggesting there were limits to God's blessing, most notably Carter in 1980 but also John Kerry. This mostly Democratic argument suggested that because there were limits to God's blessings, the American people needed to live responsibly and even make sacrifices.

A few candidates have cast their campaign as a *spiritual mission*, most notably Ronald Reagan and George W. Bush. With this theme, political campaigns were baptized in order to establish the candidate as something of a religious revival leader. Most candidates invoked God or quoted scriptures at times to explain their political philosophy or *public policy* views, but this was most often utilized by George W. Bush, Bill Clinton, Jimmy Carter, and Barack Obama. By explaining and justifying their policy positions with scriptural citations and biblical teachings, the candidates pointed to religion as an important influence in making governance decisions.

Two conflicting arguments consistently emerged on issues of church and state. Democrats urged respect for separation of *church and state*, with their arguments ranging from the strict separation of Walter Mondale and especially Michael Dukakis to the more nuanced rhetoric of religious freedom by Bill Clinton and Barack Obama. Republicans advocated polices that violated the traditional interpretation of separation of church and state, while paying lip-service to the principle and yet at the same time advocating policies that crossed the church-state line. At times, religious rhetoric was used to attack one's opponent, most notably by Walter Mondale, John Kerry, Jimmy Carter in 1980, and Bill Clinton in 1992, with the attack usually charging an opponent for going too far with their interjection of religion into the political process.

These themes—with notable partisan patterns—defined the religious-political rhetoric of the candidates praying to ascend to the Oval Office since 1976. For each campaign cycle, the nominee who used religious rhetoric more frequently, explicitly, and comfortably was victorious on election day. Together, presidential candidates since 1976 have brought a new religious style to campaign rhetoric that stands in stark contrast to the religious-political discourse of previous presidential nominees. The key characteristics that define a new confessional era of politics—based upon the descriptive themes detailed in this chapter and the previous two—are explored in the next chapter and used to test the principles of the civil-religious contract.

Chapter Five

Confessional Politics

Beginning with a born-again Southern Baptist Sunday school teacher in 1976, religious rhetoric began to play a new and substantially more important role in presidential campaigns. Both parties have found electoral success with religiously outspoken candidates. Ronald Reagan and George W. Bush led the Republicans to victory, and other Republicans—like Pat Robertson and Mike Huckabee—outperformed expectations with their heavily religious campaign appeals and followers. Jimmy Carter, Bill Clinton, and Barack Obama led their party to the White House, and other Democrats—like Jesse Jackson—have gained support while talking openly about religion on the campaign trail. Meanwhile, presidential candidates over the last thirty years who have mostly avoided the topic of religion—especially those reticent to talk about their personal faith while campaigning—have been rejected at the ballot box. Democrats Walter Mondale and Michael Dukakis, as well as Republicans Bob Dole, Rudy Giuliani, and Fred Thompson, all suffered a similar fate as they downplayed God-talk during their campaigns.

Jimmy Carter, who preached his way to victory in 1976, backed away from some of his most pronounced religious-political appeals in 1980 and lost to Ronald Reagan, who readily proclaimed the religious message desired by many conservative Christian voters. George H. W. Bush, the patrician Episcopalian whose apparent comfort with talking about religion paled in comparison to that of his predecessor and his son, was able to at least out-God-talk the more rhetorically secular Dukakis in 1988, only to be ousted four years later by the more fluent Bible-quoting Clinton. Bush's showing among evangelicals dropped 20 percentage points in 1992 when compared to his 1988 electoral coalition (Sullivan, 2008). Although election results represent a complex mix of factors—such as economic problems in 1980, 1992, and 2008, popular incumbents in 1984 and 1996, and scandals of previous administrations in 1976 and 2000—since 1976 there appears to be a strong connection between the rhetorical religiosity of presidential candidates and their electoral success. As discovered in the previous three chapters, the nominee who seemed the most *rhetorically* religious—in apparent comfortableness, frequency, and explicitness with their God-talk—won the general election. Thus, there appears to be a rhetorical religious test that our presidential candidates must now pass that represents a critical part of the equation to being viewed as a viable and competitive candidate.

This chapter argues that the heightened religious rhetoric in presidential campaigns since 1976 has created a new confessional era of presidential politics that has replaced the 1960 John F. Kennedy model of privatizing one's religious faith while running for public office. Our presidential campaigns are often regarded as crusades—a term that Ronald Reagan and Bill Clinton both used to describe their campaigns—and also as a religious mission to save the nation. In fact, many of our national party conventions during this confessional period have been compared to religious revival meetings, and nearly every election cycle has heard claims from commentators and critics that religion is now playing an unprecedented role in presidential politics. During this confessional period, candidates started to more openly testify about their personal religious beliefs and spiritual practices, often to the point that their policy positions were justified with biblical rather than constitutional foundations. Also, candidates worked to more openly profess their faith and allegiance to the Christian God rather than merely faith in the American democratic experiment, and began to place their electoral hopes on their prayers to God rather than leaving their fate just in the hands of the voters. As presidential candidates invoked God, quoted scriptures, and talked about religion in their campaign discourse, several key characteristics have emerged that describe the religious-political rhetoric of the confessional era. These four categories—testimonial, partisan, sectarian, and liturgical discourse—stand in strong opposition to the elements of the civil-religious contract proposed by Hart (1977) and others to describe how religious rhetoric should function within presidential rhetoric and political campaigns. The new characteristics of candidates' religious-political campaign rhetoric demonstrate that the civil-religious contract has been rendered null and void as presidential candidates now freely and successfully mix religion and politics. While the last three chapters identified key themes that candidates' religious-political rhetoric covered, this chapter explores the overall religious-political style that has emerged during the last three decades. This chapter outlines the features of these four categories and how they mark a substantial shift in the role religious rhetoric plays in presidential politics.

TESTIMONIAL

A significant violation of the civil-religious contract "would be confusing what should be quite distinct (private and public) priorities" (Hart and Pauley, 2005, p. 86). Hart claimed about this private-public divide: "In actuality, of course, most Americans make just such distinctions each day. Most Americans do not expect to find a confessional stance in the remarks of their elected officials" (Hart and Pauley, 2005, p. 86–87), by which he suggested that Americans did not desire or expect to hear political candidates discuss their private religious lives. Hart offered as an illustration Gerald Ford declaring his faith to be personal. However, born again Sunday school teacher Jimmy Carter clearly violated such a principle—and defeated Ford—by not only speaking openly about his personal faith and spiritual practices, but even confessing to praying as often as twenty-five times a day and to violating biblical dictates by lusting in his heart for women. Other candidates have followed Carter's pattern of testifying publicly about their personal faith and conversion experiences, often finding electoral success along the way. Much as Christians testify about their faith in evangelical denominations, our presidential candidates now publicly profess their faith to the electorate. This testimonial nature of confessional politics occurs when presidential candidates talk about their personal religious background and about their religious conversion. Such confessions include the narratives and arguments from the personal faith theme developed in the previous chapters. In contrast to the private morality Hart found with Ford and his predecessors, the more confessional politics since Carter has seen candidates crafting campaign appeals by talking about their personal religiosity.

Personal Religious Background

The first testimonial aspect of confessional political rhetoric occurs when candidates discuss their personal religious background. This type of testimony includes talk of their frequent church attendance, religious teachings they received during childhood, their faithful praying and reading the Bible, and, for some, evidence of their commitment to God by having once considered entering a religious vocation like the priesthood. With these arguments, the candidates attempt to prove their Christian pedigree and credentials. Such discussions helped propel Jimmy Carter to the presidency as he mentioned his prayer life and frequent meditating on the Bible. For instance, he stated during the 1980 campaign:

> The Bible and the study of it is a very important part of my life, on an
> absolutely daily basis, I never miss. And I try to understand God's guidance to
> me, expressed in the Old Testament and the New Testament. (Carter, 1980n, p.
> 2387)

Asked during his 1976 campaign why he was so open about his personal
faith, Carter argued it was both his patriotic and religious duty: "I've won-
dered to talk about it at all. . . . But I feel I have a duty to the country—and
maybe to God—not to say 'no comment'" (Fraker, 1976, ¶6). Other candidates followed Carter's model of testifying about their personal religiosity.
During a 1992 speech at Notre Dame University, Bill Clinton talked about
how attending a Catholic school added a different perspective to his religious
beliefs from his Southern Baptist upbringing:

> If elected, I will be the first president to graduate from a Catholic college,
> Georgetown University. . . . I wondered when I went there whether I would be
> out of place, a Southern Baptist who had rarely been far from home. Thankful-
> ly, both the students and the faculty there held to the scriptural commandment
> to befriend the stranger in their midst, and together we found much common
> ground that Baptists and Catholics could walk together. (Clinton, 1992k, ¶13,
> 15)

George W. Bush talked about his personal devotion and reading during the
2004 campaign to connect with religious citizens who shared his devotional
habits. Referring to the author of the book *My Utmost for His Highest*, a
popular title among evangelical Christians, Bush stated, "Personally, I do
rely upon the Almighty. I'm reading Oswald Chambers. If you've read Oswald Chambers, you'll understand that Oswald Chambers is a pretty good
gauge to test your walk" (Bush, 2004c, ¶470–71). As John Kerry attempted
to unseat Bush in 2004, he also testified about his religious background:

> I value my faith. I was an altar boy as a kid. It carried me through Vietnam. I
> believe what I believe, and it's part of who I am. And it gives me values and it
> gives me a sense of place, of proportion, and humility, may I add. (Kerry,
> 2004e, ¶426)

He added during the January 6, 2004, Democratic primary debate, "There
was a period in my life where religion was a huge part of my life, and I even
thought perhaps as a young man of going into the priesthood." During the
2008 campaign, Barack Obama declared, "I am a Christian and I pray every
night" (Matthews, 2008, ¶68). Mike Huckabee soared to the front of the
Republican pack in 2008 in large part by talking about his service as a
Southern Baptist minister. With these comments, the presidential candidates

opened up about their religious background and their spiritual practices. As they testified about their religiosity, the candidates declared themselves to be Christians and offered personal illustrations to support their claim.

Christian Conversion Experience

The second testimonial element of religious-political rhetoric is found in candidates' talk of their religious conversion experience. This type of testimony includes testifying first about accepting Jesus as one's personal savior, and next discussing the impact of this experience on one's life. Such rhetoric plants the candidates' rhetoric firmly within the evangelical tradition of having a "born-again" experience that requires a public profession to be considered truly genuine. During the 1976 primary, Carter explained his conversion:

> I recognized for the first time that I had lacked something very precious—a complete commitment to Christ, a presence of the Holy Spirit in my life in a more profound and personal way. . . . I've had an inner peace and inner conviction and assurance that have transformed my life for the better. (Politicians are discovering, 1976, ¶11)

During the 1992 campaign, Bill Clinton confessed that he was a sinner who needed and accepted God, which he connected to his ability to be a good person:

> My faith tells me that all of us are sinners, and each of us has gone in our own way and fallen short of glory of God. . . . Religious faith has permitted me to believe in my continuing possibility of becoming a better person every day. If I didn't believe in God, if I weren't, in my view, a Christian, if I didn't believe ultimately in the perfection of life after death, my life would have been much more difficult. (Balmer, 2008, p. 137)

During the 2000 campaign, George W. Bush told Larry King and the nation about how evangelist Billy Graham led him to his born-again experience. Although Bush felt the need to profess his Christian salvation, he still appeared a bit uncomfortable in making this profession of his personal salvation on national television:

> [Graham] planted the seed in my heart that grew over time. I got into the Bible. I read Scripture. I read the Bible everyday now. I'm into prayer. There is a gradual warming of the heart, as we Methodists like to say. . . . I felt something change when I had a talk with him in Kennebunkport, Maine, and I—you know, I—it just—and the only thing I can tell you is the Lord works in mysterious ways, the Lord does. (King, 1999, ¶313, 319)

Addressing ministers from Bob Jones University, Bush declared with more certainty, "I believe in Jesus Christ as my personal savior" (Foer, 2003/2004, p. 25). Similarly, when asked at a campaign rally in 2008 about his faith, Barack Obama confessed:

> I'm a Christian. . . . And what that means for me is that I believe that Jesus Christ died for my sins and that his grace and his mercy and his power, through him, that I can achieve everlasting life. So that's what I believe. (Obama, 2008d, ¶165, 167)

As the candidates bared their souls about their religious beliefs, they testified to the media and voters about their personal spiritual conversion. With such professions of love for and commitment to Jesus, the candidates often turned their campaign speeches, interviews, and debates into something of a church testimony night.

Some presidential candidates have even argued that a president should make a personal confession of their faith as evidence of fitness for office, thus affirming the new rhetorical religious test of the confessional era that candidates testify publicly to voters about their private religious beliefs. When asked if religion guided his decisions as president, Ronald Reagan argued in 1984, "Yes, religion is a guide for me. To think that anyone could carry out the awesome responsibilities of this office without asking for God's help through prayer strikes me as absurd" (Reagan, 1984x, ¶36). During the 1992 campaign, George H. W. Bush stated, "More than ever, I believe with all my heart that one cannot be president of our great country without a belief in God, without the truth that comes on one's knees" (Bush, 1992j, ¶16). Bill Clinton argued during the 1992 campaign that the *first* test for presidential fitness is a belief in God:

> What makes a President fit to command in my view is faith in God, belief in the greatness of our nation and the goodness of our people, a commitment to keeping America the strongest nation in the world militarily, economically, and morally, and understanding the essential character of the American people. (Clinton, 1992g, ¶15)

In 2004, George W. Bush also argued that he thought it essential for a president to believe in God: "I happen to believe that it would be very difficult to be the President without believing. I believe that—I know it's been an important part of my presidency" (Bush, 2004f, ¶175). By arguing that presidents should believe in God, these candidates affirmed the expectations placed upon them that they testify about their private spiritual beliefs and Christian conversion. Thus, they not only testified about their faith, but affirmed the expectation that they offer such insights into their private religiosity.

In defending the civil-religious contract's expectations of candidates remaining circumspect about their personal morality, Roderick Hart argued:

> Politicians, then, must be vigilant about their private and public personae. In this connection, Richard Nixon's White House tapes did the unthinkable—they permitted his private morality to be displayed in public. His civil-religious heresy was not so much that he crossed the indistinct line of ethical principle but that he was not publicly circumspect. As adherents of a national civil religion, Americans can forgive many things in their national leaders but public gaucheness is not one of them. (Hart and Pauley, 2005, p. 87)

What doomed Nixon—instead of actual unethical behavior—was the public revelation of his private transgressions. Today, no such private-public boundaries exist for political candidates' religiosity. Although public disclosure of some candidates' private moral failures has harmed their political campaigns (such Gary Hart in 1988), many candidates have found electoral success by allowing the public to know all about their private religious lives. Others—such as Bill Bradley and Fred Thompson—mounted unsuccessful campaigns as they clung to a bygone time in presidential politics by insisting that their religious beliefs should remain private. Thus, the expectation now appears to be for a candidate to not *be* religious but, perhaps even more importantly, to go public with their religious beliefs and commitment. American presidential elections have shifted substantially since John F. Kennedy's declaration to the Greater Houston Ministerial Association in 1960: "I believe in a President whose views on religion are his own private affair, neither imposed upon him by the nation, nor imposed by the nation upon him as a condition to holding that office" (Kennedy, 1960a, ¶8). Today's candidates instead openly testify about their religious beliefs as they seek to prove to the nation they are sufficiently religious—and Christian—to be elected leader of the free world.

PARTISAN

During the contractual period, a substantial difference between our nation's official civil religionists—those individuals who were actually in mainstream positions of religious and political power—and unofficial civil religionists—those on the fringe of religious or political life—was that only the latter would be "distinctively partisan" with their religious-political rhetoric (Hart and Pauley, 2005, p. 28). Official civil religionists would instead follow the civil-religious contract and avoid using religious rhetoric in a partisan and activist manner. The leaders within the mainstream who worked within the constraints of the civil-religious contract would avoid the temptation "to act out their political and religious convictions" (p. 28). However, this study suggests that the nonpartisan nature of the civil-religious contract has been replaced by religious discourse that invokes God and scripture to support a specific partisan agenda or candidate. The partisan aspect of confessional politics includes those statements that function in a decidedly partisan manner as candidates justify their public policy positions with religious rhetoric, as candidates credit God with their electoral success, and as candidates use religious rhetoric to attack their political opponents. This category of confessional politics is built on the public policy and political attack themes described in the previous chapters. Far from a universal God observing from the political sidelines, as described in the civil-religious contract, presidential candidates today rhetorically offer visions of a God who takes sides in policy debates and campaigns.

Political Philosophy and Public Policies

The first type of partisan religious-political rhetoric occurs when candidates use their religious beliefs to explain and justify their public policies or political philosophy. Candidates would sometimes justify their overall political philosophy in religious terms. In 1984, Ronald Reagan contrasted the Republican political philosophy with that of the Democrats, with the former's philosophy likened to the "Kingdom of God" and the latter to "Big Brother":

> The difference between the path toward greater freedom or bigger government is the difference between success and failure; between opportunity and coercion; between faith in a glorious future and fear of mediocrity and despair; between respecting people as adults, each with a spark of greatness, and treating them as helpless children to be forever dependent; a drab, materialistic world where Big Brother rules by promises to special interest groups, and a world of adventure where everyday people set their sights on impossible dreams, distant stars, and the Kingdom of God. We have the true message of hope for America. (Reagan, 1984b, ¶7)

In 1992, George H. W. Bush declared in an address at Notre Dame University that his work as president was to bring about God's kingdom: "Together, we can lift our nation's spirit, and together we can give our material, political and economic accomplishments a larger, more noble purpose: to build God's kingdom here on earth" (Bush, 1992d, ¶20). The man who ousted Bush, Bill Clinton, similarly claimed as president to be building God's kingdom on earth during his address to the National Baptist Convention, USA:

> I was thinking today about two years ago when we were together in New Orleans. We talked then about what we could do to build the kingdom of God here on Earth. I want to look at the progress we have made since then and about what we have to do together. (Clinton, 1996g, ¶14)

In 2008, while speaking at a campaign forum, Barack Obama cast his political vision as an extension of his religious beliefs:

> Now, what I also believe in is a gospel of not just words, but deeds. And I believe in doing right here on Earth and treating people with the dignity and respect that is inherent in them being children of God, all people. And so my faith has always been one that says, "How can I apply Jesus' teachings in a very concrete way in my day-to-day life?" That means caring for the poor; that means being [inaudible] social distinctions, treating everybody from the least of these to the mightiest with respect and dignity. It means following the golden rule of doing unto others as you'd have them do unto you. (Obama, 2008d, ¶168, 170, 172)

In a campaign brochure that detailed Obama's religious beliefs and declared him to be a "committed Christian," Obama proclaimed, "My faith teaches me that I can sit in church and pray all I want, but I won't be fulfilling God's will unless I go out and do the Lord's work" (Alessi, 2008, ¶11). From claims about building the "Kingdom of God" to establishing a "New Covenant" to doing the "Lord's work," candidates have used religious rhetoric to support their partisan political philosophy.

Candidates also relied on scripture and God-talk throughout the campaigns to justify their positions on various public policy issues. Some even explained that they looked to religious teachings for guidance when making various policy decisions in general. Jimmy Carter claimed during his 1976 campaign, "I try to utilize my religious beliefs as a constant guide in making my decisions as a private or public citizen" (Carter, 1978a, p. 458). Similarly, Al Gore claimed during the 2000 campaign that the "bedrock" of his approach to dealing with important issues would be to ask, "WWJD," which he explained stood "for a saying that's popular now in my faith, 'What would Jesus do?'" (Quinn, 1999, ¶34). In 2004, John Kerry argued:

> Scripture teaches us it's not enough, my brother, to say that you have faith when there are no deeds. Faith without works is dead. . . . I am running for president because it's time to turn the words into deeds and faith into action. (Kerry, 2004b, ¶26–27, 34)

Key issues where religious rhetoric was utilized included foreign policy issues—primarily concerning the Middle East—environmental concerns, and issues of morality in media and society. Jimmy Carter stated in 1976, "The land of Israel has always meant a great deal to me. As a boy I read of the prophets and martyrs in the Bible—the same Bible that we all study together" (Carter, 1978a, p. 216). In 2004, George W. Bush frequently cast the Iraq War as part of doing God's will by bringing the gift of freedom to the world. During the 2008 campaign, John McCain referred to the Bible and religious ideas as he defended his support for the Iraq war during his address at a meeting of the Family Research Council. He argued that, like Christianity, the war effort had not been given a chance to be completely enacted and—rather ironically—that his religious respect for life actually justified war:

> The Bible's call to do just that [reminds] me of the saying, that Christianity has not been tried and found wanting so much as it has been found difficult and not tried. The consistent message of the Gospels calls us to recognize that all life is sacred because all human beings are created in the image of God, a truth—a truth recognized as central in the founding documents of our nation. . . . And our humility, commanded by our faith and our ideals and in a just and loving God, gives us the strength to resist the unnecessary sacrifice of our faith in the necessary cause of defeating our enemies. (McCain, 2007c, ¶16–17)

The United States's foreign policies were often cast as God's foreign policy.

On the domestic front, God was also called upon to help our nation's leaders craft various policies. On the environment, Jimmy Carter stated during the 1980 campaign:

> Democrats believe that our air ought to be pure and that our water ought to be clean and that the land God gave us over which to be stewards would still be productive and not spoiled by poisons. . . . I signed a reforestation bill that will make provisions for this whole area through here to reseed our forests and to build more trees. And God's going to help us, right? (Carter, 1980o, p. 2421)

Although Democrats most often invoked religion to discuss environmental issues, several Republican candidates also made this link. For instance, Ronald Reagan stated in 1984 during a speech at a National Geographic Society ceremony:

> You are worried about what man has done and is doing to this magical planet that God gave us. And I share your concern. . . . But we also know that we must do this with a fine balance. We want, as men on Earth, to use our resources for the reason God gave them to us—for the betterment of man. (Reagan, 1984j, ¶18, 21)

Candidates also dealt with policy issues of morality in media and society with God-talk. In an address to a religious meeting during the 1996 campaign, Bill Clinton cited scripture to explain his support for legislation supporting a V-chip in televisions to protect children:

> Don't we have to remember—you know, there are a lot of people that in public life love to quote the Scripture, and all of us probably do it selectively. But there are hundreds of admonitions in the Bible—hundreds—to take care of the

children, especially the poor children. "Even as you have done it [unto] the least of these, you have also done it unto me." If that was true for Jesus, surely it must be true of America. (Clinton, 1996c, ¶75)

George W. Bush frequently used religion to talk about the need to reform society by dealing with crime and supporting faith-based initiatives. He remarked during the 2000 campaign that America's leaders needed to follow God's will: "Getting tough on crime is easy compared to loving our neighbors as ourselves. . . . The truth is, we must turn back to God and look to Him for help" (Dionne, 2008, p. 97). During his October 13, 2004, debate with John Kerry, George W. Bush connected his policy of government funding for faith-based initiatives with his religious beliefs: "I believe we ought to love our neighbor like we love ourself, as manifested in public policy through the faith-based initiative where we've unleashed the armies of compassion to help heal people who hurt." Throughout various campaigns, candidates invoked their religious beliefs to explain and justify various public policy positions. With such claims, the candidates argued their policies were supported by divine teachings and thus unquestionably justified.

Political Success

The second aspect of partisan confessional rhetoric is found in candidates' use of religion and God's blessings to explain their political successes. Ronald Reagan told the Conservative Political Action Conference in 1984 that Republicans would win if they trusted in God, which he framed in biblical terms as fighting the good fight and finishing the race: "If we trust in Him, keep His word, and live our lives for His pleasure, He'll give us the power we need—power to fight the good fight, to finish the race, and to keep the faith" (Reagan, 1984b, ¶47). Al Gore also explained his electoral chances in 2000 by comparing it to a miracle described in the Old Testament:

> And you know that however far down we find ourselves, we can be lifted up. You know that even in the valley of the dry bones, the Lord breathed life into those bones. And bone came to bone and sinew came to sinew, and there rose up a mighty army. (Gore, 2000d, ¶80)

Similarly, Hillary Clinton after winning the West Virginia primary in 2008—when she was already nearly without a chance of capturing the nomination—had faith she could still win:

> They say, "Give up. It's too hard. The mountain is too high." But here in West Virginia, you know a thing or two about rough roads to the top of the mountain. We know from the Bible that faith can move mountains. (Clinton, 2008, ¶3–4)

A couple of candidates even credited God with their primary victories. After placing second in Iowa, Pat Robertson declared, "I have to give God credit" (Sullivan, 1988, ¶7). And after several victories on "Super Tuesday" in 2008, Mike Huckabee began his victory speech with multiple biblical allusions of how the underdog or less fortunate would be victorious:

> Tonight we are making sure America understands that sometimes one small smooth stone is even more effective than a whole lot of armor. And we've also seen that the widow's mite has more effectiveness than all the gold in the world. (Huckabee, 2008, ¶2)

By referring to these biblical miracles, Huckabee suggested he received the same divine assistance that David received in killing Goliath and that Jesus referred to in a teaching to his disciples about giving. With such remarks, candidates not only placed their hopes and prayers in God but also literally invoked God's partisan assistance and involvement in the success of their campaigns and governance. In these comments God is called upon as an active player in partisan politics who grants political salvation to faithful candidates.

Political Attacks

The final form of partisan religious-political rhetoric occurs when candidates use religion to attack their political opponents. As opposed to merely claiming that God supports their policies or is on their side, some candidates at times would go even further by arguing that God opposed their opponents for being unfaithful to scriptural commands. While Reverend Jesse Jackson campaigned in a church to make a competitive run for a 1984 Democratic nomination, he mixed his biblical analogies as he compared President Ronald Reagan to the Pharaoh persecuting Jesus and his earthly father Joseph:

> Do you know that Jesus would have been in trouble under Pharaoh Reagan? Joseph, a part-time carpenter! . . . Joseph couldn't have come home and kept food assistance at the house under Reagan. Jesus couldn't have had the head-start program under Reagan. Under Pharaoh Reagan they couldn't have gotten any money to weatherize their stable! . . . You know if the Lord couldn't have gotten food and job training under Reagan you are in trouble! (MacPherson, 1984, ¶43–44)

In a speech during the 1992 campaign, Bill Clinton quoted a biblical passage in his attack on George H. W. Bush's lack of vision: "But his ship of state lacks a compass and a vision, and the Scripture says that, 'Where there is no vision, the people perish.' We are in the process of living out that admonition" (Clinton, 1992c, ¶5). In using religious rhetoric to attack George W. Bush during the 2004 campaign, John Kerry referred to a parable of Jesus to critique Bush's policies on poverty:

> Four years ago, George Bush came to office calling himself a "compassionate conservative." Well, in the story of the Good Samaritan we are told of two men who pass by or cross to the other side of the street when they come upon a robbed and beaten man. They felt compassion, but there were no deeds. Then the Good Samaritan gave both his heart and his help. It is clear: For four years, George W. Bush may have talked about compassion, but he's walked right by. He's seen people in need, but he's crossed over to the other side of the street. (Kerry, 2004f, ¶15–16)

Religiously infused attacks were usually lobbed by Democratic opponents against incumbent Republican presidents, often for hypocrisy as the Democrats accused their Republican opponents for failing to live up to the very biblical standards the Republicans claimed to faithfully follow. However, George H. W. Bush attacked the Democrats during the 1992 campaign for not showing reverence for God: "The other party took words to put together their platform, but left out three simple letters: G-O-D" (Wood, 1992, p. 727). With such arguments, religion became a political weapon with which to attack one's opponent. Far from using religious rhetoric in a nonpartisan manner, with these attacks the candidates claimed that God took sides against an opposing party or candidates.

Presiding during a different time, Richard Nixon's religious-political rhetoric followed the civil-religious contract by avoiding using religion to support partisan policies: "It is particularly noteworthy that almost none of Nixon's theologically embellished speeches dealt avowedly with partisan politics, welfare, higher education, international diplomacy, the natural environment, or other workday vicissitudes of American life" (Hart and Pauley, 2005, p. 63). Far from Nixon's discourse, candidates from Jimmy Carter to George W. Bush, from Ronald Reagan to Bill Clinton, from John McCain to Barack Obama used God-talk and scriptural admonitions to justify their partisan politics and policy positions like education, international diplomacy, and the environment. They rhetorically brought God into their campaigns to support their public policies, explain their political successes, and attack their political opponents. As the candidates made these remarks, they called for God's intervention and even divine judgment to help decide partisan elections. In 1960, John F. Kennedy promised those at the meeting of the Greater Houston Ministerial Association that he would not allow his religion to dictate his public policy positions:

I do not speak for my church on public matters; and the church does not speak for me. Whatever issue may come before me as President, if I should be elected, on birth control, divorce, censorship, gambling or any other subject, I will make my decision in accordance with these views—in accordance with what my conscience tells me to be in the national interest, and without regard to outside religious pressure or dictates. And no power or threat of punishment could cause me to decide otherwise. (Kennedy, 1960a, ¶19)

Today's candidates have rejected the Kennedy model as they not only use religion to justify their public policy positions but even declare that they would seek the counsel of the Pope or other religious leaders.

SECTARIAN

Much as the civil-religious contract demanded that religious-political rhetoric not become too partisan, it also required that the rhetoric not become too sectarian by favoring one religious faith or group. Rather, religious-political discourse was to be "a rhetoric . . . tempered by religious pluralism" (Hart and Pauley, 2005, p. 77), providing equal voice and opportunity to the many religious sects in our society:

One of the inescapable facts of U.S. history is that it has been a theologically pluralistic society from the beginning. . . . Contemporary Americans have learned these lessons of history well. The need for a symbolically compact and integrative discourse, a rhetoric around which all denominationalists and partisans can rally, continues to press upon them. (Hart and Pauley, 2005, p. 81)

The civil-religious contract's nonsectarian nature was grounded in a respect for American pluralism, a spirit that John F. Kennedy appealed to in his famous address to Protestant ministers in Houston. Kennedy declared that the specific religion of a presidential candidate should not matter because in America "religious liberty is so indivisible that an act against one church is treated as an act against all" (Kennedy, 1960a, ¶5). Since then, however, candidates have shown a much more sectarian spirit, such as a Jimmy Carter supporter questioning Morris Udall's Mormonism, attacks on Carter's evangelical beliefs by Gerald Ford's campaign, Walter Mondale and other Democrats criticizing Ronald Reagan for not attending church and Mondale's running mate attacking Reagan for not being a "good Christian," a Mike Huckabee supporter attacking Sam Brownback for converting to Catholicism, Huckabee attacking Mitt Romney's Mormonism, and Hillary Clinton and Republicans attacking Barack Obama's church and former pastor.

With such attacks, the presidential candidates and their supporters have adopted a sectarian requirement that seems to exclude candidates because of where they do or do not worship. Coupled with the most recent attacks on Muslim congressman Keith Ellison, and false rumors attacking Barack Obama for being a Muslim, today's confessional politics stands in stark opposition to Kennedy's principle of not rejecting candidates based on their specific brand of religion and his strong support for separation of church and state. Replacing the Kennedy model is a rhetorical sectarianism that shows preferences for specific faiths, adopts an evangelistic tone to convert people to a specific faith, and discounts the historic principle of separation of church and state. This element of our now confessional politics is supported by the themes detailed in the previous chapter of America's special relationship with God, depicting campaigns as part of a spiritual mission, and issues of church and state. As our presidential candidates developed an evangelical Christian message on the campaign trail, the civil-religious contract's notion of religious pluralism was quickly left behind.

Religious Preference

The first sectarian aspect of confessional political rhetoric is when candidates show preferences for certain religious faiths and thereby exclude others. With such comments, candidates often take sides in religious issues by arguing that all Americans trust in God, even though many Americans do not believe in a god or are part of a faith without a single god as in the Jewish, Christian, or Muslim sense. As a result, America is cast as more of a Christian nation rather than a nation that happens to include many Christians. Jimmy Carter stated during his 1980 campaign:

> But throughout a time of trial and tribulation, of testing, questioning, Americans have always turned to basic unchanging principles, moral beliefs, deep religious convictions, and they have turned to God for guidance in managing the secular challenges which confront us. (Carter, 1980a, p. 49)

Ronald Reagan argued in a speech during 1984 that we are a pluralistic society, but then contradicted that message as he invoked God as a singular belief, thus exposing the underlying sectarian nature of his rhetoric: "We are and must remain a pluralistic society, but we're also one nation together. We're brothers and sisters equal in the eyes of God and equal under the law" (Reagan, 1984t, ¶37). In other speeches, Reagan talked about the importance of America continuing to trust in God. Similarly, George W. Bush also offered rhetoric that excluded those who do not worship God as he declared in 2004 that all Americans turn to God: "Americans of every faith and every tradition turn daily to God in reverence and humility" (Bush, 2004e, ¶26). Mitt Romney, who sought the 2008 Republican presidential nomination, claimed in his speech on faith in America that "[f]reedom requires religion" and argued that America should recognize and honor God (Romney, 2007, ¶14). Such comments sparked criticism for suggesting that those who do not believe in God were not fully part of the American community. Also during the 2008 campaign, Republican nominee John McCain even argued that since "this nation was founded primarily on Christian principles," he would vote for a Christian instead of a Muslim for president because he would "prefer someone who I know who has a solid grounding in my faith" (Gilgoff, 2007e, ¶2). By declaring that all Americans trusted in and prayed to God, candidates have often excluded those who are part of a minority religion or profess no religious faith. Additionally, as the candidates—all of whom professed to be Christians—used Christian language and scriptures to discuss God, it suggests that their God-talk was primarily references to the Christian God. As a result, a sectarian test for citizenship was advanced as candidates defined those of a minority or of no faith to not be fully included in the America that they led or wished to lead.

Evangelistic Approach

The second type of sectarian rhetoric in confessional politics occurs when a candidate becomes evangelistic in their campaign messages by encouraging people to adopt a particular faith. With these statements, the candidates adopted the role of a revival preacher instead of a political leader. During the 1976 campaign, Jimmy Carter often talked about his previous missionary service and even cast his *Playboy* magazine interview as "an opportunity to witness," explaining that among the publication's readers were many "who may not ever go to church and may not know what Christians believe" (Carter, 1978b, p. 973). In a 1980 speech to the National Religious Broadcasters annual meeting, Carter bragged about his evangelistic efforts with foreign leaders. Justifying why he should be chosen again as the nation's commander-in-chief, Carter depicted himself as the nation's evangelist-in-chief as a result of his attempts to witness to other nations' leaders about God:

> I have had a chance to talk about the Gideons' work and Bibles with the Vice Premier of the People's Republic of China, Deng Xiaoping, and about the need for him to open up the gates of China once again for missionaries to bear the word. I've shared my faith with leaders of Korea, Poland, and other nations that I've visited. And I've found a sense of brotherhood with a Moslem leader of Egypt, Anwar Sadat, and a Jewish leader of Israel, Menahem Begin, as we worked together to find the ideal of Christ: peace on Earth. (Carter, 1980b, p. 181)

Ronald Reagan similarly bragged about evangelizing as president when visiting foreign leaders in remarks in 1984 upon returning from a visit to China:

> Many of the Chinese people still don't understand how our democracy works or what impels us as a people. So, I did something unusual. I tried to explain what America is and who we are—to explain to them our faith in God and our love, our true love, for freedom. (Reagan, 1984i, ¶17)

For Reagan, to explain America was to first talk about God. In 1992, Bill Clinton urged those at a campaign rally to join him in praying for specific individuals in our nation, creating a moment similar to one that can be found in many church services with an altar call of prayer requests. Here, Clinton notes the many struggles faced by Americans with a specific prayer request for each struggling situation:

> Tonight when you go home . . . in the quiet moments before you go to bed, remember that nothing has yet been done to change the lives of the people, and our battle has just begun. And so I ask you to say a prayer for the men and women of this city and our nation who are dying of AIDS but living with hope. Say—say a prayer for the children who cry themselves to sleep in this nation every night because their homes are filled with their parents' tension and fear, the heartbreak of unemployment, and broken dreams. (Clinton, 1992b, ¶19)

Also in 1992, George H. W. Bush took a sectarian evangelistic stance by calling for a spiritual revival in the nation, much as his predecessor Ronald Reagan had:

> We need a moral and yes, a spiritual revival in our nation so that families unite, fathers love mothers, stay together in spite of pain and hard times, because they love their children and look forward to another generation growing up tall and confident in the warmth of God's love. (Bush, 1992f, ¶52)

During the 2000 campaign, George W. Bush described the job of the president in a way that sounded more like the job of a revival preacher: "The role of the president is to say to the people of faith, you're welcome to help change America, because changing hearts will change America for the better, as far as I'm concerned" (Bush, 1999a, ¶69). Similarly, Barack Obama invoked God and the Bible at the Alfred E. Smith Memorial Dinner to urge Catholics and other people of faith to work to improve their nation:

> Scripture says God creates us for works of service. We are blessed to have so many organizations like this one in the Catholic Diocese that perform these acts of God every day, but each of us also have that responsibility. Each of us has that obligation—especially now. (Obama, 2008i, ¶30)

With these remarks, the candidates not only endorsed a specific religious faith but encouraged others to accept that faith and join in prayers and worship to the Christian God. In doing so, they often assumed the role of national preacher rather than political leader and thus adopted a sectarian approach to campaigning.

Separation of Church and State

The third form of sectarian religious-political rhetoric concerns the timid support—or even blatant attack—on the principle of separation of church and state. With this area, a significant difference between Republican and Democratic candidates was evident, although most candidates from both parties fell well short of John F. Kennedy's declaration, "I believe in an America where the separation of church and state is absolute" (Kennedy, 1960a, ¶4). For Republicans, the shift from the Kennedy model is most noticeable as they proposed policies like government sanctioned prayer in public schools and government support of religious schools or faith-based organizations. Although Republican presidential candidates sometimes gave lip-service to the concept of separation of church and state, they not only advocated policies that the Supreme Court had ruled violated the principle, but even attacked interpretations and applications of the separation principle. During the 1980 campaign, Ronald Reagan told the evangelists present at the Religious Roundtable's National Affairs Briefing meeting, "I think it's quite strange in this country that . . . we've interpreted separation of church and state to mean separation of state and country from religion and I think that's wrong. We are a nation under God" (Curtis, 1980, ¶10). During the 1984 campaign, Reagan frequently pushed for a constitutional amendment supporting prayer in school while also trying to dispel criticism that he was violating the separation of church and state:

> Now, I can't think of anyone who favors the Government establishing a religion in this country. I know I don't. But what some would do is to twist the concept of religion, freedom of religion, to mean freedom against religion. . . . At the same time, we call for the right of children once again to pray voluntarily in our public schools, and that stand is in the spirit of the Constitution as our Forefathers wrote it and as we have lived it for most of our history. (Reagan, 1984s, ¶17–18)

Reagan even suggested at times that the separation principle went too far and therefore the Constitution had to be amended to fix this original error that he saw in our First Amendment freedoms. In 1992, George H. W. Bush connected his belief in America's special relationship with God to his proposals for prayer in public schools. He also linked his support for prayer in public schools—which he stated often—to his belief that the principle of separation of church and state had been taken too far: "And some people seem to believe that freedom of religion requires government to keep our lives free from religion. Well, I believe they are just plain wrong. Our government was founded on faith" (Bush, 1992b, ¶17). During the 2008 campaign, Republican hopeful Mitt Romney attempted to dispel questions about his Mormonism. While he argued in his speech on faith in America that his religion should not be held against him in the campaign, he attacked the notion that religion should be kept separate from government and public life:

> No religion should dictate to the state, nor should the state interfere with the free practice of religion. But in recent years, the notion of the separation of church and state has been [taken] by some well beyond its original meaning. They seek to remove from the public domain any acknowledgement of God. . . . It's as if they're intent on establishing a new religion in America: the religion of secularism. They're wrong. (Romney, 2007, ¶39–42)

With these remarks, the Republican candidates not only advocated policies in opposition to the principle of separation of church and state, but even attacked how the concept was applied. As they attempted to ignore the separation of church and state, the Republican candidates were abandoning a principle that played a foundational role in the civil-religious contract.

Although Democratic candidates did not generally advocate policies considered in opposition to separation of church and state or attack the principle outright, successful Democrats in the confessional era were much less forceful in declaring their support of the principle than John F. Kennedy during his speech to the Protestant ministers in Houston. It was during his unsuccessful campaign in 1980—as opposed to his 1976 bid—that Jimmy Carter most strongly argued for preserving separation of church and state. He also linked this principle to the absence of a religious test for office as he found himself under attack from the newly created Moral Majority:

> I don't think there ought to be any religious test for political acceptability, and I don't think there ought to be any political test for religious fellowship. I believe that the people will make a sound judgment, recognizing the necessity for the separation of church and state. . . . I believe most Americans want to preserve that proper separation of church and state. (Carter, 1980q, p. 2509)

Since Carter lost to those he attacked for crossing the line separating church and state, it would seem his prophesy that Americans wanted to preserve the separation principle was incorrect. Walter Mondale in 1984 and Michael Dukakis in 1988 also stressed the importance of the principle, although neither of them made a personal religious connection to the separation principle as Jimmy Carter made in 1976 and 1980. In a 1992 campaign speech to a meeting of the Jewish group B'nai B'rith, Bill Clinton stated:

> We believe everyone ought to have the freedom to worship God in his or her
> own way. We believe in the strength of our country and our churches and
> synagogues to draw from the constitutional separation between church and
> state. (Clinton, 1992i, ¶26)

However, Clinton more often spoke about the importance of religious freedom than specifically advocating separation of church and state, and he also
connected this belief to his personal religious faith. Clinton's language about
religious freedom highlights the importance of one being able to practice
religious beliefs uninhibited—one side of the separation principle—but
leaves fairly silent the idea of keeping government from undue religious
influence. Al Gore followed Clinton with this shift in rhetorical focus, but
did not do so as eloquently or with as strong of a connection to his personal
religious faith. Barack Obama also expressed support for the principle of
separation during the 2008 campaign, but he also took a more Republican
approach of advocating governmental support for faith-based organizations—as had Gore in 2000. During a December 1, 2007, Democratic primary debate, Obama explained that although he would alter the current faith-
based programs, he would continue governmental support of religious organizations:

> And so there's no doubt that we can use the faith-based institutions that exist
> in our society for all sorts of good, but the reason we set up separation of
> church and state, the reason the founders set it up was not just to protect the
> state from the church, it was to protect the church from the state. . . . So what I
> want to be able to do is to partner and work with faith-based institutions, but
> there are ways of doing it that don't violate the separation of church and state.

Although Democratic candidates offered stronger support for the separation
of church and state than Republicans, their voices in support of the principle
usually did not match that of previous candidates like John F. Kennedy.
Additionally, only Jimmy Carter in 1976 and Bill Clinton in 1992 and 1996
managed to offer their support for separation and win the general election
during the confessional era. However, both of these candidates connected the
principle to their personal religious faith. Additionally, Carter stressed the
principle less forcefully during his successful 1976 campaign than his unsuccessful 1980 campaign, and Clinton spoke more about the importance of
religious freedom. Candidates taking a stronger position for the separation
principle—such as Jimmy Carter in 1980, Walter Mondale, and Michael
Dukakis—lost their presidential bids.

Religious-political rhetoric during the period guided by the civil-religious
contract was not sectarian as it offered generic deity references, "bland fare
usually served up at national political events," and avoided "Christo-centered
utterances" (Hart and Pauley, 2005, p. 27). Since that time, however, our

presidential candidates have invoked the name of Christ and offered sectarian religious statements. In 2000, for example, Republican presidential candidate and Texas Governor George W. Bush declared a day in June to be "Jesus Day" in Texas just as the presidential campaign was heating up (Hanson, 2000). Additionally, Jimmy Carter gushed during his 1976 campaign, "The most important thing in my life is Jesus Christ" (Carter, 1978b, p. 965). Rather than serving as "bland fare," God-talk has become quite explicit and even included in normal campaign events instead of reserved only for national ceremonies. As presidential candidates have offered more sectarian statements and even become evangelistic in promoting not only faith in America but also commitment to a specific religion, many have also discounted the separation of church and state that was essential to the civil-religious contract. In his speech to the Greater Houston Ministerial Association, John F. Kennedy emphasized the nonsectarian nature of governance as he advocated strict church-state separation:

> I believe in an America where the separation of church and state is absolute; where no Catholic prelate would tell the President—should he be Catholic—how to act, and no Protestant minister would tell his parishioners for whom to vote; where no church or church school is granted any public funds or political preference, and where no man is denied public office merely because his religion differs from the President who might appoint him, or the people who might elect him. (Kennedy, 1960a, ¶4)

Far from Kennedy's pluralistic model for separation, prohibition on public funding of religious groups, and the inability of religion to dictate the political process, today's candidates offer a decidedly more sectarian agenda for America.

LITURGICAL

Under the civil-religious contract, religious-political rhetoric was primarily ceremonial and thus lacking the spiritual significance of sectarian religious statements. For official civil religionists who adhered to the contract, the use of ritualistic religious rhetoric included "certain ground rules" that "must be observed when deploying such themes" in political discourse: "(1) they must be brief, (2) they must commence or terminate an address (but usually not both), and (3) they must normally (i.e., during peacetime) be appended to ceremonial, as opposed to policymaking or policy-endorsing, speeches" (Hart and Pauley, 2005, p. 78). However, candidates since 1976 have offered extended theological discussions throughout their campaign addresses, including policymaking speeches. Far from being ceremonial in nature, the candidates have often embraced deeper spiritual meanings. Even the more ritualistic statements have been less ceremonial than liturgical; that is, our presidential candidates and would-be leaders in the confessional era have used religious symbolism as part of an act of public worship. As the candidates have searched for political salvation, they have explained their theological beliefs and acted as national worship leaders for their political flock. Far from keeping their religious remarks brief, presidential candidates have offered detailed explanations of their theological beliefs. Far from keeping their religious remarks ceremonial, candidates have offered deeply religious expressions like those found in Christian worship services.

Theological Explanations

The first liturgical aspect of confessional political rhetoric is seen in candidates detailing the specifics of their theological beliefs. For example, when asked during the 1976 primary campaign why he thought people were on earth, Jimmy Carter, sounding more like a Sunday school teacher than a political candidate, outlined his theology about creation and the purpose of life:

> I could quote the Biblical references to creation, that God created us in His own image, hoping that we'd be perfect, and we turned out to be not perfect but very sinful. And then when Christ was asked what are the two greatest commandments from God which should direct our lives, He said, "To love God with all your heart and soul and mind, and love your neighbor as yourself." So I try to take that condensation of the Christian theology and let it be something through which I search for a meaningful existence. (Carter, 1977, p. 90)

In 1984, Ronald Reagan, using the example of his own prayerful approach as an athlete, offered a mini-devotional covering the critical theological issue of praying:

> You can't pray to win. We're all God's children, and how is He going to favor one side and not the other? So, knowing that was impossible, I'd figured out for myself that I would pray that I did my best, didn't make any mistakes, that no one would be injured on either side, and that the best team would win, and that we would all be content and satisfied, we wouldn't have any regrets of saying, "Oh, why did I do this or not do that?" when the game was over. (Reagan, 1984v, ¶7)

That same year Reagan also declared to a Catholic group, "God makes the world turn on its axis and keeps the Sun and the stars in place, but you are the people who keep America going, who make America happen every day" (Reagan, 1984n, ¶7). When asked about applying his faith in response to Bill

Clinton's sex scandal, Al Gore talked during the 2000 campaign about his theological beliefs regarding sin, "I'm taught in my religious tradition to hate the sin and love the sinner. I'm taught that all of us are heir to the mistakes that—are prone to the mistakes that flesh is heir to" (Gore, 1999b, ¶164). George W. Bush commented in 2000 about his theological views during his acceptance address at the Republican National Convention:

> I believe in tolerance, not in spite of my faith, but because of it. I believe in a God who calls us not to judge our neighbors but to love them. I believe in grace because I've seen it, and peace because I've felt it, and forgiveness because I've needed it. (Bush, 2000c, ¶235, 237, 239)

In a 2004 speech, Bush outlined his theological beliefs about prayer that seemed quite similar to a church sermon or theology lecture on the importance of trusting in God:

> In prayer, we offer petitions, because the Maker of the Universe knows our cares and our needs. . . . Prayer also teaches us to trust, to accept that God's plan unfolds in His time, not our own, that trust is not always easy, as we discover in our own lives, but trust is the source of ultimate confidence. (Bush, 2004e, ¶38, 42)

During the 2008 campaign, John McCain told those at a meeting of the National Council of La Raza:

> In my recent visit to Mexico, I visited the Shrine of the Virgin of Guadalupe, and was greatly moved by the experience, and came to appreciate all the more your deep devotion to the God who created us and loves us all equally.(McCain, 2008b, ¶20)

Asked about the biblical story of creation during a June 5, 2007, Republican primary debate, Mike Huckabee quoted scripture and the initiator of the Protestant Reformation to mark his political position as a theological stance:

> "In the beginning, God created the heavens and the Earth." To me it's pretty simple, a person either believes that God created this process or believes that it was an accident and that it just happened all on its own. . . . I believe there is a God. I believe there is a God who was active in the creation process. . . . And as the words of Martin Luther, "Here I stand. I can do no other." And I will not take that back.

When Luther made the famous remark that Huckabee quoted, it was at the closing of his speech before Catholic leadership deciding if he should be excommunicated. Similarly, Huckabee was proclaiming that he would not shy away from declaring his theological beliefs, even during a political campaign. As the candidates sought political votes, they often talked about their theological beliefs, often acting more like a Sunday school teacher, minister, or biblical scholar explaining important theological points about the purpose of life, God, and prayer. By outlining their theological beliefs and visions, the candidates, at times, appeared to be auditioning for the role of the nation's religious leader.

Worship Leader

The second type of liturgical religious-political rhetoric occurs when candidates engage in and even lead religious worship. With this type of discourse, our presidential candidates used political events to promote religious worship. Ronald Reagan ended his acceptance speech at the 1980 Republican National Convention by leading those present in a time of silent prayer: "Can we begin our crusade joined together in a moment of silent prayer?" (Reagan, 1980, ¶106). Addressing the energy crisis with a group of ministers in 1980, Jimmy Carter encouraged these religious leaders to conduct special worship services to bring attention to the matter and generate possible solutions:

> I understand that you are considering a conservation Sabbath weekend. And I hope that you'll go forward with this idea, because I know that the common approach is very good. And the individual exploration—as you commune with God, as you study holy texts, as you apply ancient principles and commitments to a modern-day challenge—can open up ideas for our Nation to explore that have not yet been understood or considered by me as President. (Carter, 1980a, p. 51)

Thus, the president filled the role of a denominational leader planning a special emphasis Sunday that would influence what the ministers preached to their congregations. At a campaign rally in Texas during his 1980 campaign, Carter urged those present to heed the Third Commandment to not use the Lord's name in vain. His plea ended with a revival-style call for people to respond by raising their hands, just as some evangelists urge people present to raise their hands in religious sermons if they are willing to make a commitment to accept Jesus as their savior:

> I notice that your illustrious Governor was not here to see me. I asked some of the students at your great colleges nearby where he might be. They said, "He might be home reading the Third Commandment." Now, for those of you who don't know what the Third Commandment is, I suggest that when you get home, you get your Bible if you've got one—I'm sure you have—turn to Exodus 20 and read the Third Commandment. . . . Well, don't forget now when you get home, read the Bible, okay? How many of you will look it up? Okay. Keep your promise. (Carter, 1980u, p. 2627)

George H. W. Bush concluded his speech to the National Religious Broadcasters during the 1988 campaign by reciting a prayer from a liturgical book and imploring those present to praise God:

> You know, in my book of common prayer, there's a phrase that goes, "Oh, God, whose service is freedom." That's always been a beautiful passage to me and to Barbara, and it can mean so many different things. . . . And I just want to close by sharing His Spirit in saying to you, "Praise God, whose service is freedom." (Bush, 1987, ¶22)

During the 2000 campaign, Al Gore, invoking the language of a preacher selecting a text for a sermon, led those present at an NAACP meeting to meditate on a biblical passage:

> I remembered what scripture teaches in the book of James, Chapter 2, Verse 18: Yea, a man may say thou has faith and I have works. Show me thy faith without thy works and I will show thee my faith by my works. That is my text for today. Now, look more closely at this text. . . . You know from a hard history and a long struggle that talk is cheap. It's deeds that matter. (Gore, 2000a, ¶139)

Al Gore started another speech by declaring, much as a minister might at the start of a church service, "All praise be to the Lord. Now that's: All praise be to the Lord" (Gore, 2000d, ¶1). On a similar liturgical note, Barack Obama began his announcement speech for the 2008 campaign by praising God: "Look at all of you. Look at all of you. Goodness. Oh, thank you so much. Thank you so much. Oh, giving all praise and honor to God for bringing us together here today" (Obama, 2007a, ¶1). Not only have many of our presidential candidates spoken in church services while campaigning during the confessional era, but they have also "preached" during campaign speeches by offering praise to God, encouraging prayer, and reflecting on scripture and actual liturgical writings.

At times it seemed that the candidates even created their own religious-political holy sites and liturgy for use on the campaign trail. In 1996, Bob Dole told of stopping to pray at the Lincoln Memorial: "I like Lincoln very much, too. In fact, on the way, on the campaign trail today, I stopped by the Lincoln Memorial for a little inspiration, reflection, and a little silent prayer about the party and the country" (Frost, 1996, ¶61). During the 2000 campaign, John McCain canonized a humorous prayer for campaigning previously offered by a 1976 Democratic presidential candidate:

> Having been on the campaign trail for months now, I have a prayer of my own—first uttered by a fellow Arizonan who was no stranger to this state, the late Mo Udall. "Oh Lord, help me to utter words that are tender and gentle, for at some future time I may have to eat them." (McCain, 2000a, ¶3)

As if he were reciting from a book of prayers prepared for worship, McCain used the Udall prayer. During the 2004 Democratic primary, Howard Dean took a pilgrimage to former President Jimmy Carter's church. After the church service, Carter introduced Dean as "a fellow Christian." Dean then linked his candidacy and character with Carter's:

> I particularly want to thank President Jimmy Carter, one, for getting me into politics and, two, for providing a moral example for all Americans. Because what we need is to restore the honor and the dignity and the morality in the White House in foreign leadership and domestic leadership, so that ordinary Americans can have their country back. (Dean, 2004)

With these reflections, candidates not only borrowed from actual liturgical prayers and writings, but even on a few occasions helped create some of their own to bring inspiration and reflection to the campaign trail.

Writing about the more ceremonial era of religious-political rhetoric that characterized the civil-religious contract, Hart concluded, "God may be something of a cosmic afterthought in American political discourse" (Hart and Pauley, 2005, p. 78). He also claimed that "[t]he most frequent manifestation of civil-religious tenets is the passing references found in political and religious oratory" (Hart and Pauley, 2005, p. 78) and "that most civil-religious discourse is quite abstract and necessarily so" (Hart and Pauley, 2005, p. 81). Since this period, however, candidates have moved God to the forefront of their campaign rhetoric and seem to have found it necessary to offer detailed and concrete discussions of theological issues. Perhaps more significantly, they have not only preached about God but also led their political followers in religious worship as they seek to become America's religious-political leader. Far from being merely ceremonial, these liturgical moments have often resembled the importance and sacredness of a religious worship service. John F. Kennedy declared during his 1960 speech to the Greater Houston Ministerial Association:

> I want a Chief Executive whose public acts are responsible to all and obligated to none, who can attend any ceremony, service, or dinner his office may appropriately require of him to fulfill; and whose fulfillment of his Presidential office is not limited or conditioned by any religious oath, ritual, or obligation. (Kennedy, 1960a, ¶10)

Today's candidates have rejected the stance of the civil-religious contract— as embodied by Kennedy—that religion should play a merely ceremonial role in politics. In campaign speeches during our confessional era, God is no longer "a comic afterthought."

SUMMARY

In detailing the civil-religious contract, Hart conceded that the contract could one day be voided: "Naturally, when the American people find the contract to be attractive no longer, they will urge their religious and political leaders to abrogate the agreement" (Hart and Pauley, 2005, p. 79). Although Hart added that he did not see such abrogation as likely, such a substantial shift in the religious-political rhetoric of candidates actually occurred before the ink was even dry on his original 1977 thesis. Although he has maintained in a later edition that the contract still exists, Hart did not offer any detailed analysis of presidential campaigns since 1972. In fact, Hart (2002) still maintained that "[h]eads continue to roll in the United States when politicians become too confessional" (p. 137–38). Rather than losing their heads, confessional candidates like Jimmy Carter, Ronald Reagan, Bill Clinton, George W. Bush, and Barack Obama have instead become the head of state. Candidates since 1976 are apparently unfamiliar with the contract and its guidelines for how our presidential candidates are supposed to talk about religion.

After limited analysis, Hart concluded that even George W. Bush has not broken the contract but instead "follows [the rules] carefully" (Hart and Pauley, 2005, p. 11). However, Hart's two examples—lack of confirmation of "right-wing jurists" (Hart and Pauley, 2005, p. 188–89) and the ignoring of religious leaders like Jerry Falwell and Ralph Reed when making governance decisions—were quickly disputed later in the same year that Hart's revised text was published. Bush was successful in getting justices John Roberts and Samuel Alito confirmed to the U.S. Supreme Court, and the withdrawal of his nominee Harriet Miers occurred largely because of criticisms by conservative religious leaders. More significantly, Hart's defense of Bush was based on governance actions and not on campaign discourse. It is possible that the system of governmental checks and balances could extend the life of the civil-religious contract in the realm of governance long after the contract has expired on the campaign trail. As a presidential candidate, Bush named Christ as his favorite philosopher, talked about his sins and the grace he found in Jesus, opened up about his private prayer and devotional reading habits, and invoked God and quoted the Bible to justify public policies. Thus, candidate Bush clearly violated the civil-religious contract with his campaign rhetoric.

Hart claimed in his revised text, "Political compromise, not sectarian creeds, is the dominant language of America politics" (Hart and Pauley, 2005, p. 189). Such a statement may describe presidential governing discourse but offers little resemblance to the presidential campaign rhetoric of the past thirty years. Although remnants of the civil-religious contract may still hold during governing, and particularly in official presidential pronouncements and addresses that seek to appeal to the widest possible audience, it is quite obvious that campaign appeals' since Jimmy Carter are not bound by the civil-religious contract.

What has emerged in the era of confessional politics is a religious-political rhetoric that is testimonial, partisan, sectarian, and liturgical. Presidential candidates now regularly and loudly testify about their religious background and their Christian conversion experiences. Leading the use of such testimonial rhetoric has been Jimmy Carter, George W. Bush, and Barack Obama. Today, our candidates make partisan claims with religion to justify public policies and to attack their opponents, while also using God to explain electoral success. In particular, such partisan religious claims were advanced by Ronald Reagan, Bill Clinton, and Barack Obama. Our presidential candidates now offer sectarian remarks that exclude those of minority religions or those of no faith while also offering evangelistic altar-calls and attacking the principle of separation of church and state. Ronald Reagan, George W. Bush, and Jimmy Carter especially employed such sectarian arguments. Presidential candidates have also created liturgical moments as they detailed their theological beliefs and led the polity in worship. In particular, George W. Bush, Ronald Reagan, and Jimmy Carter offered such liturgical rhetoric. Overall, the trendsetters in enacting the confessional political electoral model include George W. Bush, Ronald Reagan, and Jimmy Carter, with Barack Obama and Bill Clinton also following suit. As a result, the civil-religious contract no longer has a prayer of keeping political leaders from becoming too religious.

As Jimmy Carter and Ronald Reagan brought a new religious-political discourse to presidential campaigns, many candidates and political commentators still tied to the older era characterized by Hart's contract criticized the new role religious rhetoric was playing in politics. Among the early critics was 1964 Republican presidential nominee and conservative icon Barry Goldwater, who has often been credited for setting the stage for Reagan's eventual 1980 victory. Yet, during Reagan's presidency, Goldwater strongly attacked the role religion and religious leaders played in political decisions. Demonstrating a drastically different campaign philosophy from that articulated by Reagan and later conservative presidential candidates, Goldwater argued:

> I'm frankly sick and tired of the political preachers across the country telling me as a citizen that if I want to be a moral person, I must believe in the "A," "B," "C," and "D." Just who do they think they are? And from where do they presume to claim the right to dictate their moral belief to me? And I'm even more angry as a legislator who must endure the threats of every religious group who thinks it has some God-granted right to control my vote on every

roll call in the Senate. And the religious factions will go on imposing their will on others unless the decent people connected with them recognize that religion has no place in public policy. (Greenawalt, 1994, p. 145)

Such declarations during today's confessional era would quickly find a candidate politically excommunicated and unable to capture their party's nomination or especially the presidency. Although Jesus challenged the religious leaders of his day, presidential hopefuls from both parties instead seek endorsements and photo-ops with prominent clergy. It is the impact of these "political preachers" on creating confessional politics that the next chapter explores.

Chapter Six

Societal Religious-Political Shifts

Just eight years after John F. Kennedy overcame the so-called Catholic question, his brother Robert sought the Democratic nomination without his own Catholicism raised as an issue during his campaign (Feinsilber, 1979). That same year, Republican George Romney sought the 1968 Republican nomination without facing serious scrutiny or questions about his Mormonism (Balmer, 2008). Over the next thirty years, however, Catholic and Mormon presidential candidates would face questions and political attacks regarding their faiths. In addition to issues raised about Catholics John Kerry in 2004 and Rudy Giuliani in 2008, even the third Kennedy brother, Edward, faced criticism for not being a "good" Catholic during his 1980 campaign (Diehl, 1980). Walter Mondale's Catholic running mate in 1984, Geraldine Ferraro, also received criticism—including from her own bishop—for not adhering to the Church's orthodoxy in her public policy position on abortion. As for Mormons, Morris Udall was attacked during his 1976 campaign even though he had already left the church, and George Romney's son, Mitt, faced intense scrutiny of his Mormon faith during his 2008 presidential race. Additionally, although no minister had ever offered a serious challenge for a major presidential nomination prior to 1976, three—Jesse Jackson in 1984 and 1988, Pat Robertson in 1988, and Mike Huckabee in 2008—have mounted competitive bids since then. Indeed, American politics and society has changed so dramatically during this period that, as Jesus told his followers, the new wine could not be put in old wineskins.

Although the religious-political rhetoric of our presidential candidates shifted dramatically from the earlier contractual period to the current confessional era, this rhetorical shift represents more than just a change in campaign strategies. After all, candidates have not just become more confessional, they have found electoral success in using such religious-political appeals.

A majority of the polity have apparently offered their blessing to this new religious-political tone. John F. Kennedy certainly could not have used the religious rhetoric of George W. Bush, who proudly claimed that he would consult the Pope for political advice, would use his faith to make political policy decisions, and criticized the separation of church and state. Kennedy was a successful candidate, in part, because he advocated the exact opposite positions. Likewise, Kennedy's arguments regarding the role of religion and politics would not prove very successful today as our political climate has become, in the words of the apostle Paul, "a new creature."

Although some claim that religious rhetoric by presidential candidates is a "god strategy" used to win elections (Domke and Coe, 2008), a largely unanswered question is why does this rhetorical strategy now work? What are the rhetorical exigencies that demand such religious appeals from our presidential candidates? Specifically, what has created in our society a situation where candidates must prove they are a "good" Christian who prays to God and seeks his guidance for their public policy decisions? Overall, how did the relationship between religion and politics change in our nation over the last fifty years? Such questions demand a historical examination of how our religious-political environment has shifted. This chapter explores six important religious-political shifts during the 1960s and 1970s that must be considered as one seeks to understand the current state of our nation's religious-political union. These shifts include: changes in Catholicism, the impact of the civil rights movement, shifts in American religious life, significant court decisions, the aftermath of Watergate and Vietnam, and increasing religious-political activism. Together, these changes helped create new rhetorical exigencies for our presidential candidates that led to a new era of confessional politics. Such an exploration not only provides insight into how and why the rhetorical shift outlined in chapter 5 occurred, but also demonstrates the rhetorical exigencies that presidential candidates must meet in order to remain politically viable.

These changes in American society do not merely represent the background or context for the confessional political style, but rather explain how this style has come to prominence. Whereas the civil-religious contract once dominated American presidential campaigns, these societal shifts have led to the confessional political style reigning supreme. As McGee (1990) argued, it is inaccurate for a critic to attempt to separate the "text" from the "context." Instead, he concluded:

> *Discourse ceases to be what it is whenever parts of it are taken "out of context."* Failing to account for "context," or reducing "context" to one or two of its parts, means quite simply that one is no longer dealing with discourse as

it appears in the world. . . . Put another way, the elements of "context" are so important to the "text" that one cannot discover, or even discuss, the *meaning* of "text" without reference to them. (p. 283, emphasis in original)

The rise of the confessional political system, therefore, cannot be truly understood without understanding the circumstances that gave it birth. Similarly, Bitzer (1968) detailed the importance of considering the "rhetorical situation" in which a message resides. He argued that "rhetorical discourse comes into existence as a response to a situation, in the same sense that an answer comes into existence in response to a question, or a solution in response to a problem" and that "the situation controls the rhetorical response in the same sense that the question controls the answer and the problem controls the solution" (pp. 5–6). Thus, it is not enough to simply declare the confessional political system to a political strategy. How this system arose and why it remains powerful must also be considered.

CHANGES IN CATHOLICISM

One significant religious-political development during the 1960s and 1970s was the collaboration between evangelical Protestants and conservative Catholics. Although John F. Kennedy's 1960 election and earlier elections saw an important partisan divide between religious denominations—particularly Catholics voting Democratic with evangelical Protestants voting Republican—the "God gap" since the 1970s has coalesced around a partisan divide based on church attendance and theology. Now, more observant Catholics and evangelical Protestants vote Republican and less observant Catholics and evangelical Protestants vote Democratic (Green, 2007). Three important developments helped turn former political foes—conservative Catholics and conservative evangelical Protestants—into political allies: John F. Kennedy's presidency, the Second Vatican Council, and the abortion issue. These issues helped unite evangelicals and Catholics, thus creating a voting bloc that could not be ignored by presidential candidates.

As John F. Kennedy attempted to dispel Protestant concerns about his Catholicism, he promised in his speech to the Greater Houston Ministerial Association to adhere to the separation of church and state and not allow Catholic leaders to dictate public policy for him. During his short presidency, Kennedy abided by this promise. The Pope made no visit to the White House and Kennedy avoided the Vatican. Additionally, Kennedy did not appoint a representative to the Vatican, as had Franklin Roosevelt and Harry Truman. Richard Nixon would later appoint a personal representative to the Vatican, but it would not be until Ronald Reagan that there would be an official U.S. ambassador to the Vatican; and every president since Reagan has appointed one. Kennedy's adherence to separation of church and state during his presidency demonstrated that the prophecies issued by his critics during the 1960 campaign were simply false. A Catholic could be trusted as president.

Kennedy's presidency actually helped to relieve much of the anti-Catholic sentiments among Protestant voters. *Washington Post* columnist E. J. Dionne (2008) claimed that Kennedy's election "symbolized the full entry of Roman Catholics into the mainstream of American civic life" (p. 35). George Mason University public affairs professor Hugh Heclo (2007) insisted that "America's first Catholic President became a settled and harmless reality, helping to make evangelicals' anti-Catholicism a moot point" (p. 110). However, despite representing a milestone for Catholics, it also lessened the cohesiveness of the Catholic voting bloc. Brookings Institution senior fellow James Reichley (1986) suggested that Kennedy's election ironically led some Catholics to feel "less reason to maintain loyalty to the Democrats as the party of outsiders" (p. 32). Thus, Kennedy's 1960 opponent, Richard Nixon, in 1972 became the first Republican presidential candidate to win a majority of the Catholic vote, defeating George McGovern and his Catholic running mate Sargent Shriver (who replaced fellow Catholic Thomas Eagleton on the ticket). Later Republicans would also win the Catholic vote, including George W. Bush in 2004 when facing Catholic John Kerry. With the fear of a Catholic president removed for most Protestants, one barrier separating Catholics and evangelicals was eliminated. Rather than condoning anti-Catholicism, as many Republicans did during the 1928 and 1960 campaigns of Catholics Al Smith and John F. Kennedy, later presidential candidates would distance themselves from charges of aligning with anti-Catholic religious leaders, such as George W. Bush did with Bob Jones in 2000 and John McCain with John Hagee in 2008.

Overlapping Kennedy's presidency was the start of the Second Vatican Council, during which the bishops from around the globe met for a session each fall from 1962–1965 (McGrath, 2002). During these meetings, the bishops discussed and adopted changes to Catholic doctrines and practices, including allowing Mass to be performed in languages other than Latin. More significantly for the American political-religious landscape, however, was the support offered for separation of church and state and allowing clergy more freedom to speak out on political matters. Historian Garry Wills (2007) noted, "The Council repudiated the old libel that Jews were Christ killers, and finally recognized the validity of pluralist societies—the old position was that governments should recognize a monopoly of 'the one true religion'" (p. 457–58). One principle offered from Vatican II directly influenced the clergy's role in politics: "The Church should have true freedom . . . to pass moral judgments even in matters relating to politics . . . wherever the fundamental rights of man or the salvation of souls requires it" (Sullivan, 2008, p. 55).

These changes offered new freedom for American Catholic clergy, particularly on the issue of abortion that would eventually serve as a unifying political issue, joining conservative Catholics and evangelical Protestants.

In the wake of Vatican II, the National Conference of Catholic Bishops (NCCB) was created in 1966 to provide the means for American Catholic bishops to meet, discuss, and engage in social and political matters. This organization would help lead the Catholic Church's efforts to fight abortion and push for a pro-life amendment to the U.S. Constitution less than a decade later (Sullivan, 2008). Demonstrating its clear political—rather than religious—aims, the organization outlined its pro-life strategy in a 1975 document that called for creating a grassroots pro-life group in every congressional district instead of each Church diocese (Sullivan, 2008). A NCCB delegation met with both 1976 presidential candidates as they pressed support for their pro-life agenda. Although both candidates assured the Catholic leaders of their personal opposition to abortion, the major-party platform offered clearly opposing positions on the issue as the Republicans adopted a pro-life plank and the Democrats adopted a pro-choice one. Cardinal Joseph Bernardin, NCCB president, avoided offering an official presidential endorsement but signaled his favor by publicly stating he was "disappointed" in Carter and "encouraged" by Ford (Sullivan, 2008, p. 65). In an effort to reduce Catholic leaders' concerns, Carter actually distanced himself from the Democratic Party's platform on abortion, saying on several occasions that it did not represent his position and that he had hoped for a different statement that was not as strongly pro-choice.

In the early 1980s, Cardinal Bernardin led the effort to move the U.S. Catholic Church from its singular focus on abortion to "a consistent ethic of life" that included issues of capital punishment and nuclear disarmament, but his efforts were not successful with many Catholic bishops (Sullivan, 2008, p. 72). A bishop in San Diego in 1989 barred a pro-choice Catholic state legislator from taking communion (Sullivan, 2008). In 1990, Cardinal O'Connor of New York and Archbishop Apuron of Guam threatened excommunication for Catholic legislators voting pro-choice, and Bishop Reiss of Trenton banned Catholic politicians who were pro-choice from speaking at any event sponsored by the diocese or a local church (Sullivan, 2008). A retired archbishop of New Orleans warned in 1996 that it would be a sin for a Catholic to vote for Mary Landrieu, a pro-choice Catholic candidate for the U.S. Senate, and Bishop Trautman actually banned pro-choice Catholic politicians in 1998 from attending a Catholic church in the diocese (Sullivan, 2008). Most notably, several bishops declared during the 2004 campaign that they would not serve communion to Democratic presidential nominee John Kerry. Four years later, Republican presidential hopeful Rudy Giuliani faced similar communion threats, as did Kansas Governor Kathleen Sebelius, who was often mentioned as a potential running mate for Democratic presidential nominee Barack Obama. Scott Appleby, a Catholic professor at Notre Dame, argued that the Catholic Church's focus on the issue of abortion created a sectarian test now applied to many Catholic politicians:

> The Catholic Church concedes a position it once enjoyed in the mainstream, pluralistic public and says, 'Okay, we're not going to live with that diversity and flexibility with our own church and be players, because (we cannot represent that.) We're going to be pure and sect and smaller and prune ourselves from the John Kerrys and Ted Kennedys.' And I do think that was an important moment, and I think we're still trying to figure out where it's headed and whether or not the church will really move more in that sectarian direction. (Suarez, 2006, p. 206)

Following Vatican II and the rise of the abortion issue, many conservative Catholic clergy used communion to create a sectarian test for Catholic politicians.

Abortion largely remained, at first, a Catholic issue. In fact, the largest Protestant denomination, the conservative evangelical Southern Baptist Convention, adopted resolutions at its annual meetings throughout the 1970s that called for a limited government approach and for allowing abortions in the situation of rape, incest, severe deformity, or the damage to the health of the mother (Balmer, 2008). Even Southern Baptist fundamentalist W. A. Criswell, who appeared in a Gerald Ford television ad in 1976, prayed at Ronald Reagan's Republican National Convention in 1984, and helped launch the rightward shift in the SBC, endorsed a relatively pro-choice position in 1973:

> I have always felt that it was only after a child was born and had a life separate from its mother that it became an individual person . . . and it has always, therefore, seemed to me that what is best for the mother and for the future should be allowed. (Balmer, 2008, p. 94)

Additionally, televangelist and Moral Majority founder Jerry Falwell apparently did not preach about abortion until 1978 (Martin, 2005). It was not until influential evangelical writer Francis Schaeffer brought attention to the issue in the late 1970s that abortion became a significant issue among evangelicals. His 1976 book and film *How Should We Then Live?* and his 1979 book and film *Whatever Happened to the Human Race?* helped to draw attention to abortion among Protestant evangelicals (Martin, 2005). The latter work was a collaborative effort with C. Everett Koop, who would later become Ronald Reagan's Surgeon General (Martin, 2005). By the early 1980s, conservative Catholics and evangelicals were working together to outlaw abortions.

Interestingly, despite the importance of the abortion issue to religious leaders since the mid-1970s, the presidential candidates' rhetoric explored in previous chapters revealed little discussion of the issue on the campaign trail in religious terms. Candidates also largely avoided using religious rhetoric to discuss the other major "moral issue" for many religious citizens—homosexuality. It could be that presidential candidates, although addressing the topic of abortion and homosexuality, leave the religious aspects of the controversial issues to religious leaders. Or, perhaps for conservative candidates to merely mention these issues is enough to capture the attention and support of conservative Christians. As Domke and Coe (2008) argued about abortion and same-sex marriage, "Not all symbolic issues are created equal" (p. 113) and just talking about abortion—even if not framed in religious terms—sends a strong message to conservative religious voters. University of Notre Dame historian Mark Noll argued that the abortion issue is inherently tied to considerations of a candidate's religiosity:

> Seventy-five years ago, if a churchgoing Baptist knew somebody else was a Catholic, he would have doubts over whether that person was a serious Christian. . . . Today, if the churchgoing Baptist knew a supporter of abortion rights, you would not ask if the person was Catholic or Protestant, you would say, "Well, I have serious doubts." (Gilgoff, 2007c, ¶16)

Due to the influence of conservative evangelicals and Catholics, successful Republican candidates now proclaim a pro-life position, even if they do not use religious rhetoric to explain their position. For example, George H. W. Bush, formerly pro-choice, espoused a pro-life position by 1988 to be a viable Republican presidential candidate (Shires, 2007).

In addition to the collaborative efforts of Catholics and evangelicals, there has also been the rise of evangelical Catholics, such as Virginia Governor Bob McDonnell, former Florida Governor Jeb Bush, and former Speaker of the House Newt Gingrich. Some, like Louisiana Governor Bobby Jindal—often mentioned as a running mate for 2008 Republican presidential nominee John McCain—even use the term "born-again Catholic." One important development coming from this movement was the document "Evangelicals and Catholics Together," signed by many prominent Catholic and evangelical Protestant leaders to create dialogue and outline areas of agreement (Wills, 2007). The first such document in 1994 focused on abortion as a primary area of agreement. Other areas of shared concern included the lack of prayer in public schools and the desire to protect private religious schools (Wills, 2007). Jerry Falwell estimated that Catholics constituted nearly one-third of the membership of the Moral Majority, and Ralph Reed, the first executive director of the Christian Coalition, noted that about one-sixth of the Christian Coalition's members were Catholic (Reed, 1996). After Pat Robertson met with the Pope in the fall of 1995, the Christian Coalition began a division called Catholic Alliance to increase its involvement among Catholics (Reed, 1996).

With the rise of prominent evangelical Catholics, the union between the two groups has created an even stronger political force. These various changes have altered the political relationship between candidates and Catholic leaders. Discussing the role religion plays in presidential campaigns, the 2004 Democratic presidential nominee John Kerry explained in 2007:

> But the bottom line is that the Catholicism that I grew up with is quite different from the Catholicism that we have today, and that is partly due to Vatican II and to a reevaluation within the church about how the church would reach out and talk to its flock. . . . Nowadays, it's much more evangelical, and by evangelical, something is evangelical when Christ is at its center and the Bible is at its center. ("Faith and the public dialogue," 2007, ¶17).

Kerry also talked about the issue of abortion. These significant changes regarding the role the Catholic Church plays in presidential politics has affected the relationship between Catholics running for higher office and the leadership of their church.

As president, John F. Kennedy avoided the fears of evangelical Protestants who thought he would turn the White House over to the Pope and seek the counsel of Catholic leaders. However, evangelical Protestant presidents during the confessional era of politics have drastically reversed Kennedy's model. Bill Clinton recognized Archbishop Joseph Bernardin—who as head of the NCCB helped make abortion a significant issue in presidential politics—with the presidential medal. Clinton called Bernardin "one of our nation's most beloved men and one of Catholicism's great leaders" and "both a remarkable man of God and a man of the people" (Clinton, 1996h, ¶7). Ronald Reagan's 1984 campaign placed ads in Catholic newspapers that showed the president meeting with the Pope (Smith, 2006). More significantly, Presidents Jimmy Carter and George W. Bush actually welcomed the Pope to the White House. Talking about Pope John Paul II's 1979 visit to the White House—the first papal visit ever to Washington, D.C. (Carter, 2006)—Carter joked at the 1980 Alfred E. Smith Memorial Dinner:

> There were dire predictions made then that should John Kennedy become President, the Pope soon would be standing on the White House steps. And in fact, that prediction came true. The Pope did stand on the White House steps, but the year was 1979. And the President who greeted him was a Southern Baptist. (Carter, 1980m, p. 2314)

As evangelicals Jimmy Carter, Ronald Reagan, Bill Clinton, and George W. Bush proudly affirmed U.S. Catholic leaders and even embraced the Pope, it was clear that the once strong divide between Catholics and evangelicals seen during the 1960 campaign would become an issue only for historians to study.

CIVIL RIGHTS MOVEMENT

As the divide between Catholics and evangelical Protestants was beginning to dissipate, an eloquent Bible-quoting Baptist minister, Reverend Martin Luther, King, Jr., led an important social movement that also changed the American religious-political landscape. King's civil rights movement—and to a lesser extent the anti-Vietnam War movement that he was also part of—brought religious rhetoric squarely into public policy debates and created a model for later religious activists seeking political influence. In describing the civil-religious contract, Roderick Hart (1977) dismissed "The Curious Case of Doctor King" as "clearly an anomaly in the pages of civil-religious history," but added that "while King may have rejected much of the civil religious contract, it seems clear that he respected its underlying rhetorical essence" (p. 81–82). Although Hart struggled to explain away King and his rhetoric, King clearly fits within the confessional style of politics. In many ways, he served—like the biblical John the Baptist—as "a voice crying out in the wilderness" that paved the way for a new religious-political rhetoric.

King built a movement that urged religious leaders and citizens to leave the church sanctuary and march into the streets. Historian Garry Wills (2007) noted that the civil rights movement was led by "black religious leaders" (p. 468) and "supported by black Evangelicals" (p. 469). He added that the movement's power came from the evangelical influence: "It was the energy and raw Evangelical eloquence of the black preachers that fired and uplifted the more cerebral theologians of the North. . . . The power of it was Evangelical. The protesters marched to hymns and spirituals" (p. 470). With evangelical fervor, King frequently quoted scripture and invoked God in his speeches calling for racial and social justice. King clearly articulated that he believed his work was God's work: "If we are wrong, God Almighty is wrong! . . . If we are wrong, Jesus of Nazareth was merely a utopian dreamer and never came down to earth!" (Dionne, 2008, p. 26). While arguing the importance of connecting one's faith to one's policies, 2008 Democratic nominee Barack Obama pointed to King and other political activists:

> Look, Martin Luther King, the abolitionists, the suffragettes, Dorothy Day—we have a long history of reform movements being grounded in that sense, often religiously expressed, that we have to extend beyond ourselves and our individual immediate self-interests to think about something larger. (Obama, 2007d, ¶75)

Few political figures have invoked God and cited scripture as explicitly and eloquently as the Reverend Martin Luther King, Jr.

With his God-talk, King captivated the nation and brought significant changes in public policy, thus serving as a forerunner for a religious-political strategy that would be commonly used in the decades following his death. During the 1976 presidential campaign, Jimmy Carter credited the civil rights movement with changing the U.S. political scene so that he could make a competitive run for the White House. Carter, a longtime advocate of the civil rights movement, spoke frequently about civil rights in his presidential campaigns. He also clearly linked himself to the movement as the Reverend Martin Luther King, Sr.—father of the slain civil rights leader—offered the benediction at the 1976 Democratic National Convention. "Daddy King" declared before praying, "Surely the Lord is in this place. Surely the Lord sent Jimmy Carter to come on out and bring America back where she belongs. I'm with him" (Martin, 2005, p. 154). Today, Martin Luther King, Jr.'s religious-political rhetoric appears much less "curious" in the confessional era with candidates like Carter.

In addition to offering a new religious-political voice, King directly served as a primary instigator for the birth of the liberal evangelical movement. Although the conservative evangelical movement that created the Moral Majority and the Christian Coalition has often wielded more influence and received more media attention, the religious left has also played an important role in American politics. Evangelical professor of Christian ethics David P. Gushee (2008) noted that "the founding generation of 'card-carrying' black evangelicals in the United States . . . emerged in the 1960s and 1970s" along with the civil rights movement (p. 105). He also argued that the 1960s essentially saw the creation of the "evangelical left":

> This indigenous agenda goes back to the very origins of the evangelical left in the 1960s. Martin Luther King Jr., who in some ways might be seen as a founder and certainly remains an icon of the evangelical left (as he is for so many others), often grouped together as "triple evils" the triad of poverty, racism, and war. He linked them all in his famous April 1967 criticism of the Vietnam War, but they appeared as a group in his writings before that time. (p. 75)

Yale University professor Stephen L. Carter (2000) argued that although the existence of the "Religious Left" is not touted nearly as much as that of the "Religious Right," the former had "great triumphs" with the civil rights and anti-war movements of the 1960s, which he viewed as more significant than the accomplishments of the "Religious Right" during the 1980s (p. 189). Carter's book, *The Culture of Disbelief*, in which he compared the God-talk of the civil rights movement with that of the 1992 Republican National Convention, suddenly became a national best seller after President Bill Clinton read and praised it, explaining that he agreed that religion should be allowed in the public square (Kuo, 2006). Liberal evangelicals like Jim Wallis and Tony Campolo have based much of their rhetoric on the model established by Martin Luther King, Jr.

In addition to helping inspire liberal evangelicals, King also served as a role model for the larger conservative evangelical movement, even for those that opposed his civil rights efforts. George Mason University public affairs professor Hugh Heclo (2007) insisted that "the passage of civil rights legislation in the 1960s formally neutralized an issue on which evangelicals were immensely vulnerable" (p. 110). Ralph Reed (1996), the first leader of the Christian Coalition, argued that his group followed the religious-political tradition of the civil rights and other social movements. He even admitted that "the Christian Coalition has adopted many elements of King's style and tactics" (p. 63) and claimed, "I draw much of my own inspiration from the example of Martin Luther King, Jr." (p. 280). He added that if the Christian Coalition succeeded as a movement, "it will be because we have followed King's example" (p. 65, 67). Reed (1996) even compared King's efforts in Montgomery to efforts in 1993 in Jackson, Mississippi when conservative Christians "protested the suspension of two hundred students for praying over the school intercom" (p. 67). One religious critic of King, Reverend Jerry Falwell, would also later claim to follow King's example. Portending an approach he would take years later toward Bill Clinton, Falwell distributed literature attacking King for leading a communist movement. Falwell argued during the civil rights movement:

> Believing the Bible as I do, I would find it impossible to stop preaching the pure saving Gospel of Jesus Christ and began doing anything else—including the fighting of communism or participating in the civil rights reform. . . . Preachers are not called to be politicians, but to be soul winners (Martin, 2005, p. 69–70)

However, when Falwell entered the political arena less than two decades later, he pointed to the civil rights movement as his role model. Falwell's dramatic conversion offered less insight about his beliefs of racial equality than his desire to gain political influence:

> I can be true neither to my country or my God if I separate my religious convictions from my political views. This is not "radical" fundamentalist theory. It is the basic belief that drove the Pilgrims to our shores—and the spirit with which Rev. Martin Luther King, Jr., took his message of racial harmony and equality from the pulpit to the streets. (Heineman, 1998, p. 146)

Understanding how King mobilized churchgoers into an important political movement, Reed and Falwell set their own sights upon creating a similar religious-political movement. As a mostly white conservative evangelical movement mobilized in the 1980s and 1990s, the leaders of this new voting bloc looked to King's words and efforts for inspiration. Thus, King's religious-political rhetoric appears to be no longer an "anomaly" in a confessional age with religious-political leaders like Jerry Falwell and Ralph Reed mobilizing Christian voters for political battle.

RELIGIOUS SHIFT

A significant development in American religion in the 1960s and 1970s occurred as evangelical Protestants overtook mainline Protestants as the largest religious group in America. Evangelicals brought with them a strong focus on publicly professing one's faith and relying on the Bible as a guidebook for living, and brought their unique rhetorical practices and demands with them into the political arena. In addition to evangelical denominations like the Assemblies of God, Pentecostal churches, and Southern Baptists, there are also evangelical groups within the Methodist, Episcopal, Presbyterian, and Lutheran traditions that have left the larger mainline bodies of these traditions, as well as evangelical Catholics.

Evangelicals began to experience growth and greater influence during the 1940s and 1950s. The National Association of Evangelicals, founded in 1942, represented an effort to bring evangelical churches together for collaboration and provide a public face for the community (Green, 2007). The organization also served as an alternative to the Federal Council of Churches (now National Council of Churches) that united the mainline denominations (Sullivan, 2008). Also aiding the rise of evangelicals was the founding of *Christianity Today* in 1956 and the rise of Billy Graham as pastoral advisor to the presidents (Wills, 2007). David L. Weeks (1998), political science professor at the evangelical Azusa Pacific University, argued about the writings of *Christianity Today*'s first editor Carl F. H. Henry: "By the mid-1970s, evangelical leaders were primed and ready to go—the groundwork had been laid. It was now legitimate to talk about and get involved in politics" (p. 96). With these developments, evangelicals were poised to surpass mainline Protestants in size and societal influence during the 1960s and 1970s and then assert themselves politically.

Since the 1950s, the growth of mainline denominations failed to keep up with that of evangelical ones or even the general population. From 1950 to 1979, evangelical denominations posted large increases in membership: the Southern Baptist Convention increased 88.9 percent, the Assemblies of God increased 201 percent, and the Church of God increased 238 percent (Peele, 1984). Meanwhile, the United Presbyterian Church in America declined 2.2 percent, while other mainline denominations posted only modest increases during this three decade period: the United Methodist Church increased less than one-tenth of 1 percent, the Episcopal Church increased 17.5 percent, and the Lutheran Church in America increased 21.9 percent. Membership declines in mainline denominations have continued since the 1980s. Oxford theology professor Alister McGrath (2002) noted that by 1990 the mainline denominations "had lost between one fifth and one third of their 1965 memberships, at a time when the population growth of the United States had surged," therefore representing "a massive slump in the proportion of America's population" (p. 42).

Although evangelicals grew from barely one-sixth of the U.S. adult population in 1944 to almost one-quarter in 2004, mainline Protestants shrank during that time period from more than two-fifths to less than one-fifth (Green, 2007). This dramatic shift has also played out in voting trends. Evangelicals grew from 29 percent of the electorate in 1960 to 33 percent in 1996 while mainline Protestants shrank from 45 percent to 22 percent (Carter, 2000). During this time period, evangelicals became the largest religious group among the overall electorate and mainline Protestants dropped from first to third as they also fell behind Catholics (Carter, 2000). Representing this shift, the evangelical Southern Baptist Convention passed the mainline United Methodist Church in 1967 to become the largest Protestant denomination in the country (Reeves, 1996).

As a result of their numerical decline, mainline Protestants have lost much of their cultural influence. Christian theology professor Gabriel Fackre at Andover Newton Theological School, the oldest graduate theological seminary in the United States, argued that the mainline churches have retreated to the "sideline" (Fackre, 2000, p. 26). Philip Wogaman (2000), a mainline pastor who was a spiritual advisor to the evangelical President Bill Clinton following Clinton's Monica Lewinsky sex scandal, offered: "The question is whether even the mainline churches have become marginalized in the Western cultural setting. The high visibility and political successes of the evangelical right in the closing decades of the twentieth century suggest that may be so" (p. 141). Charles Marsh (2007), professor of religion at the University of Virginia, commented on this change: "There is no longer a representative mainline Protestant voice, as there is no longer any identifiable mainline Protestant culture" (p. 97). That mainline culture has been replaced by an evangelical one.

The decline of mainline Protestants and the simultaneous rise of evangelicals represented opposite indicators of the same cultural shift. Liberal evangelical preacher and author Tony Campolo (2004), who is a minister in the mainline American Baptist Churches, USA, noted that "mainline churches are rapidly losing members and that many of them are drifting into nondenominational evangelical churches" (p. 3). He argued that the problem began in part because of differing political agendas of clergy and laity:

The differences between clergy and laity became especially pronounced between the late 1950s and the mid-1970s, when the United States was trauma-
tized by the civil-rights movement and the antiwar movement. As mainline
church leaders lent their voices to these movements, they often encountered a
laity committed to resisting their socially liberal rhetoric. When the national
assemblies of denominations related to the National Council of Churches
passed resolutions, the people back home in local congregations increasingly
deemed themselves under attack by the leadership of their churches. To conservative lay Christians, it seemed almost as though their denominational leaders were taking positions that were designed to appeal to those persons who
were least likely to attend their churches. (p. 5)

Many of the Christians who felt disconnected from their church's leadership
eventually found themselves worshipping and learning in an evangelical congregation. As these individuals joined evangelical congregations, many
adopted the evangelical approach to expressing their faith. Pastor and author
Dave Tomlinson (2003) argued that these individuals changing churches
quickly became part of an evangelical "subculture with its own church services, festivals, concerts, conferences, magazines, books, merchandise,
record companies, mission organizations, training schemes, vacation clubs,
and celebrities. They will also encounter distinctive social attitudes and be-
havioral expectations" (p. 27). He added, "The bottom line is that upon
entering this strange, new world of evangelicalism individuals are expected
to change, and generally *do*" (p. 27, emphasis in original).

Additionally, cultural changes led to a shift in the strength of the two
religious tradition. Preston Shires (2007) posited in *Hippies of the Religious
Right* that many of the youth who entered the counterculture movement of
the 1960s and 1970s eventually joined the conservative religious-political
movement of the late 1970s and 1980s. This transition saw these individuals
leaving mainline congregations to enter the counterculture movement but
joining evangelical churches when they left the counterculture movement.
Shires cast the counterculture movement as a "spiritual quest" as many youth
were looking for a deeper spiritual meaning to life than they found in the
mainline churches. After all, parts of the countercultural movement, like the
"Jesus People" and street evangelists, were passionately religious. Shires
(2007) pointed to Francis Schaeffer, a popular evangelical author and speaker, as an important "bridge between countercultural Christianity and the
Christian Right" (p. 90):

[Schaeffer] not only rejected the mainstream, he also rejected his liberal or
secular parents' worldview. . . . Schaeffer said things, and in such a way, that
made him sound like one of the sixties' youth. But not only did Schaeffer's
language and gospel presentation sound harmonious to many young listeners,
his lifestyle also was in tune with theirs. Francis Schaeffer was a tailor-made
evangelist to countercultural youth. He was an eccentric who wore knickers,

smoked a pipe, and, tucked away in the Alps, he exuded a hint of avant-garde intellectualism in spite of his blue-collar childhood in Pennsylvania. Furthermore, L'Abri, Switzerland, where he lived and worked, was something of a commune. (p. 89)

Yet, Schaeffer was also very orthodox and conservative in his theology and helped mobilize the evangelical community to address the issue of abortion. The transition in the mid and late 1970s from the countercultural movement to evangelicalism included high-profile—albeit relatively short-lived—born-again conversions of former Black Panther member Eldridge Cleaver and musician Bob Dylan (Shires, 2007). As American society transitioned, evangelicals quickly adapted to increase their numbers.

Adding to the religious shift from mainline Protestants to evangelicals was the growth of the evangelical movement within mainline denominations. During the 1960s, 1970s, and 1980s, various dissident organizations sprang up, including the Presbyterian Lay Committee, Good News Movement (United Methodist Church), Episcopalians United, American Baptist Evangelicals, Biblical Witness Fellowship (United Church of Christ), and Lutherans for Religious and Political Freedom (Reeves, 1996). Another organization, the Institute on Religion and Democracy, was founded in 1981 to work within the Anglican, Episcopalian, and Methodist denominations to promote a conservative religious and political agenda. Liberal evangelical mainline minister Tony Campolo (1995) urged mainline churches to "pick up on the positive developments of modern evangelicalism" in order to "make a comeback" (p. 116). By doing so, he declared that "[m]ainline denominations *can* be saved" (p. 197, emphasis in original). Campolo, who is often attacked as a liberal by conservative evangelicals in the Southern Baptist Convention, claimed that his use of altar calls and evangelical preaching resulted in some American Baptist leaders viewing him as a "fundamentalist" and "out of place in modern mainline denominational life" (p. 21, 23). Oxford theology professor Alister McGrath (2002) said of the mainline churches that "usually the only sections of those denominations, incidentally, which show any signs of life" are the evangelical movements within them (p. 44).

With the shift from an America where mainline Protestants were the largest religious tradition to an America dominated by evangelicals, our nation's religious-political culture changed. Evangelicals brought with them a focus on publicly testifying about one's faith and relying heavily on biblical teachings. It is not that America became a more religious nation as a result of this religious transformation, but that our nation became a more *rhetorically* religious nation. While mainline Protestants insist they do not wear their religion on their sleeves, evangelicals proudly and frequently proclaim their faith and doubt the religiosity of those who do not. To be a Christian in the evangelical world is to openly talk about it. Consider, for instance, the difference between Episcopalian Gerald Ford and Southern Baptist Bill Clinton. Ford, as he adhered to the civil-religious contract, offered the mainline Protestant perspective in declaring his faith to be "a very personal thing" and "not something one shouts from the housetop or wears on his sleeve" (Hart and Pauley, 2005, p. 87). Clinton, a product of the confessional political era, offered the evangelical line as he declared that his faith was "a source of pride to me" and insisted, "We all have the right to wear our religion on our sleeves" (Clinton, 1992k, ¶25). As evangelicals became the dominant religious force in America, they instilled their rhetorical focus into our nation's religious-political character. Not only do evangelicals talk about their faith, they expect their leaders to do so as well.

Pastor and author Dave Tomlinson (2003) explained about evangelicals: "They assert that this faith must be personal, leading to an experience of conversion. They stress the importance of declaring the gospel to nonbelievers" (p. 27). John C. Green (2007), a political science professor at the University of Akron and a senior fellow at the Pew Forum on Religion and Public Life, explained how evangelical beliefs lead to "an emphasis on personal, unmediated relationship with Christ" and "an intense focus on 'evangelizing,' that is proselytizing to make converts" (p. 27). He identified a key belief of evangelicals is the "imperative to proclaim this message of salvation and make converts among nonbelievers" (p. 25). The call for public proclamations of one's personal faith and the expectation to evangelize others by sharing the testimony of one's born-again conversion is often seen as a key to the success of evangelical churches. Liberal evangelical Tony Campolo (2008) argued that the rhetorical focus of evangelicals on public professions of faith influences their political expectations:

> Evangelicals tend to put great stock in candidates who give evidence that they have had born-again experiences and who declare themselves a part of our spiritual community. . . . A candidate who regularly prays and considers, in light of Scripture, how controversial issues should be decided is a comfort for fellow believers. There will always be cynics who raise questions about how sincere such candidates are in their religious declarations, but many of us are encouraged to learn that certain candidates take God seriously and look for divine guidance when making political decisions. (p. 207–8)

Demonstrating this evangelistic zeal and expectation, former Moral Majority official Cal Thomas ended an interview in the late 1990s with former Senator and 1972 Democratic presidential nominee George McGovern by asking if McGovern could offer the "confession" that "Jesus is Lord and . . . that God has raised him from the dead" (Thomas and Dobson, 1999, p. 209). Evangelicals have posed this question to many presidential candidates since Jimmy Carter, who popularized such professions of faith in his own presidential campaign.

Georgetown University professor Jacques Berlinerblau (2008) explained that another important difference between mainline and evangelical Protestants is their view of the Bible. While evangelicals often hold the Bible to be inerrant and offering literal instructions for daily living, mainline Protestants are more likely to believe the Bible could contain transcribing errors and place greater importance on considering context of the biblical accounts. As a result, Berlinerblau argued that evangelicals are more likely to hold the Bible as the sole guide for making decisions—including our nation's public policies—and stress the importance of a singular correct interpretation. Similarly, pastor and author Dave Tomlinson (2003) explained about evangelicals: "They hold to the supremacy of Scripture over all other sources of authority. . . . Evangelicals also universally believe in the actual, historical nature of events like the virgin birth, the miracles, and the death and bodily resurrection of Christ" (p. 27). Their focus on the extreme importance of understanding and following biblical commands guides how evangelicals approach politics and candidates. Richard Cizik, who was at the time a vice president for the National Association of Evangelicals that unites millions of evangelical organizations and churches, argued:

> What we're talking about is an evangelical view that you can't compartmentalize religion and civil government. If Christ is redeemer, over not just the private (the church) but the public (the state), then the state itself can be redeemed in a positive state. You cannot, to the evangelical, relegate faith to the private arena only. . . . So by our very pietistic influence, evangelicals are challenging, I would say, the biases of Western political foundation. (Suarez, 2006, p. 8)

Presidential candidates during the confessional age have responded in kind by invoking God and quoting scripture to explain and justify their public policy positions.

As evangelicals have gained numerical strength in American society, they began to use that influence to affect American politics. Significant shifts occurred within evangelical organizations that led them to take more political positions. The largest of the evangelical denominations—the Southern Baptist Convention—serves as a clear example of this politicization. In 1979, Paige Patterson and Paul Pressler began a movement to take over the SBC, which resulted in a shift rightward with the organization becoming more politically active. Three years later, the new SBC passed a resolution supporting a constitutional amendment allowing prayer in schools, which marked a significant break from the historic Baptist defense of separation of church and state. The first president elected by this new movement—Adrian Rogers—was the pastor of conservative activist Ed McAteer, who founded the Religious Roundtable and helped persuade Jerry Falwell to start the Moral Majority (Martin, 2005). Rogers publicly lobbied for school prayer legislation, which angered some SBC leaders who felt Rogers betrayed the Baptist belief in separation of church and state (Mann, 1980). With the organization's next three presidents—Bailey Smith, Jimmy Draper, and Charles Stanley—also having close ties to leaders of the new religious-political activism of the late 1970s and early 1980s, the SBC was led from 1979 to 1988 by presidents highly connected and involved with other evangelical leaders who were working to politically mobilize Christians.

Other sections of evangelicalism also developed this new political focus. For instance, in 1978 the National Association of Evangelicals "moved toward a decisive expansion of its public policy engagement . . . when it enlarged its Washington office and enlisted Rev. Robert Dugan to be its leader" (Gushee, 2008, p. 95). Evangelical professor David P. Gushee (2008) explained:

> Dugan and the NAE seized on the election of Ronald Reagan as an opportunity for an expansion of evangelical influence in Washington, and today the NAE Web site still celebrates the "unprecedented access to the White House" that the organization came to enjoy during that period. Reagan himself addressed NAE conventions in 1983 and 1984. (p. 95)

Although the NAE had been in existence for a few decades, Dugan led the group to assume a stronger political voice.

As America's religious landscape changed, evangelicals emerged as the largest religious group in the United States. When they replaced their mainline Protestant brethren, they brought with them a focus on publicly testifying about one's personal faith and relying on the Bible as the ultimate guidebook for decisions. Evangelicals maintained this rhetorical focus as they entered the political sphere with their new strength and influence. Then, along came a proudly evangelical presidential candidate—Jimmy Carter. As *Time* magazine's Amy Sullivan (2008) explained, Carter's public claims of being born-again resonated with evangelicals:

> Evangelicals, on the other hand, were delighted—and more than a little surprised—to find their faith suddenly in the national spotlight. They seized the opportunity to publicize their message. In a nationally televised evangelistic service that spring, Billy Graham observed, "Everybody is asking, 'What does it mean to be born again?'" He then explained the phrase and invited viewers to partake. Convicted Watergate conspirator Charles Colson, who had become a believer in prison, rushed out a spiritual autobiography entitled *Born Again*, and it became an instant best seller. In evangelical pulpits around the country, preachers expounded on the subject with renewed vigor. *Born-again* was working its way into the cultural vernacular. (Sullivan, 2008, p. 34–35, emphasis in original)

No wonder *Newsweek* magazine declared that year, 1976, to be "the year of the evangelical." In reality, however, it was the launch of the era of the evangelical. As evangelicals grew and gained influence, they not only changed our cultural vernacular, they also changed our nation's politics.

COURT DECISIONS

At a prayer breakfast held in conjunction with the 1984 Republican National Convention, Ronald Reagan preached on a theme that resonated with many conservative evangelicals who felt that society had negatively changed. He argued that American society used to be more open and tolerant to religion. Reagan then declared:

> [I]n the 1960s this began to change. We began to make great steps toward secularizing our nation and removing religion from its honored place. In 1962 the Supreme Court in the New York prayer case banned the compulsory saying of prayers. In 1963 the Court banned the reading of the Bible in our public schools. From that point on, the courts pushed the meaning of the ruling ever outward, so that now our children are not allowed voluntary prayer. . . . Once religion had been made vulnerable, a series of assaults were made in one court after another, on one issue after another. (Reagan, 1984p, ¶13–15)

Reagan listed other attacks on religious expressions, such as those to remove God's name from U.S. currency and the Pledge of Allegiance. In doing so, Reagan forcefully articulated many of the very issues that helped spark greater political involvement by many religious citizens. Court decisions in the 1960s and 1970s sparked outrage among many conservative evangelicals and helped spur them into the political arena.

Most significant among the changes of the 1960s and 1970s were Supreme Court decisions that many evangelicals felt removed God from society. In 1962, the Supreme Court ruled in *Engel v. Vitale* that a school-led prayer violated the establishment clause of the First Amendment. This decision was followed in 1963 with two more decisions on religion in public schools. The Court's decision that year consolidated two cases, *Abington Township School District v. Schempp* and *Murray v. Curlett*, ruling that the reading of Bible verses at the start of each school day was unconstitutional. Other Supreme Court decisions that many Christians viewed as taking God and religion out of public schools included the *Epperson v. Arkansas* decision in 1968 that struck down a ban on teaching evolution in schools, the *Wallace v. Jaffree* decision in 1986 that declared as unconstitutional a minute of silence for prayer at the start of the school day, and *Lee v. Weisman* in 1989 that dealt with religious leaders praying at graduation ceremonies. Although there had been numerous controversies surrounding these common practices that violated the spirit of the religious disestablishment efforts of individuals like Thomas Jefferson and James Madison, most were previously resolved at the local level rather than litigated up to the Supreme Court (Zimmerman, 2009). Once the Court began to enforce the legislation, many evangelicals were outraged. Historian Garry Wills (2007) explained how many evangelicals viewed such decisions: "God was swiftly being removed from places where his presence has been taken for granted all through American history. Evangelicals responded with a spontaneous indignation that was gradually organized to become a political force" (p. 481).

Evangelical leaders did indeed respond with indignation and calls for political reform. Reverend Tim LaHaye justified the prominent role religion was playing in the 1984 presidential campaign by casting it as a natural reaction to the Supreme Court decisions evangelical Christians opposed:

> I think this is all very healthy, where we have watched a pendulum swing in our country from being a nation under God and a nation that requires our public officials to swear their allegiance to America on the Bible, to where we have expelled God from public education, we've expelled prayer—we've become a secularized nation. And I think that the liberal secular humanists and secularists of our political mainstream have brought all of this on themselves. (McNeil and Lehrer, 1984, ¶42)

Pat Robertson pointed to the Supreme Court's 1962 decision on school prayer during a February 28, 1988, Republican primary debate to explain his political vision:

> Now, the second thing is that through a succession of court decisions, back to '62, we have stripped the basic ability of our children to defend themselves in moral values. We are not transmitting the moral values of our society to our young, and I want to see a time once again in America where we teach moral values, and where little children can pray once again in the public schools of America.

As Mike Huckabee emerged as a competitive candidate during the 2008 Republican presidential primary race, he voiced his opposition to attempts by the courts to stop governmental recognition of religious symbols:

> And so when there are efforts made, whether it's because of political correctness or court decisions that have run amuck where you say you can't have a Nativity scene or a menorah on capitol grounds, that's absurd. We ought to be able to welcome the discussion of faith in the public square. (Schieffer, 2007, ¶27)

As religious and political leaders mobilized evangelicals toward the ballot box, Supreme Court decisions regarding public expressions of religion became a major rallying cry and therefore the issue of potential Supreme Court nominations figured heavily in presidential endorsements. Thus, many Republican presidential candidates—illustrated in the previous chapters—strongly supported greater governmental support of religious organizations and allowing prayer in public schools.

In addition to the Supreme Court decisions on governmental recognition of religion, court decisions related to the tax-exempt status of private schools also sparked the ire of many evangelicals. Randall Balmer (2006), professor of American religious history at Columbia University, recounted a conference he attended with religious conservative leaders where Moral Majority cofounder Paul Weyrich argued that it was not abortion that mobilized the conservative religious-political movement but the IRS revoking the tax-exempt status of Bob Jones University (BJU). The 1964 Civil Rights Act included a provision whereby schools could be penalized for failing to desegregate. In 1971, the Supreme Court ruled in *Green v. Connally* that since a school was not a charitable institution, it could lose its tax-exempt status for remaining segregated. In 1976, the IRS revoked BJU's tax-exempt status. According to Balmer (2006), Weyrich blamed Jimmy Carter for the action against BJU, even though the case began prior to Carter's presidency. The case ultimately went to the Supreme Court, which ruled against BJU in 1983. Prior to the Supreme Court hearing the case, President Ronald Reagan intervened and attempted to have the case against BJU dropped. The Christian Coalition's first leader, Ralph Reed (1996), confirmed the impact of this dispute:

> The greatest spark of the movement was not abortion but an attempt by the Carter-appointed head of the Internal Revenue Service to require Christian and parochial schools and academies to prove that they were not established to preserve segregation or they would risk losing their tax-exempt status. (p. 105)

He added that "[f]or conservative evangelicals it was nothing less than a declaration of war on their schools, their churches, and their children" (p. 105). As the BJU case prompted religious leaders and citizens to switch their allegiance from Carter to Reagan in 1980, the societal impact of the civil rights movement once again indirectly helped usher in a new confessional era of politics.

Other Supreme Court decisions that provoked many evangelicals—as well as conservative Catholics—were the 1973 *Roe v. Wade* and 1973 *Doe v. Bolton* cases legalizing abortion, and other cases concerning issues of sexuality. In 1965, the Supreme Court ruled in *Griswold v. Connecticut* that bans preventing married women from buying birth control were unconstitutional, and extended the ruling to unmarried women in the 1972 case *Eisenstadt v. Baird.* Since "many evangelicals consider [birth control pills] abortifacients," many Christian pharmacists have fought for the right to refuse filling prescriptions for them (Goldberg, 2006, p. 156). Building on the privacy rights developed in the *Griswold v. Connecticut* decision, the Court's ruling in the 2003 *Lawrence and Garner v. Texas* case that struck down sodomy laws governing private sexual acts among homosexuals also angered evangelicals. This ruling helped spark nearly two dozen states over the next few years to pass state constitutional amendments banning same-sex marriage. Bruce Wilkinson, president of Walk Through the Bible Ministries, included military defense along with the issues of sexuality as representative of evangelicals' most pressing political motivations: "Evangelicals in the past have been quiet, almost like an underground. . . . I believe issues like homosexuality, abortion and military defense have become public issues and that evangelicals have decided it's time to go public too" (Briggs, 1980b, ¶14). With these issues, political and religious leaders have been able to galvanize many religious citizens on election day.

As the Supreme Court ruled against governmental expressions and support of religion, many conservative evangelical leaders began preaching against the separation of church and state. Although there had been some religious leaders offering this argument previously, they—as Hart (1977) noted—were not in the mainstream of religious or political life and thus were "political animals who stalk the American people from lairs far removed from 1600 Pennsylvania Avenue" (Hart and Pauley, 2005, p. 24). Today, however, prominent and mainstream religious leaders who attack the principle of separation often have direct presidential access and even meet with sympathetic presidents in the Oval Office to make their case. Pat Robertson called separation of church and state "a lie of the left" and Jerry Falwell said it was used to "rape the Constitution" (Dershowitz, 2007, p. 110). Robertson also argued that the phrase was not in the U.S. Constitution, but a similar version was in the constitution of the Soviet Union, which he believed proved "[p]eople in the educational establishment have attempted to impose Soviet structures on the United States" (Wallis, 1996, p. 1). Vision America founder Rick Scarborough (1999), who helped organize the Values Voter Debate during the 2008 Republican primary and helped Republican Mike Huckabee's 2008 campaign take off in Iowa, wrote in his book *In Defense of . . . Mixing Church and State* that separation of church and state is "a lie introduced by Satan and fostered by the courts" (p. 9).The intellectual descendents of those who used to "stalk" from afar have now joined the mainstream of American politics.

However, the shift among evangelical leaders on the separation of church and state has not merely been the result of new religious leadership, but a change of opinion among even the old guard. For instance, although Baptists have historically been among the staunchest of defenders of the separation principle and religious liberty, they have now become among the harshest critics—as seen from Baptists Jerry Falwell and Rick Scarborough. Ironically, Southern Baptists Jimmy Carter and Bill Clinton connected their support for the separation principle to their Baptist faith. As Carter stated regarding the Baptist denomination during his 1976 campaign, "the Baptist Church, perhaps more strongly than any other denomination, believes in complete separation of church and state" (Carter, 1978a, p. 446). Carter correctly noted the historic position of Baptists. For instance, the first Baptist in America, Roger Williams, created the first colony with true religious freedom, Rhode Island (McBeth, 1987). The U.S. Constitution's First Amendment religious freedoms are largely the result of the campaigning of influential Baptist minister John Leland (McBeth, 1987). President Thomas Jefferson penned his letter referring to a "wall of separation between church and state" to an association of Baptists. Other Baptist ministers, like Thomas Helwys and Isaac Backus, were among the strongest and earliest voices for religious liberty with their sermons and writings (McBeth, 1987). Resolutions and official statements of the Southern Baptist Convention, the largest Protestant denomination in the nation, continued to offer unwavering support for the principle until the 1980s.

W. A. Criswell, who is often considered the grandfather of the movement that led to the rightward shift in the SBC from 1979 onward, changed his opinion on separation of church and state just as the confessional period of politics was emerging. Criswell pointed to the separation principle to explain his opposition to John F. Kennedy in 1960 since the pre-Vatican II Catholic Church did not recognize the principle: "It is written in our country's constitution that church and state must be, in this nation, forever separate and free" and that "there can be no proper union of church and state" (Balmer, 2008, p. 36). However, he claimed during the Republican National Convention in 1984 that the separation principle did not exist: "I believe this notion of the separation of church and state was the figment of some infidel's imagination" (Balmer, 2008, p. 39). Meanwhile, the SBC as a body also changed its official position on separation of church and state. When the SBC revised its confession of faith in 2000 (from the 1963 version), language supporting separation policies was dropped, such as the statement, "This state has no right to impose taxes for the support of any form of religion" (Carter, 2006, p. 60). This change opened the door for the support of parochial schools and the eventual government funding of faith-based groups. *Washington Post* columnist E. J. Dionne (2008) noted:

> This is a huge historical shift. There was once a time when the separation of church and state was a cardinal commandment of Southern Baptists and nearly all evangelical Protestants. For most of these Protestants, to spend even a dime

of public money on religious schools or church programs was to assail the
Founders, destroy religious freedom, and turn God into a servant of the state.
(p. 38)

Due to this shift, Balmer (2006) asked, "Where have all the Baptists gone?"
(p. 35).

As the evangelical community—epitomized by Baptists—changed their
stance on the issue of separation of church and state, presidential candidates
responded by similarly shifting their rhetoric on this issue. Republican candidates—detailed in previous chapters— advocated policies that violate historic interpretations of the separation principle or even stopped expressing support for the principle altogether; successful Democrats, meanwhile, also
shifted rhetorically by talking more about religious freedom and why such
policies are important to religion. This rhetorical slight-of-hand has not been
unintentional. *Time* magazine's Amy Sullivan (2008) noted advice that John
Kerry's religious strategist, Mara Vanderslice, offered his campaign:

> Within a month of her arrival, Vanderslice convinced Kerry's senior advisers
> that the phrase "separation of church and state" should be stricken from the
> candidate's vocabulary. . . . What was once a resonant phrase that described a
> valuable principle had become a dodge, at least to the ears of voters. . . . When
> Kerry spoke instead about not wanting to "impose [his] articles of faith," the
> formulation assured listeners that he respected church/state separation without
> triggering the radar of skeptics. (p. 120–21)

Similarly, Georgetown University professor of Jewish civilization Jacques
Berlinerblau (2008) praised 2008 Democrats Barack Obama, Hillary Clinton,
and John Edwards for offering a "'commonsense' view of church/state separa-
ation, which differs markedly from the absolutist position that tends to char-
acterize northeastern liberals" (p. 100). He called this approach a "*rhetorical
shift to 'lite' readings of the First Amendment*" (p. 100, emphasis in original). With this rhetorical shift by presidential candidates wooing religious
voters, an important position of the contractual period has been replaced by
more sectarian discourse.

Seeking support of evangelical leaders, George H. W. Bush told the National Religious Broadcasters during the 1988 campaign that he understood
and supported their political motivation:

> Everyone in this room knows why the evangelicals returned [to politics]. You
> had no choice. . . . Now in your absence, the rights of school children to pray
> silently and voluntarily to their God was denied; and in your absence, the
> rights of unborn children were abolished; and in your absence, our children's
> textbooks became value neutral, with the historical role of religion in

American society and American history totally repudiated; and in your absence, there was a lessening of the spiritual fiber of this country, a country which was, after all, created as one nation under God. (Bush, 1987, ¶4–5)

As Bush and other presidential candidates expressed their agreement with evangelical grievances regarding Supreme Court decisions, the religious leaders offered not only their "amens," but, more importantly, their votes.

AFTERMATH OF WATERGATE AND VIETNAM

When Jimmy Carter assumed the White House, it represented the result of a significant cultural change that enabled a little-known politician to preach his way to 1600 Pennsylvania Avenue. As he testified about his born-again faith and its political impact, his revivalistic rhetoric resonated with millions of Americans who helped him unseat the incumbent President. Americans were disillusioned, cynical, and worn out from the unprecedented scandals and resignations of top American officials. It was in this void that Carter appeared. Thus, much of the attraction to Carter came from his personal morality. Televangelist Pat Robertson argued in 1974, after President Richard Nixon's foul language was exposed on Nixon's secret recordings, that the Christians who voted for Nixon were "the victims of a cruel hoax" (Heineman, 1998, p. 66). Robertson later went on to brag he had "done everything this side of breaking FCC regulations" to help elect Carter in 1976 (Balmer, 2006, p. xvi). Ron Fournier, an *Associated Press* political writer, noted, "Stoicism was the standard for generations of American politicians, many of whom kept physical and emotional troubles under wraps. . . . But Watergate and Vietnam left Americans wanting to know more about the inner workings of their leaders" (Dart, 2003, ¶20).

As the 1976 campaign neared, many Americans—particularly evangelicals—were looking for someone who could bring a renewed sense of trust and morality to our nation. For instance, Cal Thomas, who would later become the Moral Majority's vice president of communications and support Ronald Reagan in 1980, voted for Carter in 1976 because he believed Carter "to be a serious churchman, a moral man, and a breath of fresh air following the disastrous Watergate years" (Thomas and Dobson, 1999, p. 11). Ultimately, evangelicals provided Carter with his 1976 victory—and, ironically, his 1980 defeat. As *Time* magazine's Amy Sullivan explained, "Carter ended up winning nearly half of the evangelical vote—more than twice what Democrats had managed in the previous two elections—and won the presidency by 3 percentage points. Born-again Christians had provided the victory margin" (p. 37). Carter himself acknowledged during the 1976 campaign that societal changes had enabled him to find success on the campaign trail:

> No other generation in American history has ever been subjected to such a battering as this. Small wonder then that the politics of 1976 have turned out to be significantly different from years past. I doubt that four years ago or eight years ago a former Southern governor with no national reputation and no Washington experience would have been able to win the Democratic nomination for President. But this year many voters were looking for new leaders, leaders who were not associated with the mistakes of the past. (Carter, 1977, p. 139–40)

As Carter's religious rhetoric resonated with American voters in the new political landscape, it represented a substantial shift from the role religion played in presidential campaigns just a few years earlier.

The focus on Carter's personal religious faith as a measure of presidential trustworthiness and competence did not end with the 1976 campaign. Rather than being used for one cleansing election cycle in the aftermath of the failures of the Vietnam War and especially the Watergate scandal, the personal faith of candidates has continued to serve as an important barometer throughout the confessional period. In 1976 and subsequent campaigns, many evangelicals have come to expect candidates to not only be moral but to talk openly about their religion as proof of their morality. Reverend Harold Lindsell, editor of the conservative evangelical magazine *Christianity Today*, explained his opposition to Carter following the *Playboy* interview by claiming that "any analysis of a candidate running for public office must take into account his personal life and his language, as well as his gifts and abilities for occupying the office to which he aspires" (Heineman, 1998, p. 83). In 1976, Southern Baptist minister Bailey Smith declared in a speech to the pastors' conference at the Southern Baptist Convention's annual meeting that America "needs a born-again man in the White House . . . and his initials are the same as our Lord's" (Martin, 2005, p. 157). Smith, however, led the charge against "J.C." four years later as a result of Carter's policies that Smith and others did not feel reflected Christian values. Smith—who was then serving as president of the SBC—met with Carter in the White House in 1980 and declared, "We are praying, Mr. President, that you will abandon secular humanism as your religion" (Carter, 2005, p. 32). For Smith and other evangelicals, Carter went from savior to devil in just four years.

Other religious leaders also argued that our presidential candidates should offer evidence of their Christian beliefs. Famed evangelist Billy Graham endorsed political efforts of evangelicals in an interview in 1985 on Pat Robertson's *The 700 Club*:

I'm for evangelicals running for public office and winning if possible and getting control of the Congress, getting control of the bureaucracy, getting control of the executive branch of government. I think if we leave it to the other side we're going to be lost. I would like to see every true believer involved in politics in some way, shape, or form. (Rudin, 2006, p. 57)

Jerry Falwell argued that the "leadership of godly men is the best available" (Viguerie, 1981, p. 126). Televangelist Jim Bakker—who would later fall from grace during a sex and money scandal—explained in 1980, "We want to see more and more politicians in office who believe what we believe" (Mayer, 1980, ¶2). The first leader of the Christian Coalition, Ralph Reed, argued, "What Christians have to do is take back the country. . . . I honestly believe that in my lifetime we will see a country once again governed by Christians . . . and Christian values" (Dershowitz, 2007, p. 106). Beverly LaHaye, head of Concerned Women for America, offered, "America is a nation based on biblical principles. . . . Christian values dominate our government. Politicians who do not use the bible to guide their public and private lives do not belong in government" (Rudin, 2006, p. 44). Then-Arkansas Governor Mike Huckabee (1997), who later ran for the 2008 Republican presidential nomination and previously served as a Southern Baptist pastor, argued that "[o]ur country is falling apart" and thus Christians needed to "run for public office or support candidates who share [their] Christian standards" (p. 2). Prominent Southern Baptist pastor Ed Young explained his support of George W. Bush in 2000: "He talks to God. That's all I need to know" (Smith, 2006, p. 373). With these and other comments, many evangelical leaders clearly articulated their expectation that our nation's leaders not only be Christian but must demonstrate their fitness for office by testifying about their Christian beliefs.

Part of the argument offered by religious leaders for why presidential candidates should provide rhetorical proof of their Christian beliefs is the sectarian assertion that America is a Christian nation that should only be led by Christians. Pat Robertson explained, "Christians were intended by God to be the leaders" and that Jesus "came to give us a Christian country" (Wallis, 1996, p. 166). He declared that people need to realize that Jesus "is Lord of the government" and all other areas of society (Dershowitz, 2007, p. 83), and that:

The Constitution of the United State, for instance, is a marvelous document for self-government by Christian people. But the minute you turn the document into the hands of non-Christian people and atheist people, they can use it to destroy the very foundation of our society. (Wallis, 1996, p. 1)

Lou Sheldon, head of the Traditional Values Coalition, said of Christians: "We were here first. . . . We are the keepers of what is right and what is wrong" (Dershowitz, 2007, p. 105). Jerry Falwell argued that "any diligent student of American history finds that our great nation was founded by godly men upon godly principles to be a Christian nation" (Dershowitz, 2007p. 82). He also proclaimed, "We must never allow our children to forget that this is a Christian nation. We must take back what is rightfully ours" (Dershowitz, 2007, p. 106). Influential evangelical author and speaker Francis Schaeffer (1981) wrote that "the United States was founded upon a Christian consensus" and that "we today should bring Judeo-Christian principles into play in regard to government" (p. 18). As evangelical leaders urged presidential candidates to discuss their Christian beliefs, the religious leaders based this demand in their belief that America has a special relationship with God because it was founded by Christians as a Christian nation. As described in previous chapters, many successful presidential candidates—especially Ronald Reagan—explicitly developed this theme.

Due to this testimonial expectation, presidential candidates since Jimmy Carter have tried to learn how to speak to evangelicals. Religion and public policy professor William Martin (2005) argued that Ronald Reagan learned to speak the language evangelicals were looking for from a candidate, noting that although Reagan did not seem to know how to answer the question if he was "born-again" during the 1976 campaign, he had it down by 1979. After 1980 Republican hopeful Texas Governor John Connally stumbled with a question during a meeting with Christian leaders about why he should go to heaven, some of the same ministers also asked Reagan their presidential vetting question of why God should let him into heaven. According to former Congressman John Conlan of Arizona, after Reverend James Kennedy asked the question:

> Reagan dropped his eyes, looked at his feet and said, "I wouldn't give God any reason for letting me in. I'd just ask for mercy, because of what Jesus Christ did for me at Calvary." And, hey, BOOM! To a man and woman in that room, they said "Let's go!" and they went all out for him. (Martin, 2005, p. 209)

Doug Wead, whose father was an Assemblies of God minister, advised George H. W. Bush how to reach out to evangelicals as the 1988 presidential election neared. For instance, he encouraged Bush to read parts of *Mere Christianity* by C. S. Lewis and books by Francis Schaeffer so that he could understand evangelicals and refer to the books when meeting with them (Martin, 2005). Wead also coached Bush on answering the question if he was "born-again" and working in buzzwords for evangelicals in campaign messages (Martin, 2005). As a result of evangelical expectations, presidential candidates lacking the personal religious connection that Jimmy Carter brought to the campaign trail have had to learn how to open up about religion.

As Carter appeared on the national scene, he turned out to be the right man at the right hour, offering religious voters the hope they were seeking in the aftermath of the disillusionment of Vietnam and Watergate. Historian Randall Balmer (2008) argued:

> The Kennedy paradigm of indifference toward a candidate's faith, having held through the 1972 election, dissolved dramatically following the Watergate scandal and Richard Nixon's resignation. Suddenly, in the wake of the Nixon administration's culture of corruption and Nixon's manifold prevarications, a candidate's faith seemed to matter. It was a perfect opening for a Washington outsider, a Southern Baptist Sunday school teacher who offered himself as a kind of redeemer to a deeply divided nation. Indeed, given his relative obscurity as a one-term governor of Georgia, it's difficult to imagine Carter's meteoric rise to the Oval Office under any other circumstances. (p. 156)

After Carter successfully used religion to assume the presidency, other presidential candidates quickly began co-opting his religious-political strategy. Ironically, Carter was ousted four years later as many of the very same evangelicals he helped mobilize—including Pat Robertson, Cal Thomas, and Bailey Smith—turned to support Ronald Reagan, who had been granted his own political salvation at Calvary.

RELIGIOUS-POLITICAL ACTIVISM

Societal changes during the 1960s and 1970s caught the attention and ire of many evangelicals, leading many Christian citizens to become more involved in political activism. Historian Garry Wills (2007) argued, "Almost every aspect of the Rights Revolution of the 1960s was offensive to Evangelicals' values" (p. 480). He pointed to abortion, gay rights efforts, promotion of condoms, and the contraceptive pill as examples that "shocked and revolted Evangelicals" (p. 480). Liberal evangelical preacher and author Tony Campolo (2004) explained, "Evangelicals created a politically active constituency largely as a reaction to some of the things that were happening in Washington during the 1970s" (p. 21). These changes were perhaps best reflected in the attitudes of Pat Robertson and Jerry Falwell. Robertson cited his calling as a minister for why he refused to campaign for his own father's U.S. Senate reelection in 1966; but just two decades later he ran for president himself and founded the Christian Coalition to affect political elections according to his religious calling and convictions (Martin, 2005). Falwell preached against political involvement during the civil rights movement in 1965; but by 1979 he began the Moral Majority to encourage ministers to become politically involved (Martin, 2005). Although they remain the best known of the religious-political organizations, the Moral Majority and the Christian Coalition were merely part of the overall evangelical infrastructure built to affect politics.

In the early 1960s, U.S. Presbyterian minister Francis Schaeffer relocated to the Swiss Alps to found the L'Abri community. Over the next two decades, evangelicals from the United States and other nations would flock to L'Abri to study under Schaeffer and learn about political engagement. President Gerald Ford's son, who studied for the ministry at an evangelical seminary, was among those who spent time at Schaeffer's L'Abri (Shires, 2007). Richard Land (2007), head of the Southern Baptist Convention's Ethics & Religious Liberty Commission, credited Schaeffer with helping abortion become a significant political issue:

> What happened in the period between *Roe v. Wade* and 1980 that contributed to the Republican Party's revitalization? One of the things that happened was that an odd-looking little man named Francis Schaeffer began writing and speaking against abortion-on-demand. He became arguably the most influential conservative, religious activist of the modern era. He wielded enormous influence in getting Evangelical Christians involved in the political system, especially in response to *Roe v. Wade*. (p. 8)

Land argued that the abortion issue "was reaching critical mass in the period between 1976 and 1980" and that the Republican Party's adoption of a pro-life platform helped the Party recover from the Watergate scandal (p. 8).

Various Christian media organizations were created that helped promote the religious and political messages of evangelicals who no longer needed to work through traditional media channels. In 1961, Pat Robertson began his CBN radio and television programs that would eventually turn into a media empire. In 1973, Trinity Broadcasting Network (TBN) launched, which would eventually beam religious programming around the nation and world twenty-four hours a day. The program "PTL Club," which was started by Jim and Tammy Faye Bakker, began in 1974. These broadcasters exercised political influence since the mid-1970s through their programming, along with the National Religious Broadcasters meetings at which several presidential candidates have spoken, including Gerald Ford, Jimmy Carter, Ronald Reagan, and George H. W. Bush.

In 1970, Hal Lindsey's book *The Late Great Planet Earth* was published and became the best-selling nonfiction book of the decade (Boyer, 2005). This book, along with the 1972 film *A Thief in the Night*, helped popularize the end-times theology that focused on an apocalyptic end of the world. Additional books and films over the next three decades continued to provoke interest in end-times theology, such as the immensely popular *Left Behind* books and *The Omega Code* movie. Adding to the end-times emphasis among many conservative evangelicals and fundamentalists is the strong political support given to the nation of Israel, which plays a central role in end-times theology. In addition to writings supporting Israel and demanding that the United States always support Israel and not ask Israel to trade land for peace, Christians have also started organizations to promote this particular political position. Jerry Falwell received a Lear jet from Israel in 1979—the same year he cofounded the Moral Majority (Cohn-Sherbok, 2006). The following year he became the first non-Jew to receive The Vladimir Ze'ev Jabotinsky medal for Zionist excellence from Israel's Prime Minister (Cohn-Sherbok, 2006). When Israel's Prime Minister Menahem Begin bombed an Iraqi nuclear plant in 1981, he first called Falwell to inform him of this action even before he contacted President Ronald Reagan (Cohn-Sherbok, 2006). Rabbi Dan Cohn-Sherbok (2006), a professor of Judaism at the University of Wales, Lampeter, linked the rise of Zionist politics with other religious changes occurring in the mid-1970s:

> With the American bicentennial in 1976, a number of trends converged on the American scene. First, fundamentalist and evangelical churches became the fastest growing sector of American Christianity while mainstream Protestant and Roman Catholic movements saw a decline in their numbers. Second, Jimmy Carter, an evangelical from the Bible Belt, became president of the United States, thereby giving increased legitimacy to the evangelical movement. Third, Israel gained a larger share of the US foreign and military budgets, thereby becoming a pillar of the US strategic alliance against the Soviet bloc. Fourth, as support for Israel increased in the evangelical sphere, Roman Catholic and Protestant denominations began to develop a more balanced approach to the Middle East. . . . Finally, the election of Menahem Begin as Prime Minister of Israel evoked a positive response from the American Christian right. (p. 165)

As seen in the presidential candidates' religious-political rhetoric in previous chapters, Israel has attention in religious terms. With such arguments, successful candidates of both parties addressed an issue that is close to the heart of evangelicals—and that evangelicals claim is close to the heart of God.

Beginning in the 1970s, numerous religious-political groups were organized to influence American society. Phyllis Schlafly, a Catholic, started Eagle Forum in 1972 primarily to lead efforts against the Equal Rights Amendment (Gushee, 2008). Schlafly and her organization continue even today to push the conservative position on issues of sexuality, family and taxes as well as fighting for educational and judicial changes. Historian Garry Wills (2007) noted "the Equal Rights Amendment, passed by Congress in 1972, was never ratified by the states—thanks largely to an effective lobbying effort against it by the antifeminist Catholic leader Phyllis Schlafly" (p. 472). Although Schlafly had gained attention within the Republican Party during the 1960s—most notably for her 1964 book, *A Choice, Not an Echo*, which would serve as a slogan for eventual Republican nominee Barry Goldwater—it was her creation of the Eagle Forum that began her religious-political activism.

Over the next two decades, numerous religious-political organizations were created to fight for codifying the religious agenda of conservative evangelicals. With this growing infrastructure, evangelicals were able to exert considerable political influence in presidential campaigns. The most significant and visible of these new religious-political organizations was Reverend Jerry Falwell's Moral Majority. In May of 1979, Paul Weyrich, Howard Philips, Ed McAteer, and Robert Billings met with Jerry Falwell to convince him that he should start the organization that became the Moral Majority (Martin, 2005). During the first two years, Falwell claimed the organization had four million members and a chapter in each state (Sullivan, 2008). During the 1980 campaign, Moral Majority leaders hosted rallies in churches—often avoiding media attention—where they urged ministers to be involved in politics and passed out pamphlets entitled "Ronald Reagan: A Man of Faith" (Evans and Novak, 1981). The flier laid out Reagan's pro-life and pro-family positions and quoted him arguing, "The time has come to turn to God and reassert our trust in Him for the healing of America" (Evans and Novak, 1981, p. 208).

Among the other notable religious-political activist organizations founded in the late 1970s and early 1980s were businessman Ed McAteer's Religious Roundtable to bring Christian leaders together for dialogue and planning meetings four times a year (Viguerie, 1981); Michael Farris's Home School Legal Defense Association to advocate for the right to homeschool, which later led to the creation of Patrick Henry College in Virginia that provided many White House interns for George W. Bush's administration and helped launch the Joshua Generation initiative that sent homsechooled teenagers as campaign volunteers for Bush in 2004 (Goldberg, 2006) and Mike Huckabee in 2008; James Dobson's Family Research Council—first led by later Republican presidential candidate Gary Bauer—to focus on political issues and activism instead of the more religious agenda of Dobson's Focus on the Family organization (Goldberg, 2006); Don Wildmon's American Family Association that led numerous boycotts targeting advertisers in pornographic magazines and television shows deemed immoral (Gushee, 2008); Reverend Robert Grant's Christian Voice, whose political activities included launching a "Christian for Reagan" get-out-the-vote effort during the 1980 presidential campaign, (Mintz, 1980), and sponsoring ads attacking Jimmy Carter for supporting homosexual rights (Koza, 1980); Reverend Louis Sheldon's Traditional Values Coalition to get churches and church leaders involved with supporting its political agenda on items of sexuality, life, and patriotism (Gushee, 2008); televangelist Pat Robertson's Freedom Council in 1980 to build a grassroots network focused on changing the nation for God, which—along with the audience of his TV program *The 700 Club*—would serve as a base for his 1988 presidential run (Reed, 1996); and Reverend Tim LaHaye's Council for National Policy (CNP), a secret organization "where U.S. conservative politicians, financiers, and religious leaders meet to discuss policy and funding for Religious Right projects" (Garrison, 2006, p. 76) and often hear speeches from Republican presidential candidates like George W. Bush before the 2000 campaign and Mitt Romney and Fred Thompson before the 2008 campaign. These organizations were among the most influential of dozens of others that created an important religious-political infrastructure during the 1970s and 1980s.

An especially important moment for the new religious-political movement was the 1980 National Affairs Briefing—a meeting of evangelists hosted by the Religious Roundtable at which Ronald Reagan spoke. Reverend James Robison, a televangelist influential in putting the meeting together, declared, "We are holding up a standard and trusting that the whole nation will adhere to it—that our politicians will follow the standard of God rather than the ways of the world" (Herbaugh, 1980, ¶10). He also proclaimed, "Not voting is a sin against almighty God!" (Sawyer, 1980, ¶4). Also speaking at the National Affairs Briefing were Phyllis Schlafly, Jerry Falwell, Pat Robertson, and Tim LaHaye (Martin, 2005). Robison later took credit for giving Ronald Reagan the line about how the group could not endorse him but that he endorsed them (Martin, 2005). Mike Huckabee, who later ran for the 2008 Republican presidential nomination, worked for Robison at the time and assisted with organizing the event (Kantor and Kirkpatrick, 2007). Robison would emerge twenty years later as the evangelist that George W. Bush told prior to running for president: "God wants me to do this, and I must do it" (Gaddy, 2005, p. 45). Reagan's appearance at the 1980 meeting granted him enthusiastic support from many within the evangelical community. In an attempt to recreate the success of the 1980 National Affairs Briefing meeting, the Religious Roundtable hosted another National Affairs Meeting in 1992 just days after the 1992 Republican National Convention. In addition to George H. W. Bush, other speakers included Jerry Falwell, the Eagle Forum's Phyllis Schlaffly, the Southern Baptist Convention's Richard Land, Reverend Tim LaHaye, the Family Research Council's Gary Bauer, the American Family Association's Donald Wildmon, and prominent Southern Baptist ministers W. A. Criswell and Adrian Rogers (Wood, 1992).

In the 1960s and 1970s, an evangelical left movement emerged with publications like *The Other Side* in 1965 and *The Post-American* (now called *Sojourners*) in 1971 (Gushee, 2008). The latter, founded by Jim Wallis, became part of a larger organization that included the establishment of an intercity residence and ministry in Washington, D.C., in 1975 (Gushee, 2008). In 1973, younger and more liberal evangelicals released the Chicago Declaration to offer their perspective on critical sociopolitical issues like racism, poverty, and war. Liberal evangelical preacher and author Tony Campolo (2004), who would later serve as one of President Bill Clinton's spiritual advisors in the aftermath of Clinton's Monica Lewinsky sex scandal, pointed out that "[s]ome of those who signed this declaration were the beginning of what might be called 'the evangelical left'" (p. 203). One of the signers, Ron Sider, later remarked about the document, "We wanted to get evangelicals politically engaged. . . . We never expected that the Moral Majority would be the result" (Sullivan, 2008, p. 16). In 1978, Sider founded Evangelicals for Social Action (ESA) to work toward the principles laid out in the Declaration. ESA, which generally works with liberal causes and organizations, adopted a pro-life position (Campolo, 1995). Although not nearly as large or influential as their conservative counterparts, liberal evangelicals have continued to offer their voice in presidential politics. For instance, a primary leader of the liberal evangelical movement has been Jim Wallis of *Sojourners*. Christian ethics professor David P. Gushee (2008) observed that Wallis has been "in demand as a speaker at Democratic Party consultations and events" since his 2005 book *God's Politics* and Gushee accused Wallis of acting more like a "political strategist" trying to "help the Democrats learn to speak the language of faith" (p. 84). In addition to leading sessions for Democratic politicians on how to speak the language of faith, Wallis also delivered the Democratic response to one of President George W. Bush's weekly radio addresses in 2006.

Additional religious-political groups continued to arise even after the late 1970s and early 1980s. Most significant of these was the Christian Coalition, founded in 1989, to mobilize the network Pat Robertson created during his 1988 Republican presidential run and to fill the void left by the recent disbandment of the Moral Majority. Robertson selected a young Republican activist, Ralph Reed, as the organization's first executive director. By mid-1992, the organization had a budget of more than $10 million, included over 350,000 members, and its members made up nearly 40 percent of the delegates at the 1992 Republican National Convention (Kuo, 2006). Goldberg (2006) explained:

> The Christian Coalition's grassroots, under-the-radar strategy was hugely effective, so that by 1992 religious activists had more influence in writing the GOP's platform than the party's presidential candidate, George H. W. Bush. Nearly half of the delegates at the 1992 party convention were evangelical Christians, and despite Bush's objections, they succeeded in getting a plank in the platform calling for a constitutional amendment to ban abortion without exception. (Goldberg, 2006, p. 15)

The 1992 Republican National Convention included appearances by Christian Coalition founder Pat Robertson, Southern Baptist Convention President Ed Young, Reverend James Kennedy, National Association of Evangelicals President Don Argue, and Reverend E. V. Hill, while Reverend Jerry Falwell sat with Vice President Dan Quayle (Wood, 1992). Later campaigns have seen similar political efforts by religious leaders and their religious-political organizations.

As the religious-political groups developed and grew, many presidential candidates began seeking their support. For instance, after Republican nominee Bob Dole received criticism from Christian Coalition leaders, he quickly changed his campaign plans so he could address their annual meeting. Muir (1992) noted the impact of Reagan's addresses to meetings of religious groups, such as the National Affairs Briefing with evangelists during the 1980 campaign:

> They were galvanized by the president's words and thrust themselves into the debate raging within the religious community. They took his ideas into the discourse of the ministry. . . . When the clergy went home to their congregations and the broadcasters returned to their studios, their memory of the president, dealing with the theological and social problems at the center of their ministry, must have reinvigorated them. And with that extra vigor these communicators, these counselors to others, these *verbal* men and women, spread the president's words. (p. 145, emphasis in original)

Less than three months later, Reagan became the fortieth president of the United States. Other candidates have also sought political salvation from religious-political groups, such as the National Religious Broadcasters, the National Association of Evangelicals, the Christian Coalition, the Southern Baptist Convention, and the National Baptist Convention, USA. With each appearance, our presidential candidates demonstrated the political power of our nation's religious leaders, who had become the new "king makers" in the confessional era.

SUMMARY

During the 1960s, 1970s, and 1980s, American society underwent significant changes that helped usher in a religious-political period. During this time, many Americans were overcome with feelings of disillusionment and cynicism. It was in this void that Jimmy Carter emerged promising to never lie to the American people and talking about his born-again beliefs. With evangelicals rising amidst other societal changes, Carter arrived on the scene as the right man at the right moment. However, American society was still in transition and Carter would find himself swept out of office four years later—in large part as former evangelical supporters campaigned against him. Although Carter lost ten points nationwide in 1980 from his showing four years earlier, he lost eighteen points in the counties with the highest Baptist population (Dionne, 2008). Having jettisoned Carter, evangelicals threw their full support behind Reagan. Although key issues like abortion saw little progress, he made important policy gestures like arguing for Bob Jones University to maintain its tax-exempt status and pushing for a failed school prayer amendment in 1984. Perhaps more importantly, he offered presidential access to Jerry Falwell and other evangelical leaders, and addressed religious meetings with language that clearly resonated with their members' religious-political concerns.

After several galvanizing Supreme Court decisions in the 1960s and 1970s and the disillusionment following Watergate and Vietnam, many evangelicals began looking for political redemption. Coupled with their new level of cultural influence and a growing relationship with Catholics, white evangelical leaders looked to the civil rights movement for inspiration as they began political organizations and increased their political activism. As evangelicals gained media attention and political influence, presidential candidates began looking for ways to speak the language of this newly influential voting bloc. With evangelicals now the largest religious group in the nation, their rhetorical expectations—which included publicly testifying about one's religious beliefs—began to influence how our would-be leaders discussed their personal faith and issues of religion.

With this new religious-political approach, religious leaders have argued that religion should be used to support partisan public policy decisions and that politics should become sectarian. For instance, when asked just after the 2004 election why he thought it was the Christian duty to support Bush for reelection, Jerry Falwell responded by listing the Christian issues he believed God supported: "I don't vote Republican. I vote Christian. And I believe that [God] is pro-life, pro-family, pro-Israel, strong national defense, faith-based initiatives for the poor, et cetera" (Garrison, 2006, p. 71).Offering a similar partisan message, Richard Land, president of the Southern Baptist Convention's Ethics & Religious Liberty Commission, argued:

> God has a side when it comes to the sanctity of all human life from conception to natural death and everywhere in between. God is pro-life. And God has a side when it comes to society trying to redefine His institution, holy matrimony, to be something other than marriage between one man and one woman for life. (Johnson, 2008)

Far from a distant or uninterested God, today's politically influential religious leaders argue that God supports their policies.

The old civil-religious contract fell apart as American society changed and a new confessional style of presidential politics emerged. John F. Kennedy's model of separation and privatized faith would no longer be successful as it has now been replaced by the confessional rhetoric characterized by George W. Bush, Ronald Reagan, and Jimmy Carter. Gary Bauer, former head of the Family Research Council and an unsuccessful Republican presidential candidate in 2000, explained:

> When John F. Kennedy made his famous speech that the Vatican would not tell him what to do, evangelicals and Southern Baptists breathed a sigh of relief. . . . But today evangelicals and Southern Baptists are hoping that the Vatican *will* tell Catholic politicians what to do. (Page, 2004, p. 2A, emphasis in original)

As evangelicals shifted their positions, they changed society and thus the expectations placed upon presidential candidates. Not surprisingly, then, our presidential candidates now utilize religious rhetoric frequently and explicitly, especially when addressing religious audiences.

Although Hart (2002) argued that "[h]eads continue to roll in the United States when . . . preachers [become] too ideological" (p. 137), today the heads roll when our presidential candidates do not submit to the ideological preachers. In this confessional era of politics that evangelical religious leaders helped shape, evangelical candidates—or those familiar and comfortable with the evangelical approach of offering public professions of faith—gain a considerable political advantage over their opponents. Jimmy Carter's press secretary Jody Powell—also a Southern Baptist—argued that it was Carter's religious appeals that attracted voters in 1976 looking for a politician they could trust:

> For a lot of people . . . the idea that this was a man of religious faith gave them some measure of hope that he meant what he said, that he would do what he said, that he would abide by the law, that he would behave in a way that was moral and decent and just. That is one of the things religion is supposed to do for us. (Martin, 2005, p. 148)

Today, this confessional style continues to dominant presidential discourse. As Ted Olsen of the evangelical *Christianity Today* declared in 1999 after religious declarations by candidates George W. Bush and Al Gore, it seemed the two were attempting to "out Jimmy Carter each other" (Flint and Porter, 2005, p. 48). These changes in American society are not merely background or context for the rise of the confessional political style—they explain why such style has arisen and come to dominate American presidential elections. With the rhetorical expectations placed on candidates by our nation's largest religious voting bloc—and the electoral advantage granted by those who pass this rhetorical religious test—the nature of presidential campaign rhetoric has significantly shifted as American society has changed. Since the civil-religious contract has now been replaced by a confessional political system, the impact of this transformation on American democracy must be considered. It is this question that the next chapter explores.

Chapter Seven

Implications from the Confessional Booth

During a June 4, 2007, Democratic forum sponsored by CNN and the liberal evangelical group Sojourners, candidates Barack Obama, Hillary Clinton, and John Edwards were grilled about their religious faith and its political implications. At one point, CNN's moderator, Soledad O'Brien, asked Edwards:

> Senator, I'm going to have you sit while I ask you another question, if you don't mind. Thank you. And while this is not exactly a confessional, there are a whole bunch of people out there—we certainly have enough clergy here—so I'll ask you this. . . . What is the biggest sin you've ever committed?

Edwards jokingly responded, "Just between you and me?" He then added:

> I'd have a very hard time telling you one thing, one specific sin. . . . I sin every single day. We are all sinners. We all fall short, which is why we have to ask for forgiveness from the Lord. I can't—to try to identify one particular sin that was worse or more extreme than the others, the list is too long.

As clergy and the American people watched, Edwards confessed his sinful nature in hope that they would offer him political absolution and view him as a pious and worthy leader. After dropping out of the presidential race, Edwards would admit to having an affair. The other Democratic candidates joined him in baring their souls during the forum. Also in the same campaign, Republican Mitt Romney offered what he called "a confession of my faith" during his much anticipated speech on "Faith in America" in which he addressed questions about his Mormon faith (Romney, 2007, ¶25). Romney confessed, "I believe that Jesus Christ is the son of God and the savior of mankind" (Romney, 2007, ¶28).

Throughout the confessional political era, candidates have offered American citizens the opportunity to stand in judgment of not only their political philosophies and policy positions but also the would-be leaders' religiosity. After all, Jimmy Carter famously confessed to *Playboy* magazine during the 1976 campaign that he had lusted in his heart after women: "I've looked on a lot of women with lust. I've committed adultery in my heart many times. This is something that God recognizes that I will do—and I have done it—and God forgives me for it" (Carter, 1978b, p. 964). Although Carter received widespread criticism for the interview, it was because of the actual venue and not his confession. Even Carter acknowledged this point during his October 22, 1976, debate with Gerald Ford: "If I should ever decide in the future to discuss my—my deep Christian beliefs and uh—condemnation and sinfulness, I'll use another forum besides *Playboy*." In the confessional era, candidates are now expected to discuss private religious matters and confess their sins, but clearly not in an interview with a publication deemed morally inappropriate by evangelicals.

Other candidates have also offered public confessions of their sins and explained their private faith since Carter's confessions. During the 1984 campaign, Reverend Jesse Jackson quoted scripture while apologizing for using the anti-Semitic slur "hymie": "Christ said let he who is without sin cast the first stone, and no one moved, because everyone makes mistakes" (Sullivan, 1984, ¶12). George W. Bush lost the 2000 Michigan primary to John McCain following repeated attacks on Bush for speaking at the anti-Catholic Bob Jones University. Afterward, Bush wrote a letter—publicly released by his campaign—to New York Cardinal John O'Connor confessing his error, "On reflection, I should have been more clear in disassociating myself from anti-Catholic sentiments and racial prejudice. It was a missed opportunity causing needless offense, which I deeply regret" (Kuo, 2006, p. 130). Barack Obama in 2008 confessed to Diane Sawyer on *Good Morning America*, "I say a little prayer at night for my family's safety, forgive me my screw ups, and then to ask that I'm an instrument of his work" (Sawyer, 2008, ¶16). With such statements, today's presidential candidates feel compelled to publicly confess their sins before God—and the nation—in hopes of finding political salvation in the confessional voting booth.

As the religious-political landscape changed over the last half of the twentieth century—detailed in the previous chapter—the shift brought new demands upon presidential hopefuls. Our presidential candidates responded to such exigencies by putting aside the outdated expectations of the civil-religious contract and instead offering religious-political rhetoric that is testimonial, partisan, sectarian, and liturgical in nature. Such a dramatic shift in the religious-political rhetoric of presidential candidates raises questions about the potential impact of such discourse on American democracy. Despite the U.S. Constitution's prohibition of religious tests for office, a rhetorical religious test has been applied to our presidential candidates during the confessional era. These rhetorical expectations and constraints affect the electoral process and, particularly, who is considered to be a viable candidate since one's faith and religious beliefs are used to determine fitness for holding public office. Although confession may be good for the soul, is it good for democracy? This chapter first describes our confessional society, next considers and reworks Michel Foucault's work on the confession, and, finally, critiques our current confessional political system.

CONFESSIONAL SOCIETY

Each weekday, millions of Americans turn on their television sets to watch celebrities and other individuals enter the public confessional. On various talk shows and other television programs, individuals bare their souls and confess their transgressions for all to hear. Perhaps none of the celluloid priests has developed such a confessional focus and following as well as Oprah Winfrey. Marcia Nelson (2005), author of *The Gospel According to Oprah*, pointed out, "Confession is the show's signature" (p. x). Nelson, who compared Oprah's approach of listening to her guests to the Catholic sacrament of confession, added, "Just as [Oprah] encourages confession from others, she is willing to engage in it herself. She has talked about being abused as a child, and her ongoing battle with weight amounts to a running story line on the show" (p. xiii). Nelson also noted that Oprah's magazine, *O*, frequently includes quotations about the healing nature of confession and articles explaining how confessing helps individuals overcome life's struggles. With other TV talk show hosts like Dr. Phil, Montel Williams, Ellen DeGeneres, Larry King, and Jon Stewart all urging their guests to open up about private and intimate parts of their lives, it seems that the television set has nearly replaced the church as the confessional booth of choice.

A 2008 television show on Fox, *The Moment of Truth*, featured contestants answering questions about their lives and personal thoughts before their family and friends—as well as the studio audience and millions watching at home. Their innermost revelations are subjected to a lie detector test with the contestant winning money only if they tell the truth. For instance, contestants have been asked if they ever cheated on their spouse, if they were attracted to one of their spouse's sisters, and if they had stolen from the family business—all of which received answers in the affirmative. In their quest for money, the contestants publicly confessed their transgressions—and in the process of gaining television fame and fortune risked ruining relationships with their spouses, family, and friends. An editorial in the evangelical magazine *Christianity Today* compared the "public confessional" show's studio audience, who started booing when a contestant did not answer a potentially embarrassing question, to "the bloodthirsty crowds in *Gladiator*, who jeered fighters who would not kill" (Hertz, 2008, ¶4). Americans have come to expect those in the public spotlight to confess their innermost secrets.

Robert Thompson, director of the Center for the Study of Popular Television at Syracuse University, argued that as a result of societal changes over the last several decades "we have been moving to becoming a highly confessional culture" (Leonard, 2006, ¶18). Today, Americans not only watch public confessionals on their television sets, but even join in confessing online with the use of blogs and social networking websites. Americans now pour their hearts out and post their intimate secrets for all to read. For example, Frank Warren created the Post Secret website (www.postsecret.com) encouraging people to send postcards confessing their deepest secret, which are then posted on the website. The project quickly caught on with more than one million online visitors a week and about 1,000 postcards received each week, leading to the publication of a book containing many of the most salacious confessions (Rutowski, 2007). With the Internet now democratizing the classic Catholic sacrament, individuals have the opportunity to create their own e-confessional booth. One can listen in on others' confessions and even offer one's own judgment. From high ratings for television shows to the growth of blogs and social networking websites, Americans have come to desire and even demand public confessions.

The Catholic Church, no less, has attempted to accommodate our society's increasingly public confessional tastes. The formal sacrament of confession declined in use among American Catholics during the last half of the twentieth century, often blamed on a theological shift from Vatican II (Alter, 2007). However, some Catholic priests have noticed a revival for confession following the Church's public relations campaign using radio ads and billboards stressing the importance of confession, with the ads focusing on the therapeutic aspect of confession—now known officially as the sacrament of reconciliation—instead of the punitive side (Alter, 2007). Many parishes also hold special communal reconciliation services where there is a public prayer service followed by private confessions to the priest, with such services often drawing many more parishioners than would normally come for private confession (Marchocki, 2007). As Michele M. Dillon, sociology professor at University of New Hampshire, explained, "One way the church has made the sacrament more palatable to some people is having some sort of community ritual of confession" (Marchocki, 2007, ¶34). Some priests have found success from hearing private confessions in public locations like shopping malls or taking confessions for twenty-four straight hours (Alter, 2007). Although still keeping the moment of confession private, these popular actions have added a more public element to the rite.

It is not just the Catholic Church catering to the confessional expectations of society, but also our presidential candidates as they enter the public confessional booths of TV shows like those hosted by Oprah, Larry King, or Jon Stewart. This trend particularly developed after Bill Clinton's highly publicized appearance during the 1992 campaign on *The Arsenio Hall Show*, as well as his highly confessional video, "The Man from Hope," shown at the Democratic National Convention in which Clinton revealed that his alcoholic stepfather beat his mother and also discussed his own marital problems. During the 2000 campaign, for instance, both George W. Bush and Al Gore appeared on Oprah's show. Oprah asked Bush to "[t]ell us about a time when you needed forgiveness" and then interrupted his generic response with "I'm looking for specifics" (Bush gets personal, 2000, ¶6). As our candidates seek electoral support, they willingly sit on Oprah's couch to discuss their private lives. Keith Hearit, a communication professor at Western Michigan University, argued that the public's desire for knowing the intimate details of a politician's life is "driven by the Oprahization of our contemporary culture. It's a confessional culture" (Booth, 2002, ¶11). Stanley Renshon, political scientist and psychoanalyst at City University of New York, offered, "It's absolutely a product of our times, a product of a therapeutic bent in our culture, and a product of people wanting to get a sense of who the person really is that we put into the White House" (Dart, 2003, ¶17). Today, the path to the White House seems to include mandatory visits with the high priests and priestesses of TV, with candidates revealing all in exchange for votes.

As our society demands presidential candidates confess the details of their private lives—including their religious beliefs and spiritual practices—such expectations drastically change the nature of presidential campaign communication. Today's religious confessional expectations—arising as a result of the religious-political shifts discussed in chapter 6—have clearly moved presidential candidates away from the civil-religious contract to the confessional style of politics detailed in chapter 5. Our presidential candidates have abandoned John F. Kennedy's model of private religious-political discourse, which affects the political chances of potential presidential candidates and affects our overall democratic process. Is this confessional style of politics healthy or appropriate for our candidates, democratic ideals, or religious faiths? To answer these important questions, Michel Foucault's work on the Catholic confession will be utilized.

FOUCAULT'S CONFESSION

French philosopher Michel Foucault provides a critical theoretical foundation with his work on the Catholic confession and sexuality that can be used
to consider the impact of our presidential candidates' confessional political
style in today's confessional society. Foucault developed the concept of pastoral power where the political leader serves as the shepherd of the people, or
flock, rather than ruling as the king. In this role the leader is expected to
protect, direct, and nurture the people under their care. Such leadership
creates a "form of power which does not look after just the whole community, but each individual in particular, during his entire life" (Foucault, 1983,
p. 214). Foucault developed this notion of political power in contrast to the
king's style of enforcing decrees and killing foes. The people are expected to
fully rely on the leader's guidance because only the shepherd-leader can truly
lead them to salvation. In fact, failure to follow the leader's guidance places
one's spiritual well-being in danger.

Foucault (1999) argued that the development of the pastoral model of
power was "a very important phenomenon" (p. 122) as societies moved from
sovereignty—rule of the monarch—to governmentality—a totalizing rule of
the government characterized by surveillance and through citizens internalizing power. He added that prior to the rise of this Christian idea, "Politicians
had never been defined in Greek and Roman literature as pastors or shep-
herds" (p. 122), particularly noting the silence on this theme in political
writings from Greek and Roman philosophers. Foucault (1983) claimed:

> It has often been said that Christianity brought into being a code of ethics
> fundamentally different from that of the ancient world. Less emphasis is usual-
> ly placed on the fact that it proposed and spread new power relations through-
> out the ancient world. (p. 214)

With the new political ideas introduced through Christianity, Foucault offered a more democratic form of power where control is internalized into the
thoughts and bodies of the people. This new "bio-power" worked to both
control people's individual bodies and behaviors, as well as control the population in general.

With pastoral power comes the notion of a self-sacrificial leadership
where the shepherd-leader acts in the best interest of the people, which is
only possible through an intimate knowledge of the people. Foucault (1983)
therefore locates the power of this relationship in the confession, arguing that
pastoral power "cannot be exercised without knowing the inside of people's
minds, without exploring their soul, without making them reveal their innermost secrets. It implies a knowledge of the conscience and an ability to direct
it" (p. 214). In order to lead as a shepherd, the pastor "must know, certainly,

everything that his sheep do, everything done by the flock and by each member of the flock at each moment" and "he must also know . . . what goes on inside the soul, the heart, the most profound secrets of the individual" (Foucault, 1999, p. 125). Thus, Foucault (1999) insisted, "The Christian must confess without cease everything that occurs within himself to someone who will be charged to direct his conscience" (p. 125). As a result, Foucault (1999) argued that "the pastorate brought with it an entire series of techniques and procedures concerned with the truth and the production of truth" (p. 125). For Foucault, the confession remained essential to the pastoral style of political leadership.

Due to the importance of the confession, pastoral power forced citizens to submit to the shepherd-leader's authority through confessing. Foucault (1999) explained, "This knowledge of the interior of individuals is absolutely required for the practice of the Christian pastorate" (p. 125). He added that with this approach, "the Christian will be obliged to tell his pastor everything that occurs in the secrets of his soul" as part of an "exhaustive and permanent confession" (p. 125). As a result, Foucault explained how the confession was used to force individuals to submit to the pastor. Foucault (1999) argued, "The power of the pastor consists precisely in that he has the authority to require the people to do everything necessary for their salvation: obligatory salvation" (p. 124). But, he added, to seek this "obligatory salvation" requires that "one accepts the authority of another" as one "will have to be able to be known by the pastor" (p. 124). In essence, the individual allows the confessor to know and judge every aspect of the individual's life.

As a form of disciplinary power, the confession created and represented another way of the internalization of discipline. Since it is important for an individual to report all of their sins, the individual is required to police and report on themselves. The confession provides a reminder that one is constantly being watched (by God through the Church) and thus one need not only recognize their failings but attempt to eliminate shortcomings.

Rather than freeing the individual, the confession actually created new ways for control and surveillance. Foucault (1990) argued that the "internal ruse of confession" is the idea that "[c]onfession frees" when in fact "truth is not by nature free—nor error servile—but that its production is thoroughly imbued with relations of power" (p. 60). After all, Foucault believed that an individual could not escape from power but merely move from one realm of power to another. Dreyfus and Rabinow (1983) explained that Foucault argued the confession was "a central component in the expanding technologies for the discipline and control of bodies, populations, and society itself" (p. 174). Thus, although confession was said to be a way for an individual "to know himself" it actually presented a way for the surveillance and discipline of the individual:

> The cultural desire to know the truth about oneself prompts the telling of truth; in confession after confession to oneself and others, this *mise en discours* has placed the individual in a network of relations of power with those who claim to be able to extract the truth of these confessions through their possession of the keys to interpretation. (Dreyfus and Rabinow, 1983, p. 174, emphasis in original)

Dreyfus and Rabinow added that through confession "the most particular individual pleasures, the very stirrings of the soul could be solicited, known, measured, and regulated" (p. 176).

Additionally, Foucault (1990) argued that this power of the confession works to control and normalize sexuality. He pointed out, for example, that prior to the changes he was exploring in the eighteenth and nineteenth centuries there was no such thing as the homosexual. Instead, this classification was discursively created in order to define certain behaviors as outside the normal or acceptable boundaries. Foucault explained that although there had been sodomy (the act), society—guided by the church during a time when church and government leaders were closely aligned—now created the concept of the homosexual (the person). One's sexual acts thus shaped one's identity, leading Foucault to also argue that this period led to the creation of sexuality (or a sexual identity). This creation becomes much more than a semantic issue because, with his belief that power/knowledge are inseparable, Foucault argued that once a person is inherently defined as aberrant this allows for more severe punishment than would be used for someone who merely committed an aberrant act.

For Foucault, the confession represented Christianity as he called Christianity "a confessional religion" (Carrette, 2000, p. 27) and even claimed "Christianity is a confession" (Foucault, 1999, p. 182). Foucault (1999) explained that there are two aspects of Christianity as confession. First, "there is the obligation to hold as truth a set of propositions which constitute dogma, the obligation to hold certain books as a permanent source of truth, obligations to hold certain authorities in matters of truth" (p. 182). This proclamation that one believes what the Church considers truth could be called the confession of faith. The second type of confession is confessing one's sin and inner self:

> Everyone in Christianity has the duty to explore who he is, what is happening within himself, the faults he may have committed, the temptations to which he is exposed. Moreover, everyone is obliged to tell these things to other people, and hence to bear witness against himself. (pp. 182–83)

Foucault argued that these two types of confession—"those regarding the faith, the book, the dogma and those regarding the self, the soul and the heart"—remain "linked together" (p. 183). Although Foucault focused his analysis of the confession on issues of sexuality, his overall argument was about how all aspects of an individual's life and thoughts were now under constant surveillance as individuals were expected to openly confess the intimate details of their lives. Confession was more than just a time to offer repentance for one's sins—as it is commonly miscast—but instead a time when one offers up all of their life for display. It is a full confession of one's sins, one's faith, and one's life.

Ultimately, Foucault was concerned with the growth of the confession from a Christian sacrament to a societal function. As Dreyfus and Rabinow (1983) explained, with his discussion of the confession, Foucault was not attempting to offer a "traditional history" or even a "simple unity of meaning or function" of the confession (p. 119); rather, they added, Foucault was pointing to "the confession as an important ritual of power in which a specific technology of the body was forged" and thus he was claiming that "confession is a vital component of modern power" (p. 119). Foucault explored "the history of the confession in the seventeenth century for the purposes of writing 'a history of the present'" (Dreyfus and Rabinow, 1983, p. 119). Foucault (1999) argued that the confession within the Catholic Church spread to create "within Western Christian culture" a governing system that demands individuals to "speak truthfully about himself and his faults, his desires, the state of his soul, etc." (p. 154) as the "development of confessional techniques . . . helped to give the confession a central role in the order of civil and religious powers" (p. 58). He explained the development of confession as a significant part of the Catholic Church:

> Thus up to the middle of the sixteenth century the Church only supervised sexuality in a fairly distant manner. The requirement of annual confession, with its avowal of the different kinds of sins committed, ensured that in fact one wouldn't have to relate very many sexual adventures to one's curé. With the Council of Trent, around the middle of the sixteenth century, there emerge, alongside the ancient techniques of the confessional, a new series of procedures developed within the ecclesiastical institution for the purpose of training and purifying personnel. Detailed techniques were elaborated for use in seminaries and monasteries, techniques of discursive rendition of daily life, of self-examination, confession, direction of conscience and regulation of the relationship between director and directed. (Foucault, 1980, p. 200)

Foucault (1990) argued that "the scope of the confession—the confession of the flesh—continually increased" as a result of the Counter Reformation and its push for "the yearly confession in the Catholic countries" (p. 19). Thus, Foucault (1990) concluded, "We have since become a singularly confessing society. The confession has spread its effects far and wide. It plays a part in justice, medicine, education, family relationships, and love relations" (p. 59). He added, "One confesses in public and in private, to one's parents, one's educators, one's doctor, to those one loves" (p. 59). With the spread of the confessional model to schools, prisons, and other institutions, "a power nexus occurred" as "the individual was persuaded to confess to other authorities, particularly to physicians, psychiatrists, and social scientists" (p. 176). The confession—and its demands—has spread well beyond the confessional booth.

Along with the confession comes a focus on individuals talking publicly about their private lives. Bernauer (2004) explained, "regular confessions to another" are important since "verbalization of thoughts is another level of sorting out the good thoughts from those that are evil, namely, those that seek to hide from the light of public expression" (p. 80). Foucault (1980) explained, "What I mean by 'confession' . . . is all those procedures by which the subject is incited to produce a discourse of truth about his sexuality which is capable of having effects on the subject himself" (pp. 215–16). The act of confession "is not simply to affirm that one believes but also the fact of this belief; it is to make the act of affirmation an object of affirmation, and thus to authenticate it either for oneself or before others" (Foucault, 1999, p. 154–55). Foucault (1990) added:

> An imperative was established: Not only will you confess to acts contravening the law, but you will seek to transform your desire, your every desire, into discourse. . . . The Christian pastoral prescribed as a fundamental duty the task of passing everything having to do with sex through the endless mill of speech. (p. 21)

Eventually, this opening of one's self to another led to "the nearly infinite task of telling—telling oneself and another, as often as possible, everything that might concern the interplay of innumerable pleasures, sensations, and thoughts" (p. 20). Caputo (2004) summarized Foucault's confessional approach: "in short, to talk, talk, talk, for in talking is the cure" (p. 124). Cutrofello (2004) described Foucault's work tracing the rise of the Catholic sacrament of confession as tracing "the shift from confessional showing to confessional saying, from monstration to articulation" (p. 159). Foucault's confession is, at its foundation, a consideration of public discourse about previously private matters.

BAPTIZING FOUCAULT

The concept of the confession appears to provide a useful framework for examining presidential candidates' personal religious rhetoric as they bare their souls before the electorate in today's confessional society. Yet, Foucault's theorizing about the confession does not yield direct correlations for democratic presidential campaign dialogue since his work used the hierarchical Catholic Church rather than a more democratic setting. Foucault, who said he was "not ashamed" of his "very strong Christian, Catholic background" (Foucault, 1999, p. xvi), clearly theorized from a Catholic perspective. Bernauer and Carrette (2004) argued that "Foucault's critical thinking is born out of his own French Catholic context" and that his work reveals a "privileging of certain Catholic concerns" (p. 6). Interestingly, a number of presidential rhetoric scholars have utilized priestly metaphors to describe the president-polity relationship, although not the confession. Hart declared the president to be "the high priest of the national faith" who has "an exalted perspective" (Hart and Pauley, 2005, p. 34). John K. White (1998) argued, "In many respects the American dream has assumed religious trappings, with the president acting as a high priest" (p. 33). Domke and Coe (2008) frequently employed priestly or Catholic metaphors in their examination of religious governance rhetoric used by presidents. They insisted that presidents act "as political priests by speaking the language of the faithful" (p. 19) and serve as "America's 'high priest' in times of crisis, national celebration, political turmoil, or tragedy" (p. 31). Drawing from the Jewish tradition of a "high priest," this phrase fits nicely with Catholic polity as it includes priests and even a high priest (the Pope). Additionally, scholars rely on religious metaphors like communion and pilgrimages to analyze religious-political proclamations by presidents.

The problem with such Catholic metaphors—and thus with using Foucault's notions of confession as developed—is that such a framework provides little useful analytical guidance for analyzing presidential campaign discourse. Although the Catholic confession and other metaphors might fit somewhat better when examining presidential governance rhetoric—as with Domke and Coe's (2008) work—the process of selecting a Catholic priest is one of appointment from the Church hierarchy rather than a democratic election by the congregation. Even the one democratic selection within the Catholic Church—that for the office of Pope—is a behind-the-scenes process for a lifetime term. However, within the congregations that emerged from the more radical wing of the Protestant Reformation—such as Baptists—a congregational style of church polity developed that differed substantially from the episcopal polity of a local church's hierarchical leadership or the presbyterian polity of a board of elders leading a local church. None other than presidential candidate Jimmy Carter himself explained the democratic nature of the congregational church during his 1976 campaign:

> Every Baptist church is individual and autonomous. We don't accept domina-
> tion of our church from the Southern Baptist Convention. . . . We don't believe
> in any hierarchy in church. We don't have bishops. Any officers chosen by the
> church are defined as servants, not bosses. . . . So it's a very good, democratic
> structure. (Carter, 1978b, p. 963)

With the more democratic approach found in congregational-ruled churches,
the process of selecting a new minister is substantially different than that of a
Catholic or hierarchical congregation—and more closely mirrors how our
nation's presidents are chosen.

In congregational churches, the people elect their pastor instead of having
a priest appointed by the church hierarchy. A prospective pastor, often called
a candidate, is subjected to a public interview process that includes talking
about their beliefs and plans for the church (or their policy agenda), and
preaching a prospective sermon (or campaign speech). Pastoral candidates
are asked questions by the congregants, during which the would-be leader
functions as the confesser and not the one hearing the confession. Many
churches even consider multiple candidates before selecting one to be the
church's leader. Once one becomes pastor of the church, there is an element
of serving as confessor even within Protestant denominations even though
there is not the official sacrament. As Dixon (2004) explained, "Each denomination, whether congregational or hierarchical in nature, has elements of
confession in their pastor/congregant relationship. These confessional discourses, often termed pastoral counseling, take place when the congregant's
life is in some sort of crisis" (p. 44). The minister then serves until deciding
to leave or until being voted or forced out by the congregation.

This more democratic congregational model is particularly important in
American churches, and thus offers a radically different situation from that of
Foucault's European influence. Notre Dame history professor Nathan O.
Hatch (1989) explained in *The Democratization of American Christianity*
that compared to Europe:

> [A] distinctive feature of the religious scene in modern America is the pres-
> ence of a remarkable set of popular leaders, persons who derive their authority
> not from their education or stature within major denominations, but from the
> democratic art of persuasion. (p. 211)

He added that ministers like Billy Graham, Jerry Falwell, and Pat Robertson
"continue a long tradition of democratic religious authority" (p. 211). Thus,
he concluded that "a central force" for American Christianity "has been its
democratic or populist orientation" (p. 213). Similarly, Peele (1984) argued,
"Historians of religion in the United States have noticed how all of its
Churches have developed features which reflect the democratic environment
of the country and which make American denominations more like each

other than like their European counterparts" (p. 90). In many ways, American democracy and American Christianity influenced each other during the early years of the American experiment. Religion and philosophy professor Stephen H. Webb (2004) argued, in America "a distinctively Protestant rhetoric has developed that is inseparable from the American cultural landscape" (p. 124).

The rhetorical influence of evangelicals remains strongly embedded in American society and politics. Eidenmuller (2002) explained that "the rhetorical style of American evangelicalism remains a testament to the unifying power of democracy and religion in America" (p. 81). Susan Wise Bauer (2008) added the evangelical expectation for public confession has spread well beyond merely the evangelical community: "Even Catholic priests and secular politicians found themselves pressured into public confession by followers who were neither evangelical nor Protestant. Public confession had become the most powerful means by which leaders acknowledged the power of their followers" (p. 4). The evangelical rhetorical expectations have become cultural expectations in contemporary America. Thus, it is within the Protestant tradition that a more fitting example can be found by which to consider American presidential elections and candidates' confessional rhetoric.

Such a democratic framework of the minister as the confesser offers insights for rethinking Foucault's confession in order to critically examine the implications of our would-be national leaders baring their souls in the age of confessional politics. By democratizing Foucault's concept of the confession, his work becomes more useful in considering issues in democratic elections. Just as the early Anabaptists of the Protestant Reformation declared that Christians needed to be baptized as adult believers—or rebaptized if they had been baptized as infants in the Catholic Church—so Foucault's work on the confession needs to be rebaptized to fit the more democratic setting found in some Protestant congregations. The model for such theoretical retooling can be found in the selection process of a church's pastor who must first confess to the congregation before becoming the confessor. Thus, when considering U.S. presidential campaigns, the would-be presidents are the ones who must first confess to the people. Although as president one may become the nation's "high priest" or "pastor-in-chief," and therefore serve as the nation's *confessor* in caring for the national flock, as a presidential candidate one is the *confesser* who must bare their soul to the electorate.

Adjusting Foucault's confession also aligns it more closely to how the confession has found a revival in evangelical Protestant churches in recent years. As evangelicals have shown a renewed interest in confessions, they have adjusted the concept to make it more public and have actually reversed the direction of the confession. Several evangelical churches have set up websites inviting people to publicly post their deepest secrets and sins for everyone to read. For instance, www.mysecret.tv allows people to confess and to browse the confessions made by others. The homepage banner quotes the Bible: "If we confess our sins, he is faithful and righteous to forgive us our sins and to cleanse us from all unrighteousness." Another site, www.ivescrewedup.com, also allows one to confess and read others' confessions. The website declares that "[c]onfession is good for the soul" and "[t]he bible says, 'Confess your sins to each other and pray for each other.'" Bobby Gruenewald, a pastor at the megachurch that runs www.mysecret.tv, noted that the website received 7,500 confessions in the first two years and that people at the church pray for the people submitting confessions. He added, "We do believe there is value in confessing our sins to each other. . . . This process may be a more modern way of people discovering the value of that tradition" (Salmon, 2008, ¶21). The church even showed video confessions during a sermon entitled "My Secret," and other churches have posted video confessions on YouTube (Alter, 2007). Many evangelical churches now observe a confession time by having members write their sins on a piece of paper and then drop them off at a cross at the front of the sanctuary (Salmon, 2008).

In addition to creating public confessions, many evangelical Protestants have also created reverse confessionals. For instance, a chapter of the evangelical group Campus Crusade for Christ constructed a confessional booth on campus at the University of Florida. However, students walking by were not asked to confess their sins but to listen to a confession of sins from a Christian on behalf of Christians (Sanders, 2008). Author and pastor Donald Miller, who wrote about creating a reverse confession in *Blue Like Jazz*, has inspired other evangelicals to try the idea. After recounting a few of the discussions in the confessional booth, he reflected:

> I felt very connected to God because I had confessed so much to so many people and had gotten so much off my chest and I had been forgiven by the people I had wronged with my indifference and judgmentalism. (Miller, 2003, p. 126)

Dan Merchant (2008), a Christian writer and filmmaker, was inspired by Miller's confession and constructed his own confessional booth at a gay pride parade where he apologized for the way Christians had treated homosexuals. Merchant even filmed his reverse confessions to publicly present later in his film and book *Lord Save us from Your Followers*. Similarly, Springcreek Church, a megachurch in Garland, Texas, published a full-page ad apologizing for their mistakes. The ad, which ran in the *Dallas Morning News*, declared:

We followed trends when we should've followed Jesus. We told others how to live but did not listen ourselves. We live in the land of plenty, denying ourselves nothing, while ignoring our neighbors who actually have nothing. We sat on the sidelines doing nothing while AIDS ravaged Africa. We were wrong; we're sorry. Please forgive us. ("We were wrong," 2008)

The idea of reversing the confessional in public settings captures exactly what is needed for Foucault's work to be applied to presidential campaigns—it is our leaders, or would-be leaders, that must confess to the people instead of the people to the leaders.

Since Foucault's work on the confession remained incomplete at the time of his death in 1984, additional theoretical development, reflecting societal shifts, is warranted. He discussed the confession in the first of three published volumes of *The History of Sexuality* and in other writings and lectures, but the fourth volume was to focus on the confession and Christianity. Although it reportedly was mostly completed, Foucault had demanded that none of his unfinished work be posthumously published (Carrette, 1999). As a result, Carrette (2000) argued that "the unfinished project left many theological and theoretical problems" (p. 38). One such problem left unresolved is the powerful position of the priest in the confession. Foucault (1980) famously declared about the reliance on a sovereign approach to theoretical considerations of power: "At the bottom, despite the differences in epochs and objectives, the representation of power has remained under the spell of monarchy. In political thought and analysis, we still have not cut off the head of the king" (pp. 88–89). Although Foucault attempted to overcome the problem of relying on the sovereign with his conceptualization of more democratic forms of power, his own analysis of the confession failed to cut off the head of the priest. His conceptualization of the confession—the heart of pastoral power—actually left the priest in a highly powerful position. Unlike Foucault's analysis of the Panopticon prison—where even the guards are under surveillance and thus discipline themselves—Foucault's priests do not appear to face such scrutiny. It becomes clear that disciplinary power has pervaded many areas of our confessional society, but the shepherd-leader remains immune to the confession. With the reverse confession, our would-be national leaders must first enter the confessional booth as the confesser before they can later—as the pastoral leader—serve as the confessor. Thus, the reverse confession goes beyond Foucault's confession by placing even the priest under the polity's surveillance.

Although the theoretical adjustment proposed in this chapter provides a dramatic new reading of Foucault's confession—essentially flipping who sits in the two sides of the confessional booth—it follows Foucault's own development of the confessional. He argued that there had been important "shifts and transformation" in the confession as a "form of knowledge-power" (Foucault, 1990, p. 70). For instance, Foucault traced the development of confessional techniques beyond the Catholic Church, such as in the field of psychiatry, which Dreyfus and Rabinow (1983) described as Foucault providing "a change of locale for the confession" (p. 178). Foucault clearly established the confessional approach as extending into much of society. As Carrette (2000) argued, "It soon becomes clear that Foucault is not attempting to establish a single 'framework' for confession, or 'reduce' confession and psychoanalysis to the same thing. Rather, he is strategically utilising 'confession' to exemplify a number of underlying practices" (p. 38). The specific sacrament of confession was for Foucault merely an exemplar to use in exploring societal issues of power/knowledge, control, normalization, and discourse.

With the reverse confession, our presidential candidates come to us—the American people—to confess their sins, their faith, and the innermost details of their lives. Foucault (1999) argued that with the confessional, the pastor "must know what is going on, what each of them does—his public sins" and "must know what goes on in the soul of each one, that is, his secret sins, his progress on the road to sainthood" (pp. 142–43). By reversing the confession, it is our presidential candidates who must discuss their "public sins" and "what goes on in [their] soul" on the road to the White House. If, in hopes of finding their political salvation, presidential candidates confess to the electorate, they then submit themselves and their personal religious matters to the judgment of the American voter. Foucault (1999) explained about the power of the pastor over the people:

> This new form is ensured by the pastor, who can require the people to do everything that they must for their salvation, and who is in a position to watch over them and to exercise with respect to them, in any case, a surveillance and continuous control. (p. 124)

With the reverse confession, it is the people who can require their would-be leaders to do what they must for their political salvation, and it is the people who remain in control. Not only are presidential candidates' every move literally under surveillance by the media—including tracking and frequently reporting if and when the candidates attend church—but as candidates discuss their personal faith they offer their souls up for political consideration. Foucault's confession, after all, is a matter of discourse. As Carrette (2000) explained about Foucault's perspective: "Christianity is a religion of utterances, a submission into speaking, believing and acting" (p. 27), thus "Christianity is clearly established as one of the powers which not only restricts discourse but demands it in the confession" (p. 34). With today's confessional expectations, our would-be national leaders are now required to talk about their religious faith and personal lives. This discursive demand creates significant problems for American democracy and society that can be critiqued with the framework of the reverse confession.

WHAT THE FOUCAULT?

Carrette (2000) argued that Foucault's work on the confession was essentially "a critique of religious authority in the demand for confession" and placed it at the heart of Foucault's "political spirituality" (p. 4). Similarly, with the reverse confessional framework, the demands of a confessional society now placed upon our presidential candidates can be critiqued to determine the effects of such a political system on American democracy. In their quest for political salvation, our would-be leaders have attempted to meet the rhetorical demands of our confessional society shaped largely by the significant religious-political changes discussed in the previous chapter. As a result, candidates have tossed aside the once binding civil-religious contract and instead now serve up a political rhetoric that is testimonial, partisan, sectarian, and liturgical in nature. The successful presidential candidates have been those most willing to offer the confessions sought by religious leaders, their followers, and the media. In doing so, they have helped reify the rhetorical demands of the confessional political era. Although politicians may have discovered political redemption with such religious-political discourse, a key question to examine is just how has this political discovery affected the American democratic process? As Jesus asked his disciples, "What good is it for a man to gain the whole world, yet forfeit his soul?" Similarly, can one gain political power while forfeiting the very principles of democracy upon which our nation was founded? Several problems emerging from the confessional political system illustrate how America's political soul has been placed in jeopardy.

Religious Test for Office

The rhetorical demand that presidential candidates confess their faith amounts to a rhetorical religious test for the presidency—despite Article VI of the U.S. Constitution clearly declaring that "no religious test shall ever be required as a qualification to any office or public trust under the United States." As detailed in the previous chapter, evangelicals expect presidential candidates to publicly proclaim their Christian faith, and—as chapters 2 through 5 demonstrated—successful presidential candidates have skillfully met this demand by testifying about their personal religious beliefs, their prayer habits, and their Christian conversion experiences. Candidates unwilling to enter this public confessional often find themselves rejected in the

ballot box on election day. For instance, 2008 Republican presidential hopeful Rudy Giuliani often refused to talk about his private life. After being
asked during an August 5, 2007, Republican primary debate to confess a
mistake made in life, he said to questioner George Stephanopolous: "George,
your father is a priest. I'm going to explain it to your father, not to you,
okay?" Giuliani also stated on another occasion, "My religious affiliation,
my religious practices and the degree to which I am a good or not-so-good
Catholic, I prefer to leave to the priest" (Brune, 2007, ¶4). Numerous other
candidates refusing to enter the public confessional booth have also failed to
assume the high throne of the Oval Office.

To find political salvation in our confessional era, presidential candidates
must talk about their faith and detail their spiritual beliefs and practices. As
Foucault (1999) stated, "a man needs for his own salvation to know as
exactly as possible who he is and . . . he needs to tell it as explicitly as
possible to some other people" (p. 159). Candidates willing to explicitly
discuss their faith with voters have been able to pass the religious test and
assume office as our high political pastor in the confessional era. Whether
they do willingly or not, however, presidential candidates today are pressed
to explain their faith and how it impacts their political decision-making. In
the "confessing society," Foucault (1990) argued, "One confesses—or is
forced to confess. . . . Western man has become a confessing animal" (p. 59).
As religious leaders and the public demand that presidential candidates confess their faith, they are establishing a rhetorical test for office that can only
be met by a candidate publicly baring their soul.

Much as evangelicals look to public declarations of one's faith as the true
sign of a sincere believer, they also look to a candidate's public religious
rhetoric even more so than the candidates' private faith or spiritual practices.
For instance, Bobbie Greene Kilberg, who worked in George H. W. Bush's
White House public liaison office, noted that even though Bush shared the
same policy positions as leaders of the "Religious Right," they still did not
trust him. Kilberg added, "I think it comes down to cultural factors. He
doesn't wear his religion on his sleeve. His faith was a very deep and real
thing, but it was a private thing and he didn't like talking about it much"
(Martin, 2005, p. 310). As a result of being uncomfortable in publicly discussing his personal faith, George H. W. Bush never gained the support of
conservative evangelical leaders as did Ronald Reagan or George W. Bush.
As an Episcopalian World War II veteran from the Northeast—all groups of
people famously reticent about publicly proclaiming their faith—George H.
W. Bush hardly had a prayer of passing our nation's rhetorical religious test
for higher office, except against an even more rhetorically secular Northeastern candidate from a soft-spoken denomination as seen with Michael Dukakis in 1988.

Indeed, the rhetorical expectations placed upon presidential aspirants have created a barrier to the White House for certain candidates. For instance, during the 2008 primary election, 25 percent of all Americans and 36 percent of white evangelicals said they were less likely to vote for a candidate who was a Mormon (Hill, 2007). Christian author Tricia Erickson argued that if Republican hopeful Mitt Romney could not realize that Mormonism was a false religion then she felt he did not have the "discernment [nor] the judgment to be able to adequately and objectively run our country" (Groening, 2007, ¶6). A Florida evangelist urged Christians not to vote for Romney. He argued, "Having Romney as president is no different than having a Muslim or Scientologist as president. . . . I'll stay home and not vote before I vote for Satan, since if you vote for Romney you are voting for Satan!" (Stacy, 2007, ¶9). A supporter of Democratic candidate Hillary Clinton helped spread false rumors in the key early caucus state of Iowa that declared Barack Obama was a Muslim. The email also read, "Since it is politically expedient to be a CHRISTIAN when seeking major public office in the United States, Barack Hussein Obama has joined the United Church of Christ in an attempt to downplay his Muslim background" (Sargent, 2007, ¶4). Republican nominee John McCain declared that he would support a Christian over a Muslim because he would "prefer someone who I know who has a solid grounding in my faith" (Gilgoff, 2007e, ¶2). Even Romney, who was facing questions about his own religious beliefs, stated that he could not even "see that a Cabinet position would be justified" for a Muslim, although he added that he "would imagine that Muslims could serve at lower levels of my administration" (Iftikhar, 2007, ¶3–4). Thus, in the confessional political era, it appears that for a Muslim or other non-Christian, the hurdle in seeking high public office is too high.

In addition to the religious faith barrier, the current demand for political God-talk has created a geographical and dialectical barrier to the White House. As Georgetown University professor of Jewish civilization Jacques Berlinerblau (2008) explained:

> If the misfortunes of [Howard] Dean, [Joe] Lieberman, and [John] Kerry offer lessons to be learned for 2008, then one of them might be summarized as follows: it's hard to win if you are not, sociologically speaking, Bill Clinton or a reasonable facsimile thereof. Oh, how un-Bill-like they all were! All three were New Englanders. All three were northern liberal elites. . . . And all failed, I think, because God-talk in the United States is articulated in either a southern, Midwestern, or mountain region drawl (p. 92–93)

Perhaps it is not surprising that the only three Democrats to find presidential success in the confessional era have been Southern Baptist evangelicals Jimmy Carter and Bill Clinton and African American evangelical Barack Obama. Concerning John McCain, Berlinerblau wrote:

When it comes to religious oratory, he is the strong and silent type. . . . This reluctance to emote about faith in public might be expected from an Episcopalian and a war hero descended from two generations of four-star admirals. It is also to be expected from someone who is not an evangelical and does not share their unique style of testifying to the glory of God. (p. 121)

He added, "Nor are Jews and Catholics particularly at home wearing their faith on their sleeves. Emoting publicly does not come naturally to them. . . . Testifying publicly, King James in hand, is not something a Catholic can do with ease" (p. 131). Perhaps it is true that the rhetorical religious test of the confessional era means that Northeasterners and those outside the evangelical tradition need not apply at 1600 Pennsylvania Avenue.

With the confessional era has come the expectation that our presidential candidates will talk about their personal lives, including their religious beliefs and spiritual practices. Candidates refusing or unable to offer such confessions of faith may find themselves unable to capture the presidency. As Gerald Ford, Walter Mondale, Michael Dukakis, George H. W. Bush, Bob Dole, and John Kerry could all attest, being uncomfortable talking openly about one's personal faith yields devastating results at the ballot box. With the death of this part of the American dream, American democracy loses some of its luster. As Domke and Coe (2008) argued, American democracy is weakened by our confessional faith test:

Imposing a test of public religiosity on a candidate is more than a disservice to that individual; it is a disservice to the nation. Democracy is at its best when good candidates run for office and the finest of those candidates has a chance to win. (p. 142)

Now, as our presidential candidates are politically excommunicated for their confessional sins, the full measure of our nation's democratic dream goes unfulfilled.

Disenfranchised Classes

Related to the exclusion of potential presidential candidates is a second problem of the confessional era where entire groups of Americans are virtually ignored, or at least rendered second-class citizens, in the electoral process. C. Welton Gaddy (2005), a Baptist minister and head of the Interfaith Alliance complained that the testimonial nature of the 2000 campaign made it seem that the candidates thought it was "a competition to win the title 'Holy Man of the Year' rather than an electoral race for the presidency of the United States" (p. 45). He added:

The president of the United States is a political leader, not a spiritual leader. Every person who occupies the Oval Office carries a constitutional mandate to serve as a leader for all of the people in the nation, not as a leader exclusively for citizens who share his particular faith or find meaning in the language of his personal religious tradition. (p. 45)

As candidates tailor their rhetoric with evangelical buzzwords and conversion experiences, they downplay or even ignore the religious experiences— or absence of such experiences—of other Americans, even though as president they must serve as leader of the entire nation. Much as today's confessional society has led to the exclusion of some candidates who cannot pass the ruling rhetorical religious test, it has also led to some American citizens assuming a diminished role in the electoral process.

The confession at its heart works to define and exclude many individuals as aberrations. Dreyfus and Rabinow (1983) argued that Foucault used the confession—much as he had used the Panopticon prison—"to localize and specify how power works, what it does and how it does it" (p. 110). Additionally, they explained that Foucault explored how the confession and the Panopitcon prison "define what is normal" and "define practices which fall outside their system as deviant behavior in need of normalization" (p. 198). That which is constructed as normal and that which is cast as deviant is "political" work since "normalizing society has turned out to be a powerful and insidious form of domination (Dreyfus and Rabinow, 1983, p. 198). Foucault argued that the confession helps to normalize which behaviors are sinful—and thus worthy of confessing—and who is a sinner. This type of disciplinary power discursively defines what and who is normal and thus uses such classifications to control individuals. Those who fail to submit to the confessional are excluded from the possibility of redemption. Similarly, by normalizing a specific religious experience, our confessional political system results in the exclusion of entire groups of Americans.

For example, not only would it be impossible in today's religious-political climate for a Muslim to mount a competitive bid for the presidency, but even Muslim citizens find themselves ignored by presidential candidates. Barack Obama, the 2008 Democratic nominee whose own candidacy was plagued with false claims that he is a secret Muslim, has been accused himself by Muslims of avoiding public interaction with them. After two Muslim women in headscarves, both Obama supporters, were banned by Obama staffers from standing behind the candidate during a speech—and thus an image that would have been captured by television coverage—Safiya Ghori, government relations director for the Muslim Public Affairs Council, stated, "The community feels betrayed" (Elliott, 2008, ¶15). Although Obama frequently speaks in Christian churches and even some Jewish synagogues during the campaign, he did not appear once at a mosque (Elliott, 2008). In fact, after U.S. Congressman Keith Ellison of Minnesota, the very first Muslim elected to the U.S. Congress and a staunch Obama supporter, volunteered to speak at an Obama rally originally scheduled to be held at a mosque, the event was canceled by the Obama campaign because they wanted to avoid controversy and sought to maintain "a very tightly wrapped message" (Elliott, 2008, ¶3). Ellison also criticized Obama for arguing that calling him a "Muslim" is somehow a smear on his character, suggesting there is something inherently wrong with being a Muslim. Altaf Ali, executive director of the South Florida chapter of the Council on American-Islamic Relations, argued "Since 9/11, our community has been portrayed as inherently evil, and what Obama is doing is adding to the negative stereotype. . . . His message is about change, and he has to appeal to every minority group" (Reinhard, 2008, ¶10). Additionally, Safiya Ghori said about the apparent political liability for candidates to appear with Muslims, "The joke within the national Muslim organizations . . . is that we should endorse the person we don't want to win" (Elliott, 2008, ¶39). However, considering the democratic consequences of such exclusion from full participation in the electoral process, such a problem hardly seems like a joke.

Other groups of Americans have also been deemed "untouchables" in our confessional political era. For instance, much as being an atheist is the top factor that would lead American voters to not vote for a particular candidate (Luo, 2007b), atheists in general are deemed untrustworthy by many Americans. A survey asking Americans if a number of different groups "share everyday Americans' vision of society" found that the least trusted group was atheists, followed by Muslims (Miller, 2006, ¶3). The project's leader, University of Minnesota sociology professor Penny Edgell, said of atheists: "They're the new outsiders" (Miller, 2006, ¶3). She added, "It tells us about how Americans view religion. . . . Many Americans seem to believe some kind of religious faith is central to being a good American and a good person" (Aquino, 2006, ¶2).

People excluded by our confessional politics are not just those citizens who hold religious beliefs other than Christianity or perhaps Judaism, but also other citizens who are viewed by evangelicals as transgressing their codes of "normality" or accepted beliefs and behaviors. One such group is homosexuals, which fits closely with Foucault's original focus with the confession. During the 2008 campaign, for example, Republican presidential hopefuls participated in numerous debates for special interest audiences. However, every Republican candidate declined an invitation to appear at a forum focused on homosexual rights, although most Democratic presidential contenders attended. Jack Majeske, past president of the Broward County Log Cabin Republican Club argued that the Republican candidates skipped the debate because "[t]hey're all afraid of the Christian right" (Fisher, 2007,

¶6). Just four years earlier, an important part of George W. Bush's reelection strategy—and the election strategy of other Republicans—was pushing for state constitutional amendments banning same-sex marriage.

Even Democratic candidates sometimes seem willing to ignore the concerns of their homosexual supporters in a quest for religious voters. For instance, as Barack Obama targeted religious voters by holding gospel music concerts in South Carolina, one of the main musicians for the concerts was criticized for making antihomosexual remarks. The singer, Reverend Donnie McClurkin, claimed God delivered him from a homosexual lifestyle and called homosexuality a "curse" (Wapshott, 2007, ¶2). Although Obama added a gay minister to the event—who had a much smaller role than McClurkin—many homosexual rights groups still condemned and protested the concerts. It seemed that for Obama's campaign, winning religious voters—particularly African Americans—was more important than repudiating someone considered hateful by a smaller part of the electorate. College of Charleston political science professor Jeri Cabot explained Obama's rationale: "He can win without [the gay vote]" (Burris, 2007, ¶6).

With their sectarian rhetoric—as detailed in previous chapters—our presidential candidates rhetorically exclude or even demonize segments of the American polity. Gaddy noted that George W. Bush often spoke as if he were the nation's religious leader and not just its political one, such as when he suggested that astronauts who died in the space shuttle Columbia disaster went to Heaven. Gaddy pointed out that not all of the astronauts were Christians, and the family members of those that were not might very well have been offended by Bush reading from the Christian New Testament. Likewise, on the campaign trail presidential candidates quote Christian scriptures and talk about their faith in the Christian God, suggesting that all Americans are united only in Christian beliefs. As Gaddy (2005) concluded:

> Any time that the president embraces doctrinal declarations when speaking as the nation's leader, he implicitly suggests that people who hold a different theological point of view do not matter to him as much as those who share his particular religious point of view. (pp. 46–47)

Similarly, Princeton University religion professor Jeffrey Stout (2004) argued:

> Claiming to speak for the people as a whole on religious topics, the politicians imply that citizens who refuse to be spoken for in this way are less than full-fledged members of the people. When dissenters object, they are demonized as secularists. Symbolic sacrifice of the secularist scapegoat is itself a ritual essential to the public religion that some politicians would have the nation adopt. (p. 199)

With sectarian religious messages, our presidential candidates rhetorically—
and even literally—avoid Americans who do not fit the evangelical Christian
standard that has been created in the confessional era. Thus, entire groups of
Americans are prevented from full participation and having much influence
in our nation's political process.

Although all Americans are supposed to be treated equally as citizens, it
seems clear that in a confessional era of politics new classes of civic lepers
have been created that—as in biblical times—must be avoided at all costs.
With our leaders, evangelical and political, arguing that this is a Christian
nation, such pronouncements inherently construct many Americans as not
true or full American citizens. It seems that for many evangelicals and presidential candidates, secularism has become the new communism that must be
found and removed from all parts of our society. The exclusionary confessional discourse of our presidential candidates may help them win elections,
but it harms the democratic ideals of equality and representation of all citizens.

Preferential Treatment

Another problem in the confessional political system is found in the emer-
gence of certain evangelical Christian leaders as influential "kingmakers"
with their followers receiving preferential treatment from the government, as
well as government policies crafted on the tenets of the evangelical faith.
Much as confessional politics excludes some Americans from having an
equal voice in the democratic process, it also allows others to have a greater
voice. Presidential candidates embark on pilgrimages to meet with evangelical leaders and speak to evangelical voters. With such access to presidents
and presidential candidates comes even greater evangelical influence in the
electoral process as the presidential candidates seek the public endorsements
of key evangelical leaders. While candidates may shy away from Muslims,
atheists, gays, or other supposed non-God-fearing groups of Americans, our
would-be leaders often beg evangelicals to join them for their religious-
political campaign events.

During the 2008 campaign, for example, John McCain attempted to re-
ceive penance for his 2000 remark that Reverend Jerry Falwell was one of
the "agents of intolerance." As a result, McCain traveled to Falwell's Liberty
University in 2007 to deliver an address and literally embrace Falwell.
McCain also appeared on the Trinity Broadcasting Network with Paul
Crouch, Jr. and later met with revered evangelist Billy Graham and his son
Franklin Graham to provide evidence that he cared about and listened to the
concerns of evangelicals. His Democratic opponent, Barack Obama, trekked
to Saddleback Community Church, a megachurch led by evangelical preach-
er and author Rick Warren, and also held meetings with influential evangeli-

cal ministers. Such presidential access often continues in the White House as ministers like Billy Graham, Jerry Falwell, Jimmy Swaggart, Bill Hybels, Tony Campolo, and others have frequently visited with the presidents and their top advisors to offer advice and be heard on policy issues important to evangelical Christian voters.

As presidential candidates use evangelical buzzwords, meet with evangelical leaders and voters, and discuss public policy in religious terms, they legitimize the confessional demands and thus increase the level of influence of evangelical leaders. Foucault (1980) claimed that the confessional techniques would continue to spread, "Power never ceases its interrogation, its inquisition, its registration of truth: it institutionalises, professionalises and rewards its pursuit" (p. 93). Since power never ceases, it continues to spread its influence into more areas of society. As Dreyfus and Rabinow (1983) explained about the growth of confessional techniques:

> In the confessional paradigm, the more the subject talks (or is forced to talk), the more science knows; the more the scope of legitimate examination of consciousness grows, the finer and wider the web of confessional technology. As this power spread, it became clear that the subject himself could not be the final arbiter of his own discourse. (p. 179)

Tracing this confessional growth in society was an essential aspect of Foucault's argument about the confession—its practice and power spread not only in the church but to other areas of society. As evangelicals gain the attention of candidates, it increases their electoral power, thus increasing the likelihood that future presidential candidates will show reverence to these kingmakers.

A few recent examples demonstrate the problems that arise when one group gains extraordinary influence over our nation's political leaders. In 2005, George W. Bush nominated his close friend and White House legal advisor, Harriet Miers, to the Supreme Court. When asked why he chose someone with her limited legal experience, Bush actually responded by pointing to her evangelical church background: "People ask me why I picked Harriet Miers. . . . They want to know Harriet Miers's background, they want to know as much as they possibly can before they form opinions. And part of Harriet Miers's life is her religion" (Bumiller, 2005, ¶2). For Bush, one's religion constituted a prime qualification for holding a lifetime appointment on our nation's highest court. Ironically, the strongest criticism and eventual veto of Miers's nomination came from evangelicals who wanted someone with an even clearer record on issues important to them like abortion. After much pressure from conservative leaders, Miers withdrew her nomination. Due to the importance that evangelicals place on Supreme Court decisions— and having been burned by a George H. W. Bush appointee, David Souter, who turned out to be more liberal than expected—these religious leaders now demanded clear assurances that future court nominees would support their religious-political agenda. Religious activists like Phyllis Schafly and Gary Bauer led the public opposition to Miers (Bolton, 2005). Although influential evangelical James Dobson had initially offered support for Miers—after he received a phone call from presidential advisor Karl Rove explaining the choice two days before the public announcement of her nomination—Dobson later admitted he had lost faith in Miers after her pro-choice statements from decades earlier emerged (Gorksi, 2005). One evangelical activist, Reverend Rob Schenck, grilled Miers in person on religious questions and later turned on her because he discovered that, although she had been a member of a conservative evangelical church in Texas, she made the mistake of attending a liberal mainline church in Washington, D.C. (Roddy, 2005). In this example of the mixing of religion and politics, one's lack of appropriate religious credentials clearly became a disqualifier for our nation's high court and religious leaders practiced their God-given right to veto the president's Supreme Court nomination.

When nine federal prosecutors were fired in 2006, many commentators and politicians accused George W. Bush's administration of playing politics with our nation's supposedly independent judiciary. At the center of the scandal was Monica Goodling, an aide to U.S. Attorney General Alberto Gonzales. Goodling, who ultimately resigned and testified before Congress after receiving immunity, seemed highly unqualified herself to make evaluative decisions about the qualifications of federal prosecutors since she had limited legal experience. However, her apparent qualification was having graduated from Pat Robertson's Regent University School of Law. In fact, Goodling was just one of more than 150 Regent University graduates to be hired as federal employees during George W. Bush's presidency (Savage, 2007). Even though the school's programs are generally not highly rated—the law school is listed in the bottom tier of law schools in the nation—the large number of federal government hires occurred after a Regent dean was appointed by Bush to be the director of the U.S. Office of Personnel Management (Savage, 2007). The U.S. Department of Justice's report into Goodling and the firing of the federal prosecutors found that Goodling wrote notes like "pro-God in public life" after interviewing potential prosecutors (*An Investigation*, 2008, p. 38). She also noted positions on "god, guns + gays" as "Cons" about a candidate (p. 104), even though federal laws prohibit discrimination on the basis of religion.

Additionally, through Bush's Office of Faith-Based and Community Initiatives, ministries led by Chuck Colson, Pat Robertson, Herbert Lusk, and other evangelical leaders who supported Bush have received millions of federal dollars. David Kuo (2006), who was second-in-command in the faith-based office, noted that explicitly Christian organizations were ranked higher than other charities, and thus received more funds. Kuo also lamented that the funding was used by Bush to score political points for the 2004 election. An organization created by Pat Robertson was promoted by FEMA as a preferred charity in the aftermath of Hurricane Katrina, even as Robertson's *The 700 Club* blamed the victims of the region for their plight (Blumenthal, 2005). It literally pays to be an evangelical leader in today's confessional political environment. Evangelical religious leaders have received incredible government access, opportunities, and support after supporting presidential candidates' campaigns, with such blatant political patronage helping bring about the literal fulfillment of Pat Robertson and Jerry Falwell's vision that America is a Christian nation that should be led only by Christians.

In yet another example of the attempt to create a Christian nation—defended by Christian soldiers—several cadets at the Air Force Academy have complained over the past few years about the evangelical tone of their military training. For instance, the football coach hung a banner in the Academy locker room declaring his players "Team Jesus," the cadets were taught by one general to make a "J for Jesus" hand sign, and more than 250 officers and faculty at the academy signed an ad in the campus newspaper that stated, "We believe that Jesus Christ is the only real hope for the world" (Cooperman, 2006c, ¶22). Much of the Academy's evangelistic influence stems from religious groups working with military families, such as Focus on the Family that is headquartered—along with the Air Force Academy—in Colorado Springs, and the Officers' Christian Fellowship that says its mission is to create "a spiritually transformed military, with ambassadors for Christ in uniform, empowered by the Holy Spirit" (Cooperman, 2006c, ¶8). After stricter religious guidelines were adopted by the Air Force in response to criticisms of the evangelistic activities, the new guidelines were later eased in response to criticism from evangelical organizations (Cooperman, 2006a). Similar complaints of preferential treatment for evangelicals have also been made at West Point and the Naval Academy (Banerjee, 2008). In 2003, a U.S. Army general verbally attacked Muslims while speaking in uniform at evangelical churches (White, 2007). In 2005, seven military officers—including four generals—appeared in uniform in a fundraising video for the evangelical group Christian Embassy (White, 2007). In 2006, an Air Force general sent an email to military officials to raise money for a Republican congressional candidate, citing the candidate's Christian faith as why he should be supported (Cooperman 2006b). With such actions, the U.S. military has been baptized and seems well on its way to becoming God's army—helping to fulfill George W. Bush's claim that bringing democracy to Iraq was God's gift and will.

These three examples are among the many instances of evangelicals receiving preferential treatment in today's confessional political age. Whether it be extra attention and greater voice on the campaign trail or receiving special positions or input on policy decisions, evangelical leaders have gar-nered for themselves a significant role in our democratic process—often at the exclusion of other voices and views. Presidents in their first term espe-cially have learned to keep the door to the Oval Office open to evangelicals or else they may follow the fate of Jimmy Carter—who many evangelicals felt ignored them once Carter was in office—and thus risk losing reelection. Although the Christian kingmakers benefit from such attention and treat-ment, their influence restricts the input and opportunities for other citizens, thus undermining basic democratic principles of equality and the rights of the minority.

Restricted Public Dialogue

Yet another problem with confessional politics is the demand for God-talk often prevents productive discussions on important public policy issues. With the attention given to religious concerns, other more critical issues are ignored. Additionally, religious language creates a difficult obstacle for dem-ocratic dialogue since couching one's policies as the biblical or godly deci-sion stifles considerations of other competing perspectives. Thus, with relig-ious-political discourse assuming the partisan and sectarian style that charac-terizes our confessional politics, it actually undermines efforts to increase democratic dialogue essential for a pluralistic society.

Even though many within the electorate may not notice how religious rhetoric is preventing democratic discussion, religious issues and rhetoric steers presidential campaign discourse down a particular path. Foucault argued that disciplinary techniques have become such a natural part of soci-ety, so that many people do not even question the surveillance and control. Noting the development of Catholic schools, Foucault (1995) pointed out that a hierarchy and system of surveillance was developed to not only moni-tor the educational progress of students but also to observe and report on who did not follow specific rules and religious requirements, such as "who did not have his rosary" or "who did not comport himself properly at mass" or "who committed an impure act" (p. 176). As a result, Foucault argued that the system created a "[h]ierarchized, continuous and functional surveillance" by which "disciplinary power became an 'integrated' system, linked from the inside to the economy and to the aims of the mechanism in which it was practised" (p. 176). In a similar manner, the rhetorical demands of confes-sional politics often go unnoticed but still manage to often dominate cam-paign discourse as an integrated part of the campaign mechanics.

As religious issues now frequently overshadow other public concerns, this displacement of priorities could result in voters ignoring more important qualifications for holding office or candidates giving less attention to critical public issues. Liberal evangelical author and pastor Tony Campolo (2008) insisted that just because candidates can talk about religion does not mean they are the best candidate:

> If we are honest, we will admit that there are many who believe in Christ and maintain a regular devotional life but who may be more guided by party allegiances than biblical values when it comes to government policy. . . . What concerns me is the tendency to consider a declaration of faith enough to convince us that such candidates deserve our votes. That a person seeks God's will is no assurance that he or she will find it. (pp. 207–8)

With a focus on the rhetorical religiosity of a candidate, more important considerations for determining who may be the most qualified leader for the nation may be overlooked. Such a focus might also divert attention away from more critical issues. Historian Randall Balmer (2008) argued that Americans seem to be moving toward applying "some sort of catechetical test" on presidential elections where our commander-in-chief is wrongly viewed as our "high priest" or "pastor-in-chief" (p. 162–63). He feared that such attention created standards that were not the best judge of one's governance ability and "the vetting of a candidate's religion has diverted our attention from other important questions" (p. 168). John F. Kennedy made a similar argument during his 1960 speech to the Greater Houston Ministerial Alliance:

> While the so-called religious issue is necessarily and properly the chief topic here tonight, I want to emphasize from the outset that I believe that we have far more critical issues in the 1960 campaign; the spread of Communist influence, until it now festers only 90 miles from the coast of Florida—the humiliating treatment of our President and Vice President by those who no longer respect our power—the hungry children I saw in West Virginia, the old people who cannot pay their doctors bills, the families forced to give up their farms—an America with too many slums, with too few schools, and too late to the moon and outer space. These are the real issues which should decide this campaign. And they are not religious issues—for war and hunger and ignorance and despair know no religious barrier. (Kennedy, 1960a, ¶2)

In our confessional era of politics, religious issues—or so-called religious perspectives on various public issues—dominate public policy discussions, with less attention given to other national concerns. As Kennedy warned, our religious focus could result in our citizens and leaders ignoring the important solutions that our nation needs. Unfortunately, when faith trumps empirical facts, public deliberation and decision-making often suffers.

Additionally, the use of religious rhetoric can effectively foreclose deliberation on an issue when candidates frame their policy positions as God's
will or the only biblical position. Journalist Ray Suarez argued in his book
The Holy Vote:

> The difference between "God-talk" and other policy discussions is that relig-
> iously tinged speech almost entirely releases a politician from accountability.
> The assertions are not checkable. There is no "other side" that can be put
> forward without calling into question the politician's sincerity and religious
> faith. A promise to reduce the budget deficit in three years can be analyzed and
> checked. A declaration that God has given the gift of freedom of humanity
> cannot. (Suarez, 2006, p. 53)

Not only does it make one's arguments harder to attack, but such God-talk
suggests that one's opponents are ungodly and unbiblical. Former Moral
Majority leader Ed Dobson—who has since insisted that Christians should
not be so political—claimed that the problem comes when Christians argue
"that there is a proper Christian position on nearly every political issue" and
thus "implying that disagreements with their political positions is, in fact,
disagreement with Jesus" (Thomas and Dobson, 1999, p. 80). James Wood
(1980), editor of the *Journal of Church and State*, also pointed to the problem of using God-talk to prevent further policy discussions: "By confusing
moral absolutes with public policy, anyone who dissents is identified with
immorality and is in conflict with the will of God" (p. 420). As our presidential candidates call upon God and quote the Bible to justify their political
views, their discourse often sends the message that their perspective is beyond criticism by mere humans. Such rhetoric paints one's opponents as
ungodly and prevents meaningful dialogue when deciding the best public
policies to adopt.

Presidential campaign rhetoric in the confessional era often highlights the
religious faith of the candidates and links public policy proposals to religion.
Such religious-political discourse could result in the ignoring of more important political concerns and the stifling of dissenting perspectives. As C. Welton Gaddy of the Interfaith Alliance argued, "God-talk in the public square
. . . *threatens the vitality of democracy*. Not infrequently God-talk has been
used in attempts to shut down debate on an issue or to silence voices of
opposition to an issue" (p. 56, emphasis in original). Thus, the rhetoric frequently used to win a democratic election actually undermines democratic
principles.

Politicization of Religion

A final major problem with the confessional political system is that it reduces the sacredness of religious faith. Although the other four problems focus on harm done to the democratic process when religion and politics mix too closely, religion is also damaged. America remains an incredibly religious nation with polls consistently finding more than 90 percent of respondents claiming to believe in God—a rate far higher than found in most other industrialized nations. Americans have also enjoyed immense religious freedoms. Unlike many European nations, America has never established a denomination as its official state church supported by tax dollars. In fact, the First Amendment of the U.S. Constitution expressly prohibits such a marriage between church and state. As historian Garry Wills (2007) explained, "The separation of the churches from the state has not led to the suppression of religion by the state. Just the opposite. It meant the freeing of religion" (p. 549). In this environment, American Christianity has thrived. However, the delicate balance between church and state is threatened as religious leaders allow or even encourage the politicization of religion and the religiousization of politics.

Although the confessional era has offered evangelicals greater influence and access, this does not mean they are immune from the consequences of the confessional political society. Foucault (1995) argued about the naturalizing of surveillance:

> This enables the disciplinary power to be both absolutely indiscreet, since it is everywhere and always alert, since by its very principle it leaves no zone of shade and constantly supervises the very individuals who are entrusted with the task of supervising; and absolutely "discreet," for it functions permanently and largely in silence. (p. 177)

In essence, everyone is subjected to surveillance, even those seemingly in charge. Such a democratized sense of power is understandable since, for Foucault (1995), power "is not possessed as a thing, or transferred as a property" (p. 177). Thus, all individuals—even those in positions of power—are caught in the "machinery" of power (Foucault, 1995, p. 177) since "power is neither given, nor exchanged, nor recovered, but rather exercised, and . . . only exists in action" (Foucault, 1980, p. 89). Foucault (1980) also argued that "power *is* 'always already there,' that one is never 'outside' it, that there are no 'margins' for those who break with the system to gambol in" (p. 141, emphasis in original). Dreyfus and Rabinow (1983) explained that for Foucault, "power is exercised upon the dominant as well as on the dominated" since "power comes from below and we are all enmeshed in it" (p. 186). Therefore, Foucault argued that one did not find freedom from power in the confessional but merely entered another realm of power. Even religious leaders are thus confronted with consequences from the very confessional system they helped create.

As religion becomes politicized, it loses its religious message. C. Welton Gaddy (2005) of the Interfaith Alliance argued, "God-talk in the public square, especially God-talk employed for political purposes, *compromises the integrity of religion.* Bombarded by religious comments intended to advance political concerns, individuals lose sight of the real substance of religion" (p. 55, emphasis in original). On a similar note, former Democratic presidential contender Gary Hart (2005), who previously studied for the ministry at seminary, proclaimed:

> Organized religion that seeks to occupy political power loses its purity and its purpose. Jesus sought to change people's hearts, not their political parties. . . . When faith becomes an instrument of politics, it is no longer a religious faith. It is simply a political instrument like all others. (p. 34)

In particular, when religious leaders and organizations focus on political efforts, they risk being viewed as a political group instead of a religious one. Former Moral Majority leaders Cal Thomas and Ed Dobson (1999) critiqued the political focus of religious leaders in *Blinded by Might*:

> The damage to church is caused by those who appear to the "unchurched" to be interested in ushering in the kingdom of God by force . . . It is transformed from a force not of this world into one that deserves to be treated as just one more competitor for earthly power. It is seen as just another lobbying group to which politicians can toss an occasional bone to ensure loyalty. (p. 189)

Making a similar argument about the danger of politicizing the church, Reverend Jim Wallis (2005), a key leader of the evangelical left, wrote:

> When either party tries to politicize God, or co-opt religious communities for their political agendas, they make a terrible mistake. The best contribution of religion is precisely not to be ideologically predictable nor loyally partisan. Both parties, and the nation, must let the prophetic voice of religion be heard. Faith must be free to challenge both right and left from a consistent moral ground. (p. xiv)

Although Thomas, Dobson, and Wallis have inserted religion into presidential campaigns, they also recognize the problems that occur if religion and politics become too intertwined. As religious leaders and groups become more political, they lose their religious focus and therefore may fail to fulfill their religious teachings and obligations.

In addition to religious groups losing their focus, the politicization of religion can also result in blasphemous discourse. In particular, as our leaders and would-be leaders are expected to talk about religion, their theological discourse sometimes misuses religious ideas. Duke Divinity School professor Stephen B. Chapman (2004) argued that President George W. Bush's religious-political rhetoric is often sectarian and unorthodox to the point that it becomes "blasphemous speech" and perhaps "outright idolatry" (p. 96). In particular, he points to comments by Bush that uses messianic language to describe America. Chapman described:

> The rhetorical move in question neither shows sufficient respect for the Christian faith nor avoids privileging it. Instead, coded Christian language is used to advance a political agenda at great remove from what Jesus actually taught. The state is ever alert for opportunities to use the authority of Christ as a talisman for its advancing armies. If Christians do not insist on safeguarding that authority, the state will be only too glad to put Christ to another use. (p. 96)

David Kuo (2006), who has served as a religious speechwriter for several politicians—including Jack Kemp, John Ashcroft, Bob Dole, and George W. Bush—has come to regret using biblical verses and religious hymns for political purposes: "This *should* have been driving me nuts. . . . We were bastardizing God's words for our own political agenda and feeling good about it" (p. 61, emphasis in original). Often, religious language about God's work was used to describe the government's work, such as Bill Clinton's 1992 campaign theme of a "New Covenant" that described the people's salvation as coming from good government instead of Jesus. Similarly, when George W. Bush spoke of the "power, wonder-working power" in his 2003 State of the Union Address, he was referring to the work of the government and not the phrase's original meaning in a well-known Christian hymn about the sacrifice of Jesus. These types of comments are cited by scholars (e.g., Domke and Coe, 2008; Lincoln, 2004) as ways that politicians subtly incorporate religious buzzwords in their discourse to win the support of religious voters, yet the evangelicals so wooed apparently are not concerned by the blasphemous use of these religious words and texts. Perhaps as evangelicals have become more politicized they have come to applaud any attempt by presidential candidates to use their language, even when such comments actually subvert the true religious message of evangelicals.

As evangelicals have mobilized for political campaigns they have brought with them to the public square their own unique rhetorical religious-political language and style. In the process they risk over-politicizing their faith to the point they undermine their key religious values and even condone blasphemous statements. These religious leaders, however, are caught in the same confessional system they helped created and thus can find themselves under attack and forced to confess their inappropriate religious-political rhetoric, as occurred during the 2008 campaign with Reverend Jeremiah Wright and televangelist John Hagee. After Hagee's sermons attacking Catholicism were publicly criticized—leading 2008 Republican presidential nominee John McCain to reject Hagee's endorsement—Hagee apologized to and received forgiveness from Catholic League President William Donohue. Sometimes those demanding the confessions must offer their own, in the true spirit of the reverse confessional. As long as religious leaders like Hagee cast themselves as important political players, they may have to shed more of their religious beliefs in order to remain politically useful.

SUMMARY

University of Chicago social and political ethics professor Jean Bethke Elshtain (1999) argued in aftermath of Bill Clinton's confession of infidelity at a White House prayer breakfast that this presidential plea for forgiveness was just further proof of our confessional society:

> We are awash in confession these days. There is the low form on daytime television talk shows and the slightly higher form in bookstores. Rectitude in personal matters has given way to "contrition chic," as one wag called it, meaning a bargain-basement way to gain publicity, sympathy, and even absolution by trafficking in one's status as victim or victimizer. (p. 11)

As our presidential candidates have campaigned in this confessional era, they have often entered the very public and reverse confessional to discuss their religious faith before the entire electorate. Along the way, however, a problematic confessional political system has arisen that is harmful to our electoral process, democratic ideals, and religious faith. By confessing, our presidential candidates have helped firmly establish such rhetorical expectations as the norm for other candidates. In her Foucauldian analysis of a Spanish-language talk show hosted by a Catholic priest, Acosta-Alzuru (2003) argued that "these shows further perpetuate confession as a mode of internalizing social norms" (p. 157). Similarly, our evangelical leaders and presidential candidates continue to further perpetuate the confession in today's political environment. The confession has become so strongly a part of the electoral process that merely confessing is seen as a smart political strategy. For instance, on James Dobson's radio program in 2007, former House Speaker Newt Gingrich confessed he had an affair during the time of President Bill Clinton's impeachment hearings several years earlier. Gingrich's confession was seen by many as a sign that he was preparing for his own presidential run (Sullivan, 2008).

As America's would-be leaders campaign, it often seems similar to the questioning a prospective pastor might receive during an interview at a local church—being asked if they believe every word of the Bible, what the purpose of life is, and why God allows evil to exist. This pastoral approach—as opposed to the priestly metaphor—aptly depicts our modern presidential selection process. Some of the presidential candidates have even embraced pastoral descriptions. For instance, Jimmy Carter told the National Religious Broadcasters meeting in 1980, "A television station or the Oval Office is a powerful pulpit" (Carter, 1980b, p. 182). Earlier in his political career, Carter described his state senate district as "a church with 80,000 members" (Nielsen, 1977, p. 32). Carter even described himself as a religious figure when he said during his 1976 campaign that he prays for people during campaign rallies as they bring him their concerns: "Going through a crowd, quite often people bring me a problem, and I pray that their needs might be met" (Carter, 1977, p. 181). Mike Huckabee (1997), while Governor of Arkansas and years before his Republican presidential bid, described his pastoral duties as governor while helping people after a natural disaster: "In many ways I was more of a pastor than a governor during that time. There are times when I feel I'm pastoring a 2.5-million-member church" (p. 90). Perhaps as president he would have thought of himself as pastoring a 300-million-member church. Richard Cizik, then a vice president for the National Association of Evangelicals, justified viewing presidents as pastoral figures when he defended President George W. Bush's use of religious language in the lead-up to the 2003 Iraq war:

> [Presidents] have every right to use theological language. Why? Because in our form of government, they're not just the head of [their] party but the head of the state. In that role, it's a president's job to be "national healer and consoler." (Chapman, 2004, p. 93)

When our nation's would-be presidential leaders campaign to become our nation's Commander-in-Chief, they now often appear to be running for the position of Pastor-in-Chief. However, before they can become the nation's confessor, they must first assume the role of a confesser on the campaign trail to win in today's confessional voting booth.

Michel Foucault's confession, with appropriate modification, clearly demonstrates the problems of a confessional political system: establishment of a religious test for office, disenfranchised classes of Americans, preferential treatment for "chosen" Americans, restricted public dialogue on important issues, and the politicization of religion. As our religious-political landscape has changed and ushered in a new era of confessional politics, the civil-religious contract has been quickly tossed aside. It is America's loss that this vital contract expired. Stephen Carter (1993) noted the partisan nature of religious comments during the 1992 Republican convention, which he called "the frighteningly antidemocratic (small *d*) character of the push by a national party to replace secular politics with an appeal to religiosity" (p. 47, emphasis in original). He added, "In a nation founded on the principle of religious liberty, it might even be called un-American to imply, as some at the Republican Convention did, that those with a different set of religious precepts deserve whatever they get" (p. 47). Without the civil-religious contract to protect presidential candidates, citizens, American society, and churches, it remains likely that there will be even more antidemocratic discourse and erosion of democratic values.

Until more Americans recognize the dangers of confessional politics and cease demanding such appeals, presidential candidates will likely continue to engage in the testimonial, partisan, sectarian, and liturgical religious-political discourse that is harming our electoral process, our democratic ideals, and religious faiths. Foucault might chide such a suggestion that Americans could undo their confessional system as unrealistic optimism since the disciplinary techniques are so ingrained in our society. However, Hart (1977) was confident that the civil-religious contract would continue, even though it came to an end just as he was making his prediction. Although the confessional political style continued unabatedly in 2008, it is possible that the tide could change once again. As candidates preach hope and change, perhaps they will bring true hope and true change to our democracy by refusing to submit to the demands of the reverse confessional. Maybe the American people will even come to the point of accepting the wisdom of the Protestant reformer Martin Luther, who suggested he would even support a Muslim leader: "I would rather be governed by a competent Turk than by an incompetent Christian." Until then, however, it seems the United States remains without a prayer of returning to the religious-political model and wisdom of John F. Kennedy.

Chapter Eight

Conclusion

During the 2008 presidential campaign, influential evangelical leader James Dobson of Focus on the Family often offered his thoughts and judgments about the candidates on his national radio program. For instance, he early on declared that he could never vote for then-Republican front-runner Rudy Giuliani. Late in the Republican primary, Dobson endorsed Mike Huckabee and said he could never vote for John McCain nor Democrats Barack Obama and Hillary Clinton. Despite his discomfort with McCain, Dobson later blasted Obama for having a "confused theology" and for "deliberately distorting the traditional understanding of the Bible" (Gorski, 2008c, ¶8). Dobson also accused Obama of "dragging biblical understanding through the gutter" and offering a "fruitcake interpretation of the Constitution" (Gorski, 2008c, ¶9, 12).

However, Dobson's most significant hit during the 2008 campaign came as he attacked potential Republican hopeful Fred Thompson, whose candidacy was being pushed by evangelical leaders like Gary Bauer and Richard Land. Dobson's verdict regarding Thompson's presidential fitness was cast as judgment on Thompson's soul: "I don't think he's a Christian; at least that's my impression" (Gilgoff, 2007b, ¶2). Thompson's spokesperson quickly insisted that the former Tennessee U.S. senator was indeed a Christian and had been "baptized into the Church of Christ" (Gilgoff, 2007b, ¶3), although Thompson now rarely attended church. In response, Focus on the Family spokesman Gary Schneeberger clarified Dobson's remark by explaining that Dobson "has never known Thompson to be a committed Christian— someone who talks openly about his faith. . . . We use that word—Christian—to refer to people who are evangelical Christians" (Gilgoff, 2007b,

¶4–5). Such remarks are quite revealing about Dobson's mindset—one must be an evangelical and talk openly about their personal faith in order to be considered a Christian.

Speaking about Dobson's religious vetting of the presidential candidates, University of Notre Dame historian Mark Noll noted:

> Evangelicals have always had a pretty narrow understanding of who is a Christian in the proper sense of the term. . . . Catholics and most Lutherans and Episcopalians would say that anyone who has been baptized is a Christian, but most evangelicals would not agree. They see baptism as an initiation ceremony that may or may not indicate the presence of true faith. (Gilgoff, 2007c, ¶10)

For Dobson—and many evangelicals—to be a true Christian one must talk openly about their personal faith, which is to say that one must be, or at least talk like, an evangelical. More significantly, one must pass this rhetorical religious test in order to be considered a worthy presidential candidate. Evangelical leaders today often wield immense influence and serve as the conduits through which presidential aspirants must go when seeking the support of evangelicals; and these kingmakers also demand that candidates "talk the talk" to prove their Christian pedigree.

To garner support of the critical evangelical voting bloc, a presidential candidate must talk about religion in very specific ways—and many politicians seem more than willing to make such discursive adjustments in order to reach the White House. For instance, Gary Bauer pointed to Republican John McCain's talk of America being a "Christian nation" as proof that the candidate was appropriately reaching out to evangelicals to gain the Republican nomination:

> Just like in 2000, he can't get it [the nomination] without getting a significant number of us. . . . When he said that [Christian nation], he took it on the chin, but it was the kind of thing that would get our people to sort of sit up and take notice and take another look. (Feldmann, 2007b, ¶49)

Eight years after McCain failed in his quest for the Republican presidential nomination, in large part because of the religious-political opposition to his campaign by those he called "agents of intolerance," McCain found political redemption in 2008 once he himself embraced the religious-political strategy he previously eschewed. But at what cost? When a candidate must seek public penance from religious leaders like Jerry Falwell and James Dobson and recite the confessional statements of religious activists like Gary Bauer, such pandering may help one win elections but harms our democratic process. As journalist Bill Moyers argued, "If you have to talk about God to win elections, that doesn't speak well of God or elections" (On journalism, 2007, ¶40). Indeed, it is this simple premise that guides this study. In order to further our understanding of the critical role religious-political rhetoric now plays in the selection of our nation's highest political leader, this chapter summarizes the study's significant findings and briefly considers the potential impact of these findings on the 2012 presidential race.

SUMMARY OF FINDINGS

This study offers several important findings to our understanding of religious-political discourse in presidential campaigns. First, this study detailed the demise of the civil-religious contract. Although Hart (1977) astutely captured the religious-political environment he analyzed, our nation's political and cultural environment has drastically changed since Hart's original thesis. Far from remaining impersonal and maintaining a private-public divide, presidential candidates since born-again Sunday school teacher Jimmy Carter have often openly professed their personal religious faith. Rather than offering their religious rhetoric in nonpartisan ways, today's presidential candidates invoke God to support their partisan policy positions. Instead of using generic and inclusive religious references, our presidential candidates now make sectarian arguments as they rhetorically exclude some Americans. Finally, presidential candidates today no longer include religious rhetoric in their speeches for merely artful ceremonial purposes, but instead assume the role of national worship leader. With these changes, our presidential candidates have rendered the civil-religious contract null and void.

However, many scholars of presidential rhetoric continue to utilize the civil-religious contract to examine rhetoric that no longer conforms to the contract's requirements. In fact, these scholars have used the civil-religious contract as a guiding framework in explorations of such noncontractual rhetors as Jimmy Carter, Jerry Falwell, and George W. Bush. In these studies (e.g., Erickson, 1980; Friedenberg 2002; Goldzwig, 2002; Hart and Pauley, 2005), the contract's rhetorical template serves as something of a theoretical blinder, limiting consideration of rhetorical features that do not fit the contract's demands. Although the civil-religious contract might still offer some insights for analyzing presidential governance discourse, it no longer serves as an instructive tool for investigations of campaign discourse. Thus, it is imperative that presidential rhetoric scholars acknowledge the limitations of the civil-religious contract when selecting theoretical perspectives to explain religious-political discourse and incorporate alternative perspectives that more fully illuminate our new era of presidential campaign rhetoric. As Boase (1989) concluded after noting the uniqueness of the religious rhetoric of Jimmy Carter and Ronald Reagan, "Perhaps all future aspirants to the Oval Office will have to testify to a second birth, even as some nineteenth-century presidential hopefuls felt compelled to claim a log cabin as a birth-place" (p. 7). With candidates now claiming a heavenly mansion as their born-again home, it becomes clear that once-accepted tenets of the civil-religious contract no longer hold. The "New Deal" of Franklin Roosevelt has been replaced by the "New Covenant" of Bill Clinton.

A second significant finding from this study is the description of a new style of religious-political discourse that has emerged following the demise of the civil-religious contract and the creation of a new model of candidates' religious-political rhetoric. The new religious-political approach—christened in this study as the confessional political style—represents a substantial shift from the religious rhetoric found in presidential elections during the contractual period. In the confessional political era, our successful presidential candidates have been those whose religious-political discourse has been testimonial, partisan, sectarian, and liturgical in nature. With their testimonial statements, candidates have talked openly about their personal religious beliefs and their Christian conversion experiences. In a clearly partisan manner, our presidential candidates have invoked God and quoted scripture to justify their public policies, explain their political successes, and attack their political opponents. With sectarian flair, today's candidates use religious-political rhetoric that excludes some Americans, is evangelistic in nature, and attacks or offers minimal support for the separation of church and state. Finally, presidential candidates use liturgical rhetoric as they detail their theological beliefs and lead the nation in worship of a Christian God.

Candidates who best embody this confessional political style win presidential elections, with the most rhetorically religious winning in each election from 1976 to 2008. Jimmy Carter, who helped instigate the confessional style, captured the White House with his God-talk. Four years later, Carter toned down his religious-political claims and was ousted by Ronald Reagan, who was more willing to meet the rhetorical expectations of evangelical leaders. Reagan easily won reelection over Walter Mondale, who was much less open about his religious beliefs. In 1988, George H. W. Bush, who was fairly uncomfortable discussing his faith, defeated an even more rhetorically secular candidate, Michael Dukakis. Yet, Bush was defeated four years later by an evangelical Southern Baptist Democrat—Bill Clinton. With Bob Dole, another Republican reluctant to discuss religion, Clinton easily secured a second term. In 2000, the evangelical George W. Bush managed to narrowly out-God-talk—and out-maneuver—his Democratic opponent, the evangelical Al Gore. As Bush increased his religious rhetoric four years later, he overcame the religiously reticent John Kerry. In 2008, a Bible-quoting Democrat, Barack Obama, defeated John McCain, who was uncomfortable with speaking openly about his personal faith.

It is important to reiterate that the presidential candidates who have experienced electoral success with their talk of religion have not necessarily been those who were the most religiously devout or most active in their church. Rather, it has been the candidate most outspoken in affirming their religious beliefs on the campaign trail, which is not always the candidate most religiously devout. In short, it has been the candidate who is the most *rhetorically* religious. As Stephen Carter (1993) noted, while Jimmy Carter taught Sunday school classes as president, it was Ronald Reagan who rarely attended church services yet remained popular with conservative Christians:

> The point is that many opinion shapers on the religious right argued in the course of the 1980 campaign, and again in 1984, that Ronald Reagan was one of them and that a vote for Reagan was, in effect, a vote for God's candidate. By 1984, it was inconceivable that these churchmen could have mistaken Reagan's patent lack of personal interest in things religious for a deep commitment of faith. . . . In his public rhetoric, and sometimes in his public acts, Reagan took this obligation quite seriously, and so did other members of his administration. (p. 98–99)

Reagan defeated the more active churchmen Jimmy Carter and Walter Mondale by out–God-talking them. Reagan found success not because he "walked the walk," but because he "talked the talk." Similarly, John Kerry attended church more frequently than George W. Bush, yet Bush won on election day after employing more religious rhetoric on the campaign trail (Sullivan, 2008). The religious test for office in the confessional political era remains a rhetorical one. However, as a rhetorical-critical examination of religious-political discourse, this study is unable to make causal claims suggesting any sort of direct relationship between religious rhetoric and electoral outcome. The evidence provided by this study supports a convincing argument for the apparent relationship between a candidate's religious rhetoric and their ability to secure the presidency, but it is not the only or even most important factor. There are many factors that shape the outcome of a presidential election and thus this study points to a candidate's religious rhetoric as a contributive, not determinative, factor.

A third important contribution of this study is that it reveals that such a rhetorical shift among our presidential candidates did not occur in a vacuum, but instead emerged as important societal religious-political shifts developed. When John F. Kennedy sought the presidency in 1960, he faced questions about if he was too Catholic. Since then, Catholics have faced questions about if they are Catholic enough, and other candidates have also been questioned about if they are religious enough to be president. It is not that Kennedy was more religious than John Kerry or Rudy Giuliani. In fact, Jacqueline Kennedy remarked during the 1960 campaign, "I think it's so unfair of people to be against Jack because he's Catholic. . . . He's such a poor

Catholic" (Balmer, 2008, p.12). In larger measure, the shift from the civil-religious contract to our confessional political era has occurred due to a changing American society rather than changes in candidates' rhetorical preferences.

Although some scholars have referred to a "god strategy" used by presidents for political gain (Domke and Coe, 2008), such analysis fails to acknowledge why this strategy is needed and has been successful today when the very same appeals would have failed in 1960. This study offers insights into why the contractual period was replaced by the confessional approach, including changes in American Catholicism, the impact of the civil rights movement, our nation's religious shift from mainline Protestantism to evangelicalism, reactions to Supreme Court decisions, the aftermath of Watergate and Vietnam, and the rise of a religious-political activist infrastructure. These changes, coupled with attempts by evangelical leaders to use their new positions of influence, ushered in a new confessional era where our presidential candidates are expected to talk about their religious beliefs and make clear how their beliefs would guide their public policies. As atheist Michael Shermer, publisher of *Skeptic* magazine, complained about the religious focus of presidential campaigns: "Legally, there is no religious test for office, but culturally there obviously is" (Non-believing, 2007, ¶14). This study has documented the creation of an unwritten rhetorical religious test for the presidency of the United States and the rhetorical exigencies that helped create this qualification for office.

A final major finding from this study is found in the development of theory by which to critically examine the impact of confessional political discourse on our democracy. This study advanced a significant adjustment to Michel Foucault's work on the confession by democratizing, or rebaptizing, the confession in line with the evangelical Protestant tradition's use of confessionals that are very public and which reverse the nature of the confession. This new perspective on Foucault's confession provides scholars an important analytical tool to utilize in other explorations of confessional discourse with attendant elements of power/knowledge, control, and normalization.

Demonstrating the usefulness of the new theoretical perspective on the confession, this study critiques the impact of confessional politics on our democracy. In particular, our current confessional political system excludes some candidates from presidential consideration, disenfranchises entire groups of Americans from the political process, provides preferential treatment for evangelicals, limits the ability for public dialogue, and hurts religion by politicizing it. Thus, confessional politics harms our electoral process, democratic ideals, and religious faiths.

What American politics desperately needs is a revival of the ideals underlying the civil-religious contract as embodied by John F. Kennedy in his speech to the Greater Houston Ministerial Association. Instead, what remains is a rhetorical religious test that not only violates the spirit of Article VI of the U.S. Constitution that "no religious test shall ever be required as a qualification to any office or public trust under the United States," but also harms basic democratic premises undergirding our nation. In developing his work explaining the functioning of the modern rhetorical presidency—as discussed in chapter 1—Tulis (1987) argued that although our president's constitutional powers were not technically changed by constitutional amendment, within the age of the "rhetorical presidency" a "Second Constitution" has now been imposed on top of the first, thus creating "a rhetorical fitness test" for presidential leadership (p. 184). Similarly, while the demands of the confessional political era have not technically changed Article VI of the U.S. Constitution, a defacto rhetorical religious test has now been imposed to guide the selection of our presidents. America has not officially ratified a confessional political system like in Lebanon where the president must be a Maronite Christian, the prime minister must be a Sunni Muslim, and the speaker of the Parliament must be a Shi'a Muslim. The United States's confessional political system, however, is not formally dictated by the Constitution and is not intended to promote religious diversity in leadership. In today's confessional system, presidents do not necessarily have to be an evangelical Christian, but they must be able to speak like one. Even though our confessional system is not officially codified, such rhetorical expectations are still powerful. As Foucault (1999) argued, with pastoral power the pastor "can demand of others an absolute obedience . . . as a function of his own ruling, without even the existence of general rules or a law" (p. 124). Similarly, our current and harmful religious test for presidential selection was never legislated or constructed through judicial means, instead emerging as part of the religious confessional era.

AN EYE ON 2012

With a clear connection for three decades between rhetorical religiosity and success in the presidential general election, some insights can be offered concerning the 2012 presidential election. Until all the candidates are known and they begin their rhetorical appeals, one cannot know for certain who will more fully embody the confessional political style. However, assuming the rhetorical religious test for office continues through the next election, there are a few different scenarios that could arise. The first important unknown variable is whether President Barack Obama will be more like Jimmy Carter or Bill Clinton as he shapes his reelection discourse. If he takes the route of Carter and tones down his religious-political rhetoric, he could find himself vulnerable to being out-God-talked by his Republican challenger and thus politically vulnerable due to the confessional political expectations. The other main unknown is who will emerge as the Republican challenger. Will they run someone like Ronald Reagan who freely injects religious rhetoric into campaign messages or will their standard-bearer be someone like Bob Dole who is uncomfortable with public religious appeals. Considering the religious-political trend of the past three decades, a candidate like Mike Huckabee, Rick Santorum, or Bobby Jindal would likely give the Republicans a better shot of retaking the White House than someone like Mitch Daniels or Haley Barbour. Mitt Romney provides a more difficult scenario. He clearly demonstrated his willingness to utilize the confessional political style during the 2008 election. However, as a Mormon he also faced the judgment of the confessional political system that placed him outside the evangelical Christian mainstream. The issue of his Mormon faith would be unlikely to go away for many Republican primary voters in 2012. Similarly, Newt Gingrich's recent conversion to evangelical Catholicism places him rhetorically within the confessional political style, but his divorces and affairs could cause problems with many evangelical voters.

Four different main matchups present themselves at this point: still religiously outspoken Obama versus religiously quiet Republican, still religiously outspoken Obama versus religiously outspoken Republican, religiously quieter Obama versus religiously quiet Republican, and religiously quieter Obama versus religiously outspoken Republican. Assuming the confessional political system remains intact for 2012, the first matchup could help Obama gain reelection while the last matchup could assist a Republican victory. The other two scenarios could be closer and thus would depend on the degree of religious outspokenness or quietness, much as in 1988 when a relatively religiously quiet George H. W. Bush beat an even more religiously quiet Michael Dukakis. Thus far, Obama has shown little sign of moderating or quieting his religious-political rhetoric as he has continued George W. Bush's faith-based initiatives and continues to quote scriptures in his speeches. If this trend continues, it would appear that the Republican's only prayer for success would be to find a candidate who can comfortably pass our nation's rhetorical religious test. However, the confessional demands placed upon our candidates could change. When Hart (1977) penned his initial description of the civil-religious contract, it came just as the contract's hold on presidential rhetoric was coming to an end. Likewise, it is possible that after thirty years the confessional political era could also be replaced or modified. Perhaps the pendulum will swing back to the civil-religious contract or perhaps yet another distinctive style of religious-political discourse will arise.

CONCLUSION

In 1976, as America celebrated its two hundredth birthday, a new relationship between religion and politics was emerging. Thirty years later, this confessional political style still dominates presidential campaign rhetoric. Despite undermining our democratic ideals, American voters—led by evangelical leaders—continue to demand that candidates meet the confessional political expectations. Candidates who refuse find themselves watching from afar on inauguration day as a more religiously outspoken candidate places their hand on a Bible and solemnly swears to uphold the Constitution of the United States.

An incident during Reform Party nominee Ross Perot's 1996 speech at a Christian Coalition meeting illustrates the rhetorical demands of the confessional era. Arguing that his 1992 candidacy was not responsible for the election of Bill Clinton, Perot was interrupted when he stated, "I ask you, as honest, religious people . . ." by a voice from the audience shouting out "Christian" (Perot, 1996, ¶38–39). A startled Perot recovered and adjusted his remarks: ". . . to please go—honest Christian people; however you want it—honest Christian people, to please go to the library and study the exit polls from the 1992 election" (Perot, 1996, ¶40). Not only did Perot seek an audience with the Christian Coalition—demonstrating the political influence of these evangelicals—but he quickly, although rather awkwardly, adopted the language that they literally demanded. The question is how long will evangelical leaders and citizens remain able to successfully demand our presidential candidates meet their rhetorical demands?

Afterword

In September of 2010—just as this book originally went to press—former U.S. Senator Rick Santorum traveled to Houston, Texas to deliver a speech on the role of religion in politics. In the speech, entitled "A Charge to Revive the Role of Faith in the Public Square," the life-long Catholic articulated his religious-political vision as he prepared for his upcoming presidential run. However, he also presented the speech as a rebuke to another Catholic politician. Santorum deliberately trekked to Houston to deliver the speech just days before the fiftieth anniversary of then-Democratic presidential nominee John F. Kennedy's famous speech on religion and politics. While Kennedy perfectly captured the rhetorical expectations of his era, Santorum demonstrated how dramatically those expectations had changed. When former Massachusetts Governor Mitt Romney delivered his speech on religion and politics in Texas during the 2008 campaign, he subtly tried to draw comparisons to Kennedy while rhetorically articulating a dramatically different message (Kaylor, 2011). While Santorum painted a religious-political vision similar to that of Romney—whom Santorum endorsed during the 2008 campaign—Santorum offered a more explicit critique of Kennedy's political doctrine.

During his Houston speech, Santorum argued that while Kennedy broke the barrier preventing Catholics from moving into 1600 Pennsylvania Avenue, Kennedy did so by starting "the construction of another, even more threatening wall for our society—one that sealed off informed moral wisdom into a realm of non rational beliefs that have no legitimate role in political discourse" (Santorum, 2010, ¶1). Santorum added, "Kennedy chose not just to dispel fear, he chose to expel faith" (Santorum, 2010, ¶3). While Kennedy advocated a strict separation of church and state, Santorum quickly turned his rhetorical fire on the concept. Santorum derided the historic principle Kennedy advocated by arguing Kennedy's approach resulted in making "people of faith increasingly feel like second-class citizens" (Santorum, 2010, ¶13). While Kennedy argued that public policy matters could be decided independently from religious teachings, Santorum insisted the two are inherently intertwined. Thus, Santorum ended his speech by claiming Kennedy "undermined the essential role that faith" plays in U.S. politics and society and helped create an environment that results in "repressing or banishing people of faith from having a say in government" (Santorum, 2010, ¶58-59). With that, the man who would win the 2012 Iowa caucuses—primarily due to his faith-based appeals that won over conservative evangelical voters (who made up nearly 60 percent of the voters in the Hawkeye State)—staked a position 180 degrees from that which helped Kennedy remove the "no Catholics" sign from Oval Office. A half century had brought substantial religious-political changes.

CONTINUING THE TREND IN 2012

Santorum's religious appeals hardly stand out as unique during the 2012 Republican presidential primaries. Throughout much of the primary season, most of the Republican candidates appeared to be on a quest to out-God-talk one another. With the exception of Jon Huntsman—whose distant third place finish in New Hampshire was not "a ticket to ride"—each of the candidates frequently engaged in confessional politics (and Huntsman, a Mormon who cast himself as spiritual instead of religious, at times tried confessional politics). Although some of the candidates saw their campaigns end due to verbal gaffes (U.S. Representative Michele Bachmann and Texas Governor Rick Perry) or allegations of sexual misconduct (Herman Cain), their rapid rise in the polls came largely due to their faith-based appeals to evangelical voters. Bachmann, who often spoke during Sunday church services while campaigning, mobilized evangelical voters to win the Iowa Straw Poll in August of 2011. Perry launched his campaign by hosting a prayer rally in a football stadium. Perry, Bachmann, and Cain all spoke about being "called" by God to run for president. Former Speaker of the House Newt Gingrich again confessed his past moral failings and spoke about finding God's forgiveness. As Perry ended his presidential run after his dramatic fall from grace following poor debate performances, he justified his endorsement of Gingrich by talking about his faith: "Newt is not perfect, but who among us is. The fact is, there is forgiveness for those who seek God. And I believe in the power of redemption, for it is a central tenet of my Christian faith" (Perry, 2012, ¶21-22). Gingrich's strong victory in the South Carolina primary came as he matched former Arkansas Governor and Southern Baptist pastor Mike Huckabee's 2008 showing among evangelicals in the Palmetto State. Gingrich's victory in South Carolina suggests, as was argued in this study, that a candidate's rhetorical confessional appeals can outweigh his personal behavior and religiosity. U.S. Representative Ron Paul launched "Evangelicals for Ron Paul" and he rhetorically reached out to evangelicals by increasing his use of biblical references in speeches and stressing his pro-life record. Paul's efforts came due to the assistance of Doug Wead, who advised both George H.W. Bush and George W. Bush on religious-political outreach. Throughout the early states, Paul more than doubled his 2008 showing—and his evangelical outreach helped him nearly match Bachmann in the Iowa Straw Poll.

Even former Massachusetts Governor Mitt Romney's campaign again tried to utilize confessional politics, such as with campaign fliers in South Carolina that stressed his "faith" (although without referencing Mormonism). Despite these efforts, Romney actually fared worse among evangelicals in Iowa and New Hampshire than he had four years earlier and continues to struggle with voters who classify themselves as evangelicals or say they care about the religious beliefs of candidates. Worried that the splitting of the anti-Romney vote would help Romney capture the nomination—much as Senator John McCain benefited from the vote being split between Huckabee and former U.S. Senator Fred Thompson—more than 150 conservative evangelicals even gathered for an unprecedented gathering on a Texas ranch to try and coalesce around a single candidate. Meeting between the New Hampshire and South Carolina primaries, the group emerged to declare Santorum as their favored candidate—with Gingrich also receiving a number of votes. Thus, the evangelical Protestant leaders cast their support for two evangelical Catholics over Perry, an evangelical Protestant. Santorum, who called himself a "Jesus candidate" while campaigning, touted the endorsement and urged evangelical voters to choose a candidate who could speak their language:

> I feel blessed that over 150 Christian leaders could 'miraculously' come together and support my candidacy. . . . But my question to you this morning is will the people of South Carolina vote their conscience or let others who don't speak our language choose our candidate. (Stanley, 2012, ¶3)

Once again, a candidate's ability to "talk the talk" helped in the campaign. Although the effort by evangelical leaders may not stop Romney from capturing the nomination, it does represent the continuing political influence of evangelical Catholics. Despite the concerns about Romney's faith, many conservative evangelicals will likely quickly find ways to justify voting for Romney against Obama in the general election—just as James Dobson and others quickly pivoted from attacking McCain during the 2008 primaries to supporting him in the general election.

Not to be outdone, President Barack Obama appears determined tack closer to the religious-political reelection strategy of Bill Clinton than Jimmy Carter. In late 2011, the Democratic National Convention hired Reverend Derrick Harkins, an African American Baptist pastor in Washington, D.C., to lead its religious outreach. Harkins, a board member for the National Association of Evangelicals, is well connected within evangelical circles. Joshua DuBois, who led Obama's religious outreach during the 2008 campaign, now heads the White House Office of Faith-based and Neighborhood Partnerships. Obama also continues to frequently invoke God and quote scriptures in speeches, even periodically offering highly personal, confessional moments. Thus, he seems unwilling to cede the topic of religion to the Republicans in 2012. As the rhetoric of Obama and his Republican challengers suggest, the trend of the past nearly four decades appears to be continuing.

CONCLUSION

As speakers blared the O'Jays song "For the Love of Money," a triumphant Donald Trump waltzed up the stairs and waved to the cheering crowd. Approaching the podium to the singing of "money, money, money, money," the twice-divorced businessman who built multiple casinos found himself the star at a gathering of conservative evangelical activists from around the nation. While flirting with a presidential run in the summer of 2011, the business tycoon and reality TV host went through many of the normal motions of a would-be presidential candidate. This included joining the other candidates on a pilgrimage to the annual meeting of the Faith & Freedom Coalition, which was founded by the former Christian Coalition leader Ralph Reed. Joining Trump in the weekend's lineup were Republican presidential hopefuls Michele Bachmann, Herman Cain, Jon Huntsman, Ron Paul, Tim Pawlenty, Mitt Romney, and Rick Santorum. Events hosted by the conservative evangelical group event not only bring together a "who's who" list of conservative politicians and activists, but are also among the expected stops on the way to the Republican presidential nomination.

Although Trump had weeks earlier slowed down speculation of a presidential run by signing up for another year of hosting his television show *The Apprentice*, he kept suggesting he might still run later since he did not like any of the candidates. As he took the stage at the conservative evangelical event, Trump started his speech by showing a picture of his confirmation class at First Presbyterian Church in Jamaica, N.Y. He held up a copy of the picture as the image was also displayed on the large video screens—as if he needed to prove he had been in the class. Trump told the group he kept a copy of the photo on his desk. As the room of about 1,000 evangelical pastors and activists erupted in applause, a smiling Trump responded, "Good, right? That doesn't always play, but in this crowd it plays." With that, Trump demonstrated he understood today's era of confessional politics—presidential aspirants need to prove their Christian faith by publicly talking about it. As the on-again, off-again candidate left the stage to applause and an encore of his "money, money, money, money" theme song from *The Apprentice*, his presence at the event—as well as that of the more serious candidates—demonstrated that, like money, faith can move mountains and voters.

Similarly, the rhetorical expectation to offer such public expressions of piety are so great that even faux presidential candidate Stephen Colbert started his short-lived 2012 campaign by praying publicly to determine if—like Bachmann, Cain, and Perry had suggested about themselves—God wanted him to run for president. After a brief pause with his head bowed, Colbert looked up and declared, "Okay, God's good with it." While Colbert comically pokes fun at such religiously-based campaigning, it raises serious concerns about the actual state of U.S. politics. After evangelical leaders meeting in Texas voted to back Santorum in hopes of stopping Romney from garnering the nomination, Colbert returned to the topic to offer his disappointment in the selection: "Personally, I would not have gone with Santorum. If I were God, I would have gone with me." Colbert, a Catholic Sunday School teacher, then listed his religious-political credentials—much like actual candidates do while seeking religious voters. Despite the entertainment Trump and Colbert add to presidential politics, the troubling consequences of confessional politics detailed in this study remain. Perhaps in a future campaign cycle, politicians and voters will leave such God-talk to television personalities. Until then, however, would-be presidents must seek political salvation in the confessional voting booth.

January 31, 2012
Brian T. Kaylor

REFERENCES

Kaylor, B. T. (2011). No Jack Kennedy: Mitt Romney's "Faith in America" speech and the changing religious-political environment. *Communication Studies, 62*, 491-507.
Perry, R. (2012, January 19). *Withdrawal announcement*. Retrieved January 30, 2012 from www.blog.chron.com/rickperry.
Santorum, R. (2010, September 9). *A charge to revive the role of faith in the public square*. Retrieved January 24, 2012 from www.eppc.org.
Stanley, P. (2012, January 15). Republican candidates vie for evangelical vote at SC prayer breakfast. Christian Post. Retrieved January 23, 2012 from www.christianpost.com .

References

Acosta-Alzuru, C. (2003). Change your life!: Confession and conversion in Telemundo's *Cambia Tu Vida*. *Mass Communication & Society, 6*, 137–59.

Albright, M. (2006). *The mighty & the almighty: Reflections on America, God, and world affairs*. New York: HarperCollins Publishers.

Alessi, R. (2008, May 15). In Kentucky, Obama ads stress that he's a Christian. *Lexington Herald-Leader*. Retrieved June 13, 2008 from LexisNexis.

Alpern, D. M., Fuller, T., Manning, R., Doyle, J., Agrest, S., & Kasindorf, M. (1980, May 5). Campaign '80: The third man. *Newsweek*, 46. Retrieved April 25, 2008 from LexisNexis.

Alter, A. (2007, September 21). Confession makes a comeback. *Wall Street Journal*, p. W1. Retrieved September 4, 2007 from www.wsj.com.

An investigation of allegations of politicized hiring by Monica Goodling and other staff in the office of the attorney general. (2008, July 28). Retrieved February 22, 2009 from www.usdoj.gov.

Aquino, J. (2006, March 24). Survey: U.S. trust lowest for atheists. *Minnesota Daily*. Retrieved July 8, 2008 from LexisNexis.

Artz, M. (2007, March 14). Stark gives confession. *Inside Bay Area*. Retrieved October 28, 2007 from LexisNexis.

Babington, C. (2007, July 12). Hindu clergyman from Reno makes history: Senate prayer disrupted. *Associated Press*. October 28, 2007 from LexisNexis.

Balmer, R. (2006). *Thy kingdom come: How the Religious Right distorts the faith and threatens America*. New York: Basic Books.

Balmer, R. (2008). *God in the White House: How faith shaped the presidency from John F. Kennedy to George W. Bush*. New York: HarperOne.

Banerjee, N. (2008, June 25). Religion and its role are in dispute at the service academies. *New York Times*, p. A14. Retrieved July 2, 2008 from LexisNexis.

Bauer, S. W. (2008). *The art of the public grovel: Sexual sin & public confession in America*. Princeton, N.J.: Princeton University Press.

Beamish, R. (1984, November 5). President, challenger fill airwaves with ads. *Associated Press*. Retrieved April 14, 2008 from LexisNexis.

Beasley, V. B. (2002). Engendering democratic change: How three U.S. presidents discussed female suffrage. *Rhetoric & Public Affairs, 5*, 79–103.

Bellah, R. N. (1967). Civil religion in America. *Daedalus, 96*, 1–21.

Bellah, R. N. (1975). *The broken covenant: American civil religion in time of trial*. New York: Seabury Press.

Bellah, R. N. (1992). *The broken covenant: American civil religion in time of trial*. Chicago: University of Chicago Press.

Beloit College's mindset list for the class of 2011. (2007). Retrieved August 30, 2007 from www.beloit.edu.

Benson, J. M. (1981). The polls: A rebirth of religion? *Public Opinion Quarterly, 45*, 576–85.

Berlinerblau, J. (2008). *Thumpin' it: The use and abuse of the Bible in today's presidential politics*. Louisville, KY: Westminster John Knox Press.

Bernauer, J. (2004). Michel Foucault's philosophy of religion: An introduction to the non-fascist life. In J. Bernauer & J. Carrette (Eds.), *Michel Foucault and theology: The politics of religious experience* (pp. 80–97). Burlington, VT: Ashgate Publishing Company.

Bernauer, J., & Carrette, J. (2004). Introduction: The enduring problem: Foucault, theology and culture. In J. Bernauer & J. Carrette (Eds.), *Michel Foucault and theology: The politics of religious experience* (pp. 1–16). Burlington, VT: Ashgate Publishing Company.

Billups, A. (2008, April 14). McCain keeps his faith out of politics. *Washington Times*. Retrieved April 14, 2008 from www.washingtontimes.com.

Bitzer, L. F. (1968). The rhetorical situation. *Philosophy and Rhetoric, 1*, 1–14.

Blosser, J. B. (1983, May 20). Mondale criticizes Reagan education cuts. *United Press International*. Retrieved April 22, 2008 from LexisNexis.

Blumenthal, M. (2005, September 7). Pat Robertson's Katrina cash. *The Nation*. Retrieved July 16, 2008 from www.thenation.com.

Blumenthal, S. (1990). *Pledging allegiance: The last campaign of the Cold War*. New York: HarperCollins Publishers.

Boase, P. H. (1989). Moving the mercy seat into the White House: An exegesis of the Carter/Reagan religious rhetoric. *Journal of Communication and Religion, 12 (2)*, 1–9.

Boller, Jr., P. F. (1979). Religion and the U.S. presidency. *Journal of Church and State, 21*, 5–21.

Bolton, A. (2005, October 18). Right ups ante on Miers. *The Hill*, p. 1. Retrieved July 2, 2008 from LexisNexis.

Booth, M. (2002, December 18). 'Sorry' seems to be the hardest word: Lott walks rocky path toward second chance in America's confessional culture. *Denver Post*, p. A01. Retrieved June 25, 2008 from LexisNexis.

Boyer, P. S. (2005). Biblical prophecy and foreign policy. In C. H. Badaracco (Ed.), *Quoting God: How media shape ideas about religion and culture* (pp. 107–22). Waco, TX: Baylor University Press.

Brachear, M. (2007, June 24). Obama tells church right 'hijacked' faith. *Chicago Tribune*. Retrieved March 3, 2008 from LexisNexis.

Briggs, K. A. (1980a, June 9). Handling Anderson's position on religion poses a dilemma for his campaign effort. *New York Times*, p. B12. Retrieved April 25, 2008 from LexisNexis.

Briggs, K. A. (1980b, August 19). Evangelicals turning to politics fear moral slide imperils nation. *New York Times*, p. D17. Retrieved May 31, 2008 from LexisNexis.

Brockriede, W. (1974). Rhetorical criticism as argument. *Quarterly Journal of Speech, 60*, 165–74.

Broder, D. S. (1984, July 17). The Mondale logic. *Washington Post*, p. A19. Retrieved April 14, 2008 from LexisNexis.

Brune, T. (2007, August 8). The art of getting personal. *Newsday*. Retrieved August 14, 2007 from www.newsday.com.

Bruni, F., & Mitchell, A. (2000, March 2). McCain apologizes for characterizing Falwell and Robertson as forces of evil. *New York Times*, p. A23. Retrieved October 28, 2007 from LexisNexis.

Buchanan, P. (1991, December 10). *Presidential campaign announcement*. Retrieved March 12, 2008 from LexisNexis.

Bumiller, E. (with Kirkpatrick, D. D.). (2005, October 13). Bush criticized over emphasis on religion of nominee. *New York Times*, p. A23. Retrieved July 2, 2008 from LexisNexis.

Burris, R. (2007, November 2). Obama exposes rift between gay, black communities. *The State*. Retrieved July 8, 2008 from LexisNexis.

Bush, G. (1987, February 2). *Message to the National Religious Broadcasters national convention*. Retrieved May 13, 2008 from www.fednews.com.

Bush, G. (1988a, January 5). *National Press Club luncheon.* Retrieved May 13, 2008 from www.fednews.com.

Bush, G. (1988b, August 8). *Republican platform hearings.* Retrieved May 13, 2008 from www.fednews.com.

Bush, G. (1988c, August 18). *Republican National Convention session VI statement.* Retrieved May 13, 2008 from www.fednews.com.

Bush, G. (1988d, September 7). *Speech to B'nai B'rith international convention.* Retrieved May 13, 2008 from www.fednews.com.

Bush, G. (1991a, November 1). *Speech to Bush/Quayle '92 event.* Retrieved March 12, 2008 from LexisNexis.

Bush, G. (1991b, November 26). *Participates in teleconference with the Association of Christian Schools International Teachers Convention.* Retrieved March 12, 2008 from LexisNexis.

Bush, G. (1992a, January 27). *Remarks to the religious broadcasters.* Retrieved March 12, 2008 from LexisNexis.

Bush, G. (1992b, March 3). *Remarks to the annual convention of the National Association of Evangelicals.* Retrieved March 12, 2008 from LexisNexis.

Bush, G. (1992c, April 20). *Remarks to Ameriflora '92 meeting.* Retrieved March 12, 2008 from LexisNexis.

Bush, G. (1992d, May 17). *Commencement address, The University of Notre Dame.* Retrieved March 12, 2008 from LexisNexis.

Bush, G. (1992e, May 27). *Remarks to Mount Parin School community with question and answer period.* Retrieved March 12, 2008 from LexisNexis.

Bush, G. (1992f, May 29). *Remarks at town hall of Los Angeles.* Retrieved March 12, 2008 from LexisNexis.

Bush, G. (1992g, July 14). *Remarks at the signing ceremony at Sequoia Grove Trail.* Retrieved March 12, 2008 from LexisNexis.

Bush, G. (1992h, July 21). *Remarks to religious and ethnic groups.* Retrieved March 12, 2008 from LexisNexis.

Bush, G. (1992i, August 5). *Remarks to the Knights of Columbus Annual Supreme Council.* Retrieved March 12, 2008 from LexisNexis.

Bush, G. (1992j, August 20). *Remarks at ecumenical prayer breakfast.* Retrieved March 12, 2008 from LexisNexis.

Bush, G. (1992k, August 20). *Republican National Convention remarks.* Retrieved March 12, 2008 from LexisNexis.

Bush, G. (1992l, September 8). *Address to the 36th annual International Convention of B'nai B'rith.* Retrieved March 12, 2008 from LexisNexis.

Bush, G. (1992m, September 15). *Address to the National Guard Association Convention.* Retrieved March 12, 2008 from LexisNexis.

Bush, G. W. (1999a, September 24). *Remarks at home schools event.* Retrieved February 27, 2008 from LexisNexis.

Bush, G. W. (1999b, November 19). *Remarks on foreign policy.* Retrieved February 27, 2008 from LexisNexis.

Bush, G. W. (2000a, January 6). *Interviewed following GOP debate.* Retrieved February 27, 2008 from LexisNexis.

Bush, G. W. (2000b, February 29). *Takes questions following campaign event.* Retrieved February 27, 2008 from LexisNexis.

Bush, G. W. (2000c, August 3). *Delivers acceptance speech at Republican National Convention.*

Bush, G. W. (2000d, August 4). *Delivers remarks at prayer breakfast.* Retrieved February 27, 2008 from LexisNexis.

Bush, G. W. (2000e, September 8). *Delivers remarks at town hall meeting.* Retrieved February 27, 2008 from LexisNexis.

Bush, G. W. (2000f, October 30). *Delivers remarks at elementary school.* Retrieved February 27, 2008 from LexisNexis.

Bush, G. W. (2004a, March 3). *Remarks at a Bush-Cheney 2004 fund-raiser*. Retrieved March 31, 2005 from LexisNexis.

Bush, G. W. (2004b, March 11). *Remarks via satellite to the National Association of Evangelicals Convention*. Retrieved March 31, 2005 from LexisNexis.

Bush, G. W. (2004c, May 3). *Participates in an "Ask President Bush" event*. Retrieved March 31, 2005 from LexisNexis.

Bush, G. W. (2004d, May 4). *Participates in an "Ask President Bush" event*. Retrieved March 31, 2005 from LexisNexis.

Bush, G. W. (2004e, May 6). *Delivers remarks on the National Day of Prayer*. Retrieved March 31, 2005 from LexisNexis.

Bush, G. W. (2004f, May 7). *Participates in an "Ask the President" event*. Retrieved March 31, 2005 from LexisNexis.

Bush, G. W. (2004g, June 1). *Remarks at the first White House National Conference on Faith-Based Community Initiatives*. Retrieved March 31, 2005 from LexisNexis.

Bush, G. W. (2004h, June 15). *Delivers remarks at the congressional picnic*. Retrieved March 31, 2005 from LexisNexis.

Bush, G. W. (2004i, June 21). *A conversation on compassion*. Retrieved March 31, 2005 from LexisNexis.

Bush, G. W. (2004j, July 9). *Remarks at "Ask President Bush" event*. Retrieved March 31, 2005 from LexisNexis.

Bush, G. W. (2004k, July 20). *Remarks at Kirkwood Community College*. Retrieved March 31, 2005 from LexisNexis.

Bush, G. W. (2004l, August 3). *Remarks at the 122nd Knights of Columbus Convention*. Retrieved March 31, 2005 from LexisNexis.

Bush, G. W. (2004m, September 4). *Remarks at Bush-Cheney campaign rally*. Retrieved March 31, 2005 from LexisNexis.

Bush, G. W. (2004n, September 10). *Remarks at a campaign event*. Retrieved March 31, 2005 from LexisNexis.

Bush gets personal on 'Oprah.' (2000, September 20). *Desert News*, p. A02. Retrieved June 25, 2008 from LexisNexis.

Bush stresses need for preservation of family unit. (1980, April 13). *Associated Press*. Retrieved April 30, 2008 from LexisNexis.

Campbell, K. K., & Jamieson, K. H. (2008). *Presidents creating the presidency: Deeds done in words*. Chicago: University of Chicago Press.

Campolo, T. (1995). *Can mainline denominations make a comeback?* Valley Forge, PA: Judson Press.

Campolo, T. (2004). *Speaking my mind: The radical evangelical prophet tackles the tough issues Christians are afraid to face*. Nashville: W Publishing Group.

Campolo, T. (2008). *Red letter Christians: A citizen's guide to faith & politics*. Ventura, CA: Regal.

Cannon, L. (1980, October 4). Reagan disagrees with fundamentalist teaching on prayer. *Washington Post*, p. A6. Retrieved May 5, 2008 from LexisNexis.

Caputo, J. D. (2004). On not knowing who we are: Madness, hermeneutics and the night of truth in Foucault. In J. Bernauer & J. Carrette (Eds.), *Michel Foucault and theology: The politics of religious experience* (pp. 117–39). Burlington, VT: Ashgate Publishing Company.

Carrette, J. R. (1999). Prologue to a confession of the flesh. In M. Foucault, *Religion and culture*, J. R. Carrette (Ed.), (pp. 1–47). New York: Routledge.

Carrette, J. R. (2000). *Foucault and religion: Spiritual corporality and political spirituality*. New York: Routledge.

Carroll, M. (1980, October 2). Reagan, in Manhattan, says he backs Westway proposal. *New York Times*, p. B13. Retrieved May 5, 2008 from LexisNexis.

Carroll, M. (1984, March 26). Mondale is cheered and booed on day in the city. *New York Times*, p. B9. Retrieved April 22, 2008 from LexisNexis.

Carter, J. (1974, December 12). *Address announcing his candidacy for the 1976 Democratic presidential nomination to the National Press Club.* Retrieved May 2, 2008 from www.4president.org.

Carter, J. (1977). *A government as good as its people.* New York: Simon & Schuster.

Carter, J. (1978a). *The presidential campaign 1976: Volume one part one.* Washington, D.C.: United States Government Printing Office.

Carter, J. (1978b). *The presidential campaign 1976: Volume one part two.* Washington, D.C.: United States Government Printing Office.

Carter, J. (1980a, January 10). Remarks at a White House briefing for religious leaders. *Weekly Compilation of Presidential Documents, 16,* 49–51.

Carter, J. (1980b, January 21). Remarks at the National Religious Broadcasters Association annual convention. *Weekly Compilation of Presidential Documents, 16,* 180–83.

Carter, J. (1980c, February 7). Remarks at the annual National Prayer Breakfast. *Weekly Compilation of Presidential Documents, 16,* 275–77.

Carter, J. (1980d, April 17). Remarks to the delegates attending the 4-H Club's 50th anniversary conference. *Weekly Compilation of Presidential Documents, 16,* 701–3.

Carter, J. (1980e, May 5). Remarks and a question-and-answer session at the League of Women Voters' biennial national convention. *Weekly Compilation of Presidential Documents, 16,* 828–36.

Carter, J. (1980f, July 24). Remarks to delegates attending the Boys Nation annual meeting. *Weekly Compilation of Presidential Documents, 16,* 1412–15.

Carter, J. (1980g, September 2). Remarks and a question-and-answer session at a townhall meeting. *Weekly Compilation of Presidential Documents, 16,* 1610–25.

Carter, J. (1980h, October 1). Remarks at the annual convention of the Civil Service Employees Association. *Weekly Compilation of Presidential Documents, 16,* 2003–9.

Carter, J. (1980i, October 6). Remarks and a question-and-answer session with Du Page County residents. *Weekly Compilation of Presidential Documents, 16,* 2080–89.

Carter, J. (1980j, October 6). Remarks at a Democratic National Committee fundraising reception. *Weekly Compilation of Presidential Documents, 16,* 2091–95.

Carter, J. (1980k, October 9). Remarks to residents of Forsyth County and the surrounding area. *Weekly Compilation of Presidential Documents, 16,* 2143–48.

Carter, J. (1980l, October 16). Remarks at the Alfred E. Smith Memorial Dinner. *Weekly Compilation of Presidential Documents, 16,* 2313–16.

Carter, J. (1980m, October 20). Remarks at a meeting with the congregation of the Concord Baptist Church and state and local officials. *Weekly Compilation of Presidential Documents, 16,* 2364–68.

Carter, J. (1980n, October 21). Remarks and a question-and-answer session at a town meeting. *Weekly Compilation of Presidential Documents, 16,* 2383–95.

Carter, J. (1980o, October 22). Remarks at a rally with local residents. *Weekly Compilation of Presidential Documents, 16,* 2419–23.

Carter, J. (1980p, October 23). Remarks at the White House reception for black ministers. *Weekly Compilation of Presidential Documents, 16,* 2426–30.

Carter, J. (1980q, October 29). Remarks and a question-and-answer session at a town meeting. *Weekly Compilation of Presidential Documents, 16,* 2505–23.

Carter, J. (1980r, October 29). Remarks to local ministers and community leaders. *Weekly Compilation of Presidential Documents, 16,* 2527–31.

Carter, J. (1980s, October 31). Remarks and a question-and-answer session at a town meeting. *Weekly Compilation of Presidential Documents, 16,* 2588–99.

Carter, J. (1980t, November 1). Remarks at a rally with area residents. *Weekly Compilation of Presidential Documents, 16,* 2616–22.

Carter, J. (1980u, November 1). Remarks at a rally with area residents. *Weekly Compilation of Presidential Documents, 16,* 2627–34.

Carter, J. (2006). *Our endangered values: America's moral crisis.* New York: Simon & Schuster Paperbacks.

Carter, S. L. (1993). *The culture of disbelief: How American law and politics trivialize religious devotion.* New York: BasicBooks.

Carter, S. L. (2000). *God's name in vain: The wrongs and rights of religion in politics*. New York: BasicBooks.

Carter urges international cooperation. (1976, June 26). *Facts on File World Digest*.

Carters join church formed after racial controversy. (1981, January 26). *Associated Press*. Retrieved June 24, 2008 from LexisNexis.

Chapman, S. B. (2004). Imperial exegesis: When Caesar interprets scripture. In W. Avram (Ed.), *Anxious about empire: Theological essays on the new global realities* (pp. 91–102). Grand Rapids, MI: Brazos Press.

Clendinen, D. (1980a, August 18). National desk. *New York Times*, p. B7. Retrieved May 31, 2008 from LexisNexis.

Clinton, B. (1991, November 20). *Remarks at Georgetown University*. Retrieved March 12, 2008 from LexisNexis.

Clinton, B. (1992a, January 25). *The National Rainbow Coalition presidential candidate forum*. Retrieved March 12, 2008 from LexisNexis.

Clinton, B. (1992b, April 7). *Speech following polls closing*. Retrieved March 12, 2008 from LexisNexis.

Clinton, B. (1992c, June 13). *Address at a Rainbow Coalition luncheon*. Retrieved on March 12, 2008 from LexisNexis.

Clinton, B. (1992d, July 16). *Remarks, Democratic National Convention*. Retrieved on March 12, 2008 from LexisNexis.

Clinton, B. (1992e, July 31). *Remarks at the North Little Rock Community Center*. Retrieved on March 12, 2008 from LexisNexis.

Clinton, B. (1992f, August 21). *Remarks to the Olivet Institutional Baptist Church*. Retrieved on March 12, 2008 from LexisNexis.

Clinton, B. (1992g, August 25). *Remarks to the American Legion's annual convention*. Retrieved on March 12, 2008 from LexisNexis.

Clinton, B. (1992h, August 29). *Remarks before the Arkansas State Democratic Convention*. Retrieved on March 12, 2008 from LexisNexis.

Clinton, B. (1992i, September 9). *Remarks via satellite to the B'nai B'rith conference*. Retrieved on March 12, 2008 from LexisNexis.

Clinton, B. (1992j, September 9). *Town meeting*. Retrieved on March 12, 2008 from LexisNexis.

Clinton, B. (1992k, September 11). *Remarks at Stepan Center, University of Notre Dame*. Retrieved on March 12, 2008 from LexisNexis.

Clinton, B. (1996a, February 10). *Weekly radio address*. Retrieved March 7, 2008 from LexisNexis.

Clinton, B. (1996b, May 2). *Remarks at ceremony honoring Reverend Billy Graham*. Retrieved March 7, 2008 from LexisNexis.

Clinton, B. (1996c, May 30). *Remarks at Women's International Convention of God in Christ*. Retrieved March 7, 2008 from LexisNexis.

Clinton, B. (1996d, June 12). *Remarks at the rededication of Mount Zion African Methodist Episcopal Church*.

Clinton, B. (1996e, August 12). *Remarks regarding the agreement to close New World Mine on the outskirts of Yellowstone National Park*. Retrieved March 7, 2008 from LexisNexis.

Clinton, B. (1996f, August 26). *Remarks at Bowling Green, Ohio*. Retrieved March 7, 2008 from LexisNexis.

Clinton, B. (1996g, September 6). *Remarks to the National Baptist Convention USA*. Retrieved March 7, 2008 from LexisNexis.

Clinton, B. (1996h, September 9). *Remarks at ceremony to honor recipients of the presidential medal of freedom*. Retrieved March 7, 2008 from LexisNexis.

Clinton, H. (2007, March 26). *Hillary Clinton Campaign event*. Retrieved April 12, 2008 from LexisNexis.

Clinton, H. (2008, May 13). *Post-West Virginia primary remarks*. Retrieved February 8, 2009 from LexisNexis.

Coe, K., & Domke, D. (2006). Petitioners or prophets? Presidential discourse, God, and the ascendancy of religious conservatives. *Journal of Communication, 56*, 309–30.

Cohn-Sherbok, D. (2006). *The politics of apocalypse: The history and influence of Christian Zionism*. Oxford: Oneworld Publications Limited.

Cole, E. (2007, June 15). Poll: American voters want a religious president. *Christian Post*. Retrieved October 28, 2007 from www.christianpost.com.

Cooperman, A. (2006a, February 10). Air Force eases rules on religion: New guidelines reflect evangelicals' criticism, general says. *Washington Post*, p. A05. Retrieved July 2, 2008 from LexisNexis.

Cooperman, A. (2006b, May 6). Air Force to examine fundraising e-mail sent by a general: Message praised candidate's Christianity. *Washington Post*, p. A03. Retrieved July 2, 2008 from LexisNexis.

Cooperman, A. (2006c, July 16). Marching as to war: Former Air Force officer Mikey Weinstein zeroes in on proselytizing in the military. *Washington Post*, p. D01. Retrieved July 2, 2008 from LexisNexis.

Cornell, G. W. (1980, October 3). Domestic news. *Associated Press*. Retrieved May 5, 2008 from LexisNexis.

Crockett, D. A. (2003). George W. Bush and the unrhetorical rhetorical presidency. *Rhetoric & Public Affairs, 6*, 465–86.

Curtis, D. (1980, October 4). Washington news. *United Press International*. Retrieved May 5, 2008 from LexisNexis.

Cutrofello, A. (2004). Exomologesis and aesthetic reflection: Foucault's response to Habermas. In J. Bernauer & J. Carrette (Eds.), *Michel Foucault and theology: The politics of religious experience* (pp. 157–69). Burlington, VT: Ashgate Publishing Company.

Dart, B. (2003, December 5). Personal politics: Candidates open up lives with frank revelations. *Atlanta Journal-Constitution*, p. 1A. Retrieved June 25, 2008 from Lexis Nexis.

Dean, H. (2004, January 18). *Remarks with former president Jimmy Carter*. Retrieved February 27, 2008 from LexisNexis.

Denton, R. E., Jr., & Hahn, D. F. (1986). *Presidential communication: Description and analysis*. New York: Praeger.

Dershowitz, A. (2007). *Blasphemy: How the religious right is hijacking our Declaration of Independence*. Hoboken, N.J: John Wiley & Sons, Inc.

Detwiler, T. (1988). Viewing Robertson's rhetoric in an Augustinian mirror. *Journal of Communication and Religion, 11 (1)*, 22–31.

Diehl, J. (1980, April 27). P.G. Catholics cool to Kennedy. *Washington Post*, p. B1.

Dionne, Jr., E. J. (2008). *Souled out: Reclaiming faith & politics after the religious Right*. Princeton: Princeton University Press.

Dixon, M. A. (2004). *The sword of the word: The use of sermonic discourse as organizational rhetoric in the battle for the Southern Baptist Convention*. Unpublished doctoral dissertation. University of Missouri, Columbia.

Dolbee, S. (2007, October 14). Will Christian right leave GOP at altar?: Evangelicals deserting ahead of 2008 election. *San Diego Union-Tribune*, p. A1. Retrieved October 28, 2007 from LexisNexis.

Dole, B. (1995a, April 10). *Official announcement*. Retrieved March 5, 2008 from www.4president.org.

Dole, B. (1995b, August 22). *Bob Dole for president rally*. Retrieved March 5, 2008 from LexisNexis.

Dole. B. (1995c, September 8). *Remarks at the Christian Coalition's "Road to Victory Conference."* Retrieved March 5, 2008 from LexisNexis.

Dole, B. (1996a, May 23). *Remarks at the Catholic Press Association Annual Convention*. Retrieved March 7, 2008 from LexisNexis.

Dole, B. (1996b, August 15). *Accepts nomination*. Retrieved March 7, 2008 from www.4president.org.

Dole, B. (1996c, September 14). *Remarks before the Christian Coalition annual meeting*. Retrieved March 7, 2008 from LexisNexis.

Dole, B. (1996d, October 24). *Remarks*. Retrieved March 7, 2008 from LexisNexis.

Domke, D., & Coe, K. (2008). *The god strategy: How religion became a political weapon in America*. Oxford: Oxford University Press.

Dreyfus, H. L., & Rabinow, P. (1983). *Michel Foucault: Beyond structuralism and hermeneutics.* Chicago: University of Chicago Press.

Dukakis, M. (1988a, September 7). *Speech delivered to B'nai B'rith international convention.* Retrieved May 12, 2008 from www.fednews.com.

Dukakis, M. (1988b, September 13). *Speech before the Congressional Hispanic Caucus Institute dinner.* Retrieved May 12, 2008 from www.fednews.com.

Dukakis, M. (1988c, September 14). *Remarks at Georgetown University.* Retrieved May 12, 2008 from www.fednews.com.

Dukakis, M. (1988d, September 19). *Speech at the Congressional Black Caucus.* Retrieved May 12, 2008 from www.fednews.com.

Dukakis, M. (1988e, October 10). *Winning the battle for our economic future.* Retrieved May 12, 2008 from www.fednews.com.

Dukakis, M. (1988f, October 17). *A choice of values: The fight for America's future.* Retrieved May 12, 2008 from www.fednews.com.

Eidenmuller, M. E. (2002). American evangelicalism, democracy, and civic piety: A computer-based stylistic analysis of Promise Keepers' stadium event and Washington D.C. rally discourses. *Journal of Communication and Religion, 25,* 64–85.

Elder, J. (2007, July 11). Finding religion on the campaign trail. *New York Times.* Retrieved October 28, 2007 from www.nytimes.com.

Elliott, A. (2008, June 24). Muslim voters detect a snub from Obama. *New York Times,* p. A1. Retrieved July 2, 2008 from LexisNexis.

Elshtain, J. B. (1999). Politics and forgiveness: The Clinton case. In B. Fackre (Ed.), *Judgment day at the White House: A critical declaration exploring moral issues and the political use and abuse of religion* (pp. 11–17). Grand Rapids, MI: William B. Eerdmans Publishing Company.

Erickson, K. V. (1980). Jimmy Carter: The rhetoric of private and civic piety. *Western Journal of Speech Communication, 44,* 221–35.

Evans, R., & Novak, R. (1981). *The Reagan revolution.* New York: E. P. Dutton.

Fackre, G. (2000). *The day after: A retrospective on religious dissent in the presidential crisis.* Grand Rapids, MI: William B. Eerdmans Publishing Company.

Faith and the public dialogue: A conversation with Sen. John Kerry. (2007, November 1). Pew Forum on Religion & Public Life. Retrieved November 11, 2007 from www.pewforum.org.

Farrelly, M. J. (2003, April 5). Meshing of religion with politics refreshing for some Americans, concern for others. *Voice of America News.* Retrieved November 26, 2007 from LexisNexis.

Feinsilber, M. (1979, November 3). Washington dateline. *Associated Press.* Retrieved April 30, 2008 from LexisNexis.

Feldmann, L. (2007a, June 6). Can the religious left sway the '08 race? *Christian Science Monitor,* 1. Retrieved November 26, 2007 from LexisNexis.

Feldmann, L. (2007b, October 18). How the Arizona senator, once a POW 'pastor,' finds purpose in his beliefs and survival. *Christian Science Monitor.* Retrieved October 18, 2007 from www.csmonitor.com.

Fisher, J. (2007, August 11). Republicans won't talk about equality for gays. *Lewiston Morning Tribune,* p. 6A. Retrieved July 8, 2008 from LexisNexis.

Flint, A. R., & Porter, J. (2005). Jimmy Carter: The re-emergence of faith-based politics and the abortion rights issue. *Presidential Studies Quarterly, 35,* 28–51.

Foer, F. (2003/2004, December 29/January 12). Beyond belief: Howard Dean's religion problem. *The New Republic,* p. 22–25.

Foley, T. J. (1980, May 19). "Third man's" theme: Seize political center. *U.S. News & World Report,* p, 31. Retrieved April 25, 2008 from LexisNexis.

Ford. G. (1976a, February 15). Remarks to a group of athletes in the East Room. *Weekly Compilation of Presidential Documents, 12,* 266–67.

Ford, G. (1976b, February 22). Remarks at the National Religious Broadcasters and National Association of Evangelicals combined convention. *Weekly Compilation of Presidential Documents, 12,* 270–71.

Ford. G. (1976c, March 13). Remarks and a question-and-answer session at the West Wilkey High School. *Weekly Compilation of Presidential Documents, 12*, 422–27.

Ford. G. (1976d, April 28). Remarks and a question-and-answer session at Tyler Junior College. *Weekly Compilation of Presidential Documents, 12*, 720–25.

Ford. G. (1976e, May 23). Remarks at the commencement exercises of Warner Pacific College. *Weekly Compilation of Presidential Documents, 12*, 926–27.

Ford. G. (1976f, June 15). Remarks at the 1976 Southern Baptist Convention. *Weekly Compilation of Presidential Documents, 12*, 1058–59.

Ford, G. (1976g, August 8). Remarks at International Eucharistic Congress. *Weekly Compilation of Presidential Documents, 12*, 1253–54.

Ford. G. (1976h, September 9). Remarks to the biennial convention of B'nai B'rith. *Weekly Compilation of Presidential Documents, 12*, 1320–23.

Ford. G. (1976i, October 8). Remarks and a question-and-answer session at a breakfast meeting sponsored by the San Fernando Valley Business and Professional Association. *Weekly Compilation of Presidential Documents, 12*, 1469–74.

Ford. G. (1976j, October 12). Remarks at the Yeshiva of Flatbush High School. *Weekly Compilation of Presidential Documents, 12*, 1490–92.

Ford. G. (1976k, October 21). Alfred E. Smith memorial dinner. *Weekly Compilation of Presidential Documents, 12*, 1552–54.

Ford. G. (1976l, October 23). Remarks at the South Carolina state fair. *Weekly Compilation of Presidential Documents, 12*, 1582.

Ford. G. (1976m, October 28). Remarks at a fundraising reception for Senator Robert Taft, Jr. *Weekly Compilation of Presidential Documents, 12*, 1642–43.

Ford. G. (1976n, October 28). Remarks at Fountain Square. *Weekly Compilation of Presidential Documents, 12*, 1640–41.

Foucault, M. (1980). *Power/knowledge: Selected interviews & other writings 1972–1977.* C. Gordon (Ed.), C. Gordon, L. Marshall, J. Mepham, K. Soper (Trans.). New York: Pantheon Books.

Foucault, M. (1983). *The subject and power [Afterword].* In H. L. Dreyfus & P. Rabinow. *Michel Foucault: Beyond structuralism and hermeneutics.* Chicago: University of Chicago Press.

Foucault, M. (1990). *The history of sexuality I: An introduction.* New York: Vintage Books.

Foucault, M. (1995). *Discipline & punish: The birth of the prison.* A. Sheridan (Trans.). New York: Vintage Books.

Foucault, M. (1999). *Religion and culture,* J. R. Carrette (Ed.). New York: Routledge Inc.

Fraker, S. (with Clift, E., & Doyle, J.). (1976, April 5). Carter and the God issue. *Newsweek,* p. 19. Retrieved May 2, 2008 from LexisNexis.

Friedenberg, R. V. (2002). Rhetoric, religion and government at the turn of the 21st century. *Journal of Communication and Religion, 25*, 34–48.

Frost, D. (1996, October 30). *Talking with David Frost.* Retrieved March 7, 2008 from LexisNexis.

Gaddy, C. W. (2005). God talk in the public square. In C. H. Badaracco (Ed.), *Quoting God: How media shape ideas about religion and culture* (pp. 43–58). Waco, TX: Baylor University Press.

Gannon, J. (1976, April 12). Jimmy Carter's spiritual side. *Wall Street Journal,* p. 14. Retrieved May 2, 2008 from ProQuest.

Garrison, B. (2006). *Red and blue God, black and blue church: Eyewitness accounts of how American churches are hijacking Jesus, bagging the beatitudes, and worshiping the almighty dollar.* San Francisco: Jossey-Bass.

General news. (1980, October 8). *United Press International.* Retrieved April 25, 2008 from LexisNexis.

Gerson, M. (2007, June 29). The gospel of Obama. *Washington Post,* p. A21. Retrieved July 5, 2007 from www.washingtonpost.com.

Gerstenzang, J. (1980, May 26). Reagan ready to 'let out a loud yell' over capturing GOP nomination. *Associated Press.* Retrieved May 5, 2008 from LexisNexis.

Gilgoff, D. (2007a). *The Jesus machine: How James Dobson, Focus on the Family, and evangelical America are winning the culture war.* New York: St. Martin's Press.

Gilgoff, D. (2007b, March 28). Dobson offers insight on 2008 Republican hopefuls. *U.S. News & World Report.* Retrieved July 5, 2008 from LexisNexis.

Gilgoff, D. (2007c, May 21). What is a 'real' Christian? *USA Today,* p. 15A. Retrieved July 5, 2008 from LexisNexis.

Gilgoff, D. (2007d, September 20). Mitt Romney and the Mormon question. *Washington Post,* p. B03. Retrieved October 6, 2007 from LexisNexis.

Gilgoff, D. (2007e, September 30). John McCain: Constitution established a 'Christian nation.' *BeliefNet.* Retrieved October 28, 2007 from www.beliefnet.com.

Goldberg, M. (2006). *Kingdom coming: The rise of Christian nationalism.* New York: W.W. Norton & Company, Inc.

Goldzwig, S. (1987). A rhetoric of public theology: The religious rhetor and public policy. *Southern Speech Communication Journal, 52,* 128–50.

Goldzwig, S. R. (2002). Official and unofficial civil religious discourse. *Journal of Communication and Religion, 25,* 102–14.

Gore, A. (1999a, November 15). *Remarks to Microsoft employees.* Retrieved February 27, 2008 from LexisNexis.

Gore, A. (1999b, December 14). *Participates in Town hall meeting.* Retrieved February 27, 2008 from LexisNexis.

Gore, A. (2000a, July 12). *Delivers remarks at NAACP Convention.* Retrieved February 27, 2008 from LexisNexis.

Gore, A. (2000b, August 8). *Holds news conference to announce Senator Lieberman as running mate.* Retrieved February 27, 2008 from LexisNexis.

Gore, A. (2000c, August 17). *Delivers acceptance speech at Democratic National Convention.* Retrieved February 27, 2008 from LexisNexis.

Gore, A. (2000d, November 4). *Delivers remarks at campaign rally in Memphis, Tennessee.* Retrieved February 27, 2008 from LexisNexis.

Gorski, E. (2005, October 28). Church support rapidly fell away: Nominee's 1993 statement cited. *Denver Post,* p. A06. Retrieved July 2, 2008 from LexisNexis.

Gorski, E. (2008a, February 8). Evangelical leader James Dobson endorses Mike Huckabee for GOP presidential nod. *Associated Press.* Retrieved May 27, 2008 from LexisNexis.

Gorski, E. (2008b, May 26). Pastors pose problems for McCain and Obama. *Associated Press.* Retrieved May 27, 2008 from LexisNexis.

Gorski, E. (2008c, June 24). Dobson accuses Obama of 'distorting' Bible. *Associated Press.* Retrieved July 5, 2008 from LexisNexis.

Gray, J. (1996, September 15). Christian Coalition offers Dole both cheers and sharp prodding. *New York Times,* p. A38. Retrieved October 28, 2007 from LexisNexis.

Green, J. C. (2007). *The faith factor: How religion influences American elections.* Westport, CT: Praeger.

Greenawalt, K. (1994). The participation of religious groups in political advocacy. *Journal of Church and State, 36,* 143–60.

Gring, M. A. (2002). Broken covenants and the American pantheon: Church and state 25 years after *The Political Pulpit. Journal of Communication and Religion, 25,* 115–35.

Groening, C. (2007, December 6). Former Mormon: Romney lacks discernment to be president. *OneNewsNow.* Retrieved December 6, 2007 from www.onenewsnow.com.

Gushee, D. P. (2008). *The future of faith in American politics: The public witness of the evangelical center.* Waco, TX: Baylor University Press.

Hahn, D. F. (1980). One's reborn every minute: Carter's religious appeal in 1976. *Communication Quarterly, 28,* 56–62.

Hampson, R. (1984, October 16). Al Smith Dinner combines politics, religion, humor. *Associated Press.* Retrieved April 14, 2008 from LexisNexis.

Hanson, C. (2000, November/December). God and man on the campaign trail. *Columbia Journalism Review,* 40–45.

Hart, G. (2005). *God and Caesar in America: An essay on religion and politics.* Golden, CO: Fulcrum Publishing.

Hart, R. P. (1977). *The political pulpit*. West Lafayette, ID: Purdue University Press.

Hart, R. P. (2002). God, country, and a world of wars. *Journal of Communication and Religion, 25*, 136–47.

Hart, R. P., & Pauley III, J. L. (2005). *The political pulpit*. West Lafayette, ID: Purdue University Press.

Hatch, N. O. (1989). *The democratization of American Christianity*. New Haven, CT: Yale University Press.

Heclo, H. (2007). *Christianity and American democracy*. Cambridge, MA: Harvard University Press.

Heineman, K. J. (1998). *God is a conservative: Religion, politics, and morality in contemporary America*. New York: New York University Press.

Herbaugh, S. (1980, August 23). Preachers return home to promote revival at the ballot box. *Associated Press*. Retrieved May 31, 2008 from LexisNexis.

Hertz, T. (2008, June 10). Pennies for your thoughts: What Fox TV's public confessional reveals. *Christianity Today*. Retrieved June 25, 2008 from www.christianitytoday.com.

Hill, M. (2007, December 6). Romney turns focus to faith. *Baltimore Sun*, p. 2A. Retrieved December 6, 2007 from LexisNexis.

Hornblower, M. (1980, October 23). Anderson: Steady and self-confident. *Washington Post*, p. A1. Retrieved April 25, 2008 from LexisNexis.

Hostetler, M. J. (2002). Joe Liberman at Fellowship Chapel: Civil religion meets self-disclosure. *Journal of Communication and Religion, 25*, 148–65.

Huckabee, M. (with Perry, J.). (1997). *Character is the issue: How people with integrity can revolutionize America*. Nashville: Broadman & Holman Publishers.

Huckabee, M. (2007, October 20). *Remarks at the Family Research Council Voter Values Summit*. Retrieved April 11, 2008 from LexisNexis.

Huckabee, M. (2008, February 5). *Remarks on "Super Tuesday."* Retrieved April 11, 2008 from LexisNexis.

Hughes, R. T. (1980). Civil religion, the theology of the republic, and the free church tradition. *Journal of Church and State, 22*, 75–88.

Hunt, T. (1980, August 22). Reagan says churches should be politically active. *Associated Press*. Retrieved May 5, 2008 from LexisNexis.

Hyer, M. (1980, July 25). Reagan, Carter, Anderson: Three 'born again' Christians who differ on meaning. *Washington Post*, p. A28. Retrieved May 5, 2008 from LexisNexis.

Iftikhar, A. (2007, December 1). Romney, a victim of bigotry, turns on U.S. Muslims. *Buffalo News*, p. A6. Retrieved December 6, 2007 from LexisNexis.

Into the wilderness: By demanding orthodoxy from GOP presidential candidates, the religious right risks losing its clout. (2007, October 24). *Los Angeles Times*, p. A26. Retrieved October 28, 2007 from LexisNexis.

Jackson, J. (1984, January 16). *Presidential campaign announcement in Philadelphia, Pennsylvania*. Retrieved April 28, 2008 from www.4president.org.

Jeffrey, T. P. (2008, March 3). Obama: Sermon on Mount justifies same-sex unions. *CNSNews*. Retrieved March 3, 2008 from www.cnsnews.com.

Johnson, J. (2008). *Jerry Johnson Live*. Retrieved February 26, 2008 from www.jerryjohnsonlive.com.

Kaid, L. L, McKinney, M., & Tedesco, J. C. (2000). *Civic dialogue in the 1996 presidential campaign*. Cresskill, N.J.: Hampton Press, Inc.

Kantor, J., & Kirkpatrick, D. D. (2007, December 6). Pulpit was the springboard for Huckabee's rise. *New York Times*. Retrieved December 6, 2007 from www.nytimes.com.

Kennedy, J. F. (1960a, September 12). *Address to the Greater Houston Ministerial Association*. Retrieved October 6, 2007 from www.americanrhetoric.com.

Kennedy, J. F. (1960b, September 12). *Greater Houston Ministerial Association Q&A*. Retrieved October 6, 2007 from www.americanrhetoric.com.

Kernell, S. (2006). *Going public: New strategies of presidential leadership*. Washington, D.C.: CQ Press.

Kerry, J. F. (2004a, April 23). *Remarks to the Newspaper Association of America annual convention*. Retrieved March 31, 2005 from LexisNexis.

Kerry, J. F. (2004b, July 6). *Delivers remarks at AME Church Convention.* Retrieved March 31, 2005 from LexisNexis. {African Methodist Episcopal Church}

Kerry, J. F. (2004c, July 29). *Remarks at Democratic National Convention.* Retrieved March 31, 2005 from LexisNexis.

Kerry, J. F. (2004d, July 31). *Remarks at campaign event in Greensburg, Pennsylvania.* Retrieved March 31, 2005 from LexisNexis.

Kerry, J. F. (2004e, August 26). *Remarks at campaign rally in Anoka, Minnesota.* Retrieved March 31, 2005 from LexisNexis.

Kerry, J. F. (2004f, September 9). *Remarks to the 124th annual session of the National Baptist Convention.* Retrieved March 31, 2005 from LexisNexis.

Kerry, J. F. (2004g, October 24). *Remarks at the Broward Center for the Performing Arts.* Retrieved March 31, 2005 from LexisNexis.

King, L. (1999, December 16). *Larry King Live.* Retrieved February 27, 2008 from LexisNexis.

King, R. E. (1997). When worlds collide: Politics, religion, and media at the 1970 East Tennessee Billy Graham Crusade. *Journal of Church and State, 39,* 273–95.

Klope, D. C. (2002). *Civil religion revival: (God Bless America) after September 11.* Paper presented at the annual convention of the National Communication Association, New Orleans, LA.

Knutson, L. L. (1984, November 5). Mondale, down in the polls but cheered by crowds, declares he'll win. *Associated Press.* Retrieved April 14, 2008 from LexisNexis.

Koza, P. (1980, October 29). Washington news. *United Press International.* Retrieved May 31, 2008 from LexisNexis.

Kuo, D. (2006). *Tempting faith: An inside story of political seduction.* New York: Free Press.

Land, R. (2007). *The divided states of America?: What liberals AND conservatives are missing in the God-and-country shouting match!* Nashville: Thomas Nelson, Inc.

Langer, G. (1983, May 1). Jackson takes political pulse in N.H. *Associated Press.* Retrieved April 22, 2008 from LexisNexis.

Laracey, M. (2002). *Presidents and the people: The partisan story of going public.* College Station, TX: Texas A&M University Press.

Lardner, Jr., G. (Schwartz, M.). (1984, April 1). Jackson sees bright future for 'Rainbow Coalition' and its agenda. *Washington Post,* p. A3. Retrieved April 22, 2008 from LexisNexis.

Lawsky, D. (1984, August 10). Mondale attacks Reagan in the South. *United Press International.* Retrieved April 14, 2008 from LexisNexis.

Lee, R. (2002). The force of religion in the public square. *Journal of Communication and Religion, 25,* 6–20.

Leonard, M. D. (2006, September 24). Getting Real: Blogging, TV talk and reality shows offer forums for true confessions—but is baring all a good idea? *St. Louis Post-Dispatch,* p. E1. Retrieved June 25, 2008 from LexisNexis.

Lewis, A. (1980, September 18). Religion and politics. *New York Times,* p. A31. Retrieved May 5, 2008 from LexisNexis.

Lim, E. T. (2002). Five trends in presidential rhetoric: An analysis of rhetoric from George Washington to Bill Clinton. *Presidential Studies Quarterly, 32,* 328–66.

Lincoln, B. (2003). *Holy terrors: Thinking about religion after September 11.* Chicago: University of Chicago Press.

Lincoln, B. (2004, October 5). The theology of George W. Bush. *Christian Century.* Retrieved November 20, 2007 from http://marty-center.uchicago.edu.

Lindsey, S. (2006, December 22). Va. lawmaker won't take back his comments about Muslims. *Virginian-Pilot,* p. B3. Retrieved October 28, 2007 from LexisNexis.

Luo, M. (2007a, July 7). For Clinton, faith intertwines with political life. *New York Times,* p. A1.

Luo, M. (2007b, July 22). God '08: Whose, and how much, will voters accept? *New York Times,* p. D4. Retrieved October 28, 2007 from LexisNexis.

Lynn, F. (1983, September 29). Mondale stresses his differences with Glenn at Rochester Forum. *New York Times,* p. B6. Retrieved April 22, 2008 from LexisNexis.

MacNeil, R., & Lehrer, J. (1984, September 6). *The MacNeil/Lehrer NewsHour*. Retrieved April 14, 2008 from LexisNexis.

MacNeil, R., & Lehrer, J. (1987, April 6). *The MacNeil/Lehrer NewsHour*. Retrieved May 13, 2008 from www.fednews.com.

MacPherson, M. (1980, March 6). "Wow!" said Anderson after the Tuesday count, but can his dark horse go the distance? *Washington Post*, p. D1. Retrieved April 30, 2008 from Lexis-Nexis.

MacPherson, M. (1984, May 22). Jesse Jackson: The fire and the faith. *Washington Post*, p. E1. Retrieved April 22, 2008 from LexisNexis.

Magruder, J. (1983, December 18). Jackson: First primary a chance to shed 'black candidate' tag. *Associated Press*. Retrieved April 22, 2008 from LexisNexis.

Mann, J. (1980, April 7). "Old-time religion" on the offensive. *U.S. News & World Report*, p. 40. Retrieved May 31, 2008 from LexisNexis.

Mansfield, S. (2003). *The faith of George W. Bush*. New York: Jeremy P. Tarcher/Penguin.Marchocki, K. (2007, April 1). Confessing a need. *Union Leader*, p. A1. Retrieved June 25, 2008 from LexisNexis.

Marsh, C. (2007). *Wayward Christian soldiers: Freeing the gospel from political captivity*. Oxford: Oxford University Press.

Martin, L. (1980, March 5). Vote-buying charge hits GOP campaign in South Carolina. *Globe and Mail*. Retrieved April 30, 2008 from LexisNexis.

Martin, W. (2005). *With God on our side: The rise of the Religious Right in America*. New York: Broadway Books.

Marvin, C. (2002). A newly scholarly dispensation for civil religion. *Journal of Communication and Religion, 25*, 21–33.

Matthews, C. (2000, May 31). *Hardball with Chris Matthews*. Retrieved February 27, 2008 from LexisNexis.

Matthews, C. (2008, April 2). *Hardball with Chris Matthews*. Retrieved April 12, 2008 from LexisNexis.

Matthews, T. (with Clift, C.). (1975, December 1). Carter: Early bird. *Newsweek*, p. 41. Retrieved May 2, 2008 from LexisNexis.

Mayer, A. J. (with Lindsay, J. J., Fineman, H., McGuire, S., Kirsch, J., Reese, M.) (1980, September 15). A tide born-again politics. *Newsweek*, p. 28. Retrieved May 31, 2008 from LexisNexis.

McBeth, H. L. (1987). *The Baptist heritage: Four centuries of Baptist witness*. Nashville: Broadman Press.

McCain, J. (1999, October 18). *Remarks on campaign finance reform*. Retrieved February 27, 2008 from LexisNexis.

McCain, J. (2000a, January 13). *Addresses New Hampshire State Legislature*. Retrieved February 27, 2008 from LexisNexis.

McCain, J. (2000b, February 29). *Media availability following town hall meeting*. Retrieved February 27, 2008 from LexisNexis.

McCain, J. (2007a, April 23). *Center for Strategic and International Studies (CSIS) meeting*. Retrieved April 11, 2008 from LexisNexis.

McCain, J. (2007b, June 4). *Delivers remarks on immigration at a campaign event*. Retrieved April 11, 2008 from LexisNexis.

McCain, J. (2007c, October 19). *Remarks at the Family Research Council Voter Values Summit*. Retrieved April 11, 2008 from LexisNexis.

McCain, J. (2008a, May 7). *Remarks*. Retrieved June 10, 2008 from LexisNexis.

McCain, J. (2008b, July 14). *Remarks at the La Raza Convention*. Retrieved February 17, 2009 from LexisNexis.

McCain, J. (2008c, August 11). *Prepared remarks*. Retrieved February 17, 2009 from Lexis-Nexis.

McCain, J. (2008d, September 27). *Prepared remarks*. Retrieved February 17, 2009 from LexisNexis.

McGee, M. C. (1990). Text, context, and the fragmentation of contemporary culture. *Western Journal of Speech Communication, 54*, 274–89.

McGrath, A. E. (2002). *The future of Christianity*. Malden, MA: Blackwell Publishers Inc.

McKinney, M. S., & Pepper, B. G. (1999). From hope to heartbreak: Bill Clinton and the rhetoric of AIDS. In Elwood, W.M. (Ed.), *Power in the blood: A handbook on AIDS, politics, and communication* (77–92). Mahwah, NJ: Lawrence Erlbaum.

McQuillan, L. (1984, September 7). Mixing it up over politics and religion. *United Press International*. Retrieved April 14, 2008 from LexisNexis.

Medhurst, M. J. (1977). McGovern at Wheaton: A quest for redemption. *CommunicationQuarterly, 25*, 32–39.

Medhurst, M. J. (2002). Forging a civil-religious construct for the 21st century: Should Hart's "contract" be renewed? *Journal of Communication and Religion, 25*, 86–101.

Medhurst, M. J. (2006). *The rhetorical presidency of George H. W. Bush*. College Station, TX: Texas A&M University Press.

Medhurst, M. J. (2008). *Before the rhetorical presidency*. College Station, TX: Texas A&M University Press.

Merchant, D. (2008). *Lord save us from your followers: Why is the gospel of love dividing America?* Nashville: Thomas Nelson.

Meyer, P. (1978). James Earl Carter: The man and the myth. Kansas City: Sheed Andrews and McMeel, Inc.

Miller, D. (2003). *Blue like jazz: Nonreligious thoughts on Christian spirituality*. Nashville: Thomas Nelson.

Miller, P. (2006, March 25). U of M study finds atheists are least trusted. *Star Tribune*, p. 10E. Retrieved July 8, 2008 from LexisNexis.

Mintz, M. (1980, October 5). Evangelical group plans Nov. 2 political appeal at churches. *Washington Post*, p. A5. Retrieved May 31, 2008 from LexisNexis.

Mitchell, N. E., & Phipps, K. S. (1985). The jeremiad in contemporary fundamentalism: Jerry Falwell's *Listen America*. *Religious Communication Today, 8*, 54–62.

Mohr, C. (1976a, May 18). Carter won't repudiate backer's Udall remark. *New York Times*, p. 18. Retrieved May 2, 2008 from ProQuest.

Mohr, C. (1976b, June 7). Carter gets an ovation after assuring Jews in Jersey on his religious views. *New York Times*, p. 22. from ProQuest.

Moseley-Braun, C. (2003, September 22). Announcement speech. Retrieved October 28, 2007 from www.gwu.edu/~action/2004/braun/braun092203sp.html.

Muir, Jr., W. K. (1992). *The bully pulpit: The presidential leadership of Ronald Reagan*. San Francisco: Institute for Contemporary Studies Press.

Nelson, M. Z. (2005). *The gospel according to Oprah*. Knoxville, KY: Westminster John Knox Press.

New post-election poll demonstrates political diversity of evangelical Christians. (2008, February 11). Faith in Public Life. Retrieved July 8, 2008 from www.faithinpubliclife.org.

Nielsen, Jr., N. C. (1977). *The religion of President Carter*. Nashville: Thomas Nelson Inc., Publishers.

Non-believing US voters feel demonized. (2007, December 18). *Breitbart*. Retrieved December 20, 2007 from www.breitbart.com.

Obama, B. (2004, July 27). *Keynote address at the Democratic National Convention*. Retrieved July 5, 2008 from www.washingtonpost.com.

Obama, B. (2007a, February 10). *Makes a campaign announcement*. Retrieved April 12, 2008 from LexisNexis.

Obama, B. (2007b, March 4). *Delivers remarks at a Selma voting rights march commemoration*. Retrieved April 12, 2008 from LexisNexis.

Obama, B. (2007c, March 27). *Remarks to the Communications Workers of America legislative political conference*. Retrieved April 12, 2008 from LexisNexis.

Obama, B. (2007d, September 12). *Participates in a presidential forum sponsored by Slate, Yahoo and the Huffington Post*. Retrieved April 12, 2008 from LexisNexis.

Obama, B. (2007e, October 29). *Delivers remarks at the MTV/Myspace presidential forum*. Retrieved April 11, 2008 from LexisNexis.

Obama, B. (2008a, January 21). *Remarks marking Martin Luther King, Jr. Day*. Retrieved April 12, 2008 from LexisNexis.

Obama, B. (2008b, January 24). *Delivers remarks at a campaign event.* Retrieved April 11, 2008 from LexisNexis.

Obama, B. (2008c, March 18). *Delivers remarks on race issues.* Retrieved April 12, 2008 from LexisNexis.

Obama, B. (2008d, March 26). *Delivers remarks at a campaign event.* Retrieved April 12, 2008 from LexisNexis.

Obama, B. (2008e, April 29). *Holds a news conference.* Retrieved June 10, 2008 from Lexis-Nexis.

Obama, B. (2008f, May 16). *Holds a news conference.* Retrieved June 10, 2008 from Lexis-Nexis.

Obama, B. (2008g, August 26). *Remarks.* Retrieved February 22, 2009 from LexisNexis.

Obama, B. (2008h, September 18). *Remarks at a "Change We Need" rally.* Retrieved February 22, 2009 from LexisNexis.

Obama, B. (2008i, October 16). *Remarks at the Alfred E. Smith Memorial Foundation Dinner.* Retrieved February 22, 2009 from LexisNexis.

Ofulue, N. I. (2002). President Clinton and the White House prayer breakfast. *Journal of Communication and Religion, 25,* 49–63.

O'Leary, S., & McFarland, M. (1989). The political use of mythic discourse: Prophetic interpretation in Pat Robertson's presidential campaign. *Quarterly Journal of Speech, 75,* 433–52.

On journalism and democracy: An interview with Bill Moyers. (2007, Fall). *Christian Ethics Today, 13.* Retrieved December 4, 2007 from www.christianethicstoday.com.

Page, S. (2004, June 2). Churchgoing closely tied to voting patterns. *USA Today,* p. 1A–2A.

Pauley, II, J. (2002). Religion, politics, and rhetoric: Twenty-five years after *The Political Pulpit. Journal of Communication and Religion, 25,* 1–5.

Peele, G. (1984). *Revival and reaction: The right in contemporary America.* Oxford: Clarendon Press.

Perot, R. (1992, May 1). *Remarks to the Salvation Army conference.* Retrieved March 12, 2008 from LexisNexis.

Perot, R. (1996, September 13). *Remarks to the Christian Coalition "Road to Victory" conference.* Retrieved March 7, 2008 from LexisNexis.

Peterson, B. (1983, February 24). Askew opens dark-horse White House bid. *Washington Post,* p. A1. Retrieved April 22, 2008 from LexisNexis.

Phillips, D. (1980, October 16). Commentary: Anderson's enthusiasm up as election day nears. *United Press International.* Retrieved April 25, 2008 from LexisNexis.

Politicians are discovering it's o.k. to talk religion. (1976, May 3). *U.S. News & World Report,* p. 18. Retrieved May 2, 2008 from LexisNexis.

Porter, L. W. (1990). Religion and politics: Protestant beliefs in the presidential campaign of 1980. *Journal of Communication and Religion, 13 (2),* 24–39

Powell, L., & Neiva, E. (2006). The Pharisee effect: When religious appeals in politics go too far. *Journal of Communication and Religion, 29,* 70–102.

President Reagan. (1981). Washington, D.C.: Congressional Quarterly Inc.

Pulliam, S., & Olsen, T. (2008, January 23). Q&A: Barack Obama. *Christianity Today.* Retrieved January 25, 2008 from www.christianitytoday.com.

Quinn, S. (1999, July 12). The g-word and the a-list. *Washington Post,* p. C01.

Raines, H. (1980, August 23). Reagan backs evangelicals in their political activities. *New York Times,* p. A8. Retrieved May 5, 2008 from LexisNexis.

Raines, H. (1983, July 17). Candidates begin sprint for campaign funds. *New York Times,* p. D3. Retrieved April 22, 2008 from LexisNexis.

Reagan, R. (1979, November 13). *Official announcement.* Retrieved April 30, 2008 from www.4president.org.

Reagan, R. (1980, July 18). Speech accepting the Republican's nomination. *New York Times,* p. A8. Retrieved May 5, 2008 from LexisNexis.

Reagan, R. (1984a, March 2). *Remarks at a White House luncheon for elected Republican women officials.* Retrieved April 3, 2008 from www.reagan.utexas.edu.

Reagan, R. (1984b, March 2). *Remarks at the annual Conservative Political Action Conference dinner.* Retrieved April 3, 2008 from www.reagan.utexas.edu.

Reagan, R. (1984c, March 6). *Remarks at a New York Republican Party fundraising dinner.* Retrieved April 3, 2008 from www.reagan.utexas.edu.

Reagan, R. (1984d, March 6). *Remarks at the annual convention of the National Association of Evangelicals in Columbus, Ohio.* Retrieved April 3, 2008 from www.reagan.utexas.edu.

Reagan, R. (1984e, March 13). *Remarks at the Young Leadership Conference of the United Jewish Appeal.* Retrieved April 3, 2008 from www.reagan.utexas.edu.

Reagan, R. (1984f, March 20). *Statement on Senate action on the proposed constitutional amendment on prayer in schools.* Retrieved April 3, 2008 from www.reagan.utexas.edu.

Reagan, R. (1984g, April 4). *The President's news conference.* Retrieved April 3, 2008 from www.reagan.utexas.edu.

Reagan, R. (1984h, April 13). *Remarks at the Baptist Fundamentalism Annual Convention.* Retrieved April 3, 2008 from www.reagan.utexas.edu.

Reagan, R. (1984i, May 1). *Remarks upon returning from China.* Retrieved April 3, 2008 from www.reagan.utexas.edu.

Reagan, R. (1984j, June 19). *Remarks at dedication ceremonies for the new building of the National Geographic Society.* Retrieved April 3, 2008 from www.reagan.utexas.edu.

Reagan, R. (1984k, July 4). *Remarks at a Spirit of America Festival in Decatur, Alabama.* Retrieved April 3, 2008 from www.reagan.utexas.edu.

Reagan, R. (1984l, July 16). *Remarks on signing the captive nations week proclamation.* Retrieved April 3, 2008 from www.reagan.utexas.edu.

Reagan, R. (1984m, July 24). *The President's news conference.* Retrieved April 3, 2008 from www.reagan.utexas.edu.

Reagan, R. (1984n, July 26). *Remarks at the St. Ann's Festival in Hoboken, New Jersey.* Retrieved April 3, 2008 from www.reagan.utexas.edu.

Reagan, R. (1984o, August 17). *Remarks at a White House luncheon marking the 40th anniversary of the Warsaw Uprising.* Retrieved April 3, 2008 from www.reagan.utexas.edu.

Reagan, R. (1984p, August 23). *Remarks at an ecumenical prayer breakfast in Dallas, Texas.* Retrieved April 3, 2008 from www.reagan.utexas.edu.

Reagan, R. (1984q, August 24). *Remarks to members of the Republican National Committee and the Reagan-Bush campaign staff in Dallas, Texas.* Retrieved April 3, 2008 from www.reagan.utexas.edu.

Reagan, R. (1984r, September 2). *Informal exchange with reporters on the presidential campaign.* Retrieved April 3, 2008 from www.reagan.utexas.edu.

Reagan, R. (1984s, September 4). *Remarks at the annual convention of the American Legion in Salt Lake City, Utah.* Retrieved April 3, 2008 from www.reagan.utexas.edu.

Reagan, R. (1984t, September 5). *Remarks and a question-and-answer session at the "Choosing a Future" Conference in Chicago, Illinois.* Retrieved April 3, 2008 from www.reagan.utexas.edu.

Reagan, R. (1984u, September 6). *Remarks at the International Convention of B'nai B'rith.* Retrieved April 3, 2008 from www.reagan.utexas.edu.

Reagan, R. (1984v, October 10). *Remarks and a question-and-answer session at St. Agatha High School in Detroit, Michigan.* Retrieved April 3, 2008 from www.reagan.utexas.edu.

Reagan, R. (1984w, October 15). *Remarks and a question-and-answer session at the University of Alabama in Tuscaloosa.* Retrieved April 3, 2008 from www.reagan.utexas.edu.

Reagan, R. (1984x, November 3). *Written responses to questions submitted by France Soir Magazine.* Retrieved April 3, 2008 from www.reagan.utexas.edu.

Reagan's final speech is upbeat and optimistic. (1980, November 4). *United Press International.* Retrieved May 5, 2008 from LexisNexis.

Reed, R. (1996). *Active faith: How Christians are changing the soul of American politics.* New York: The Free Press.

Reeves, T. C. (1996). *The empty church: The suicide of liberal Christianity.* New York: The Free Press.

Reichley, A. J. (1986). Religion and the future of American politics. *Political Science Quarterly, 101,* 23–47.

Reinhard, B. (2008, July 6). Obama website riles Muslims. *Miami Herald*. Retrieved July 8, 2008 from www.miamiherald.com.

Religion and the presidential vote: Bush's gains broad-based. (2004, December 6). Pew Research Center for the People and the Press. Retrieved October 6, 2007 from www.people-press.org.

Reston, M. (2008, April 26). McCain doesn't put his faith out front. *Los Angeles Times*. Retrieved May 7, 2008 from www.latimes.com.

Reynolds, F. (1980, October 13). *ABC World News Tonight*. Retrieved April 25, 2008 from LexisNexis.

Roddy, D. (2005, October 20). When religion is a litmus test. *Pittsburg Post-Gazette*. Retrieved July 2, 2008 from www.post-gazette.com.

Romney, M. (2007, December 6). *Delivers remarks on faith*. Retrieved April 11, 2008 from LexisNexis.

Rosen, J., & Dobbin, M. (2004, November 7). Reinventing themselves is Democrats' next task. *Sacramento Bee*, p. A1. Retrieved October 28, 2007 from LexisNexis.

Rosenthal, H. F. (1980, July 20). John Anderson, embarrassed by limelight, pursues the presidency. *Associated Press*. Retrieved April 25, 2008 from LexisNexis.

Rudin, J. (2006). *The baptizing of America: The religious right's plans for the rest of us*. New York: Thunder's Mouth Press.

Russert, T. (2007, January 28). *Meet the Press*. Retrieved April 11, 2008 from LexisNexis.

Rutowski, K. (2007, October 3). Confessional Web site Post Secret moves forward. *The News Record*. Retrieved June 25, 2008 from LexisNexis.

Sabar, A. (2007, September 20). John Edwards: Working-class values and a closely held faith. *Christian Science Monitor*, p. 1. Retrieved March 3, 2008 from LexisNexis.

Sacirbey, O. (2006, December 9). Conservatives attack use of Koran for Oath: Sacred and secular books have subbed for Bible. *Washington Post*, p. B09. Retrieved October 28, 2007 from LexisNexis.

Salmon, J. L. (2008, March 8). Feeling renewed by ancient traditions: Evangelicals putting new twist on lent, confession and communion. *Washington Post*, p. B09. Retrieved June 25, 2008 from LexisNexis.

Sanders, K. (2008, April 10). Christians construct reverse confessional on campus. *The Independent Florida Alligator*. Retrieved April 24, 2008 from www.alligator.org.

Sargent, G. (2007, December 5). Here's the Obama Muslim smear e-mail sent out by the county chair volunteering for Hillary. *Talking Points Memo*. Retrieved December 5, 2007 from www.tpmelectioncentral.com.

Savage, C. (2007, April 8). Scandal puts spotlight on Christian law school: Grads influential in Justice Dept. *Boston Globe*. Retrieved July 2, 2008 from www.boston.com.

Sawislak, A. (1984, April 20). Campaign takes Easter break. *United Press International*. Retrieved April 22, 2008 from LexisNexis.

Sawyer, D. (2008, January 7). *Good Morning America*. Retrieved April 12, 2008 from LexisNexis.

Sawyer, K. (1980, August 24). Linking religion and politics. *Washington Post*, p. A12. Retrieved May 31, 2008 from LexisNexis.

Scarborough, R. (1999). *In defense of . . . mixing church and state*. Houston: Vision America.

Schaeffer, F. (1981). *A Christian manifesto*. Westchester, IL: Crossway Books.

Schieffer, B. (2007, April 8). Face the Nation. Retrieved April 11, 2008 from LexisNexis.

Schlesinger, Jr., A. (1976, April 28). God and the 1976 election. *Wall Street Journal*, p. 18. Retrieved May 2, 2008 from ProQuest.

Schram, M., & Sawyer, K. (with Balz, D.). (1984, February 20). Close contestants for second place in Iowa defend attacks on Mondale. *Washington Post*, p. A4. Retrieved April 22, 2008 from LexisNexis.

Shaw, B. (1988, November 1). Inside Politics. Retrieved May 12, 2008 from www.fednews.com.

Shires, P. (2007). *Hippies of the Religious Right*. Waco, TX: Baylor University Press.

Shogan, C. J. (2006). *The moral rhetoric of American presidents*. College Station, TX: Texas A&M University Press.

Sigelman, L. (1996). Presidential inaugurals: The modernization of a genre. *PoliticalCommunication, 13*, 81–92.

Smith, B. M. (1980, February 28). Candidates' staffs trade accusations on buying black votes. *Associated Press.* Retrieved April 30, 2008 from LexisNexis.

Smith, G. S. (2006). *Faith & the presidency: From George Washington to George W. Bush.* New York: Oxford University Press.

Stacy, M. (2007, June 7). Florida evangelist criticized for anti-Romney rants. *Associated Press.* Retrieved December 6, 2007 from LexisNexis.

Steele, R. (with Doyle, J.) (1976, February 9). 1976's sleeper issue. *Newsweek*, p. 21.

Stout, J. (2004). Thoughts on religion and politics. In E. J. Dionne, Jr., J. B. Elshtain, & K. M. Drogosz (Eds.), *One electorate under God?: A dialogue on religion & American politics* (pp. 194–99). Washington, D.C.: Brookings Institution Press.

Stuckey, M. E. (1991). *The president as interpreter-in-chief.* Chatham, NJ: Chatham House Publishers.

Suarez, R. (2006). *The holy vote: The politics of faith in America.* New York: Rayo.

Sullivan, A. (2008). *The party faithful: How and why Democrats are closing the God gap.* New York: Scribner.

Sullivan, J. F. (1984, March 28). Jackson tells Syracuse students their votes in primary are vital. *New York Times*, p. B7. Retrieved April 22, 2008 from LexisNexis.

Sullivan, K. (1988, February 9). *This Morning.* Retrieved May 13, 2008 from www.fednews.com.

Swarns, R. L., & Cardwell, D. (2003, December 6). Democrats try to regain ground on moral issues. *New York Times.* Retrieved December 6, 2003 from www.nytimes.com.

Thomas, C., & Dobson, E. (1999). *Blinded by might: Can the Religious Right save America?* Grand Rapids, MI: Zondervan Publishing House.

Tomlinson, D. (2003). *The post-evangelical.* El Cajon, CA: emergentYS Books.

Tulis, J. K. (1987). *The rhetorical presidency.* Princeton, NJ: Princeton University Press.

Tulis, J. K. (2008). On the forms of rhetorical leadership. In M. J. Medhurst (ed.), *Before the rhetorical presidency* (pp. 29–34). College Station, TX: Texas A&M University Press.

VandeHei, J. (2003, November 27). A spiritual struggle for Democrats: Silence on religion could hurt candidates. *Washington Post*, p. A01. Retrieved November 28, 2003 from www.washingtonpost.com.

Viguerie, R. A. (1981). *The new right: We're ready to lead.* Falls Church, VA: The Viguerie Company.

Wallis, J. (1996). *Who speaks for God?: An alternative to the religious right—A new politics of compassion, community, and civility.* New York: Delacorte Press.

Wallis, J. (2005). *God's politics: Why the right gets it wrong and the left doesn't get it.* San Francisco: HarperCollins.

Wallis, J. (2008). *The great awakening: Reviving faith & politics in a post-Religious Right America.* New York: HarperOne.

Wapshott, N. (2007, October 26). Obama fails to quell row over an anti-gay singer. *New York Sun*, p. 1. Retrieved July 8, 2008 from LexisNexis.

We were wrong. (2008). Retrieved January 12, 2010 from www.springcreekchurch.org/wewe-rewrong.html.

Webb, S. H. (2004). On the true globalism and the false, or why Christians should not worry so much about American imperialism. In W. Avram (Ed.), *Anxious about empire: Theological essays on the new global realities* (pp. 119–28). Grand Rapids, MI: Brazos Press.

Weeks, D. L. (1998). Carl F. H. Henry's moral arguments for evangelical political activism. *Journal of Church and State, 83, 40*, 83–106.

Weinraub, B. (1983, December 26). Mondale staff worries: Will voters pick him? *New York Times*, B8. Retrieved April 22, 2008 from LexisNexis.

Welch, R. L. (2003). Was Reagan really a great communicator?: The influence of televised addresses on public opinion. *Presidential Studies Quarterly, 33*, 853–76.

West, E. M. (1980). A proposed neutral definition of civil religion. *Journal of Church and State, 22*, 23–40.

White, J. (2007, August 4). Officers' role in Christian video are called ethics breach. *Washington Post*, p. A08. Retrieved July 2, 2008 from LexisNexis.

White, J. K. (1998). *The new politics of old values*. New York: University Press of America, Inc.

Wills, G. (2007). *Head and heart: American Christianities*. New York: The Penguin Press.

Witt, E. (1979, October 23). Washington dateline. *Associated Press*. Retrieved April 30, 2008 from LexisNexis.

Witt, E. (1983, February 23). Askew makes White House bid, rejects 'quicksand of protectionism.' *Associated Press*. Retrieved April 22, 2008 from LexisNexis.

Wogaman, J. P. (2000). *Christian perspectives on politics*. Louisville, KY: Westminister John Knox Press.

Wood, Jr., J. E. (1980). Religious fundamentalism and the New Right. *Journal of Church and State, 22*, 409–21.

Wood, Jr. J. E. (1992) Religion and the U.S. presidential election of 1992. *Journal of Church and State, 34*, 721–28.

Zimmerman, J. (2009, December 21). More than a century of war on Christmas. *Philadelphia Inquirer*. Retrieved December 21, 2009 from www.philly.com.

Index

About the Author

Dr. **Brian T. Kaylor**, a graduate of Southwest Baptist University and the University of Missouri, is an assistant professor of communication studies at James Madison University. A former Baptist pastor, he is also the author of the book *For God's Sake, Shut Up!* (2007). Several of Kaylor's research articles have been published in various journals, including *Communication Quarterly*, *Communication Studies*, *Free Speech Yearbook*, *Journal of Communication and Religion*, *Journal of Gender Studies*, *Journal of Media and Religion*, *Public Relations Review*, and *Southern Communication Journal*. He has presented over fifty papers at academic conferences, and is the author of two chapters in Lexington Books publications (*The Rhetoric of Pope John Paul II* and *The Daily Show and Rhetoric*). His writings have also appeared in numerous media outlets, including CNN.com, *Birmingham News*, *Houston Chronicle*, *Kansas City Star*, *Roanoke Times*, *St. Louis Post-Dispatch*, and *Virginian-Pilot*. Kaylor won the top dissertation awards from the University of Missouri and the Religious Communication Association, the Bruce E. Gronbeck Political Communication Research Award from the Carl Couch Center for Social & Internet Research, and several other awards for both academic and journalistic writing.

CPSIA information can be obtained at www.ICGtesting.com
Printed in the USA
BVOW020106090412

287099BV00001B/6/P

9 780739 148792